BEYOND THE BLUE MOUNTAINS

AN AUTOBIOGRAPHY

GEORGE WOODCOCK

Fitzhenry & Whiteside

© George Woodcock 1987

Fitzhenry & Whiteside
195 Allstate Parkway
Markham, Ontario L3R 4T8

Typesetting by ISIS Communications Limited
Printed and bound in Canada

Canadian Cataloguing in Publication Data

Woodcock, George, 1912-
  Beyond the Blue Mountains
ISBN 0-88902-928-8

1. Woodcock, George, 1912-   — Biography.
2. Authors, Canadian (English) — Biography. *
3. Historians — Canada — Biography.   I. Title.
PS8545.062Z53 1987   C818'.549   C86-095053-0
PR9199.3.W66Z63 1987

CONTENTS

I

FIRST SPRING ON THE ISLAND

NEVER HAVE I SEEN the air so clear on the Pacific Coast as it was in the spring of 1949 when we reached Vancouver Island. A young Canadian we had met in London had bought a patch of land in what then seemed the remote village of Sooke, thirty miles west of Victoria, near the ocean end of Juan da Fuca Strait. He offered to sell us part of his plot. The day we drove out together in Doug's tinny, virtually springless army surplus truck, through the arbutus-clad and mossy cliffs of the Sooke Hills, where the views opened to the sea, we could distinguish quite clearly individual trees twenty miles away in the foothills of the Olympic Mountains across Juan da Fuca Strait. We began to skirt the double inlet, Sooke Basin leading into Sooke Harbour, which was linked in turn by a narrow channel with the open sea. The dazzling blue waters dotted with small and bosky islands had an exquisite, lacustrine beauty.

To be sure, Sooke was a rough frontier village. But we had expected that — human uncouthness facing pristine nature — and might have been disappointed otherwise. And when we turned off the main road at the store-cum-post office, and drove past the clapboard United Church and the little alder mill on the hillside beyond which Doug's land lay, an open field with gold broom rampant before a dark line of woods, we decided to seek no farther for a place to start our attempt to combine mental and manual toil.

The Europe we had known was seven thousand miles away, and so was the English literary world in which I had found a place, and so were most of our friends. Yet the very foreignness of this village, with its population of loggers, fishermen, plummy-voiced remittance men, and even stranger exiles caught on the westernmost strand of the Americas (the last frontier, as visiting Californians called it) was stimulating. Surely, a writer could not fail to find material and inspiration here.

At first everything looked promising, though we had not come with much money. Even when we had sold most of our English library, and the caravan we owned in a Buckinghamshire orchard, we had been able to bring with us only about $500. But Dwight Macdonald, who was editing *Politics* in New York and for whom I had been writing regular London Letters, lent me $1,000, and this gave us $1,500 to start building a house. And that, in 1949, did not seem an absurd proposition. Two hundred dollars bought us our first acre, and so far as the house was concerned, one could still buy lumber cheaply from the little riverside sawmills that in the 1940s had not yet been squeezed out by the big lumber combines. If we could find some way of earning enough money to compensate for the loss of freelance tasks in London, then we might survive until our land could provide us with food and a small income.

Neither calculation worked out, but this did not become evident until the following winter, and in the meantime we set about creating our new life. Ronnie and Jean England, our neighbours from whom Doug had bought his land, helped. They were barely into their twenties: Ronnie, a gangling ex-seamen, 6'3", who talked nostalgically of his single voyage to Tahiti; Jean, a big blond girl with bright blue eyes; a prow of a nose, an addictive passion for reading, and long, startling beautiful legs which she displayed all summer long as they turned the delectable colour of butterscotch under her short shorts. They had bought the farm, half scrub forest and half cleared land infested with broom, for a few thousand dollars, and now they were rearing cows, growing strawberries, and living in a big high-ceiling Victorian farmhouse with tumbling verandahs. Needing somewhere to live while we built our house, we were glad to have Ronnie bring a trailer to the farmyard. For a tiny rent we could occupy it, link up with his electricity, and get water, milk and eggs from the farmhouse.

So the trailer was installed on the edge of the farmyard, in the shade of firs populated by irascible squirrels. Inge, I and our adopted black kitten Tim took up residence. A long old sheet-metal construction on which the rain clattered loudly, shaped like a bus, with beds that turned into seats, and folding tables, it had a little cast-iron stove that smoked so badly that I can still recognize the books I owned then by their dusky edges.

A routine of work and discovery began. The farmer across the road ploughed some of our land so that we could seed it with peas and beans, root crops and cabbages. The offcuts a sawmill operator had dumped gave us fuel for two years and wood for our first rough-carpentered furniture. And I began to battle the broom that covered our land.

On long days in May and June, I sweltered mindlessly in the hot sun, hacking at broom plants or trying to rip them out. Sometimes I flushed a family of quail, or a brightly striped garter snake would glide away from my blade, or I would find a clump of blue-eyed grass vividly blossoming among the broom roots. Much of the broom was twenty feet high, and we had to borrow a tractor at weekends to root the great bushes out; Doug, driving the tractor, would haul the chain that I hooked around each thick stem. Often, working alone in this thick growth, which shut out sight and sound, I would feel all the loneliness of a solitary pioneer, and grieve for lost friendships. In that great quietness, I began to hear voices, would emerge from my thicket, and realize there was no one there.

As for the house, I knew nothing about building one and had never done carpentry more complicated than putting up a bookshelf. But Doug was working as a carpenter, and at weekends he gave me hints, and by trial and error I did everything with simple tools like handsaw, hammer, and brace-and-bit, until, to my secret astonishment, the house took shape. The trenches were dug, foundations poured, the floor joists and floors were laid, and the studded skeletons of walls rose until finally there was a shed roof on and we could work under it on wet days. And one day the walls were shiplapped in, and Dirty Sam, a spade-bearded surviving Klondike sourdough, came to spend a cursing day laying bricks for fireplace and chimney. I worked as his hodsman and listened with sceptical delight to his tall tales of Dawson City — how Bishop Bompas outsmarted the famous card-sharper Swiftwater Bill Gates, and how the quintessential mountie Sam Steele succumbed to the wiles of Diamond-tooth Gertie.

But all this took far longer than I expected, for apart from the fact that I learnt every process as I went along, and became a precariously effective electrician and plumber as well as a passable carpenter, there were endless interruptions. We had to cut stove wood, tend the garden, and walk a mile and back every noon to pick up our mail. There were weekly trips into Victoria, by bus, or hitchhiking if we were broke, to shop and to forage in the recesses of the Parliament Buildings, where the Provincial Library lent books to rural borrowers, and of the Provincial Museum, which consisted of a row of low-ceilinged basement rooms full of old glass cases crammed in disorder with thousands of Coast Indian artifacts — masks and ceremonial robes and abalone shell masks and intricate rattles and carved talking staffs; feasting bowls in the shape of mythical animals and great carved boxes and strange foods like dried clams strung on hoops of withy and the bulbs of giant kelp filled with the oil of the oolachon or candlefish — from which I first learnt the traditional splendour of the peoples who had inhabited the land I now chose to live in.

We also began to explore the Island, riding in Doug's barbarous truck over the Malahat Mountain, with the sea channels misty blue below us, to Duncan with the English accents of its retired majors and rear-admirals, and Nanaimo, with its streets of little miners' cottages. We went on swimming trips with the Englands to the Potholes in the Sooke River Gorge, where I was more interested in climbing cliffs for island flowers — dark fritillaries that were called chocolate lilies, and delicate white lilies that were called dog's tooth violets — than in plunging into the deep river pools. And once we travelled through the virgin first-growth forest where we saw the trunks of ancient Douglas firs rising, twelve feet in girth and more than two hundred feet tall, into the green darkness of their branches — to search for gold at Leech River with a lank broad-spoken barber, Len Stephenson, who had learnt his placer skills in the old mining fields of the Kootenays. We found only a few flakes of yellow gold in our pans.

WITH SUMMER THE VISITORS began to come. The novelist David Stacton, jangling his bracelets in a gay exhibitionism that in the late 1940s seemed exotic. The poet Kemper Nomland, with whom I had corresponded when we were both conscientious objectors, he in the camp at Waldport where many young American writers came together, and I in London. Two years before, Kemper had published my third book of verse, *Imagine the South*, with the Untide Press which he had taken over from William Everson; not long afterwards he was to leave his car with its engine running on the Golden Gate Bridge and leap to his death in San Francisco Bay, but nothing of the despair which drove him to this act was evident in the talkative young man, full of comic recollections of wartime experiences, who arrived at Sooke in a large car loaded with wine.

From Vancouver came the poet Earle Birney. He was one of the few Canadian writers whom I had read, for I had reviewed *The Strait of Anian*, for Muriel Spark's *Poetry Magazine*, and I immediately liked this tall thin man with his reddish beard and his western twang, and his wife Esther, whose sharp and malicious wit had been cultivated in the Jewish milieu of East London. A friendship began between me and Earle that I am sure will last our lives out. Earle revealed to me the barrenness of the Canadian literary world at the end of the 1940s, with its unadventurous publishers jobbing foreign books, and only two literary magazines of any interest, *Contemporary Verse* and *Northern Review*. His welcome extended to including me in a new anthology of Canadian poets he was editing. He told me about his friend Malcolm Lowry; *Under the Volcano* had appeared in 1947, and Lowry was still living in the cabin on Burrard Inlet where he had completed the final version — the last book he was to complete. Earle was anxious that Lowry and I should meet, and he offered us the use of his cabin near Lowry's shack at Dollarton; all the rent he would ask was that I build a deck for him. But Inge and I were too immersed in our efforts to live the Tolstoyan life during that first year on Vancouver Island,

and also too financially entangled, to move to the mainland; I never did encounter Lowry.

But, thanks to Earle, I did meet other writers, including the poet Floris McLaren, who was living in Victoria, and through her, Alan Crawley, the blind editor of *Contemporary Verse*, a man of curiosity and sensitivity who lived for Canadian poetry, to which, by running his magazine, he contributed so much. When we met he would pump me for stories and opinions about the young English poets whose company I had just left, and he educated me on the poetic scene in Canada, then in a state of restive expectation, with many poets emerging and few places for them to publish; the next decade would see a great change. Alan accepted four poems and printed them in *Contemporary Verse*. It was my first publication of any kind in Canada.

Through Earle I also received an invitation from John Sutherland to contribute to *Northern Review*. Sutherland too helped to inform me. In fact, he virtually initiated me into Canadian fiction (I had read only Stephen Leacock and Ralph Connor) by sending me the novels which Hugh MacLennan had published and asking me to write an essay about them. I recognized in MacLennan's manner the uncouth strength I found in many of the poets to whom Birney and Crawley were introducing me, notably E. J. Pratt whom I have never been able to accept as other than a highly imperfect and very conservative poet, and I was also critical of the strong strain of nationalist didacticism in *Barometer Rising* and *Two Solitudes*, yet I recognized a painstaking kind of craftsmanship and a touching sincerity which I would also find in MacLennan himself when, years later, I met him. I was impressed that, after my very critical piece appeared, MacLennan wrote me a letter of appreciation and explanation. It made me understand that I had entered a literary world which, though it was spread over the breadth of a wide continent, was in fact so small that everything a critic said reverberated. In such modest yet uncomfortably public ways my career as a critic in Canada began.

Other people, less known and less welcome, showed an interest in Inge and me at this time. One day Doug's brother, a small businessman in Victoria, came out to tell me that the RCMP had visited him, under a seal of secrecy which, being a sensible and decent man, he immediately broke. They knew we were living in the trailer on the Englands' farm; they wanted to know what we did and where our money came from. They had obviously been alerted by the Special Branch of Scotland Yard, to whom I had become known in 1945, when I had edited the anarchist magazine *Freedom* after its editors were imprisoned on sedition charges. Thus I learnt that my police file in Canada was opened on the day I landed; I am sure it has been growing ever since.

There was one trip we made during that first summer of which the Mounted Police were certainly aware; more than any other experience it gave us the sense of moving into another, different world from any we had known. I had been interested in the Russian sect of Doukhobors ever since they moved as shadowy figures of legend through my English childhood, when my father had included them among the characters in his nostalgic recollections of life in Winnipeg; strange Russians who cleared snow in the prairie towns and were given to stripping in public, regardless of sex.

I realized that the Doukhobors were something more than nudist shovellers of snow when I began to read Tolstoy and Kropotkin, who regarded them as admirable peasant radicals and Nature's anarchists. The Doukhobors' anti-militarism appealed to my own pacifism, and I accepted Tolstoy's impression of a libertarian sect which took its Christianity neat and turned its settlements into utopian communes. To meet the Doukhobors had been one of my aims.

When we reached Vancouver Island I found that a small group had migrated from the British Columbian interior, where they had been settled since early in the century, and founded a colony at Hilliers, about sixty miles north of Sooke. People in Sooke talked reluctantly about the Hilliers community, yet even their hostile comments told us something. The leader of the group, a heretical offshoot — was a prophet who called himself Michael the Archangel. He preached the destruction of marriage, and this our neighbours vaguely envisaged as a complex and orgiastic pattern of shacking-up.

Hilliers was near, but we knew already that long-term bad relations with the Canadian government had made the Doukhobors distrustful. However, I wrote to them, and by return received a letter from the secretary, Joe Podovinikoff. Welcoming my interest, he invited us to stay with them as long as we wished. I was a little surprised at the enthusiastic tone, but the reason soon became evident.

One day in August we hitchhiked northward, and it was late afternoon when the last driver turned off the seacoast road into the broad valley, hot and still of air, where Hilliers lies in the lee of the tall mountain spine that runs down the length of Vancouver Island. The non-Doukhobor village of Hilliers was a whistle-stop on the railway to Port Alberni, and the entrance to the community stood opposite a siding filled with boxcars. A high cedar fence faced the road. A large board was nailed to it with *Union of Spiritual Communities of Christ* in Russian and English. The wide gates stood open; between them a Chekhovian village met the eye. Low log cabins and unpainted shacks were scattered along a faintly marked trail that ran between grass verges to end, a furlong on, at two larger two-storeyed houses standing against the brown background of the mountains, with the grey bubble of a communal baking oven between them. Each cabin was surrounded by a picketed garden, where green rows of vegetables and raspberry canes ran over the black earth in neatly weeded symmetry, and ranks of sunflowers lolled their brown and yellow masks towards the light.

An old woman with a white kerchief shading her face was slowly hoeing in the nearest garden. I went up to her fence. Could she tell me where to find Joe? Her English was so broken that I could not follow it. By this time a little wave of younger women in bright full petticoats, and of blond, crop-headed small boys, came towards us hesitantly. There was nothing of the welcome we had expected. Inge spoke to one of the women. "Joe ain't here," she answered. "He's at the other place." She waved vaguely northward. A pick-up truck drove in through the gates, and two young men got out. The women called to them, and they talked together in rapid, anxious Russian. Then one man got back into the truck, while the other came up to us. He was dark and nervous, dressed in an old blue serge suit, with chaff whitening the wrinkles. "I'm Pete," he said. "Joe's brother. Joe's coming." He paused. "Afterwards . . . you'll see Michael . . . Michael Archangel," he added and then fell silent. The small boys went to play in the boxcars.

Joe was so different from Pete that it was hard to believe them brothers — blue-eyed, wiry, jumping out of the truck to run and pump our hands. "Michael Archangel knew you were coming a long time ago," he shouted. I had written only a week before. "A long time ago?" I asked. Joe looked at me and then laughed. "Yes, before you wrote!" Then he grabbed our rucksacks, helped us into the truck, and drove wildly a couple of miles along a rough track beside the railway to a large old farmhouse in a quadrangle of shacks and barns surrounded by propped-up apple trees that were ochre-yellow with lichen. "This is the other place," Joe explained. "Most of the young people stay here."

We went into the kitchen. Two young women, fair and steatopygous as Doukhobor beauties are expected to be, were preparing the evening meal. A small girl showed us to our room and stood, avid with curiosity, while we unpacked our rucksacks and washed our faces. Then Joe took us around the yard, showed us the new bakehouse on which a hawk-faced man was laying bricks, and tried to entice us into the bathhouse. I looked through the door and saw naked people moving like the damned in the clouds of steam that puffed up whenever a bucket of water was thrown on the hot stones. In a couple of seconds I withdrew, gasping for breath. The bricklayer laughed. "You never make a Doukhobor," he said. "Add ten years to your life," said Joe.

Everyone stood in a circle around the oval table for the communal meal. Twenty Doukhobors sang in the half-Caucasian rhythm that penetrates their music, the women high and nasal, the men resonant as bells. Most had Slavonic features, their breadth emphasized among the women by the straight fringes in which their hair had been cut across the brow. They sang of Siberian and Canadian prisons, of martyrs and heroes in the faith. "Rest at last, ye eagles of courage, rest at last in the arms of God," they boomed and shrilled.

The singing was solemn, but afterwards there was laughter and loud Russian talk; now and then our neighbours would translate. The food was vegetarian: bowls of purple borscht, dashed with white streaks of cream, and then kasha, made with millet and butter, and vegetables cooked in oil, and pirogi stuffed with cheese and beans and blackberries, and eaten with great scoops of sour cream. Slices of black bread passed around the table, cut from a massive square loaf that stood in the middle, beside the salt of hospitality, and the meal ended with huckleberries and cherries.

Afterwards Joe and Pete took us to drink tea in a room they used as an office. It was furnished with a table and benches of thick hand-adzed cedar, but a big blue enamel teapot served instead of a samovar. In the first of many long conversations the history and rationale of the community was imparted to us. This is what we were told.

It began with the experience of Michael Verigin, a backsliding Doukhobor. Michael had left his home in the mountains and his sect, joining a pentecostal group and opening a boarding-house for Russians in Vancouver, where he prospered. But after a few years he returned to the village of Krestova. Krestova is the Mecca of the Sons of Freedom, the fire-raising and nude-parading radical wing of the Doukhobor sect. Michael rejoined the Sons of Freedom and was regarded with deference because he was a distant cousin of Peter the Lordly, the Living Christ who presided over the Doukhobors' first years in Canada, and died mysteriously in a train explosion during the 1920s.

"Then Michael had a vision."

"A dream?"

"No, a vision. He was awake, and he said there was a voice and a presence."

"He saw nothing?"

"That time he didn't. The vision told him he was no longer Mike Verigin. Michael the Archangel had gone into him. He was the same man, but the Archangel as well."

"How did he know it was a real vision?"

"He just knew." Joe looked at me imperturbably. "The vision said Michael must prepare the world for the Second Coming."

The Second Coming did not mean the return of Christ. According to Doukhobor belief, Christ returns all the time in various forms. The

Second Coming was the establishment of God's earthly kingdom and the end of time and mortality.

As the chosen pioneers of this great mission, the Doukhobors must purify themselves. The Archangel proclaimed that they must renounce not only meat and fish, but also tobacco and musical instruments. Joe himself had abandoned playing the violin, which he loved. (As he told me this, a radio was loudly playing Bach in the kitchen. "That's O.K.," Joe reassured me. "A radio ain't a musical instrument.") Above all, the lust for possession must be rooted out. This meant not only a return to the traditional communistic economy from which the Doukhobors had lapsed under evil Canadian influences, but also the destruction of that inner citadel of possession, marriage. Two or three hundred of the Sons of Freedom accepted the Archangel's teaching. Their neighbours burned down the houses of those who followed Verigin. At this point the Archangel had another vision.

Two of his followers must visit Vancouver Island. There they would find a tower where a clock had stopped at half-past two; then they must proceed eastward until they saw a white horse by the gate of a farm. Joe and another man went on the expedition. They found the clock at Port Alberni, and the horse by the gate of a three-hundred-acre farm that was up for sale at a knockdown price. (After I had heard Joe's story I happened to visit Port Alberni, and there, on the tower of a fire-hall, I saw a dummy clock whose painted hands stood unmoving at half-past two.)

The farm was bought with pooled resources, and Michael the Archangel led his disciples on the exodus. Immediately after leaving the mainland he banned sexual intercourse — to conserve energies for the great task of spiritual regeneration. Complete freedom was only to be won by complete self-control. So much for the stories of Free Love rampant!

I wanted to find out the nature of Michael's power. Tolstoy once thought that, because they opposed the state, the Doukhobors lived without rulers. Other writers had suggested that the Living Christs, like Peter the Lordly, Verigin and his son Peter the Purger, had been rulers as powerful as any earthly governor.

"Michael is just our spiritual leader," Joe explained blandly.

"But he still seems to have a great say in your practical affairs."

"It depends on what you mean by say. He gives no orders. We are free men. We don't obey anybody. But he gives us advice."

"Do you always accept?"

"If we know what's good for us, we do."

"Why?"

"Because we know Michael the Archangel is always right."

"How do you know?"

"We just know."

The next day we met the Archangel. He had sent a message summoning us, and Joe drove us to the hamlet where we had arrived originally. The Archangel's house was one of the larger buildings, but we were not allowed to go in. We waited outside. The Archangel would meet us in the garden.

A tall man in his late forties came stepping heavily between the zinnia borders. A heavy paunch filled his knitted sweater, and his shining bald head loosened into a coarse, flushed face with a potato nose, a sandy moustache, and small eyes that glinted out of puffy sockets. The Archangel bowed and shook hands limply. He spoke a few sentences in Russian, welcoming us and wishing us good health, and he affected not to understand English, though we learned later that he was effectively bilingual. He picked two small pink roses from a briar that ran along the fence and gave one to each of us. In five minutes he was gone, retiring with dignified adroitness and leaving our intended questions about archangelic power unanswered. Joe led us away, loudly declaring that the Archangel had been delighted with us, and that he had given many messages which he, Joe, would transmit in due course. Our relationship with the Archangel took on this elusive, indirect form, with Joe acting like a voluble priest interpreting and embellishing the laconic banalities of the oracle.

For the rest of the second day we wandered around the community, talking to people. There were signs of strain. I found empty beer bottles in a corner of one field; in the shelter of the ten-foot plumes of corn that were the community's pride a young man begged a cigarette and smoked in heavy gulps to finish it. Yet there was also an atmosphere of dogged devotion. The land was growing heavier crops of corn and tomatoes and vegetables than any of the neighbouring farms, while the houses were surrounded by rows of hotbeds where melons and gherkins ripened. The younger people talked constantly of schemes for new kinds of cultivation and for starting light industries, but the younger people were few. There were too many children, too many old visionaries.

Sunday was the climax. Our arrival had coincided with the community's first festival. In the afternoon the only child so far born there was to be handed over to the care of the community as a symbolic demonstration against the conventional ideas of motherhood and the family. Since the Archangel had forbidden fornication we were surprised that a being whose presence seemed to defy his will should be so honoured. The Doukhobors applied a Dostoevskian equation — considering that, if the ban itself was sacred, so must be the sin against it. "Free men ain't bound by reason," one young man unanswerably concluded.

The day began with morning service in the bare meeting house. Flowers and plates of red apples had been brought in; the sunlight played over the women's white head-shawls and bright cotton dresses. Bread and salt stood symbolically on the small central table and also a great ewer of water from which anybody who felt thirsty drank as the service went on. The women ranged to the right of the table, the men to the left. On entering the hall each person bowed low from the waist, and the bow was returned by the whole assembly; the salutation was not to the man, but to the God within him. The Archangel stood at the head of the men, benign and copiously sweating; he did not attempt to offend Doukhobor precedent by acting like a priest. Today, as a child was to be the centre of the festival, the children led off the service, choosing and starting in their sharp, clear voices the Doukhobor psalms and hymns for the day. Almost every part of the service was sung, and the wild, incomprehensible chanting of the two hundred people in the small meeting house produced in us extraordinary exaltation. At the end, we all linked arms at the elbows and kissed each other's cheeks, first right then left, in a traditional token of forgiveness.

Later in the day we reassembled in the open air, forming a great V with the bread and salt at the apex. The singing rose like a fountain of sound among the drooping cedar trees, and between lines of women waving flowers and men waving green boughs the mother carried her child to the table. She was one of the young women we had met at the farmhouse on our arrival. As she stood there, her fair face grave and melancholy within the white frame of her head-shawl, she looked like the dolorous Mother of some naive ikon. The singing ended, the old bricklayer prayed before the table, and the mother, showing no emotion, handed the child to another woman. The Archangel began to speak, in high emotional tones; Pete, standing beside me, translated. The child would be named Angel Gabriel. The fruit of sin, he contained the seed of celestial nature. He would fulfil the great destiny of the Doukhobors and lead mankind back to lost Eden.

The women brought out pitchers of *kvass* and walked among the people as the orators began to speak. Emblematic banners were unfurled. One, representing women dragging the ploughs that broke the prairies during the hard early days in Canada, was meant to celebrate the coming liberation of the sect from all forms of bondage. Another, covered with images of clocks and other symbols of time, was carefully expounded by the Archangel, who found in it the fatal dates that charted the destiny of the world. Then spoke elders and young women; a Communist lawyer who had come in from the blue; even I, under moral coercion, as an enquiring Tolstoyan. It was hot and tedious work as the sun beat down into the bowl among the mountains, and Sunday trippers from Qualicum Beach gazed in astonishment through the palisades.

We walked back to the farmhouse with a Canadian woman who had married a Doukhobor. "You've seen what Mike wants you to see," she said bitterly. "You don't know all there is to know about that girl. Now she'll go up to stay in Mike's place. They won't let her talk to anyone, and they'll pay her out in every way for having a child by her own husband. Purification! That's what they talk about. I call it prison!" The mother of the Angel Gabriel was not at the evening meal. We asked Joe what had happened to her. She had gone willingly into seclusion, for her own good of course.

Joe had more important things to talk about. "You have a great part to play in the future of mankind." He fixed me with a sharp, pale eye. "Michael's vision has told him that the end of the world is very near. Now we have to gather in Jerusalem the hundred and forty-four thousand true servants of God mentioned in Revelation. This time Jerusalem will be right here."

"Here? On Vancouver Island?"

"On this very spot."

"But how do you know?"

"We ain't worrying. We just know. And the Archangel had a vision about you. A long time ago he knew you were coming. He knew you were a writer. He knew you were being sent here so you could tell the world what we're doing."

I must have looked at him dubiously, for he flapped his hands reassuringly. "I ain't asking you to do it. Nor is Archangel. We just know you will. You'll write about us, and people will come to us, and then you will come back and be marked with the sign and live for ever among the servants of God."

We left the next day. The Archangel saw us once more in the garden, gave us a white rose each, and said we would meet again before long. "It's a prophecy," Joe whispered.

And it was. One day, months later, I was broadcasting in Vancouver when the producer, Ross McLean, said he had heard Joe was locked up in the Court House. I went over, but I could not see him without a judge's order. But as I was about to leave the cell area, Michael the Archangel was brought in under escort, and for a couple of minutes, in that grim barred room, I was allowed to talk to him. He was pleased to be recognized, and even willing to talk a little English. "I am free soon," he said, as he was led away to the cells. Not long afterwards he and Joe were sentenced on nebulous charges of having incited arson in the Kootenays, which did not stand scrutiny when the sentence was appealed. Joe was released; Michael the Archangel had already died in jail.

From that first meeting came a lasting involvement with the Doukhobors. From the moment of meeting Michael I abandoned my earlier illusions that these were natural anarchists. I recognized theocracy when I saw it, and throughout my later relations with the Doukhobors I was fascinated by the combination of a sacred leader responding intuitively to the will of a people that was expressed through a gathering of inspired mystics, the *sobranie*, so that with the Doukhobors it has always been hard to tell where autocracy ends and anarchy begins. For both find their places among this people who rejected the secular state yet accorded an unbounded moral and even political authority to their leaders.

II

MOUNTAINS AND RIVERS

URING THE AUTUMN THE STREAM of visitors dried up. Our early enthusiasm for the land began to flag, and we began to experience loneliness, nostalgia, and disorientation. All this was deepened by the fact that materially things were not going as we had hoped.

Our efforts to raise money by truck gardening failed. We had been naive enough to imagine that the luxuriant growth of broom on our acre was a sign of fertility. But broom thrives on poor soil, and our land had been worked out in generations of bad farming, so that our crops were wretched. We took our French beans to the wholesalers in Victoria, who bought them derisively at the lowest price; the total income from that year's cultivation was about $10, plus the vegetables we ate and sometimes bartered for fish.

Our situation was further impoverished when the pound sterling fell from $4.20 to $2.80, which meant that my tiny remaining income from royalties in England declined sharply. I was unable to start any new books that might have increased my income, since the long hours of manual work left me without the energy or the will to sit down at the typewriter in our stuffy, confined trailer and do more than brief journalistic pieces, on rainy days. By the end of the year I realized that, for me at least, the marriage of manual and mental work was a failure. But I did not know how and when I could escape from the manual work.

As an unknown outsider, I found it impossible even to begin making a living writing in Canada, where few authors could then exist by their work alone. The two Canadian magazines that did publish my work, *Contemporary Verse* and *Northern Review*, could not afford to pay, and my only source of local income from writing for a long time was the Canadian Broadcasting Corporation. Ross McLean, then Talks Producer in

Vancouver, commissioned a few talks about contemporary British novelists; the pay for each was $25, and even when hamburger cost 33¢ a pound, it was virtually starvation payment. From CBC in Toronto, Robert Weaver, who had already read some of my books, gave me the occasional review assignment for *Critically Speaking*, which brought in $35 a talk; he also commissioned a series on the classic Russian novelists for the national network, and for this I received the princely payment of $45 a talk.

But these assignments were few and scattered, and by December the situation was building to a crisis. Winter had come, and we had not moved into our house because there was no cash to pay for door and window fittings. Even money for food was running short, and it was not the season to pick up casual work in the village; proposals I had put to the CBC were delayed in bureaucratic mazes. Wandering one day glumly into the Englands' kitchen to ask their advice, we found they were trapped in a similar predicament. Their strawberry fields would not start bearing until next summer, and they too had run out of cash. We pooled our problems and found a seasonal solution — selling Christmas trees.

So each morning we went out in Ronnie's decrepit panel wagon to a stretch of young woodland somewhere west of Sooke, where we would drive into a hidden clearing and cut a load of trees as fast as we could, since we were not sure of the legality of what we were doing. The trees were covered with wet snow that had half-frozen into glittering transparent crystals, so that we quickly became drenched and chilled, our hands numb and aching. We peddled a few trees by knocking at doors in residential Victoria, and then a gas station gave us space for selling in return for a share of the take. For two weeks before Christmas Inge and I stood every day in the bitter wind that blew up from the harbour, selling our trees while Ronnie ferried fresh loads from the farm. We ended with enough money for Christmas and six weeks after; we could even put a little aside to buy the door and window fittings that would allow us to move into our half-finished house.

It was high time, for Christmas was followed by a cold and snowy spell that made life in the trailer arctic. It was almost uninsulated, and the snow falling on the roof melted during the day from the heat of the stove; at night the water that had streamed down the sides would freeze. One morning we could not even open our door; a layer of ice had sealed us in. I shouted from the window and Ronnie came with an axe to cut us out. For ten days afterwards he did the same thing every morning, coming with an armful of kindling to start a fire in our stove so that the edge of the cold would be blunted when we got up.

Even when we had left our trailer and could relax in the space and the slighter discomfort of our house, with its secondhand and improvised furniture, life showed little improvement. Out of sight was out of mind, for my agent in England not only got me few commissions, but also slowed down in sending my meagre royalties. There were two especially tight corners. One day we were down to our last dollar. I had decided to hitch a ride into Victoria and pawn my typewriter. But before setting out I went for a stroll along the road into the back country, mulling over our problems, and all at once I saw eleven dollars lying in the ditch. Quickly grabbed, carefully spent, and supplemented with a big haunch of fishy-tasting black bear which the farmer across the way had given us, it tided us over until a cheque arrived.

A few weeks later we were again out of paper money and down to nickels and pennies. This time we went over to the Englands to try and borrow a couple of dollars. They too were broke again. Ronnie was off in Victoria trying to find work. Having told us this, Jean went without another word to her cupboard, took out her meagre stores, and divided them, tin by tin and packet by packet. Then she took the children's money box, silently opened it, counted out the contents, wrote an IOU, and then divided the cash so that she and Inge had about $4 each. It was the most shining act of mutual aid I have ever experienced. Ronnie came home next day with a job that kept him going until the spring.

About April, 1950, our luck began to change. I got work digging ditches and a septic tank for a builder. It was exhausting work for a dollar an hour, hacking away at hardpan and shovelling dirt nine feet into the air; at the end of the first excavation the builder decided I was too slow and paid me off. But then I got another spell of work as a plasterer's labourer. It wasn't as tiring as excavating deep tanks, and at least I was above ground, but I did not know how to handle lime, and ended with great painful sores that ate into my hands and took days to heal.

Then, having got a little cash together, Ronnie resumed work on his strawberry fields. He wanted manure spread among the beds, and I did it for 75¢ an hour. I wheeled heavy, sodden turkey manure from the heap behind Ronnie's barn, then forked it around the plants. The worst feature was the sour, penetrating smell that distinguished turkey shit from all other kinds. It clung in my clothes so persistently that when I left work I would stand at the back of our house hurriedly slipping off my outer clothes, which I would hang on a nail before nipping indoors in my shorts to wash.

Later there was strawberry picking, paid at piece rates so low that it was hard to make more than $3.50 in a full day, though we could take home as many berries as we liked. It was backbreaking work. The concentration of my gaze to find fruit among foliage was so intense that when I lay down to sleep at night and closed my eyes, a pattern of red strawberries and green leaves appeared on the retina and stayed until I fell asleep. Strawberry picking brought us among Indians, survivors from the once large Sooke tribe. We got on well with these shy, gentle people.

By this time we had had our fill of manual toil. Some of it I enjoyed, especially the carpentry and even, in moderation, the gardening. But my writing fell away so much that from April 1949 to April 1951, I sold only six articles to American and English magazines. I also wrote a few pieces without payment for *Freedom, Le Libertaire,* and other anarchist papers, more out of personal loyalty to old friends than from sustained conviction. After a period of great doubt about the philosophy that had once sustained me, I ended up still an anarchist, but not the simplistic propagandist of my *Freedom* days.

That came after our second spring in Sooke when, though we put in fruit trees and bushes, we were no longer serious about selling produce. Yet it was not lost time. Composing CBC talks helped me open up and colloquialize my prose, and when I started writing seriously and consistently again I did so with much more fluency and naturalness. During 1950 we also began to know British Columbia a great deal better, and to get a sense of Canada as a whole.

Earle Birney remained a most helpful mediator. When I recorded broadcasts, he and Esther put us up in the converted army shack they then inhabited at Acadia Camp at the University, and through them we encountered some of the writers then living on the mainland: such as Dorothy Livesay and her husband Duncan McNair, whom I always liked greatly, Phyllis Webb, Anne Marriott and Marya Fiamengo among the poets, as well as the short story writers Bill McConnell and his wife Alice, and George Robertson, who at this period wrote superb stories but would later virtually cease writing when he became absorbed in TV production. Some of these writers would meet in a circle they called "Authors Anonymous", whose aim seemed to be self-improvement by mutual criticism. Since I have always felt writing to be an intensely private act, whose product must be concealed until it is acceptable enough to be offered to the world, I felt uncomfortable in what seemed to be a situation of competitive exhibitionism, particularly since I found that criticism, though elicited, was usually resented. I did not realize that this practice would soon become the basic technique of a whole new academic discipline, "Creative Writing", which has always seemed to me to border on the fraudulent, since every real writer knows that his craft can only be learnt in painful solitude. I gained an early reputation for

English arrogance when I wrote about what I heard at such gatherings as "contorted prose and sheer bad poetry read by perfectly sincere people under the influence of passing literary fashions" (*Ravens and Prophets*). Perhaps I was unjust, in so far as publication in Canada was then so difficult to achieve that such reading circles were often the only means for a young writer to bring his work to the attention of others.

Earle introduced us to another world of artistic activity when he took us to Lynn Valley, which lies under the mountains of North Vancouver, where the painters Bruno and Mollie Bobak had built themselves a fine studio house. We immediately liked Mollie's exuberance and Bruno's ironic Slav humour. This was the beginning of many a whole circle of sustaining friendships with painters.

On another occasion Earle arranged for me to give a lecture at the University of British Columbia. It would earn me $50 and I would meet interesting and perhaps helpful people. It was late January 1950 when we ventured out of our snowed-in trailer and made our way to Vancouver, which was also snowed in, so that Earle, who had a theory that the only effective way to drive in snow was at top speed, landed us deep in a drift on the way to his house. The snow continued, and only a score or so of people gathered for the lecture, on contemporary English poetry, which was another beginning, since from now on the university was to occupy a continuing place in my life.

The poet Roy Daniells, whom I had encountered ten minutes before, introduced me with grace and wit I learnt to appreciate as we became close friends over the years, and that evening Earle gave a party where we met people who were to play lasting roles in our lives: Bert Binning, whom I have always felt to be an insufficiently appreciated artist, and the painter Jack Shadbolt and his wife Doris, who became and still are our closest friends in Canada.

What sealed that evening in my memory was the sudden entry of Stan Read, a Professor of English at U.B.C. Stamping the snow off his boots, he came urgently up to me. "I've just heard the BBC news," he said. "Your friend George Orwell has died." It was news I expected, yet in the middle of my sadness I felt in that moment a phase of my life was really ending and another was beginning. And so, indeed, it turned out: a friendship that attached me to England had ended; the new friendships that would attach me to Canada were being started that evening.

Ever since reaching Sooke we had meant to escape from our village base and explore western Canada, but it was a year and a half before we were able to shake free. During the summer of 1950 I persuaded an English publisher to give me a small advance on a book about British Columbia. About the same time I wrote a verse play about El Dorado, based on *Candide*, and sold it to the CBC for what then seemed the lordly sum of $125. I persuaded the Canadian Pacific and the Canadian National railways to give Inge and me free transport on their trains and coastal ships. And in October two San Francisco anarchists who had already visited us in the summer, David Koven and Audrey Goodfriend, arrived from California in a big old car, and we began our travels with a hard drive up the still unpaved Cariboo Road into the Indian country beside the Skeena River which few British Columbians had visited.

The travels, which I described in *Ravens and Prophets*, my first book on Canada, fell into four sections. First there was the dash into the gathering winter of the north of British Columbia with Dave and Audrey. They had a brief holiday period and an objective, which was to visit Fred Brown, a grandson of the famous John Brown, who had bought land in the mountains between the Bulkeley and the Skeena valleys to which he had moved with his family and where he planned to set up an intentional community. Having lived in and visited such communities in England during the war, I had a sceptical interest in his experiment, but I was more concerned with the old mining country of the Cariboo where I hoped to learn something about early white settlement in British Columbia, and the Indian villages of the Skeena where I had heard the older culture of the coast vestigially survived.

At the best of seasons, travel in this area would have been difficult, for the highway through the Fraser Canyon towards the Cariboo had not much improved since the original road was built by the Royal Engineers in the 1860s. At points it narrowly crept around towering cliffsides; at others it consisted merely of thick planks laid on a structure supported on gigantic wooden brackets attached to the cliff wall. Beyond the Canyon it became a rough gravel road that continued as far as the Skeena, and on which four of Dave's tires blew out and the springs of the ancient car were ruined. The dry summer of this country had ended, and we drove for hours through rain and often, where road construction was beginning, had to plough our way for miles through sticky mud.

Everything human in the landscape had a look of decay. The long stagnation of the depression and the war years had told on settlements already diminished by the ebbing of successive mining rushes from the 1850s to the Edwardian era, which had ravaged the country and then left it depopulated. The boom that would follow a decade after our journey, and send new roads lacing over the province, had not yet begun. The old log barns and houses of pioneers stood forlorn in farms over which the scrub was returning. Activity had almost come to an end in places like Barkerville where thousands of placer miners had once congregated, making and losing fortunes, and the decaying settlements, still awaiting their revival as "historic ghost towns", refurbished for tourists, evoked melancholy rather than enthusiasm. The only people who seemed to be employed were the cowboys, often Chilcotin Indians, whom we occasionally saw herding cattle, and most of the travellers were hunters, often Americans, coming down from the north with the corpses of deer and moose strapped to the roofs of their cars.

The landscape had the appealingly subtle colours and rolling shapes of the dry plateau country that fills so much of central British Columbia. The woods of aspen, cottonwood and birch were turning in a vivid range of yellows and oranges, and though the only big game we saw were the carcasses on the hunters' cars, the lakes were populous with ducks and geese migrating southward. Once, near Lac La Hache, we drove through a flock of bluebirds, several hundreds of them, such as we were never to see again.

Far on, after the road had turned westward at Prince George, we entered a land of mountains and great rivers. I had not even heard of the Hudson Bay Mountains until I saw them with astonishment, their glacier gleaming blue over the little town of Smithers, or of the vast bulk of the Rocher Déboulé that looms over Hazelton, and though I had heard of the Skeena, I had not expected the majestic green flow that swept westward between the vivid woodlands and the lines of high white peaks following it towards the sea. Inge and I fell in love with this country, and have returned there repeatedly since that first sight of it.

Dave and Audrey were excellent companions. Packed with all our impedimenta, including camping equipment we had no chance to use, into the same shaky car, and often sharing the same uncomfortable room at night, we were in a situation that seemed made for mutual irritability. But, as David stubbornly drove the car northward day after day, we found our discomforts binding rather than dividing us. We shared our anarchism, with its belief that a peaceful and functioning society could be built on the harmony created by people mutually working together to face the world's adversities, and here we had a perfect testing ground. Perhaps we would not have succeeded if we had not also shared an easy undogmatic attitude, amused by the absurdities of the tradition to which we belonged yet faithful to its ideals.

Audrey was short, with a dumpy ungainly body astonishingly crowned with a head that had the clear-lined, lucid beauty of an Italian madonna, but lit by restless intellectual vivacity; David was tall and powerfully built and had a slightly heavy but remarkably plastic face, so that his thoughts were perpetually and changeably on display. Audrey came of a long line of Jewish anarchists who had maintained the faith with almost rabbinical fervour; David had been born in a slum area of Brownsville, had lived a childhood on the edge of the New York underworld, and only in adulthood had joined the movement in New York. Recently they had moved to San Francisco, and had become part of the libertarian group centred around the poet Kenneth Rexroth. It was composed mainly of local poets — Kenneth Patchen and Robert Duncan as well as Rexroth — and of Italian anarchists as traditional in their adherence to Malatesta's kind of activist anarchism as Audrey's parents had been to Kropotkin's more intellectual sort.

Besides exchanging recollections, our curiosity about one another's lives, ideas, and about the land we travelled through prevented the discord that can often arise as a relief from the boredom of a journey. We still see each other often, and with a sibling ease which began to develop on that journey half a life ago.

We found Fred Brown near the top of his mountain, living with his wife, three children, three miscellaneous parents, four horses and a cow in an encampment centred on a great army tent built for Alaskan winters and set up in the middle of the two hundred acres of forest and peavine pasture he had bought for a few hundred dollars. He was a gaunt, laconic obsessed man. On the single night we spent in his camp we got drunk with him on bad fortified wine. He was already a casualty of past failed communities, in California and Oregon, and it looked as though the present one would also fail, partly because its nucleus was a tightly knit joint family unit which repelled outsiders, and partly because Fred's intellectual overbearingness had already driven away after a few weeks every one of a small stream of novices. There seemed no room for the open affinities that make a successful community. Later Fred would leave to seek a new utopia in Castro's Cuba, which after a while he abandoned in disillusionment. The last time I heard from him he was teaching the truths of community living in a third-rate Canadian university.

Fred's camp was on land that had traditionally belonged to the Gitksan Indians, and even now, disregarding white property titles, they hunted and picked berries. Their villages lay beside the Skeena and its tributaries, and here we found that the artistic traditions of the Coast Indians had lingered long after white contact and white diseases had weakened them on the coast itself. The only villages we had time to see before we started back to meet Dave's deadline for returning to San Francisco were Hazelton, which was half-white and half-Indian, and Kispiox, up a small tributary of the same name. Under the influence of missionaries the Indians had replaced the old split cedar longhouses of the past with large, ornate Edwardian villas, themselves now fast decaying into ruins of tumbling gingerbread. The "new" town of Kispiox, with its big mock-Gothic church, lay back from the river, above whose banks we could trace the foundation lines of the vanished original longhouses, and here the remaining poles stood, leaned or lay among the long grasses. There must have been two dozen of them, some much decayed, others well-preserved and showing in their carved lineage legends the lightness of touch and fancy that distinguishes Gitksan carving from that of the Haida and the Kwakiutl, doubtless because the trees so far inland were much smaller than the giant cedars used by the coastal tribes. A small boy stood and stared at us. A woman pulled aside a curtain and peeped, and that was all we saw of the inhabitants. The Indians of the Skeena were still suspicious of strangers.

To see even the vestiges of a Gitksan village — the soft grey cedar of the weathered poles on the vivid green grass, under a sombre sky beside the lacy rapids — was moving enough for the memory of it to lead us back every few years, until we became familiar with all the villages in the area where poles and other carvings survived *in situ*. They had hauntingly euphonious names: Kispiox and Kitwanga, Kitsequecla and Kitwancool (the best of all), not to mention the village the Indians made in memory of their past, 'Ksan' at Hazelton. During those later visits we observed the renaissance by which the Gitksan repossessed as much of their great neolithic past as ever an Indian can.

THE OTHER JOURNEYS THAT WENT into *Ravens and Prophets* resonate less than that first one. When we left Audrey and David in Vancouver, we took a circular railway trip through southern British Columbia — the Okanagan and the Kootenays, over the Crow's Nest Pass into Alberta, and then back through Banff and the Kicking Horse Pass and the great ranges of the Rockies, the Selkirks and the Monashee, to Vancouver. There we embarked on a coastal ship and sailed up the Inside Passage between Vancouver Island and the mainland to Ketchikan in Alaska, and back to Prince Rupert in British Columbia. From Prince Rupert we went by train along the Skeena and the Bulkeley rivers to Prince George, and thence, on the archaic little Pacific Great Eastern Railway from Quesnel down through the Cariboo and the Coast Mountains to Squamish at the head of Howe Sound, where we took another steamer filled with drunken miners down to Vancouver.

Almost everywhere we saw splendid scenery, though the winter was coming on fast and often we were unable to enjoy the country's full magnificence because the mountains were hidden in clouds or the roads were veiled in snowstorms. We realized even then that we were missing the magnificence of the late spring flowering in the interior and the grandeur of the summer skies in the high plateaus. And after Kispiox, everything human seemed physically, mean, and spiritually at best expectant. No one could have foreseen how the wretched towns and villages through which we travelled would begin to change a decade or so later as British Columbians became aware of a past and, acquiring a sense of history, began to think of shaping their futures as well as defining their origins.

On our fourth and last winter journey we hitchhiked into the Kootenays for meetings with the Doukhobors that had been arranged by Peter Maloff. Peter was one of the few intellectuals among his people, and I had been corresponding with him while I was still in England. We had stayed a day with him previously, and now thanks to him we were able to go as trusted strangers to Gilpin, a village of the Sons of Freedom which we reached by a precarious little box of an aerial ferry cranked by hand over the rocks and rapids of the winter-swollen Kettle River.

In the wooden meeting hall beside the tumbling river, where they held a *sobranie* in our honour and welcomed us with their splendid polyphonal singing, the bearded elders of the Sons of Freedom and their broad-beamed vociferous women explained that the deeds of destruction for which they were notorious had in fact been acts of self-deprivation to give symbolic value to their spritual quest. Nudism and arson were indeed forms of protest against a materially oriented and militaristic society, but they were emphasized by the fact that the perpetrator himself suffered as he shivered naked in the winter wind and saw his own house go up in the flames. What if it were a neighbour's house? Then it was a neighbourly act reminding him of his moral duties and detaching him from possessions; he should be burning the house himself. Or a public building such as a school? That was a declaration against an authoritarian system that forced children into the schools and then taught them war. Many of the people gathered in that meeting hall had joyfully served prison sentences.

But all that, we were told, had ended. A new prophet, a man of mystery, had recently appeared from nowhere, and the Sons of Freedom suspected he was Peter Iastrebov, Peter the Hawk, the lost grandson of the great leader, Peter the Lordly. In fact, Peter the Hawk had already died in one of Stalin's concentration camps, and the new leader was a Russian Baptist gospeller named Stefan Sorokin, no Doukhobor at all. He was to wield an ambivalent influence in the sect over the twenty years to come.

When we returned to Sooke after these journeys, nothing seemed to have changed. But in fact, our journeys did herald the end of our life there. Far up in the north, at Fraser Lake between Prince George and Smithers, I had realized that the deadline for Guggenheim Foundation applications was near, and decided to gamble on winning a fellowship. So I set up my typewriter on a roadside pile of railway ties and prepared a sketchy application for a grant to write the first English-language biography of the French anarchist, Pierre-Joseph Proudhon. I forgot about my application during the winter as we sorted out our land title and sold our incomplete house for little more than the cost of materials. When we had paid off our debt to Dwight Macdonald, we were left with little money and no regular income, but a friend loaned us a cabin on an old Indian shell mound at Saseenos beside Sooke Basin, and there, with a shimmering, ever-changing water mirror before me, I dug in the shell mound, but found no artifacts, and started *Ravens and Prophets*, but what preoccupied me most was my third and last try at a novel. This time I had an ambitious plot about a group of people setting off, after the collapse of the 1848 revolutions in Europe, to establish a utopian community high up the Amazons — and failing. I knew a lot about the Amazons because of my interest in the naturalist H.W. Bates (whose biography I later wrote), and I was familiar with the history of utopian socialism and of the 1848 uprisings; I had also been a member of Middleton Murry's settlement at Langham in Essex, and I knew from first hand how communities failed. At first the novel seemed to be going well, and when my agent in New York sent a few chapters to Harcourt Brace, the editor who read them responded with enthusiasm.

But in March, before I had written more than half the book, an unexpected telegram arrived; I had won a Guggenheim Fellowship — a year abroad.

III

A WANDERING YEAR

WE HAD BOOKED TO SAIL from New York, and our journey from San Francisco across the United States was knit by reunions, and meetings with those we had known previously only through long correspondence. The first night we ever spent on American soil was in the house of Wayne Burns on the shore of Lake Washington outside Seattle. Wayne, whose goateed features and plump soft body gave him a disconcerting resemblance to Napoleon III, was an anarchistically inclined Professor of English at the University of Washington, a devotee of Albert Camus and Alex Comfort who had begun to write to me shortly after my arrival on Canadian soil. Later on Wayne was to play an important role in our lives. But on this visit, though we were grateful for his hospitality and for the long evening drinking with him beside the moonlit lake which was turbulent with salmon swimming in towards the spawning rivers of the Cascades, our next day's meeting lay heavily on our minds.

During our last days in London the poet Kenneth Rexroth had introduced us to the West Coast American painter Marney George, who was living in Julian Trevelyan's studio in Chelsea. Marney was a pleasant, unexceptional painter, influenced by Morris Graves, but also an extremely attractive and charming being, and Inge and I came to love her. She had gone back to her home in Oregon about the same time as we left for Canada, and we had continued to write to each other.

But it was Rexroth, not Marney, who told us she was dying of cancer, and after we left Seattle our next destination as we travelled down the Oregon coast road, with its broad surf-beaten beaches and its cliff-top grasslands blue with dwarf irises was Bandon, a fishing port of white-painted wooden houses with a little country hospital where we found Marney.

[25]

Marney was dying; the deep luminosity of her eyes left no doubt of it. Yet she seemed entirely in control, her beauty refined with an inner translucence, her mind working as originally and sharply as ever, so that it seemed as if she were comforting *us*. She had learnt how to make every moment count; now she seemed to know how to die. We left her sadly, yet ungrieving, as she obviously wished. A few days after we saw her, she went back to her own house to die among the views she had treasured and the paintings she had made, and there she went, conscious and gentle, into her good night. Marney was never well known as a painter, though she had a genuine small talent, but I remember her as one of those rare persons whose friendship leaves an unquenchable point of light in the memory.

The day afterwards we were in San Francisco, where we stayed with David and Audrey in the big house they inhabited in the Fillmore area, then a peaceful district largely populated by Molokons, a pacifist Russian sect resembling the Doukhobors and named for their ritual obsession with milk-drinking.

Our few days in the city persuaded us that when we returned from Europe we must settle here. Guggenheim grants in those days were given to non-Americans on condition that they spend their fellowship time in the United States in order to absorb the superior benefits of American culture. I had argued that much of the research for my book on Proudhon had to be done in France, and grudgingly the Foundation had agreed that I might spend half the year in Europe. The rest I must spend on American soil and California seemed the best place to do it.

Our most memorable meeting in San Francisco was with Rexroth. I had corresponded with him since 1943, and, apart from our shared interest in anarchism, I grew to admire the lucid wisdom of his poetry. Rexroth was as eccentric as his letters had led me to expect. With his strange square face and his mane of hair, he looked like a decrepit Metro Goldwyn Meyer lion, and the oddity was enhanced by the extraordinary way his eyes would turn upwards while he was talking, until the pupils were lost under the upper lids. In his North Bay apartment, which was filled with oriental artifacts and his own declamatory paintings, he cooked a superb lunch, with which he drank the best Scotch instead of wine because, he claimed, it was good for his ulcers; afterwards he sat cross-legged on a couch and with elaborate ceremony, and much coughing and puffing, prepared the nargileh he always liked to smoke when he meant the conversation to be serious.

And serious it was until he got to personalities. Rexroth was the kind of superb polymath only a self-taught man can be; he had read enormously, and his talk was full of haphazard erudition, scientific,

philological, metaphysical, historical, as well as literary. Out of this reading he had developed a sense that all the world's cultures were interrelated
and mutually comprehensible, and that linguistic differences formed barriers that were less formidable than they were generally thought to be.

He was courteous in a stately Elizabethan way, and given to odd prim-
nesses. Describing a gay poet to Inge, he explained "You see, my dear,
he doesn't do it with ladies." His talk was peppered with such absurd
circumlocutions. He tended to be cantankerous towards the absent,
and when he recited grievances against them, his voice would take on
the harsh mid-western twang of his Chicago youth, as it did when he
decided to embark on some scandalous fragment of autobiography,
delivered out of the left-hand corner of his mouth. "When I was a boy in
Chicago, George, selling small dogs for sexual purposes . . ." He seemed
something of a mythomane, inventing his life as he went along, and in
his own way he tacitly admitted this by calling the account of his early
life *An Autobiographical Novel.*

The day before we left we went to a big anarchist picnic to celebrate
some anniversary in the libertarian calendar; it took place in the arbours
of a large vineyard belonging to an Italian comrade, and it was a pleasant
occasion, with lots of well-seasoned pasta, the wine flowing freely, and
the guitars and accordions playing Neapolitan melodies and old anarchist songs. The former Italian anarchists had taken to the Californian
climate, to which their traditional methods of farming in dry hot country
had been well adapted, and prospered with their winegrowing, orange
groves, and artichoke gardens; one fat happy man smiled complacently
when he was introduced as "the Artichoke King of California". Anarchism had become a matter of memory and sentiment for them and they
looked back through a haze of prosperity on their activist youths.

We crossed the United States by Greyhound bus, and travelled day-
and-night so that we would have a little time in New York before we
sailed to France. It was an exhausting journey, and when we arrived we
slept twelve hours in Dwight Macdonald's walkup apartment on the
edge of the Bowery.

We spent about a week in New York. It was to be my only visit to the
city, and I now find it hard to believe that then we walked out at all
hours without the least concern, whether we were crossing the Bowery
or strolling down Fifth Avenue. We went into Harlem, and in a black
revivalist church called the Mount Carmel Holy Ghost Filling Station, as
a pianist softly strummed, women dressed as angels were speaking in
tongues and writhing on the floor in ecstatic seizures. The atmosphere
was so hypnotic that we slipped away soon for fear of being swept into
the fervour.

As a host, Dwight Macdonald was as genial, humorous, and cantankerous as his letters and his articles had led me to suppose, and he lived in the heart of the New York literary and journalistic world. One evening he took us to a party thrown by the editor of *Time*. My namesake, the English trade unionist leader George Woodcock, was also in New York at the time, and one of the more bibulous women guests came up to me and said: "Jee-sus! Have you changed since I met you two days ago!" The next evening Dwight himself gave a more sober party in our honour at which Norman Mailer, Delmore Schwarz, Hannah Arendt, and Mary McCarthy appeared, but though I was glad to meet these people whose books had been important to me, I felt self-conscious, a bushed outsider in their inturned world of New York gossip and modish philosophizing. And though I dutifully visited magazine editors and literary agents, I found New York much more enclosed and much less productive in contacts and contracts than I had naively expected. I had a major disappointment when Bob Giroux of Harcourt Brace told me that he did not share his editor's initial enthusiasm for my novel, and that he was not prepared to sign a contract. So I added the typescript to the baggage I took on board the *Ile de France*, and the five days of the voyage were largely devoted to an agonized reassessment of the book.

With forced stoicism I concluded that Giroux was right. My descriptions of the Amazons were splendid; how could they be otherwise with a master like H.W. Bates? My historical background of Europe in the Year of Revolutions was accurate. My rendering of the problems of utopian communities was psychologically sure. But, except for the heroine, none of the characters seemed to live, and the heroine was a recognizable portrait of my friend Marie Louise Berneri and hence autobiography rather than fiction. The last night of the voyage I decided that the book was irredeemable, and dropped the manuscript into the Atlantic before I could change my mind. Those five days of rigorous self-criticism convinced me that, whatever kind of writer I might be, I was not a novelist. But, the experience may have made me a better critic. I knew, at least, what fiction should not be, and from that point it was only a step through the looking glass to knowing what it should be.

Shortly after we sailed from New York I was sitting in the cabin class lounge, reading a book by Hannah Arendt which Dwight had given me for the voyage, when a tall dark man with an acne-scarred face came up and said: "Are you George Woodcock?" He was the American critic Alfred Kazin. I did not tell Alfred of my problems with the novel as we talked, but during the voyage he must have realized I was going through some creative crisis, for he talked of the necessary role of the man-of-letters, particularly as exemplified by Edmund Wilson's career, and of the creativity of the non-inventive modes of writing, like criticism and biography, so that after our voyage together and our later meetings in Paris, I was no longer haunted by the sense that a silent poet, or a would-be novelist who has abandoned fiction, need be less than creative as a writer.

LANDING IN FRANCE, WE WERE at first struck by the contrast between our Old World and our New. The Norman trees in their long avenues seemed small and spindly after the great conifers of the Pacific Coast, and there was an ingrained agedness about the thatched farmhouses that made the ghost towns of British Columbia seem symbols of impermanence rather than of antiquity. Paris seemed at once familiar and astonishing, with a special vitality that lingered from the days of liberation. We settled into a small, shabby hotel in the Latin quarter, in a narrow street just west of the Boulevard St. Michel, and for a few days excitedly visited familiar places, encountering old friends — Giliane Berneri (Marie Louise's sister), Serge Senninger the poet, André Prudhommeau, the anarchist writer with whom I had spoken at the Bakunin anniversary celebration in Berne five years ago, and Frank Lea, with whom I had lived in the pacifist community at Langham.

Having shed my novel, I still had to complete my travel book on western Canada and to begin research on Proudhon. Theoretically I was here in France to do the latter, but the travel book could not be allowed to grow stale, and it was obvious that we could neither afford the rooms in Paris where work would be easy nor protect ourselves there from distracting temptations. We had to find some quiet, inexpensive retreat. Here Inge's nostaglia for her ancestral country and my need for a good working place came together.

Austria was still cheap and comparatively unvisited by tourists. The contrast, crossing the frontier by train from Liechtenstein into Vorarlberg, the easternmost Austrian province, was at first sad. The people were shabbier and obviously poorer than the Swiss, and signs of the war were still evident; there were French troops at the border station, for Austria was still under Allied occupation, and Vorarlberg, as one of the remotest, poorest provinces, had been entrusted to France as a junior partner in the alliance.

We left the train at Bludenz. At first sight it seemed an ordinary pleasant Central European small town. The architecture was baroque; there were shady stone arcades along the main street, a beautiful fountain, a church with a gilded onion dome, murals of saints and angels on the stuccoed houses. Yet it was depressing. The French garrison had roughed up some of the best buildings. A chaotic drainage scheme had ripped up almost all the streets, so that one proceeded by scaling piles of dirt and hopping over open trenches. And there was an air of habitual poverty. Vorarlberg was always badly off, even under the Hapsburgs, and had more than its share of the economic troubles that followed the breakup of the Austrian Empire in 1918. The shabby, hungry-looking, and obviously unemployed young men standing about the streets reminded me of Welsh mining towns during the Depression.

The hotels in Bludenz were full, and in the one where we stopped for a jug of red Tyrolean wine, the waiter overcharged us extravagantly. We eventually found a room in a small inn on the edge of the town. Bludenz was no place to stay. The next morning we boarded a Postauto that travelled into the Brandnerthal. The road wound through mountainside forests, and then on to more open ground where meadows and barley fields hung on slopes that seemed impossibly steep for cultivation. Every now and then we passed a shrine for the protection of travellers, and sometimes, when we looked over the chasms that yawned beside the road, we felt a little protection was not to be despised.

After seven miles of laborious uphill driving we came to the head of the valley and the village of Brand. It was the place we were looking for. It was more than a straggling mile long, of big wooden peasant houses, with enormous overhanging roofs and deep balconies. The valley floor was meadowland, and above the pine forests climbed. A great isolated crag, conical, grey, and inexpressibly solid, loomed over the village at the end of the valley, and beyond it, enclosing everything in an icy arc, were the white jagged peaks of the Rhaetikon Alps, barring us from Switzerland. We walked slowly along the dirt road and at the far end of Brand we found a large farmhouse whose balconied upper rooms looked towards the mountain peaks. When we found Herr Meyer, the blond wine-florid bauer who was scything his hay, he agreed to give us a room and breakfast for as long as we wanted to stay. We arranged with an inn at the other end of the village for our dinners.

The balcony where I set up my typewriter every morning was excellent for working, far enough above the ground to give me a sense of detachment, and enough in sight of the Austrian mountains to make me feel comfortable writing about those of Canada.

The weather was eccentric. When we climbed into the mountains during the day we were usually scorched by a fierce Alpine sun, but nightfall was often heralded by magnificent electric storms, with the thunder echoing like gunfire across the valley. Wildlife was plentiful. The roe deer came down to feed in the valley on the edge of the woods, on the lower hills we would see dark-coloured foxes and sometimes, on the mountain, chamois stood outlined. A wealth of wild flowers seemed to become more abundant and beautiful the higher we climbed above the valley. On lower slopes, in awakening summer, we walked through fields of pale blue forget-me-nots and thickets of deadly, indigo-blue monkshood. A little higher there were damp places densely covered with yellow globe flowers, and natural beds of Turk's head lilies and on the stonier ground vast drifts of crimson Alpenrosen, the dwarf azaleas of Europe. In the thin air and intense light of the higher ridges, flowers became ever purer and brighter. Beside the icy brooks from the glaciers grew tiny clear pink primulas, on the bare slopes around the high cold lakes we picked electric blue trumpets of gentians and ivory white mountain crocuses, and on the edge of the snow were the delicate purple bells of the sondanella, melting their way upward to the light.

The human life of Brand was equally unfamiliar. Brand attracted few visitors from outside, and tourism contributed less to its income than the smuggling over the mountains in which the younger men were involved. The main industries remained dairy and stock farming. During the summer the cattle were high up the mountainside, where the grass had come up rich and thick after the melting of the snow, and we only saw them when we went climbing. The fields of the valley were being kept for winter fodder, and the first of the year's three crops was got in while we were there.

Haymaking was colourful, with whole families taking part. The women wore full print skirts and vividly coloured buttoned bodices, with scarves over their heads; they favoured clear greens and reds and deep purples. They took their turn scything the grass, which was cut quite short; the slopes were too steep and irregular for machinery. After cutting, the hay was laid out on the ground for a first drying. Then stakes were driven into the earth in rows across the fields; each had two or three cross pieces and on these the wisps of hay were carefully arranged so that they would dry. The stakes were called "little hay men", and at a distance, standing in formation across the meadows, they looked indeed like the ragged caricature of a regiment of soldiers. When the grass was finally dry it was carried down the slopes on sleighs or, where the ground was too steep, in enormous bundles on men's backs, and stored in the barn for the winter.

With his extensive fields and grazing rights, Herr Meyer was one of the most prosperous of peasants. Yet, as he told us, he was worth hardly a penny. The series on inflations that had plagued Austria every since the Great War had given him a deep distrust of financial security, and although he had income from cattle dealing, cheese-making, and other sources, he put every schilling into goods. He had installed a water closet on each of the three storeys of his house, and I had copiously used the one on our floor before I realized that no plumbing had been installed, and that I must use the fly-infested earth closet in the yard. Apart from the unusable W.Cs, Herr Meyer had idle electric motors and power tools, considering that any solid object was much superior to its equivalent in shaky cash. This distrust of the future, this dread of another economic collapse or war or another customs officer's son from Austrian Braunau, was shared by everybody in the village, from the Burgermeister and the postmaster to the waiter in the inn who was learning English in order to get away and who, when he learnt we were Canadians, scrounged extra helpings for us in the hope that one day we might be useful to him.

Brand was a friendly place. I worked well there and finished *Ravens and Prophets*. Yet existence did have an elemental harshness that was not entirely hidden by hospitality or by the festiveness that would break out on holidays when the girls put on their voluminous silk skirts and braided jackets, and the village band in beaver hats, full-skirted blue coats, and black knee breeches blasted their way between the grey tumbling fences of the village road. The children often went barefoot except on holidays, and this want and frugality was thrown into relief by the proximity of happier Liechtenstein, to which, when we were tired of the simple meat and *mielspeisen* diet of the Brandnerthal, we occasionally went on foraging trips.

From Bludenz, a slow train took from us to a little station among the apple orchards, where a grumpy customs official, representative of a land of 60 square miles and 13,000 inhabitants, would peer officiously into the shopping bags of peasant women and examine our passports.

Vaduz, the capital, was not even on the railway line, and we had to take a little bus through the corn fields and vineyards. The population of the tiny metropolis was round about three thousand. It had only one street, with many wine cellars, some modern Swiss-style stores and a weekly newspaper. The whole governmental machinery was housed in a couple of nineteenth century mansions on the edge of town. The most impressive building was the post office, which did a brisk trade in the slickly engraved pictorial stamps I remembered from my philatelic childhood; my father, something of an expert, never treated them as authentic, since far more of them were sold to collectors and stamp dealers than were ever used on letters.

A steep, dark bluff dominated Vaduz and there stood the castle of the Prince, a solid mediaeval keep with a baroque wing. Keep-off notices and locked gates surrounded it on every side. Since I first saw it I have often thought that Kafka might have taken this closely kept little citadel, brooding over its tiny realm, as the model for *The Castle*. I found nothing Kafkesque about the Liechtensteiners, who seemed to me, as I wrote at the time "probably the nearest European equivalent to the inhabitants of the Friendly Islands," a judgment I would radically change twenty years later when I landed in Tonga, the real Friendly Islands. Liechtenstein was happy enough to have no army. It has remained neutral for centuries, and if its inhabitants escaped the rigour of military service, they also avoided paying for atom bombs or even for rifle bullets. In fact, they paid hardly any taxes at all and their standard of living was remarkably high. In the long run of course Liechtenstein is as much at the mercy of the great powers, the large armies, and nuclear war as the rest of us. But in this world we tend to live by the short run, and in this way Liechtenstein had managed to survive a good many years in prosperity.

WHEN WE HAD LEFT AUSTRIA in search of facts about Proudhon, we went first through Switzerland into the French Jura, to Besançon, a small baroque city of grey stone. There we found the house of Proudhon's birth and childhood, a building in a working class street, so decrepit that it seemed ready to sink into the earth as soon as we had taken a look at it. In the dour limestone countryside, so marvellously evoked in Courbet's paintings, and in the frontier provinciality of the city, with its sturdy Franco-Germanic cooking in the restaurants around the market place, its strong purple-brown *pelure d'oignon* wine and the feather quilts on its beds, one found an appropriate setting for Proudhon's uncompromising peasant anarchism.

We reached Paris early in August, in time for the annual exodus from the city, which meant that we could live in Giliane Berneri's one-room and kitchen apartment while she took her month's vacation. It was on a seventh floor on the rue St. Jacques, on the edge of the student quarter but not far from the working class areas of the rue Mouffetard and the Place Maubert, where we mostly shopped. Every morning we heard the sound of Pan's pipes, and would go out onto the balcony to see a man leading a small herd of nanny goats which he milked for his housewife customers. We spent most of our days in libraries, including the Bibliothèque Nationale, which was presided over by formidable ladies in black garments whose ferocious looks reminded one of the *tricoteuses'* during the Terror.

But the turning point of the research was the discovery of Proudhon's diaries. I knew these existed, since I had seen extracts published in a magazine round about 1910. I found that they were in the hands of a surviving granddaughter and made contact with her through a young worker-priest who had been tracing the relationship between Proudhon and Marx in the 1840s.

Suzanne Henneguy lived in a steep little street near the rue St. Jacques, and one chilly September morning we went to her second floor apartment. The door was opened by a small, round, bustling woman, with a shrill, high-pitched voice that hurled French at us with the speed of a *mitrailleuse*. This was Proudhon's granddaughter. And in her parlour, we stepped into a French room of the mid-nineteenth century in all its stuffy grandiosity. Proudhon had not lived there, but he would not have been out of place. Enormous dark red curtains and drapes, faded and betasseled with tarnished braid, hung over every doorway and obscured the windows. Sideboards and tables and whatnots of every kind and size supported a museum of bronze stags in combat and wild boar at bay, and of marble nymphs and fauns. We stood bemused as our hostess, a perfect example of the restless, indestructible energy of the French *bourgeoise*, bustled around, showing us, like an *hors d'oeuvre* to the feast, such personal relics as Proudhon's ink-pot and the little steel-rimmed spectacles he had always worn. The rich second course appeared when she went into a dark corner of the room and switched on a light over a picture. It was Courbet's celebrated portrait of Proudhon — the original. Out of a dense, dark background the face of the revolutionary philosopher shone with a lambent brilliance, the great brow of which his contemporaries always talked soaring up over the intense eyes, over the square dogged face and the shaggy beard. The impression was mingled serenity and passion; the artist had caught the twin aspects that made Proudhon so original and paradoxical.

For the rest of my visit this picture acted as a shrine, for on a table underneath it our hostess would lay out the twelve worn thick black notebooks we had come to see, and every day we worked there Proudhon's face glowed with ironic benignity.

I cannot say that I flung myself on the diaries. Rather, I opened them gingerly, and peered despairingly at the crabbed writing in an unfamiliar, foreign and antiquated hand. Sometimes the writer had hurried and his words were almost illegible. Sometimes there was a hasty note inserted in pencil that had faded in a hundred years to the ghost of a message. The damp of prison cells had taken its toll of some pages. And at times the diarist had written in a tiny hand which made a magnifying glass imperative. But as we searched day after day, we gradually adapted to the difficulties, and there remained little that was indecipherable.

It was an eccentric miscellany of material, typical of the author's restless mind. There were financial accounts, and plans for business enterprises and for great fifty-volume works that were never even started. There were

outlines of articles, notes of ideas that had suddenly occured to him, para-
doxes he was trying out for the first time. Such entries were invaluable for
tracing the development of Proudhon's thought. But the diaries also had
their personal side. Proudhon, who was an anti-feminist but also appreciative of women when they showed what he thought were their proper
excellences, dilated on love at great length. "Would you be completely
free, in reason, in imagination, in industry?" he asked himself. "Then do
not marry. Would you be free and a lover, both at the same time? The
best thing is to marry. You must decide whether you want to or can do
without love." He himself found that he could not, and married a young
woman whom he had seen going to and fro in his street. He proposed
abruptly without introduction, and the match succeeded remarkably well.

The diary was enlivened by Proudhon's impressions of famous people.
Victor Hugo, Jules Michelet, Karl Marx, Michael Bakunin, George Sand,
Liszt's mistress, the Comtesse d'Agoult, made appearances. He described
one day the visit of a sympathetic Russian named Tolstoy, with whom he
agreed on almost everything. And an angry pencil note dismissed Karl
Marx as the tapeworm of socialism. Finally, there were vivid on-the-spot
notes of events through which Proudhon had lived — descriptions of the
Paris revolution of 1848 and of the *coup d'etat* that established the Second Empire of Napoleon III in 1851.

Just as Proudhon slowly revealed himself to us, so the hospitality of his
descendants increased. We were quite unprepared for the superb dinner
to which we were invited by Suzanne Henneguy and her sister, Mme.
Fauré-Fremier on the final day. If Proudhon's portrait did not smile on
this last gathering, which took place in another room, I like to think his
spirit was there, perhaps inspiring the flavour of the excellent *gigot
d'agneau* or the dessert, *crème de marron* pudding laced with brandy, or
giving a tang to the Arbois wine he loved.

In mid-September we had to move out of the flat on the rue St.
Jacques. We went for a few days to Brussels, to consult official records
regarding Proudhon's exile there, and on our return, because of our
dwindling funds, lived in the cheapest hotels of the Latin Quarter. At
this time of the year, with competition from students, inexpensive rooms
were the hardest to get. We moved restlessly from one fleapit with
threadbare blankets and lukewarm radiators to the next, eating in *prix-
fixe* eating houses and cheap *crêpéries* until the day we left for Le Havre.

THE *SAN PEDRO*, A FRENCH FREIGHTER, took twelve days to limp
across the Atlantic. There were only twelve passengers, and the cabins
were large and comfortable, but the captain was inclined to drink, and
though we had more than enough wine (four bottles at each meal for

each table of four and more if one asked), the food was indescribably bad. The captain tried to make up by holding cocktail parties each evening, when he would use his only English to shout "Down the 'atch!" as he gulped his first martini.

We were eventually landed, in the middle of a snowstorm, at a coal wharf downriver from the main port of Québec, and since this was a freighter and the agent took no responsibility for passengers we shifted for ourselves. A Québecois passenger went off and found a truck in which we stood huddled together and drove through the falling snow into Québec, where Inge and I caught the train into Montreal. There we stayed just long enough for me to meet John Sutherland, the editor of *Northern Review*, in a hotel lounge, and then we set off to Toronto, and took a bus into the United States. The border officials seemed to have no inkling of my anarchist past.

This time we eased our journey by travelling only in the daytime and staying overnight in places like North Platte, Iowa, and Elko, Nevada, so that it took a monotonous five days, varied only by the unbelievable ugliness of Chicago, an unseasonable but terrifying thunderstorm in Iowa, some interesting observations of the madness that seizes respectable American matrons when they enter the wide-open gambling towns of Nevada, and the beautiful scenery of the Sierra going over from Reno to Sacramento.

After a week in San Francisco, we went north to the little summer settlement of Camp Meeker on the Russian River among the redwood forests. An Italian anarchist, Joe Rienzi, had lent us his cabin there for the winter, so that I could have a peaceful place to work. Joe's "cabin" was really a rambling house with no less than thirteen outside doors, one for every room including the bathroom. Though Joe was now a retired contractor much henpecked by his wife, he had served in his youth in some minor capacity in Al Capone's gang and the mania about escape routes had never left him, so that in building his house he made sure of being able to run into the forest from any room at a moment's notice. For us, the main problem was making sure that every door was locked when we went out or went to bed. In fact, though we were regularly visited by skunks, squirrels, blue jays and families of raccoons, we had few human contacts apart from occasional visits from two anarchists who lived near us, a Sardinian chicken farmer named John Vattuone and Rexroth's friend Frank Triest, who was experimenting with the musical qualities of glass vessels and had created something like a gamelin orchestra of blown glass on which he would play hauntingly ethereal tunes he called Cloud Chamber Music. As well Hilaire Belloc's son, Hilary, a stocky, bluff, bearded man of fifty, turned up at our door. He worked as a road engineer up and down California.

In northern California the spring came early, with flamboyant wild flowers blooming abundantly on the bare hills beyond the redwood forests, and the roadsides golden with mimosa. There was nothing much to Camp Meeker but the summer homes and a couple of motels beside the river, all of them deserted, but not far away, where the orange groves and vineyards began, was a quiet little town called Occidental where old men sat on benches in the sunlight and talked vehemently in Italian.

San Francisco remained our metropolis, where we would talk to Rexroth and other poets there, like Kenneth Patchen, who was by now very sick with arthritis, and James Laughlin who came for a visit, and Philip Lamantia, who scandalized the local anarchists one Saturday evening by giving a lecture in praise of masturbation, which incensed the Italians, who argued passionately that the essence of anarchism was not keeping pleasure to oneself but sharing it.

As the spring advanced we made our plans to leave. The Guggenheim Foundation would not renew my fellowship, and already, I had been forced to take a commission from a rich Californian woman to edit a batch of Emma Goldman's letters and essays, which she possessed, for $500. At first fascinated because of Emma's sheer energy, I ended the task exasperated because of her consummate vanity. Nowhere have I found the individualism which is one side of anarchism carried so far into the egotism that Max Stirner preached. I found her eminently disagreeable.

In April we safely locked the thirteen doors of the house and left for San Francisco, where I gave a lecture on William Godwin. Nearly two hundred people turned out to hear about a writer whose reputation was only beginning to stir out of a long obscurity. The next day we took the bus northward. During the months in Europe the desire to live there permanently had diminished, and the reports I had received about England — still gripped in Crippsian austerity — discouraged us from even returning for a visit to London. After I had re-established my CBC contacts and arranged to give some talks on our European travels, we made our way back to Canada for a second effort at establishing a life there. This time it was to be successful.

IV

DESTRUCTION AND CREATION

SOME PEOPLE DO NOT NECESSARILY dominate periods of our lives, but signalize them, so that when we look back to a particular time, and pour the blood into the pit like Odysseus, one figure advances out of memory to give the tone to that past. One such was Anton Kohout.

Returning to Sooke, we sailed on one of the elegant old Canadian Pacific ferry boats through the Gulf Islands from Vancouver to Victoria. It was a slow four-hours' trip in those days, on an uncrowded boat in which the first people we saw were Kohout and his American wife Natalie.

We had already known Kohout, slightly. He was a quick old man, a Czech with high Slavic cheeks, a rippling crest of white hair and a grey Hohenzollern moustache. His ice-grey eyes darted constantly. His body never rested, as though life were a constant gesture, and gesture could control the world; when his ageing car would strain at a hill, he would move his body gruntingly backwards and forwards at the wheel, as if his action could help the machine.

Kohout talked rapidly, almost incessantly, and his accent was Germanic rather than Slavic. He had been born in the Austro-Hungarian Empire and regarded himself always as one of the Hapsburg Empire's German-speaking elite. Vienna was his spiritual home, and he retained a facile Viennese wit, interspersing his conversation with bright aphorisms and stale European jokes at which he would always laugh before anyone else, in a high-pitched mad cackle like a jungle cock.

But his attachment to Franz Josef's Empire had not prevented his voting with his feet, for he had arrived in Canada not long after 1900, and though he never admitted it, I am sure he left Austria-Hungary to avoid military service. After a period in Québec he gravitated to Vancouver

Island, and may have been involved in land speculation, for he could be extremely informative about the corruption in provincial politics, particularly among the Liberals. Finally, he bought a piece of forest land on the cliffs at the entrance to Sooke Harbour, and there he built a resort hotel, the Sooke Harbour House, at the butt of Whiffen Spit, the long shingle bar that almost closes off the harbour. By the time we knew him he had sold it to a chef from Québec.

Soon after we first encountered Kohout we began to go down to his old farmhouse. We could not afford a car, and we had to walk, mostly along a narrow dirt road through the bush. The walks back along the unlit road after dark were sometimes nervous, for cougar and bear often used this piece of land as a thoroughfare from Sooke Harbour to the hills. Sometimes we were assailed by a sense of presence and, halting, heard a swish in the vegetation, perhaps a slight crack of a twig, that ended immediately after we stopped, and would know that a cougar was following us. And, though we knew that only when they were sick and starving did cougars attack human beings, we would still hurry to reach the main road.

Kohout had strange tales to relate, with a slightly contemptuous Viennese amusement, about displaced English aristocrats and remittance men who gave a pinchbecky glitter to genteel life in the region thirty or forty years before we arrived. He did not have a historical mind, but he did have a European way of valuing the past. He was an anecdotalist, with a mind full of restless memories, yet he helped to populate the tangling bush around us.

So, when we joined him and Natalie at lunch on the ferry that day in May 1952, we were receptive to his suggestions about our future. Why not remain at Sooke? Kohout suggested. I would have time to write at leisure, without the distractions of finding my feet in a city, and I could build my connections in England and the United States to make up for the lack of outlets in Canada.

Half-convinced, we protested that we now had nowhere to live. A louder cackle than most, and then Kohout declared that he had the perfect solution. He had allowed the loggers to take out the largest timber on his clifftop land, and now he was dividing it into strips, almost an acre each, with more than a hundred feet of water frontage. The price was $950, and we could pay it off at $50 a month without interest. Since we already knew how to build a house, the second time would be quicker, and he could help us. There was a cabin on one of the lots, built by an old hermit who had died a couple of years before. Anton and Natalie, having left their farmhouse, were camping there at present, but we could occupy it for the time we needed to build our house.

The morass of poverty and frustration into which we plunged in 1949 should have been lesson enough. But now, forgetting that, we went with Kohout up the sawdust road the loggers had made. Small trees and underbrush had been left as a protective band along the roadside, dominated by a single giant first-growth Douglas fir, about twelve feet in diameter. The rest of the ground was the bare forest floor, dotted with stumps, but down the cliffs the trees still grew high, and there was a steep path to a shingly beach that gave way to sand where the tide lapped up. A bald eagle sat on one of the clifftop trees; delicately roseate lady's slipper orchids were blooming among the roots of the firs. We breathed the scent of the sun-warmed conifers, and talked about the kind of house that might stand there. As all of us liked the Austrian Alps it was natural that the idea of a Tyrolean chalet emerged. Inge sat down on a stump and sketched it on an envelope: a single large room, L-shaped and swinging round to the kitchen alcove whose wood stove would keep us warm in winter, a shower and toilet, windows on all sides to keep the room light in the shadow of the trees, a front verandah, window boxes and painted shutters, and the walls covered in rough cedar to fit the woodland. And this was the house we built. For we had fallen in love with the land, not with its stumps and slash, but as it might be when we had cleared it, planted grass and fruit trees, and built a proper way down the cliff.

We completed the house in six weeks of hard work, with handsaw and hammer. Our old friend Doug helped me over a weekend with the rafters, and one day Dirty Sam brought his vast bird's nest of a beard for a cursing day of tall tales about the Klondike as he laid the bricks for our chimney. For the rest we did it all, down to the wiring and plumbing. They were long summer days, from eight in the morning until ten at night, and usually twelve hours out of the fourteen would be spent on the house; I was never so tired, or so slim, or so healthy, as at the end of those six weeks.

Kohout was fascinated. He would appear with a loping walk through the trees, and stand with his head a bit on one side and his eyes darting foxily. "My, you're doing well!" he would cackle, and then begin to offer help.

His first passion was for laying concrete. When we poured the foundation blocks for the floor beams to rest on, he helped us hand-mix with shovels, and when we poured the concrete slab for the steps he again appeared. But we found that Kohout's passion had a lurid side. I have never met a man who more exemplified such classic anarchist maxims as Proudhon's *destruam et aedificabo* ("I build up and I destroy") and Bakunin's "The passion to destroy is also a creative passion." For Kohout was fascinated by dynamite and fire.

I had not thought much about how we would get rid of the stumps on the property. I calculated that some might be grubbed out and burnt, and that the two or three large ones might be disguised with shrubs and creepers. "Impossible!" declared Kohout. "It will take you weeks to grub out the smallest. And the large ones will be an eyesore for ever! You must *dynamite* them!" His crest of hair seemed to rise up as he spat out the words, and his cackle reached a tremolo of excitement. "I will show you! We will do it together!"

Having read and written so much about the famous anarchist *dynamiteros*, I was amused that I should find myself learning how to use the legendary stuff. So I agreed, since Kohout promised to do the more delicate tasks of fitting the detonators and the fuses.

We began with a couple of small and distant stumps, and Kohout led me through digging a suitable recess, well down between the roots of a tree, bundling the five or six sticks of dynamite, attaching the detonator and fuse, then burying the charge with good stiff mud around it and tamping earth over it to make everything firm, before we finally lit the fuse and headed for cover. With intense expectation we squatted behind another stump or a pile of brush, waiting until there was a satisfying crack in the air, a thudding vibration in the ground beneath us, a shower of earth pattering among the trees, and we stood up to see smoke drifting up between the neatly lifted and bisected or trisected stump.

The biggest stump of all was at least eight feet in diameter where it had been cut six feet from the ground; it was supported by heavily buttressing roots. It stood perhaps 150 feet from the house, and we should have blown it before I even began construction. We decided that it would have to be sprung before the windows were put in, and Kohout calculated that if we laid the charge properly we could direct the blast so that the house would not be harmed. So we went ahead, excavating a sap under the stump's centre.

Kohout was in a state of extreme excitement while this was going on, and when our sap was ready he huddled into it with a great bundle of fifty sticks of dynamite. He emerged, grinning and cackling. "That should do it! But, let me see! I've some old dynamite stored away that is probably not much good any longer. But it might give a bit of an extra boost!" So off he trotted to the cellar underneath an old barn and emerged with another twenty-five sticks wrapped in an ancient newspaper. These too we packed around the fifty, and then went on with our final preparations. "Whack it hard!;" shouted Kohout as we tamped, and whack I did, fearing all the time that too hard a bang might somehow set off the detonator.

When this was done Inge and Natalie, who had watched with horrified fascination, went off into the deep woods with our black cat Tim. I ran out into the lane to make sure no cars or people were around. And then we lit the fuse and headed into the trees a hundred yards away, where we squatted down in a ferny dell. We thought that we were far enough away to avoid falling debris, but when the mine did blow with an earth-shaking roar (the old stale dynamite turning out as good as the new), we cowered as rocks and hunks of wood went flying high in the air, peppering the woods a hundred yards beyond us. I rushed back immediately, scared for the house, but Kohout's calculations had been exact. We had blown the stump apart into four vast segments and the building was not even scratched.

I became so infected with Kohout's enthusiasm that when he sold the next lot to a Danish logger and offered to blow his stumps, I gladly agreed to act as assistant blaster without pay. But it was how my career as a *dynamitero* ended. We were dealing with a moderate-sized stump that, we decided, needed ten sticks of dynamite. We lit the fuse, and retreated for cover. We squatted there. Nothing happened. When I looked into Kohout's eyes they no longer danced but were fixed and anxious. He could not explain what had gone wrong. But we could not leave the charge there.

"What can we do?" "Risk our lives," said Kohout, his cackle quavering. "We can carefully uncover the charge and disconnect it. That is very risky. Or we can dig beside it and put in a smaller charge which we hope will blow the first. That is ten per cent less risky." "I'll settle for ten per cent."

So we got to work, digging carefully, in the end with trowels, beside the first charge, put in a couple more sticks, with detonator and fuse, hurriedly filled in over the second charge, lit the fuse, and ran. This time the double charge blew in a fine fountain of soil and stones, and we embraced each other and danced crazily in relief. I never blew another stump. Nor, so far as I know, did Kohout.

But there were other ways of fulfilling the destructive urge. Fire was still needed to consume the stumps, and we would drag slash and rubbish out of the woods and pile it around them in preparation for the evening change of the wind, when the fires would burn with passion and clarity. Inge, Natalie, Kohout, and I would feed the marvellously incandescent cores of the stumps, and over the crackling of the flames we would hear the slap of the seals as they played below the cliff or the crashing splash of the killer whales proceeding towards the harbour.

But Kohout was as dangerous a man with a match as he was with dynamite. Kohout put a match to a pile of brush. It was early September now, and the last three weeks had been rainless, so that the rubbish among the trees had dried out. By a freak chance, the wind changed from the customary southwester to a southeaster, blowing right along our cliff. We had our own forest fire, the sky blazing a hundred yards away from our house.

Kohout darted along the lee of the fire, intoxicated with excitement. When I suggested we get the Sooke fire engine he was so opposed that I knew he feared prosecution for setting a fire in the dry season. "It will burn out! It will burn out!" he kept on saying. It had only to run another half-mile, I pointed out, and then it would start to burn into the thick woodland of the next big property along the coast. He still refused to go.

We had no telephone, and we feared too much for our own house for either of us to walk even the half-mile to Sooke Harbour House, which did have a telephone. So we stayed, our only weapon a garden hose which we took turns spraying on the roof to put out the sparks that blew over from the blaze. There was nothing we could do with the fire on the cliff except wait it out. When the fire had crept to the edge of the next property, the wind did shift and die down, but there were still smouldering pockets along the cliff that all night kept exploding into small fires. I went down next morning, to see our cliff black and still smoking, the rubbish burnt away and many of the smaller trees killed; fortunately the bigger trees had not been harmed.

As winter came on, Kohout, who suffered from bronchial asthma, began to disappear for spells to avoid the intensely humid coastal winter: trips to the California desert ("For drying out," as he cackled), to Corvallis where Natalie had been a professor ("For edification"), to Penticton ("For elevation"). But he would appear again, scuttling through the trees to look at our lot and say, "My, you're doing well!"

BY AUTUMN WE HAD COMPLETED a comfortable small cottage and had ploughed and seeded into a promising meadow the land between the house and the cliff. Each morning I worked with saw, axe, and wedge for an hour cutting and splitting the day's stove wood. Twice a week, when we could not scrounge lifts, we would walk four miles into the village with our rucksacks to buy provisions and collect mail. On bright days I might clear more ground for flower and vegetable beds.

Besides *Proudhon*, I wrote critical essays, and historical articles largely based on the knowledge I had gained in recent years about North America west of the Rockies. I established long-standing connections with the *Geographical Magazine* and *History Today* in England, with the *Sewanee Review*, the *New Republic* and the *Saturday Review of Literature* in the United States. In Canada I continued to give talks on the CBC networks and even sold a series of documentary programs on the history of utopian writing.

But still I was far from making a good living. When all the bills for our house had been paid we were again in debt and as soon as the weather broke in early spring, I laboured for a friend who was building his house.

One day I was working a small electrically operated concrete mixer, standing on wet ground. Suddenly, as another man pushed his barrow forward and I began to swing the handle to fill it, I felt as if my whole body had been struck a great blow, heard a strange yelling voice which I realized had been my own, and came to myself lying flat on my back; someone had switched off the power, but my hand was seared with a wide burn that took several weeks to heal. Instead of showing sympathy and concern, my friend and his wife looked at me with a suspicion verging on hostility. I realized that they feared I might try to get compensation from them. So I quietly left.

Then Inge and I persuaded a fisherman who was building a house near us to let us dig his basement. For almost two weeks we laboured with pick, shovel, and wheelbarrow, from morning often until dusk. We were paid partly in cash and partly in kind, and received $120 and as much salmon and halibut as we could eat for the next two months. We got very tired of fish. By the summer of 1953 we had decided we were really urban people. We were lonely and lost in so remote a countryside, despite the friends we had made.

One evening in Vancouver Bill McConnell took us up to Capitol Hill, where Jack and Doris Shadbolt were just completing their house on a brow looking over the harbour to the Strait of Georgia. The house was isolated, and woods extended beyond it. As we talked about our situation, Jack waved towards the trees. "You know, there's a cabin in there. It hasn't been occupied for years, but it's in good shape. I think the people who own it might even like someone to live there to keep an eye on their property." The idea stirred our hopes, and when we got back to the island we put up our cottage for sale. We waited a nervous two months until we finally sold it to a couple of women teachers who were so taken with the way Inge had arranged it that they bought it with almost everything it contained, and we set off with no more than our clothes, books, manuscripts, and our cat.

We never saw Kohout again. But not long afterwards we heard he had died in a way that seemed to fit the more grotesque side of his nature, for he was involved in a freak accident in a hotel lift. His leg was trapped and it had to be amputated; the shock killed him. I sadly remembered how, like Bakunin, he had seen the poetry of destruction; like a Zoroastrian, he had loved the leaping of the fire.

WE HAD ARRANGED SO THAT the women who bought our house would pay off what we owed to Kohout for the land. The rest of the modest payment would be paid in two installments. The first, which we received at the end of June, would enable us to start again in Vancouver; the second we had decided to spend on a long-contemplated journey to Mexico. *Ravens and Prophets* had come out a few months before and modest royalties were starting to come in, so that we were not in immediate want.

The months that followed were in their own way idyllic. The cabin, which we were allowed to use for no payment provided I made some elementary repairs, was minute — little more than a quarter the size of our last house. The floor was worn and broken, and a hideous tier of bunks dominated the small interior. But one end was entirely glass which, when we washed it, revealed a view through the trees towards the Vancouver Island mountains; there was a good wood stove, a folding table, some fitted cupboards, and by the time I had spent three or four days laying a new floor and dismantling the bunks, using their mattresses to make divans on either side, it had been turned into a snug and luminous habitation.

Nobody came into the wood except an old man who sometimes wandered through looking for berries and mushrooms, in which we also shared. From the hillside one could see the city spread every night below one like a great luminous map. There were red squirrels and pheasants, blue jays and pileated woodpeckers, brilliant western tanagers that rested in the great fir tree above the cabin and the little white-bellied field mice that sometimes found their way into the cabin, ran over our beds, and had to be captured with sheets of cardboard slid under biscuit tins and transported into the deep woods from which they would often come back.

We became part of a creative community. Jack and Doris Shadbolt did everything possible to make our life viable. The cabin was wired but there was no power connection and no water supply. But we ran a cable through the woods to the Shadbolts' house, and were given a key, getting our daily supply of water from a utility room.

As we were all living active creative lives, the Shadbolts' impulses, and ours, fed each other. Jack was then teaching at the Vancouver School of Art, but he was painting hard at the same time, already beginning to create the icons that owed so much to local Indian traditions and to gain a reputation as a superb colourist. He worked semi-publicly, responding to the world around him as he painted, and so when one lived near him one became caught up in the impetus of his creative process and willy nilly we became a participating audience. His exuberance dominated our little community. But the rest of us were equally hard at work. Doris was already a docent in the Vancouver Art Gallery, where she eventually became curator, but at home she was making beautiful silver jewellery in abstract forms. Inge, who had lived near Bernard Leach years before in Cornwall and been fascinated by his work, took up pottery, studying with Reg Dixon at the Vancouver Art School and showing a marvellous natural hand. I was making headway on Proudhon.

It was a book into which I entered deeply, emotionally as well as intellectually. For that reason I still think that, apart from my much later book on Gabriel Dumont, it is the best of my biographies. It was not merely that I found Proudhon's non-violent and mutualist kind of anarchism, with its emphasis on the network of independent workers in free cooperation and its strong peasant-craftsman basis, sympathetic. I also found so many similarities between the situation of this mid-nineteenth century peasant-printer turned into radical writer and my own that I could write of him with all the identification of one who had shared a similar predicament.

We had both endured poverty in our childhood among families with diminishing fortunes; we had both been academically brilliant boys denied a university education for lack of means and became autodidacts who learnt most we knew by personal effort, finding how to write by practicing the art. And at the time I described his misfortunes I was struggling, like Proudhon, to make a living by writing in a generally unreceptive society.

Proudhon's difficulties were due to the fact that what he wrote did not please the literati of either the left or the right in the France of the 1848 revolutions and the second Napoleonic Empire. He was isolated because of his opinions. My difficulties were due to the fact that, even if my opinions had been acceptable to the majority of Canadians, which they were not, I would still have found it difficult to live by writing here. So I was also working out my own creative frustrations and relied on the book to restart my career as a fulltime writer after the past four barren years. But it was not easy to place with a publisher, though it found a good one when Herbert Read at Routledge & Kegan Paul brought it out almost three years after completion, in 1956.

Despite difficulties, existence in Vancouver was satisfying because I was back in something like the cultural world I had known in London, with the added satisfaction of living in a setting of mountains and salt water. It was not merely the miniature community of tastes and living that we shared with Jack and Doris Shadbolt on Capitol Hill. Through the Shadbolts, the Bobaks, Earle Birney and the novelist Robert Harlow, who had taken over Ross McLean's position as Talks Producer for the

CBC in Vancouver, we become acquainted not merely with a few writers and artists of some standing, but others who were starting on the upward path, such as Arthur Erickson, then a student of architecture, and Bill Reid, the Haida sculptor, who would often be the announcer for talks I broadcasted in the old CBC studios in the Hotel Vancouver; we also met emerging painters of the 1950s like Gordon Smith, John Korner and Aleister Ball.

Our cabin, with its air of remoteness from civilization and yet its panoramic view of the city, appealed to these people, and we would entertain them at open air dinners which Inge ingeniously cooked on her tiny wood stove and a couple of hotplates. Thanks largely to the acquaintances she had made at the Art School, we came to know more painters and potters than writers, and I found the pattern so mentally broadening that even now I spend more time with visual than with literary artists. This reversed the pattern of my London years, when as an apprentice author I had felt the need for fellow writers to share my problems and reassure me. I found in Vancouver the mixture of stimulation and detachment that I need, and I have been fortunate enough to find it in a physical setting of whose beauty I have never tired. Settling in Vancouver was, in the creative sense, finding home.

V

THE BONES OF MEXICO

IN THE AUTUMN, about the same time as I finished *Proudhon*, we received the final payment on our house in Sooke, and left for Mexico. I was drawn towards Mexico partly because D.H. Lawrence (in *The Plumed Serpent* but especially in *Mornings in Mexico*) Aldous Huxley (in *Beyond the Mexique Bay*) and Graham Greene (in *The Lawless Roads* and *The Power and the Glory*) had made it part of my imaginary world, a land of violence and beauty, where life was lived more precariously and unpredictably yet perhaps more truly than in Europe or even in the rest of North America. It was easily reachable, and cheap. I hoped such a different world would stimulate my creative fires, and I had the vision that perhaps, in the three months there that we would probably be able to afford, I might win my way back into fiction by conceiving and making a good start on a novel.

We travelled by bus, down through Seattle, San Francisco, and Los Angeles, (which we found a detestable and inhuman place) and over the Sierra through the monotonous California desert into the much more spectacular Arizona one, with its natural citadels of red and purple rock and its gigantic thickets of monstrous cacti. We took three days crossing the desert to the Mexican border, and this was an appropriate prelude, for already we encountered extremities of nature and routine brutalities in human behaviour.

At a dusty hamlet called Sheffield in the Texas desert the melancholy woman who ran the sand-scoured café told us she could not make any more coffee until the wind, which had not blown in their hollow for a week, came back to turn the pumps and give them water. At a grim little town called Pecos, where we stayed a night, the temperature until sunset was about 110 degrees Fahrenheit, and we could only lie naked under the fans in the motel room until, as the sun set, the temperature fell and we were able to venture out for food. And at a bus station between San Antonio and the Mexican border, a handsome, dignified black — a teacher from a northern city — who had come with us to the counter to feed, was quietly asked by the waitress to go to the kitchen; just as quietly he went.

We crossed the border, bribed our way into Mexico because the officials ingeniously found some irregularity in Inge's status and took three days travelling through the heart of the country to Mexico City. It was a land as strange and in its own dark way as pristine as we had ever hoped to find, and still its images remain in my mind. For twenty miles, in the desert between Nuevo Laredo and Monterey our bus passed through a westward migration of butterflies, so numerous that they seemed like a blizzard of white and yellow flowers, with great swallowtails and bright orange creatures a handspan across appearing here and there among them.

A day later we entered the Huasteca, a jungle region where the Huastecan Indians still lived in self-sufficient neatness as they had done before the Spaniards came. A small and delicately built people, their round faces smooth in outline under bangs, their large eyes staring and gentle, they lived in houses of bamboo poles fastened closely together and grew orchards and sugar plantations as meticulously cultivated as Chinese gardens. From their market town of Tamazunchale we began the long drive upward through climatic zones to the high plateau. The road wound its way between tall sugarloaf peaks densely felted with vegetation, and as I watched the mists boiling out of the canyons and coiling up the crests I understood the art of the Tao, the way of nature in response to which the old Chinese painters had worked, for these were their landscapes faithfully rendered by the land itself, nature dramatically imitating art.

Then, as we climbed through the pine forests on to the plateau, came the third epiphany, which was that extraordinary flowering of the Mexican autumn that Lawrence called a "strange, inverted spring." Whole hillsides lay under a golden lustre of orange and ochre marigolds. Crimson dahlias and yellow sunflowers, little scarlet zinnias and sages of every shade of blue and purple mingled together in other places to give the appearance of a forest floor in a millifiore tapestry, and over the open meadows spread the mauve-pink flush of wild cosmos.

Vividly perceived experiences of this kind continued, and are recorded in my book *To the City of the Dead*. The city of the dead was Mitla, the ancient Zapotec city south of Oaxaca which represented the southern limit of our journey. Before we reached there we had travelled north from Mexico City to the part of the plateau known as El Bajio, and had lived for two months in the old colonial town of San Miguel Allende. From there we travelled through the higher plateau region known as Los Altos to Guadalajara, and thence through Michoacan to Patzcuaro, and eventually southward through Cholula and Puebla to Oaxaca and Mitla.

Mexico liberated the physical vision, and returned to me some of that preternatural clarity of perception, that illuminated heightening of reality, which I experienced at times in childhood. This heightened awareness, in response to light on the Mexican plateau, occured one evening near the colonial town of Ixmiquilpan on the journey to Mexico City. Here in the afterglow the stubble of the maize fields suddenly shone like square lakes of gold; the old buildings radiated a warm light from the heart of their massive stones; even the drab adobe of the little villages took on the ruddy warmth of red sandstone; bushes burned with green fire. The people were transformed into a new race; the brown of their skins had an inner intensity, as if ichor flowed in their veins, and the faded colours of their poor clothes ignited suddenly into glowing magnificence. It was a time of transfiguration. And then the dusk began to thicken with tropical rapidity, and everything was blotted out. The country around us lay dark and impenetrable beyond the long probing of the headlights.

None of the often amusing but rarely dramatic episodes in which we were involved was so important as the sense of detachment from our past life Mexico induced in me, and the shift in my view of life that was the result. There were times when this disturbing feeling became so strong that I felt as if my personality had emptied itself, as if the life I remembered so faintly had been that of another person. In San Miguel I found it hard to write anything. The most I could do was to keep a diary of observations and impressions. I soon learnt that my experience was not exceptional.

What one perceives on reaching Mexico, if one observes it with anything sharper than the most superficial tourist eye, is a ruthless stripping down of life to the bones of existence. It begins with the landscape of the plateau, the endless hills worn down to arid skeletons, the plains desiccated into sandy wastes, the lakes dried into alkali flats, the vegetable forms almost geometrical in their starkness, so that even the flow of sap seems dried into tortured angularity. One feels no organic link with one's surroundings and, at the same time, a sense of being isolated by them from any more sympathetic world. Physically, it is a country without compromise, made for the direct confrontation of man and death, across a vista of challenging indifference.

This challenge of the landscape is repeated in the existence of human and animal beings, and all the time one perceives the spark of consciousness burning clearly but meagrely. In such a life nothing is concealed; everything negative and malignant is forced on one's attention with merciless candour. Poverty, hunger, disease, inequality, injustice, violence, death — none can be ignored. The Mexican may be fatalistic about such matters, he may profit or rebel against them. But he rarely avoids them or anaesthetizes them out of his consciousness. He accepts the existential tragedy of which circumstances daily remind him, and by doing so he is often able to gain a great satisfaction from the rest of life; as Proudhon once suggested, the man who realizes that he is in the midst of death begins to live with intensity.

The visitor from other places, where social circumstances may have cushioned him, can hardly avoid an immediate sense of disturbance. It is partly a moral horror, and it is partly a feeling of guilt at the relative prosperity of his own life in comparison with the privation he sees around him. After a while such feelings lose their acuteness, not because one ever accepts the vast injustices of Mexican life, but because one realizes that, even for the poor, life is not so abysmally dejected as one has imagined.

Mexico is not a place for escape. It is a place for facing the extremities of existence, and most of the would-be escapers who drifted there in fact committed suicide either artistically or physically. There were a good many painters and writers in San Miguel who were living a kind of death of uninspired routine, and more than a few expatriates who were direct or indirect suicides. By the end of two months of drinking and creative frustration I needed to escape from the threat of becoming one of these.

In Mexico I experienced catastrophically the back-to-the-wall feeling I had sensed sometimes at Sooke. Having been there made me much more receptive to existentialist philosophies. And from that time onwards I began to read extensively the French fiction and drama one may term absurdist, and to be influenced, in my attitude to life and death and in my ideas about writing, not so much by Sartre, whom like Orwell I have always regarded as a windbag, but by Malraux and by Camus especially. I saw the overwhelming significance of the extreme moments when one faces existence stripped of all pretences, how they give meaning to life and also to dying, and out of such a recognition I also came to accept that we are self-made by our own choices, that there is no common human nature but only individual natures whose mutual tensions form the net that holds society together, and that in living with our death we define ourselves in our creative action, as the Mexicans defied the cruelty and deprivation of their lives by the splendour of their fiestas. I came to accept the belief that the justification for a life in art is that it is the supreme defiance of death. Cultures die as well as men; many have done so in Mexico. But their artifacts remain and continue to speak in a hidden language.

In later years, when we went to even poorer countries, it became evident that the experience of Mexico had inoculated us; I never again underwent such a culture shock but began to recognize the special way in which a society had to be approached and not judged, but understood. I came to see existentialism and cultural relativism going together, and fitting in with anarchism in a grand denial of moral, political, and aesthetic absolutes. Mexico changed me, and much I have done and created since has sprung from that testing encounter with the dark extremities of existence.

VI

PERSONA NON GRATA

AS SOON AS I RETURNED to Canada the writing block I had suffered in Mexico was immediately released. In two months I wrote four articles, five radio talks and a long documentary script on Shelley; before me stared a list including five articles on Mexico that had been commissioned, five reviews and critical articles, and a verse radio play on Maximilian.

Clearly, my fortunes had changed since moving to Vancouver. I was getting more radio work locally because I could maintain contact with producers by making a short trip downtown, and the Mexican experience furnished me with articles for magazines like the *New Statesman* and *Encounter*, *History Today* and the *Geographical Magazine*; Mexico was still a comparatively unknown country to most English people.

Yet sources of income were precarious, and our earnings sufficed us only because we lived rent free in our cabin, which involved its own problems, for the winter turned hard and snowy, and the little uninsulated shack was bitterly cold. To add to the precariousness of our freelance existence, the income from my books had shrunk almost to nothing, since during the past five years only *Ravens and Prophets* had been published. *Pierre-Joseph Proudhon*, had not yet found a home, and the consumption of time spent in running around after freelance work and then writing radio scripts and articles, meant that I was working very slowly on my book on Mexico.

I hoped to get some kind of teaching position at a university. I had never taught, yet in some areas, notably modern British writing, I had a broader and more direct knowledge than many professors who were teaching the subject. Moreover, the universities were interested in having me appear as a visiting speaker. The University of British Columbia held a Shaw Festival, and I was invited to give two lectures. A little later

I gave a lecture at the University of Washington on the Welsh elements in Dylan Thomas's poetry. These occasions taught me that I could hold an audience, and I began to feel more confidence. But when I approached Roy Daniells about a position at the University of British Columbia, it was obvious that my lack of university training was an insuperable barrier.

However, in the early summer a source of regular income did appear. At this time Robert Harlow was producing my radio talks and we had become good friends. One evening, at dinner, we were discussing the lack of literary magazines in Canada. *Contemporary Verse* had disappeared. *Northern Review* was becoming increasingly conservative since John Sutherland's transformation into a devout Catholic; soon it would vanish as John died slowly of lung cancer. Nobody, in Vancouver at least, seemed to have enough money to start a new journal, and the Canada Council had not yet appeared to provide funding support. Inge remarked that obviously the only source of ready funds was the CBC; why not a Little Magazine of the Air? Harlow was taken with the idea, and passed it on to Robert Weaver in Toronto. Shortly afterwards the Anthology program was launched. As a kind of reward, because Inge had suggested the idea, I was appointed an advisory editor, and several years afterwards for a monthly fee I read manuscripts.

Since my tastes in literature did not agree completely with those of Robert Weaver, who generally controlled the program, my recommendations were not always accepted. Among the manuscripts I received was a dull story by Mordecai Richler, and I recommended its rejection; it appeared in the first Anthology program. Weaver was — and is — a confirmed admirer of both Richler and Callaghan, both of whom I regard as uneven writers whose failures have outweighed their successes. But such divergences of taste never affected my good relationship with Weaver, and when he came to Vancouver that summer we had several conversations which familiarized me more with the Canadian literary scene, for Bob knew every English Canadian writer of any significance, and he had amusing, sometimes scandalous tales to tell about most of them. Also, he talked of the project which he and a few others in Toronto were developing for a literary magazine that would be in print. I agreed to join that too, as a writer and a name on the masthead. Out of such discussions, which Weaver carried on with many other writers, emerged *Tamarack Review*, the first magazine of the Canadian literary revival of the 1950s.

There was no doubt, by 1954, that the literary situation in Canada was beginning to change for the better. The report of the Massey Commission in 1951 had encouraged people in all the arts, and, though the Canada Council it recommended was not established until 1957, we were expecting that something of the kind would happen. But there were many independent signs of a stirring of life, as new writers began to appear and somehow to get their books published. Yet, aware as I was that prospects were improving in Canada, slowly but perceptibly, I was tempted southward.

DURING THE EARLY SUMMER, with the Shadbolts and the Bobaks, Inge and I went on a trip through the drylands of the British Columbia interior, where the land was flowering with a brilliance and abundance it never achieves on the rain-forested coast. When we got back, a message from Earle Birney was awaiting me. Robert Heilman, who headed the Department of English at the University of Washington, wanted a lecturer for a term to fill in for a man who had been taken ill; Earle suggested that I should get in touch with Heilman. I wondered whether I could adapt myself to the routine of teaching, and then a letter came from Heilman recollecting my lecture on Thomas, and inviting me to take the post.

I accepted. We would have no financial anxieties for three or four months, and I was touched by the fact that the Americans had shown themselves more flexible than the Canadians by hiring me with no degree and no teaching experience, just on the strength of my writing and a single lecture. I felt challenged by the idea of acquiring a new skill, and I guessed that I might have more time to work on my book than if I continued in the time-consuming freelance round in Vancouver. I got a temporary permit without difficulty from the U.S. Immigration officials at the border, and we went down to Seattle in August and found an apartment looking over Lake Washington but near the campus. There we were to stay all the academic year, for by December the man I replaced was dead and my appointment was extended.

The teaching was my main problem, since I had not only to run ahead of my students in learning unfamiliar course material, which was not difficult, but also to teach myself how to teach as I went along. The day on which I met my first class my hand shook as I handed out the course outlines I had prepared, and it was hard to control my voice. I was the most frightened person in that classroom.

But the next day I was more self-possessed, and found that I could hold students' attention as I read from my notes and kept on talking fast for fear that an interruption might put me off my balance. Very soon I found that I had a rapport with the students. I had no models but the schoolmasters of my distant past, so I kept to clear explanation, throwing in a few provocative ideas as I went along, and found it worked. My having no degree and no university background not only interested the students, but predisposed them to me; here was someone who had got on top of the system without having to go through it as they must, which they admired and which I soon learnt to exploit. Teaching is a histrionic art if it is to be done well, and by the end of my first year I had turned myself into a pedagogic actor.

Each term I taught one or two classes of freshman composition, and one or two in comparative literature, portmanteau courses that could include anything from *Don Quixote* to Silone's *Bread and Wine*. These I enjoyed because I was drawing on my accumulated knowledge and could talk about the ideas the books represented, and generally I found they attracted the more sensitive, intelligent students. The freshmen classes I endured with no better grace than the students, though I disguised my boredom more expertly. I was appalled by the standard of education they revealed.

Even at university level the teaching system was weakened by democratic concepts used in the wrong place and in the wrong way. No sooner had I arrived than I was taken aside by a friendly colleague and told that because this was a state university and not an Ivy League private college, it was assumed that people had a right not only to an education, but to pass through the system. So, I was quietly warned, "we fail students very sparingly." I was also approached by the football coach with a plea for the two gorillas from his team who were enrolled in one of my classes. I failed them, and many other functional illiterates who had found their way virtually unimpeded into the university; some of the most unteachable were later passed as proficient in English by other teachers when they repeated the freshmen course.

I found the courses undemanding of either students or professors, for I soon realized that I was expected to teach at a level no higher than that of the sixth form at a good English grammar school. As I conquered my nervousness, I quickly discovered that the only way to achieve anything in such a system was to set the level of one's teaching to the intelligence of the best students, and never to compromise by pandering to the ignorant or the frivolous-minded. One had to perform, to call upon whatever wit one possessed, in order to catch the attention of the students, and having caught it one must never relax it. A single term of teaching sufficed for me to shed most of my vague and lax concepts of progressive education. I was there to offer certain ideas, views of life, aesthetic experiences, and to open minds to receive them, and I found that by challenging lazy minds I could provoke them into response. I was glad to have had such good and exacting teachers in my youth. Often it was the memory of what I had gained from their instruction that sustained me in setting my own standards.

The circumstance I regretted most was that the school year was fragmented into three unconnected terms, and after teaching a student for less than three months one might not seen him or her again. This made it impossible to get to know one's students, and so I rarely experienced what I later found to be a redeeming pleasure of teaching: to observe and assist over a crucial year of life the awakening of a mind passing from youth into adulthood. A few individuals particularly interested in literature, with writing ambitions of their own, would seek me out for something more interesting than complaining about their grades, but my own anxieties at having to prepare classes made me too preoccupied with problems of keeping afloat to allow me to seek broader links.

As for my colleagues in the Department of English I found among them a puzzling mixture of cordiality and apprehension. I was never made to feel different from them because of my lack of formal education, and the general hospitality and helpfulness, and even the candid curiosity about my achievements and attitutdes, far exceeded anything a stranger might expect if he were newly arrived at an English or even a Canadian institution. Here I was encountering Americans at their best.

Yet there was an undercurrent of reserve which I quickly realized had nothing to do with me personally. It was related to the times through which Americans, especially academics and intellectuals, had been living. After all, 1954 was the year when Sentor Joseph McCarthy was finally defeated through his attempt to show that the U.S. Army, like the country's other institutions, was a nest of Communists. A sense of relief spread over the campus that autumn when McCarthy was removed from the chairmanship of his investigative committee and condemned by a majority vote in the senate.

But for many of the professors who were old enough to have been involved in the radical movements of the 1930s the wounds caused by fear over their past and shame over their later caution were deep and lasting. Some would not talk about the past if it touched upon their political beliefs; others — the healthier ones — talked with an irony that was often bitter and self-mocking. One man, who had associated with Hemingway and Joyce in Paris and had an encyclopedic but almost entirely unwritten knowledge of the "lost generation", told me how one night at the height of the McCarthy terror he had found his fear of investigation so crippling that he had taken all the left-wing books he had acquired during the 1930s, to a cottage in a remote corner of Puget Sound. In the middle of the night Harry Burns — for I can safely name him now thirty years afterwards — had walked out to the end of a pier and launched all these incendiary works — Marx and Engels, Lenin and Gorki, even Malraux and Aragon — on to the quenching waters. The next morning he had gone walking on the beach to enjoy his newfound feeling of immunity. He saw something dark and rectangular floating in on the tide, and as he watched with horror a gentle wave deposited *Das Kapital* at his feet. He felt, he told me, as doomed as Polycrates must have done when the great fish was opened and the priceless ring he had thrown into the sea to placate the jealous gods was handed back to him.

Very few people then believed that the relief afforded by McCarthy's departure was permanent, and sometimes I was warned to be careful what I said in class, since there were many conservative-minded students around, and any of them was capable of bearing a tale to the Dean. Actually, I never heard of this happening, but the fear was real, and most of the professors circumspectly handled controversial issues and avoided discussing them. It was a bad atmosphere for a place of learning to generate, and when it led to cautious, sometimes positively cowardly teaching, the students suffered as much as the teachers. In hindsight, it now seems to me that the rebellion of the next decade, against all things regulated and predictable, must already have been stirring.

AMONG THE CAUTIOUS AND MEDIOCRE spirits who make up most university faculties, there were some people of brilliance and personality who gave that year in Seattle its special tone. The Head of the Department, Robert Heilman, was one of the New Critics, a school with whom I have often argued, but he was an excellent Shakespearian scholar and flexible enough to have followed my work, so different in focus from his own, with a lasting interest that has kept us in touch intermittently over the past thirty years. A tall, hawk-faced Pennsylvania Dutchman, he was as capable of administering a difficult department of strongly conflicting personalities and of weaving through the Byzantine politics of a typical American university as he was of disentangling the verbal structures of *King Lear*. Though I was one of the lowest people on the academic totem pole, at first a sessional lecturer and just a step above the teaching assistants who were the real proletarians of the faculty, Heilman always treated me as a scholar and a writer, and did his best within a jealous department to give me the courses which he thought would best use my knowledge.

I had more directly to do with Jackson Matthews. Matthews, a tall, sardonic, insomniac Southerner and a close friend of Allen Tate, was a sensitive interpreter of Paul Valéry, and for the whole period I knew him, which extended some years beyond my departure from Seattle, he was preparing the definitive and many-volumed Bollingen translation of Valéry's works. He had come to the university as a Comparative Literature teacher, and ran a tiny subdepartment which consisted of him and of such part of me as was not involved in teaching freshmen how to construct sentences. With Heilman, he gave me courses in which I could effectively use my knowledge, and led me into the field of comparative literature. With Jack and his charming *belle laide* wife Martiel we passed many a bourbon-laced hour. The only occasion I remember with regret is that on which he brought me together with Allen Tate. It was at Theodore Roethke's house, in whose bibulous ambiance I got immoderately drunk, to Tate's obvious and tight-lipped disapproval, at the end of an evening that had started off with some of the most eruditely witty conversation I have heard. I always liked to listen to the Southerners talking.

Matthews is dead now, after lying for years in a coma with a rare degenerative disease, and so is Ted Roethke, that shambling bearlike infant of a man who wrote some of the most madly tender poetry of our age. Ted regarded me, because of my lack of an academic background, as his kind of man, and he was a great and understanding support to me in those difficult weeks when, as he realized, I was teaching myself to teach. I would not claim that I become his friend; few people could, for Ted was a lonely man. But we were allies.

Once I was asked to do an interview with Ted for broadcast in Canada by the CBC. It was taped on the campus radio station, and we talked a great deal about his poetry, of which he read several pieces. Ted arrived with a mickey of rye which he sipped through the interview until at the end of the hour it was finished; a whole half-bottle, and none — I am still furious to remember — tipped over to me.

Always unkempt, rather like a car salesman who has let himself go, and often drunk, Ted seemed to have an eroding sense of inadequacy, which often made him aggressive with his more academic colleagues, whose pomposities he would sometimes prick by roughly calling them "horses' arses" or "armpits", but he was very gentle with his students, who loved him as a kind of wayward father.

Ted's wife, Beatrice, who had been his student at Bennington College, was a beauty in the classic American vein; she had been a model and had at first sight a rather tubular, icy quality, with the firm jaw-line popular in Hollywood in the early 1950s. She looked unapproachable, but I found she was in some ways a very supportive, simple — though not simple-minded — woman. Towards the end of his life she tried to keep Ted for his own good within some kind of discipline. The result was resentment on his part, rarely openly expressed, and a furtive breaking of the rules. The last I heard from Ted was not long before his death in 1963, when he rang me up from Seattle — I was home in Vancouver — on some pretext I have understandably forgotten, because the real thing he had to tell me was that he thought he would be getting the

Nobel Prize. Then he asked me if I could have the call reversed, and pay for it, since Beatrice thought he was calling too many people. I recognized that joker in the Freudian pack, the non-Oedipal man. Linking the incident with Ted's poems, which show such obvious affection for and siding with his father, I saw the pattern of alliance with the father against the mother. I know the pattern — it's my own — and how it exasperates orthodox psychiatrists, as it must have exasperated Ted's.

I made much easier contact with Ted's disciple, David Wagoner, who arrived at Seattle the same day as we did. David was dark, good-looking and described by some of the women teachers as "electric". He was a good poet and a mediocre novelist. Some evenings he appeared at our flat with a case of beer, and we sat for hours talking about English and American poets. Later he arrived with Carolyn Kizer, a noisy ash-pale blonde from outside the university who turned out a fine poet. There were others with whom we maintained affectionate, memorable relationships: Margaret Duckett, who lived in the flat above us, became good friends with our cat Tim, and wrote a fine book on Bret Harte; Edward Bostetter, the gentle Romanticist and editor of Coleridge (also dead), his wife Betty and their superbly dignified Persian cat Figaro who at the age of eighteen would leap through hoops with disdainful elegance; and always Wayne Burns, at whose house by the lake I met the best of the graduate students, and especially Warren Tallman, who later moved to Vancouver and became a leading influence in the development of Canadian poetry during the 1960s.

Teaching, talking, partying, drinking; there was a great deal of them while I was in Seattle, but still I was removed from the need for continued freelance work and had time to write, at a little desk in the corner of the bedroom. In that year I abridged Proudhon, and Herbert Read finally accepted it for Routledge and Kegan Paul. I worked on *To the City of the Dead*. By the early summer of 1955 my agent John Smith had persuaded Geoffrey Faber to accept it — my association with Faber & Faber would last for the next two decades. Both books would appear in 1956.

By the end of the year I was offered a permanent post as Assistant Professor. It seemed a moment of portentous decision. If I accepted we would be abandoning our Canadian venture and opting for a future in the United States. My attachment to Canada was not yet strong enough to sway the issue. Feeling comfortable among the friends and associates we had acquired, weighing the fact of a permanent job and no more freelance anxieties, and looking to the greater possibilities for publishing my work in the United States, we decided on staying. Since we were now proposing to establish permanent residence, we had to go back to

Canada to obtain visas. At the end of June, 1955, we set off north, never doubting that some time in the summer we would return for good.

MY EXPECTATIONS OF A CAREER as an adoptive American writer, like that on which my friend Denise Levertov had already embarked, were dashed. When we got back to Vancouver, Doris and Jack Shadbolt suggested that it was pointless for us to move back into the cabin which had declined once again into a habitation for birds and mice. They invited us to stay in their house, and this we did, while the American consular service leisurely processed my visa application.

That summer the sunsets were glowing and dramatic every evening over the harbour and Georgia Strait. Jack was in his studio, painting often far into the nights on his gouaches of grass and seedscapes. I happily completed the final version of *To the City of the Dead*. Inge and Doris shared the cooking and every evening before dinner we would gather on the deck to drink martinis as the evening light grew rich and golden.

At last, in early September, the call from the consulate came. I went down in the morning, but by an oversight the secretary did not tell me that my case would not come up until the afternoon. As I sat unobserved in the waiting room over the lunch hour I heard voices through a half-open door and realized that two consular officials were discussing my case. One of them, to my surprise, was reading to the other passsages from my early polemic *Anarchy or Chaos* — naturally the most inflammatory — and exclaiming: "And this guy expects to go down into the States and teach school!"

The consulate in Vancouver had obviously unearthed information about me unknown to the immigration officials I had encountered at various border points, and I was prepared for the aggressiveness with which I was received after lunch by an official I had overheard — a young vice-consul obviously pleased about the credit he would gain for having discovered a dangerous radical trying to enter the United States. He was surprisingly knowledgeable about left-wing movements and also about my past. He knew much about my activities at the time of the trial of the British anarchists in 1945 and my subsequent editing of *Freedom*, (as I have already related in *Letter to the Past*), and he knew that I had attended the gathering in Berne in 1947 to commemorate the seventieth anniversary of Bakunin's death, which in his eyes had swollen into an important conspiratorial conference.

The vice-consul had no power to make a decision, but the next day the consul himself — the other man in the conversation — called me up. I went down again, and he told me, that, though he agreed I did not

seem to advocate violent action, I was still opposed to organized government and hence inadmissible under the McCarran Act. He hinted that if
I were willing to declare categorically that I was no longer an anarchist
and that I regretted having been one something might be arranged. I did
not respond, and he then told me he could not grant a visa. He obviously did not relish his task, and as I left he told me that if I wanted to
go down to Seattle to settle my affairs in the few days before the fact of
my inadmissibility had been filtered to the border posts, he would be
unaware that I was doing so.

I went back feeling elated rather than defeated. I knew there was a
battle ahead and enjoyed the idea, even though I suspected I would not
win. Jack Shadbolt caught my mood, and he went down into his studio to
paint a gay gouache of bottles and glasses and grape leaves to celebrate
the possibility that we would stay in Canada after all.

Since we could no longer trespass on the Shadbolts' hospitality, we
found a temporary home in Earle Birney's house on 3rd Avenue. Earle
had already begun the series of absences that ended in his parting from
Esther, and Esther offered us her basement, half of which was an immense games room we converted into a bed-sitting-room, and the other
half a kitchen designed like a ship's galley by some former owner with a
mania for boats. It even included an old ice-box, and we were among the
last people in Vancouver to whom the iceman came twice a week with
his great glassy block slung by immense tongues over his shoulder.

It was, at times, a turbulent house because of the presence in the attic
of John Pearson, the original of the reprobate academic, John Parlabane
in Robertson Davies' *The Rebel Angels*. John Pearson was almost as unbelievable as his fictional counterpart. He was a stocky man, running to
fat, with a square, pugnacious, boyish but ravaged face whose resemblance to Churchill's he would accentuate by wearing a white yachting
cap, which went with a gold-headed cane. He was a homosexual, an
alcoholic, and a waywardly brilliant man, and all three features had
combined to foster a bizarre existence; he had been a novice monk in an
Anglican Benedictine monastery in England, but had gone over the wall
after being disciplined for getting drunk on the sacramental wine. He
had held a professorship of philosophy at a prairie university until he
was expelled for his sins against propriety, and by the time we knew him
he was an academic pariah whom no college would employ.

Yet he was extremely learned in strange fields. I had fine times with
him, when he was relatively sober, discussing the history and doctrines
of those Bulgarian heretics, the Bogomils. Since I was studying the Russian Doukhobors, we enjoyed dwelling on the similarities between the
two sects and the possibilities of early contacts between them. In fact,

John convinced me that Douhoborism had its roots among the Bogomils, and I still give the idea a cautious credence.

Robertson Davies gives his character Parlabane a rather Mephistophelian quality, but any devilry John Pearson may have had was worn away by the time I knew him. He lived with all the furtive cunning of the inveterate alcoholic. Often, at night, we would be awakened while he rummaged like a great clumsy pack rat in the maze of pipes and airducts in the basement where he hid the bottles he sneaked into the house. Esther hit on manual work as a possible therapy, and allowed John to install in the garage a power saw to which he would cut the planks, out of which he began to construct neat, enormous pieces of furniture. The critical moments came when drinking and woodworking coincided. Some evenings we would stand on the lawn in the darkness, looking with tingling apprehension into the lit garage, where John in his yachting cap, reeling drunk, would be pushing planks into the saw. We did not dare go in, lest we scare him into a clumsy movement, and we decided that to cut off the power might be equally perilous, so we waited like Milton's servants, in case we might have to rush in and give first aid before the ambulance arrived. But the god that preserves drunkards always kept him from falling into that saw. When, after three months, we left for an apartment we had found in North Vancouver, Pearson was also departing, and we saw him only once again — or seemed to see him — under very odd circumstances.

This was almost three years later, towards the end of 1958. We were living in yet another apartment near the University. Our kitchen window overlooked a large corner lot occupied by a gas station, and one day, looking through the Venetian blinds, I saw John Pearson crossing the lot on the arm of a middle-aged woman. Walk, carriage, face, yachting cap, gold-headed cane: there was no doubt of it. I called Inge and said: "Look! Johnny's back in Vancouver!" She came, also looked and also recognized him. Three weeks later we ran into Esther Birney at a party, and I remarked casually: "We saw Johnny Pearson the other day." She looked startled. Then she said: "You couldn't possibly have seen him. He shot himself in Toronto three months ago!"

While we were under the Birneys' roof, I had worked hard on changing the monolithic mind of American officialdom. At the University of Washington, Bob Heilman not merely declared that the English Department was fully behind me; when I went down to Seattle to clear up my affairs he recruited the support of the University's President, one of those American conservatives who, whatever their faults in other respects, doggedly stand up for the freedom of expression. Heilman even made two journeys to Vancouver to reason with the consul; the latter stood on the letter of the law, and the letter of the McCarran Act was benightedly exclusive.

I realized that I would need more potent support within the United States, and, after sending a five thousand word letter to John Foster Dulles, stating my position as a non-violent anarchist, I wrote to people I knew in New York, notably Dwight Macdonald and Roger Baldwin of the American Civil Liberties Union, whom I had met in London. They quickly got to work, and soon I was hearing from people like Norman Thomas, the veteran American socialist, who wrote: "I trust you will not be a permanent victim of what I consider the absurdities or worse of our present law", and Sidney Hook the political philosopher, who remarked that "The grounds for barring you could serve equally well for barring Tolstoy, Thoreau and, in some of his moods, even Jefferson."

A petition was organized and circulated among leading American scholars. It gathered sixty-one signatures, among them those of David Riesman, Bruno Bettelheim, John Crowe Ransom, William Barrett, F.W. Dupee, Arthur Schlesinger Jr., Lionel Trilling, Reinhold Niebuhr, and Daniel Bell.

If the proper tactics had been pursued all this would have had a notable effect. Unfortunately a division of views appeared among my American supporters. The scholars of the eastern states believed that it was essential to give the widest publicity to the petition. But those at the University of Washington were scared of the political consequences, and told me that the offer of a post would probably not remain open if there were publicity. It seemed as though I might win the battle and lose the war, since the absence of employment would have given the American consul a reason to refuse me a visa even if the political inadmissibility clause were waived. Besides, I felt obligated to Heilman, who kept the post open for me even after the academic year began. So I accepted his advice and the petition was not published.

I am now sure that I should have exposed the situation publicly regardless of the possible consequences, as I did thirty years later, in 1983, when I was again excluded from the United States. For the result of all this activity which never reached the press was that nobody in the State Department answered the petitioners, or the American Council of Civil Liberties, which also approached Dulles on my behalf. The case ground its way slowly through the bureaucratic mills, and on June 1956, nine months after the first refusal, I received another letter from the consul telling me that the case had been reviewed and that no reason had been found for reversing his decision.

VII

FRUSTRATIONS IN ACADEME

B Y THIS TIME I had already abandoned all thought of a future in the United States, and had decided to stay in Canada. Jack Shadbolt's spontaneous painting of a celebratory picture on the day I was originally refused a visa was only the first of many expressions of Canadian good will. I quickly found myself busy with radio work. From England, Peter Quennell commissioned a series of articles for *History Today* on various North American subjects and advances arrived for two forthcoming books. We found we could afford to rent a modest apartment in the shadow of the mountains in North Vancouver and to buy our first car.

Meanwhile the drama of my rejection by the United States, and the news filtering up from Seattle that I was a good teacher of literature had changed the minds of Canadian academics regarding the possibility of employing me.

In January 1956 the Extension Department of the University of British Columbia approached me to give an evening course in modern European literature. I accepted, because it seemed to give me an academic showcase, for the payment was slight. Then in February Roy Daniells invited me to tea; Earle Birney was there, and we discussed my joining the Department of English. While wandering around Roy's winter garden, the suggestion was made that some day soon U.B.C. might decide to compete with Queen's and Toronto by publishing its own quarterly, and that I might be the person to give it a special editorial tone. When the official offer came from the university I accepted.

The spring and summer were still open and I did not let them lie idle. The CBC had started to make television programs in Vancouver, and one of the producers, the film-maker and painter Ron Kelly, invited me to do some items with him. One was with J.B. Priestley whom I had never met in England. He was enthusiastic about Vancouver's "pearly light", as he correctly described it, and surprised me by talking knowledgeably about my book on Godwin. Priestley had signed a contract to be interviewed for half an hour, and towards the end of the filming I saw him looking furtively at his watch. Suddenly he stood up, and said: "Time's oop! I want more money!" and before we could continue Kelly had to assure him hurriedly of a supplementary payment.

More important was the small film — my first — which Kelly and I did in the late spring of 1956 on Roderick Haig-Brown, the western Canadian naturalist, novelist, and essayist. Rod and his wife Ann invited me to stay with them in their large wooden house on the banks of the Campbell River on Vancouver Island. After the day's work in the garden, by the river, and in the surrounding hills and forests, following Rod on his habitual avocations, I spent the evenings drinking scotch and talking with him in his enormous study overlooking the river, with its large heterogenous library. We discovered a common enthusiasm for the classic Victorian naturalist-writers: Darwin, Huxley, Bates and Belt, whose vivid, economical, pre-jargon prose we admired as models of descriptive and expository writing. Like Aldous Huxley, Rod was a pioneer environmentalist and he was engaged in a battle against hydro and logging interests to save the habitat of the Vancouver Island elk. He was also a superb descriptive essayist, and possibly the best in Canada.

That week of film-making was the beginning of a friendship that lasted until his death more than twenty years later. Occasionally Inge and I went to stay briefly with Rod and Ann and their children at Campbell River; two of their daughters, Valerie and Mary, would become my students.

During the summer of 1956 Rod tried to get me appointed editor for the anthology of British Columbian writing that was to be published to celebrate the province's centenary in 1958. It was then that I — and he — ran up against the only negative Canadian reaction to my difficulties with the American authorities. My name was rejected by the majority of the committee because my radical past might be politically embarrassing to the Centennial, and a safe professor was appointed. Rod was as perturbed as I, but he also made a remark revealing the Attic moderation that governed his own actions. "Why did you ever *call* yourself an anarchist?" he said sadly to me. "You can hold whatever beliefs you like, and spread them far and wide and beneficially, so long as you don't give your ideas and yourself a label. Writing and isms don't really go together."

Rod's disinclination to label himself did not connote reluctance to get publicly involved. Apart from his conservationist activities, he was the local magistrate, a terror to people who shot protected birds or pit-lamped deer out of season, but an understanding man with drunks and petty thieves and a tireless counsellor in the bitter and sometimes violent family disputes that occurred among the loggers and fishermen of the wild little communities around Campbell River. He was so much more an arbitrator than a judge that he and I never got involved in the kind of extreme arguments one might have expected between an anarchist and a pillar of the law; Rod held so firmly that laws were made for men, and should be ignored or mitigated when their administration led to obvious injustices that he seemed to disarm beforehand the criticisms one felt one should, in principle, be making.

The criticism I did make, the longer I knew Rod, was that as the years went on he seemed to be allowing his public activities to submerge his writing. Rod listened patiently, and then would remark that he wrote when he had to, but that the other activities were important if one valued human community. He would quote to me the case of Aeschylus who requested an epitaph in which his dramatic works were ignored and his service in the ranks at the battle of Marathon was remembered.

Later, I came to understand that Rod was one of those writers who have certain things to say, and have found eloquent ways of saying them, but who do not feel it necessary to write for writing's sake. As the other kind of writer, addicted to words and never likely to stop putting them together as long as I live, I found it hard to understand such restraint, such willing and probably wise silence. For Rod strikes me as one of the wisest men I have known, and sometimes, when I have committed some gross verbal irresponsibility, I see his ghost rising to admonish me with a quiet, smiling remark between puffs on the pipe that was rarely away from his mouth.

LATER IN THE SUMMER, Inge and I went to Peru. Alan Pringle, my editor at Faber & Faber, was so pleased with *To the City of the Dead* and with the reception it was getting from London critics that he urged me to write another travel book, and I decided to balance the Mexican book with one on Peru, the other great centre of ancient American civilization. The advance Fabers offered and commissions from a few magazines did not give us enough funds for such a long journey, but I persuaded Canadian Pacific Airlines to provide a couple of free flights to Lima and back. Those two months of exhausting travel were eventually described in *Incas and Other Men*.

In order to see the regions of that mountain-divided country, we were forced to make several separate journeys, all starting from Lima and returning there. The first was up into the Altiplano, the high plateau of the Andes, on the railway built by the American entrepreneur Honest Henry Meiggs up the escarpments known to Peruvians as the Eyebrow of the Coast; it climbed higher than any other railway in the world, reaching almost five thousand metres above sea level by the time it crossed the divide and descended to Huancayo. Our centre was Tarma, from which we travelled through the dreary high moorlands of the copper mining region of Cerro de Pasco, and down through the descending ranges into the valley of the Huallaga and the headwaters of the Amazons.

Next we went from Lima on a great loop southward through the coastal desert almost to the Chilean border, and then eastward to the beautiful colonial city of Arequipa, from which we travelled north to Puno on the austere shores of Lake Titicaca, and through the mountain ranges to the Inca capital of Cuzco, from which we reached the remote citidel of Machu Picchu. We flew back from Cuzco to Lima, and then set off in a northerly direction through the seashore region, just as arid here as it had been to the south, as far as Trujillo, which is Arequipa's rival among the beautiful colonial cities of Peru. From Trujillo we visited the pyramids of Moche and the vast mud-walled city of Chan Chan which had been the capital of the Chimu culture before the rise of the Inca empire. We came south from Trujillo to Chimbote, whence we turned inland up the narrow valleys to the Callejon de Huaylas, the great trench lined by the noblest ranges of the Andes, where the highland city of Yungay still flourished under the mountain that later destroyed it, and thence, by other valley roads, we returned to Lima.

Except for a few recuperative days in Tarma at the end of the trip, we were on the move almost every day. We often had to travel by decrepit trucks with two seats in front and cargo piled dangerously high behind; we travelled on mountain roads that were often single-laned and sometimes half blocked by landslides, and so perilous that their verges were dotted with little crosses to celebrate those who had gone over the edge; we suffered from soroche (mountain sickness), from bad strains of dysentery, and from ear infections aggravated by flying in the unpressurized planes; we arrived at a politically insecure time, when the dictatorship of General Odria was giving way to a conservative democratic government and the country was full of suspicion and fear; we endured the insolence of the para-military Guardia Civil, with their clanking sabres, who were constantly stopping the buses and collective taxis on the highroads, and once I was taken off a car and into a guard post and alarmingly interrogated.

We found a society even more divided than that of Mexico, for up to then there had been no social revolutionary movement that raised

Indians upward from their inferior status. The threefold division of the population into *mistis* or *creoles* (whites), *cholos* (people of mixed blood), and *Indios* remained rigid. The Indians of the Sierra formed a conservative mass among whom customs hardly changed, and with whom it was virtually impossible for the passing stranger to make direct contact. While our fleeting relationships with white Peruvians and with the many central European (Hungarian, German, even Swiss) immigrants were open, often cordial, we could only observe as outsiders an archaic culture surviving among people who still mainly spoke the ancient Quechua and Aymara tongues and whose life was in many ways as it had been under the Incas, with an overlay of seventeenth century Spanish peasant culture which appeared in their costumes and the perfunctory Catholic observances mingled with stubborn paganism. These people had lost what was probably the most important element in the Inca administration, the elaborate system of food storage that provided insurance against famine. The season when we travelled was one of lasting drought, and the distress was visible in the shrunken markets and the diminished herds.

All these circumstances made Peru as harsh a country to the senses and the conscience as Mexico, yet I did not experience the same disorientation, as I had felt in Mexico. I had been inoculated, and saw it with the kind of detachment that can make action more effective.

THE FIRST YEAR AT the University of British Columbia was by far my unhappiest there, not because of the teaching itself, but because of the burden of work I found myself expected to carry.

Throughout the year I taught two sections of freshman English, and I was involved in a quixotic experiment of bringing the humanities to engineering students so that they would leave with at least some tiny inkling of a liberal education. The project was a course in utopian literature; a parallel, it was thought, might be drawn between political and mechanical constructions. I taught two seminars — one to a group of mechanical engineers who were entirely impenetrable, and the other to a group of metal engineers with whom I did establish a kind of jesting rapport, though even they regarded the whole exercise as a waste of their time — as I did of mine — and showed at most a polite interest in the austerities of Plato's *Republic* or the aestheticist felicities of *News from Nowhere*. But — with a weekly lecture to the assembled engineers — it added five hours to my six of freshman English, which meant that in the first term I was teaching 11 hours a week as against the customary departmental load of 9 hours. During the second term I was also put to teach a second-year survey course, and this brought my load to 14 hours.

As well as all this teaching during the day, I still had my evening class in European literature, so that I had to prepare four different classes and mark the papers for the day classes as well. To make matters worse, we had accepted a offer from the Shadbolts to live in their house while they were in Europe for a year. Although we loved the house and its setting, it meant travelling fifteen miles twice a day and four times a day when I gave my evening classes. Little wonder that by November I found it hard to keep up and at the same time to fulfil those minimal literary commitments which I could not afford to let go. I fell into states of nervous tension and profound discouragement which have made it the more difficult to cope with everything. I had a deep conflict between the demands of writing and teaching which I was sure that teaching would lose in the long run — or rather, as things looked, in the short run. Autodidacts like me and Proudhon I felt had no place in universities — or places only on sufferance.

My sense of being on sufferance was augmented by conditions under which I had to work. U.B.C. had few buildings to cope with the steadily rising enrolments, and as one of the newest arrivals I was assigned as an office a tiny cubicle in a used army hut which I had to share with a teaching assistant. I taught in similar shacks, and remember my classes mostly by the sound of rain beating on the thin roof above my head and the stench of chalk and damp raincoats. The only redeeming factor was that the students were better prepared than their American counterparts.

A deeply self-preservative instinct made me evade committees and avoid university politics. But I could not fail to note the negative effects of rapid expansion on Canadian universities. There were too few trained Canadians to meet the need for teachers. In 1956 I was the only Canadian among the new entrants into the Department of English; all the rest were Americans, and except for the eccentric, brilliant Warren Tallman, all were second-raters who had been unable to find posts in American universities. This situation continued for years, and produced the growing Americanization which Robin Mathews and other Canadian nationalists would denounce. I have always opposed the xenophobia with which Robin Mathews attacked good scholars from abroad, whose presence we greatly needed. My objection was to the rejects from the American academic system who lowered the quality and the imaginativeness of Canadian university teaching; this seemed to me far worse than the introduction here and there of American content into Canadian courses.

I had little time for writing. I produced some literary columns for the *Vancouver Sun* and a few talks for the CBC, working in spare hours, but I had no time to even to start work on my book on Peru. In mid-winter I was racked with violent and recurrent stomach pains. In the series of alarming tests to which the doctors subjected me no sign of either ulcers or cancer appeared; I was suffering merely from frustration, and the pains diminished as the end of the school year approached.

The principal compensation of that dreary year was the blossoming of friendships, notably with the painters Aleister Bell and John Korner, and with Roy Daniells, with whom, though we had disagreed sharply on the allocation of classes, I found a sympathy of outlook on poetry and politics emerging as I got to know better that complex man, furtive and devious as an administrator but as a friend luminous in understanding and stubborn in loyalty.

Interesting, if not always congenial, visitors found their way over the mountains or up the coast. My old friend Herbert Read had come early in the summer of 1956, when we were still living in North Vancouver, and stayed for a week of lectures. Later Norman Levine arrived, and recorded the visit and Inge's cooking in *Canada Made Me*. One day a young American came from San Francisco. He was Allan Ginsberg, still unbearded but already deeply into drug-taking in the hope of expanding his poetic consciousness. Out of a great shaggy sweater he produced a frayed, thick manuscript and thrust it at me. It was the yet unpublished "Howl". I was not impressed by this noisy non-poem, and in spite of the almost symbolic status it took on in the mythology of American post-modernism I still think I was right when I handed it back silently, and that "Howl", with its stale aura of Whitman and pot-smoke, is probably the most overrated poem of the century.

A meeting that was strange in another way took place in the summer of 1957 when Northrop Frye arrived at the University, and came out for dinner at the Shadbolts' house. It was a superb evening, the sunlight on the mountains mellowing as the sun fell lower, the shadows long and black, and the air so clear that one could see far up Indian Arm into the heart of the range, and far westward across the harbour to the blue peaks of Vancouver Island. I always felt proud to be able to take people on to the deck on such a day, and to share this vast gift of nature with them; most people responded with delight. But Frye grew visibly paler as he stood for an instant looking out. Then he turned. "Those mountains make my blood run cold," he said, as he hurried indoors. I felt in that single unexpected remark I had the clue to what had disturbed me in Frye's criticism; he created huge critical schemata because he wanted literature to appear as a construct apart from the nature he feared; he used the garrison as a metaphor describing Canadian colonial culture because he dreaded the wilderness.

In April, as the teaching year drew unhappily to a close, I was negotiating with the CBC over a dramatization of *Don Quixote* which George

Robertson intended to produce. At the same time, I was threatening to resign from the University of British Columbia unless my teaching load were lightened, and I had proposed, as the price of my staying, a Comparative Literature course in European novelists and dramatists from Stendhal to Camus. I had also applied for one of the Canadian Government Overseas Fellowships paid in blocked French funds, the precursors of the Canada Council arts awards, which were being administered by the Royal Society of Canada.

I would have been content if one of my schemes worked out. But all three did. I was commissioned to write the adaptation of *Don Quixote*, in seventeen episodes, which would enable me to do justice to that noble book. The University agreed to my terms and I agreed to stay on. Then I heard from the Royal Society that my fellowship application had been approved and that I would be financed for my year in France. So I could postpone my return to teaching and look forward to a year and a half of writing and study with no financial anxieties.

The Shadbolts would not be returning from Europe until the end of August, and we planned to leave Vancouver at the beginning of September. This gave me a clear summer once I had finished marking a small mountain of examination papers by the end of April. I concentrated on *Don Quixote*.

Cervantes, a failed playwright, had inserted much dramatic confrontation into his novel, which was also episodic in structure so that — taking advantage of radio's tolerance for fantasy — I was able to make a series of effective small plays without drastically violating the book. Radio had not yet been starved of its funds to feed television, and Robertson was able to put on a suitably baroque production, with music especially composed for the plays and a small orchestra heavy on trumpets and guitars which suggested both the Castilian setting and the mock-heroic spirit of the novel; Frank Wade, nearing the end of his acting career, played the Don with the right mixture of nobility and madness.

This was my first substantial incursion into drama, and by the time I had written the last episode and the knight was safely dead, I believed I had acquired a sound knowledge of radio drama and that it was time to start writing original plays.

Just after I had finished *Don Quixote* Jack and Doris returned and we were ready to set off for Europe. Just before I left Rod Haig-Brown wrote to me: "Don't if you can help it let Europe steal you away from us again. You are badly needed in your native land." This time, in fact, I had no thought of not returning.

VIII

THE CAVES OF THE HUNTERS

B Y THE TIME WE LEFT VANCOUVER, I was ready for a period
of recovery from a hard year. Inge and I decided to take our Beetle
with us to Europe so that we would have more freedom of travel,
and we went by road to Montreal. Beyond Calgary was *terra incognita*.

The Trans-Canada Highway was still far from complete, and cross-
country roads were in places so primitive that Canadians wishing to
cross the Rockies would usually travel via the northern United States
rather than embark on the half-day of rough going over the unpaved Big
Bend Highway that followed the curve of the Columbia River through
the Selkirks from Revelstoke to Golden. We took the Canadian route
both here and on the equally difficult northern Ontario highway through
Kapuskasing to North Bay; and thus gained an intimate sense of the
country. In the 1950s small communities were still full of life, active
centres of regional existence each with a character of its own, and not yet
the dying villages, on the edge of extinction, into which swift travel
between major centres has turned them. One had the sense of an abundant and varied rural life still going on all the way across Canada, a
sense which agriculture and commercial concentration have destroyed
except in those areas that are topographically resistant to modern large-
scale farming.

In Toronto I felt a new sense of a developing literary world. I had time
to meet literary figures like Robert Fulford and John Robert Columbo
with whom I would develop lasting relationships, to spend an afternoon
with that bizarre late Johnsonian, Nathan Cohen, and much longer with
the people associated with *Tamarack Review*, notably Robert Weaver,
Kildare Dobbs and William Toye.

The first issue of *Tamarack* had appeared in the autumn of 1956 with
a travel piece by me, "A Road in the Andes", and now I worked out with

Weaver a tentative sharing of territories in case something came of the proposals for a new magazine at the University of British Columbia with me as the editor. It was evident from its early issues that *Tamarack* was filling the gap left by the disappearance of *Northern Review* and that there was no place for a rival literary magazine of the same type. My own inclinations were towards establishing a critical magazine, and the *Tamarack* people thought that their magazine, which was concentrating more on fiction and verse with a bit of closet drama, could only gain from having a critical counterpart. I knew that in the event of the offer of a magazine at U.B.C. coming my way I would have the blessing of what then passed for a literary establishment in eastern Canada. I needed the latter's support, because I realized that whatever I produced would be an editorial disaster if it were merely an academic journal written only for professors.

ARRIVING IN PARIS, WE put up at a cheap little hotel in the Latin Quarter. The first two weeks we wandered the streets, going to museums and art galleries, buying novels, and soaking up metropolitan cultural fare. Robert Heilman and Jackson Matthews were in Paris, and we would dine together in one of the cheap and nasty restaurants which James Joyce had frequented.

Late in September we drove into the Loire valley. From our first night at St. Symphorien across the river from Toulouse, we established a pattern of picking hotels with cheap simple rooms and good food, so that one balanced off the expense of eating against the economy in sleeping. In those days this was easier in France than it is now; our St. Symphorien meal featured an excellent dish of fat river eels that was followed by a casserole of chicken cooked with white onions and bitter cherries.

We turned south from Tours and travelled down to Brives, a town of dove-grey houses on the edge of the Dordogne and the nearest place with a hotel to the caves of Lascaux. From Brives we drove to the village of Montignac and then up a dirt road to a farmhouse in the hills, whence we proceeded on foot through a spinney of thin trees to the caves themselves, on the edge of a high plateau.

Great metal gates closed behind each batch of visitors, since humidity was already becoming a problem. Electric lights had been installed, and this innovation obviously dissipated the mystery with which dim lighting and heavy shadows had invested the paintings for the hunters who made them millenia ago, yet it made the effect, as one stepped down into the first painted hall, an immediate and astounding one. Before going here I had seen many photographs of the cavern, but none of them conveyed the grandeur of those vast chestnut bulls, seventeen feet long, charging majestically across the creamy grey rock among herds of black horses and strange deer with many-tined antlers. A hundred yards or more of halls and passages are so covered. They are executed with no apparent master plan; each was an individual painting, and they were remarkably varied, so that in this primeval art gallery I was able to pick out the precursors of all the modern manners of painting. Most figures are portrayed with a realism that depends not on photographic representation so much as an empathetic understanding of the animal in movement; true magic realism. The one human figure, on the other hand, is as highly stylized as a figure by Klee, and there are patterns of coloured squares that reminded me of the geometrical compositions of Ben Nicholson.

The marvellous thing about the Lascaux paintings is that their magic is in a strange way transferred to the present so that one has no sense of their being distant or alien. Standing there, in the few minutes before the guides moved us on, I experienced a sense of recognition which seemed to make insignificant the centuries that divided the ancient hunter from a modern man. The sense of seeing through another's eyes, and the emotion that accompanied it, were immediate and seemingly irrational.

Yet I am sure that an explanation lies in the nature of the culture that produced Lascaux. Concentrating in a mystical solitude on the work of hand and eye, the Magdalenian hunter contrived to give permanence to the idealized representation of his wish. And in so doing he invented the one universal language, that of art. True, the cave man of the Dordogne did not think of himself as an artist; he thought of himself — if he was self-conscious enough to think of himself at all — as a magician. And it is there that we find the secret of his art and its undying appeal. For in the kind of totemic magic which primitive hunters practice the essential elements seems to be that man should not only represent, but also identify with his subject. Out of the emotion comes success in the hunt.

And this, I am sure, is what happens in all true art. The most successful artist is not the man who carefully plans his work and carries it out with self-conscious intelligence, but the man whose depth of feeling makes him lose all self-consciousness in identifying himself with what he creates. In this sense art is the last magic in our materialist world, and the modern artist is in his own way a magic hunter, a belated descendant of the sorcerers who painted the long-deserted caverns of the Dordogne and the Pyrenees with such time-defying mastery.

WE TRAVELLED OVER THE limestone plateaus of the Dordogne and down through deep fertile valleys clothed with dense chestnut woods turning colour with the coming of autumn, and through places whose names had evoked the magic of mediaeval romance in our minds, like Cahors, and Rocamadour spilling down into its marvellous gorge, and Carcassonne with its girdles of concentric walls. We peered at the roman-esque sculptures of Moissac and ate the fine trout of the Pyrenees in Basque inns, and ascended the high passes into the mountain republic of Andorra (finding it ruined by tourism), wandered through the hospital in Lourdes behind bands of pilgrims loudly chanting hymns for the benefit of the unfortunate patients, and came to the Roman towns of Nîmes and Arles which I had known in the 1930s, and went across country to Aix with its plane-tree concourses, and through the Cézanne country of blue hills and maquis to the pine forests of the Esterel and the sea at Cannes.

This was where we had decided to spend most of our time in France, but at first we were not certain whether it would be among the dry hills with their vibrant colours and their memories of painters we admired, or down on the coast beside the sea. We remained a few days in Nice, went inland to Grasse and Vence, looked speculatively at the strange pinnacle of Èze and at La Turbie with its Roman arch, hesitated over Cap Ferrat, but when we came to the end of the road and reached Menton, tucked into its quiet bay under the sheltering crags of the Alpes Maritimes, our minds were suddenly made up. The size and atmosphere of the town, the promising hinterland, the warmth and the clear light, all attracted us, and when we found a furnished apartment bright with new paint in a grove of ancient olive trees on the western edge of the town, we immediately moved in.

We settled quickly into a life that to others seemed idyllic. In a letter Roy Fuller remarked: "Your fellowship task sounds to me no task but pure hedonism," and I wrote to Ivan Avakumovic: "We are happy down here, blessed with sun and warmth when every other part of Europe seems to be freezing or deluged with rain." We walked each morning to the market, and we came to know the shopkeepers and stallholders better than anyone else in Menton: the peasant women from whom we would buy tender young French beans and the small delectable potatoes grown on the terraces between the olive trees, and the tall blonde girl from whom we bought great bunches of carnations, thirty for a dollar, and the woman in a street behind the market who educated us in French cheeses, and the shaven-headed White Russian butcher, a man of infin-ite politeness who, whenever one thanked him, would say "*Merci pour me dire merci!*" Sometimes we would drive into Nice, by the Grande Corniche, to shop through the old town, browse in the flea market where once I picked up a twelfth century Annamese pot for fifty cents, and visit the English library, exchanging greetings on the way with the polite whores of the rue de France. In the evenings I usually worked on my book on Peru, though often not until after we had returned from dinner in Nice or Monte Carlo or La Turbie.

Sometimes we went to Nice for its bizarre opera performances, in which the chorus would sing nasally in French while the imported stars sang in Italian, which by contrast sounded strangely flamboyant. And in Monte Carlo, we saw Thomas Beecham for a last time. By then he was 78 or 79, and had come to Monaco to avoid the English winter. He conducted the local symphony orchestra, normally an uninspired set of musicians, and everybody was curious to see what he would do with them. The theatre was crowded, with Grace and Rainier in the princely box, and Marc Chagall, who had come down from Vence, sitting three seats away from us. It was a moving, almost miraculous occasion. As he shuffled to the conductor's stand in an old greenish tailcoat, Beecham looked like an ancient beetle, and we were all prepared for disappointment and compassion. But no sooner had he faced the orchestra and raised his baton than a transformation took place. With vigour and precision, he conjured a remarkable performance from that mediocre orchestra. It was a salutary exhibition of the creative will overcoming the disabilities of the flesh.

On our frequent expeditions into the miniature grandeur of the Alpes Maritimes that lay immediately north of Menton we had to travel only twenty miles to pass through changes in terrain and climate that in other regions would take hundreds of miles. We drove along one of the narrow valleys out of the town, and came first to the mild hillsides facing the sea up which the cultivated terraces rose like the steps of Mexican pyramids. The houses were bright blue and pink against the greyish foliage of the olive groves and the dark green of the orange and lemon trees. In autumn the persimmon trees in the gardens, stripped of leaves, were loaded with fruit that glowed like great garnets against the black branches; in winter the mimosa broke in a yellow surf of blossom over the hillsides; in spring — late February and early March — the wild purple anemones and grape hyacinths came into flower under the budding peach trees, and in April the air was filled with the rich fragrance of lemon blossom.

Yet in a couple of miles all this blandness melted away among the rocky spurs of the hilltops, and we entered a region of almost Tibetan bleakness, where the slopes were deluged with the grey detritus of vast moraines. Even here spring blazed out in the carmine of innumerable rock roses and the gold of genista, but at other seasons it was a sombre maquis of parched juniper and stunted cypress. It had its own life of ugly spotted snakes and nightmare insects like the praying mantis, and once when we were sitting beside the road on this barren plateau a hoopoe with a brilliant crest and black-barred wings settled before us and then, with the derisive cry that gives it its name, disappeared into a clump of ilex trees.

Sometimes from this plateau we would go down into other valleys and search out the mediaeval stone villages that are hidden in the folds of the Alpes Maritimes, to try their local wines and goats' milk cheeses and the onion cake called pissaladière. Occasionally, in an old church, we found an alter painted with the gauche figures and clear colours of the fifteenth century Niçois primitives. At other times we went from the plateau through deep gothic gorges. The hills were becoming mountains and a little farther on the road would rise to more than five thousand feet at the pass known as the Col de Turini. And on the Col, while the coast enjoyed its balmy spring in mid-winter, the snows lay feet thick among the dense fir woods that clothed the ridges. It was as if one had travelled, in an hour or so, from a land of the easy south to a land of the rigorous north, from the Riviera to the Rockies; indeed, so much did this pass remind us of home that sometimes, when we had too much white December sunlight, we would say: "Let's make a trip to Canada", and head for the thin, biting air, and the snow, and the sombre conifers of Turini.

But even here the pilgrimage through many lands in a few miles did not end. On the other side of the Col, the pinewoods thinned into the Alpine meadows of a village with the melodic Provençal name of Peira Cava. When the snow left Peira Cava in April, the meadows became brilliant with the flowers I had associated with the Swiss and Austrian Alps — fragile mountain cyclamens, pale wild crocuses, little purple orchids, and the magnificent metallic blue trumpets of gentian.

For me the French political crisis of 1958 and de Gaulle's return to power is associated with the flowers of Peira Cava, for it was there that the waiter who brought us coffee on the terrace of the little mountain hotel told us of the generals' coup d'état in Algeria. We sat looking into the deep valley of the Vesubie, where the beech woods on the hillsides were breaking into tender green foliage, and wondered whether this might not be the end of our French interlude, with civil war raging over the countryside and the foreign embassies calling their nationals to the seaports.

We need not have been anxious. The bloodlessness of de Gaulle's rise to power became a matter of history. The next day the army was on foot in Menton and a couple of tanks took up positions in the olive grove where our apartments stood. At first we looked apprehensively at this military show, but we were never menaced or even asked for our papers, and within days we were walking nonchalantly under the muzzles of the guns and exchanging pleasantries with the bored soldiers.

IN THE KIND OF LIFE in which I should have been happy, and Inge was, I went through the darkest inner crisis of my life. The problem was within myself, and it led me into deepest despair. I was lonely in Menton, for we found it impossible to strike up personal relationships with the local French. Our conversations did not go far beyond the tradespeople, the postman, the concierge, and a couple of the neighbours. And through the winter our only visitors were Bert and Jessie Binning, who delighted us by arriving on Christmas Eve.

I also found it hard to write at first, because of a lassitude that was a reaction from the hard work of the preceding year. But after Christmas the book on Peru went forward quickly, so that I was able to finish it by the end of March, as well as reading many French novels, writing articles for *Encounter* and *Tamarack Review* on French fiction, and in *Arts* of New York on Mexican muralists. Yet even when the writing went well, I was still engulfed in a despair I could only keep at bay by working.

The crisis came in March. Inge's parents visited us, and she accompanied them for a brief trip to Italy while I stayed in Menton to finish my book. I became seized with a deep foreboding of death. No physical symptoms justified such a feeling, yet it was so strong that I did not think I would be alive when the others returned. I lay in panic, feeling that I would not even survive until the morning and that if death did not come in some other way I would have to kill myself. I was filled with fear, physically trembling with agitation, when I became aware of a presence inhabiting the room. It was not tangible or visible; it never spoke. I felt and knew its reality, yet what I knew and felt I could not describe except to say that it emanated peace. My agitation quietened until I was calm. The thought of death receded. I fell asleep and woke at dawn to walk along the seafront and enjoy everything I saw with the intensity of a reborn vision. I went home and confidently wrote the last pages of my book. Was I saved by some benign impulse emerging from my own unconscious and projecting itself into my surroundings? Was I visited by an angelic presence? I have always been content to accept it as inexplicable, just as it was invisible and intangible.

With spring the loneliness was broken. Canadian and American travellers wandering through France would stay with us a day or so, so that again there was conversation and the clash of opinions. Then, in mid-May, we gave up our apartment and set off for Italy. It was a very conventional tour — to Pisa and Florence, and thence to Siena and Arezzo, for the splendid Piero della Francesca frescoes in Arezzo, then into

Umbria, to Assisi and Perugia, over the Appenines to Rimini, and north to Ravenna, where the great mosaics seemed in their different geometries to balance the intellectual grandeur of Piero. Such works took me back into a world of imaginative achievement of which I seemed to lose the consciousness in the bland scene of the Côte d'Azur.

We were back in France by the beginning of June, anxious to see as much of it as we could before we left. We drove west along the coast to St. Raphael to Arles; across the meadows and marshlands of the Camargue, through Aigue Mortes set so starkly in its salt flats, and then, turning north, climbed to the high plateau of the Cevennes, where the Protestant Camisards, — with André Gide's ancestors among them — defied the dragoons of Louis XIV. Now the vast chestnut groves were in fresh green leaf, the high meadows were white with great drifts of poet's narcissus, and the stone walls were alive with emerald green lizards that had just come out of hibernation. We reached Le Puy amid its purple sugarloaf hills, and climbed again into the tangle of the Massif Central, on our way to Moulin and the haunting Madonna of its anonymous Mâitre. Our journey, in so far as it was an antiquarian pilgrimage, ended in Carnac in Brittany, among the ranks of menhirs aligned to play their part in the neolithic cult of the sun.

Even without their original celebrants and ceremonials, the unshaped stones, gold and green-mottled with the mosses and lichens that had accumulated in thousands of years, were still uncannily impressive as they marched across the barren Breton moorland. Yet the stones seemed only stones, and no imaginative effort could impart to them the holiness they must have had for the men who raised them. I could only think how alien were the minds that had conceived it all. Yet in many ways these Neolithic ceremonialists were men more like ourselves than the Lascaux hunters. They were men who farmed, felled forests, and built houses, and knew the meaning if not the sound of the dread word *organization*. But they were men in whose lives plastic art played no part. Their magic lay in the drama of great spectacles; the priest as actor had replaced the priest as painter — and the actor's is the most perishable of the arts.

Our French pilgrimage yielded a final ironic comment on the mystery of creativity as we wandered back to Paris by way of Chartres. We passed through a small French town, one of those nondescript places of nineteenth-century brick houses with a smell of poorly refined gasoline hanging in the afternoon silence. All at once, a sign told me it was Illiers, and I remembered that Illiers was the original of Proust's Combray. Perhaps it was fortunate that we had come upon it by chance, for I arrived without preconceptions, and saw the place as it dejectedly was on a quiet summer day in 1958, and knew it could hardly have been much different on a quiet summer day in the childhood of the two Marcels in the 1880s, except that the air would have smelt of horse dung and not of gasoline. We stopped so that I could get out and stroll through that ugly little place and wonder at the imagination that could draw out of its ineffable dullness the transfigured splendours of *Du côté de chez Swann.*

Our return to Paris was in more than one way a preparation for our return home, for we spent much of the time with congenial Canadians who were in Paris that summer like Bruno and Molly Bobak, and Phyllis Webb, who at that time projected a luminous austerity, as if she were moving through her own fire.

The centre of the group was the painter Joe Plaskett, who had begun his long residence in Paris, where he still works. Joe then inhabited an apartment on the Boulevard St. Germain reminiscent of *la belle épopue,* the vital period of Parisian life that corresponded with the Edwardian era in England. The rooms were filled with chandeliers and mirrors, and much of the period's almost obsessive preoccupation with the rendering of light entered into the paintings Joe was producing: interiors, often inhabited by hieratically envisioned women, and always illuminated by floods of silver or golden light pouring through the windows from the summer boulevard.

IX

"CANADIAN LITERATURE"

B ACK AT THE UNIVERSITY, now an Assistant Professor, I was to teach nine hours a week like my colleagues, and initiate a course in modern European novelists and dramatists. We settled into an apartment with a view of Howe Sound and the Coast Mountains, and I began to prepare my new course, which gained a large enrolment that would increase each successive year. I lectured well, and each year introduced new books. For once I enjoyed teaching without reservations, and until 1963, when I reached another arrangement with the University, teaching was my main occupation for seven or eight months of the year, yet I never felt I was a true teacher. Always I saw myself as a writer teaching for economic reasons, putting to a new use knowledge acquired for other purposes. I came to resent one aspect of teaching. Once I had thoroughly discussed a subject in the classroom, I found that I had no longer any desire to write my thoughts, and in this way over the years I talked out at least two books, to whose subjects I shall never return.

So much for my teaching career. What seemed much more important to me in the fall of 1958 was the fact that the idea of a university magazine was much alive. Some younger teachers of English and Creative Writing were talking of a general literary review. I sensed that rival personal ambitions had already become deeply involved in this venture, and that any editorial arrangement would probably end in a compromise and some kind of committee arrangement, which I had no intention of accepting. So I evaded attempts to involve me, and the journal eventually appeared without my collaboration. As *Prism* it has had an erratic course, varying from excellence to mediocrity, but it survives.

Another group talked about a magazine devoted to Canadian studies on a broad scale, but the idea was not sharply enough defined and it lapsed for lack of a real objective. Then a third group emerged, headed by Roy Daniells and consisting of older professors of English and some of the library staff. They had narrowed the original proposal down to a journal devoted to the study and criticism of Canadian literature.

On being invited to become editor my reactions were ambivalent. Here was the opportunity for which I had been hoping, to edit a magazine at the University. Yet it had not come in the form I had expected. I was then far from being a specialist in Canadian writing. I had written a few reviews of Canadian books and some essays on writers like Hugh MacLennan and Malcolm Lowry; I had by now read fairly widely in Canadian fiction and verse and knew a few Canadian writers: that was all. On the other hand, I was aware of the need for a critical magazine in Canada, and I had the experience of editing *Now* in England. I put these points forward, and the reaction was that editorial experience, a critical judgment and a literary reputation were more important than an extensive knowledge of the field. They could advise me if I needed it, but they imagined I would soon find my way.

I accepted the challenge. In any case, my initiation into teaching had accustomed me to learning as I went. So I agreed, with a promise that next year, when the publication of the magazine actually began, I would be released from one course and do six hours teaching a week instead of nine.

By Christmas the title of *Canadian Literature* was given to the new journal, the first issue of which was to appear in the autumn of 1959. Since academics are chronically addicted to collective decision-making, a committee was formed, but fortunately it was chaired by Roy, who shared my own views about the necessary independence of editors. In the event, the committee was as willing as any Cheshire cat to dissolve with a smile, and after six months, it was no longer called and the work of starting the journal was left to a few practical people. The librarians were particularly helpful as volunteer workers. Inglis Bell spent many hours on promotion, Basil Stuart-Stubbs organized mailing the journal from the University basement, and Dorothy Shields looked after advertising. As the journal became more self-supporting and Canada Council subsidies materialized these pioneer volunteers were replaced by a paid staff of one part-time worker, but to the end I did my own secretarial work, and much of the cottage industry atmosphere remained; I would occasionally organize working bees of supporters to meet emergencies.

Before I even gathered a page of manuscript, we hired Robert Read, a fine Canadian typographer, to design the journal, and he created the spacious classical format that, after a quarter of a century, the magazine still maintains. Read in turn introduced us to our printer, Charles Morriss of Victoria, and that creative association also continued. *Canadian*

Literature was the first of many literary magazines to appear from Morriss Printing, which still produces it today.

As for editorial policy, *Canadian Literature* began and has continued as a broadly critical magazine rather than as a scholarly journal. A narrowly academic publication would have been irrelevant in the Canadian context of the time, as well as alien to my tastes and temperament.

The immediate problem was how to find the critics to write in a journal that was in fact breaking new ground. There were already a few distinguished Canadian critics, like A.J.M. Smith and Northrop Frye, and literary historians, like Desmond Pacey, but there were comparatively few younger ones. Smith and Pacey rallied immediately to *Canadian Literature*: they appeared in the first and many other issues. Frye never quite approved of my approach to criticism and always, to my great regret, stood aloof. The task I faced was to establish a body of critics who would write fairly regularly but not so often as to give the impression that *Canadian Literature* was the journal of a clique. Prophets of gloom were numerous; it was often said that after a year I would run out of both critics and subjects.

And so I might have done if I had not been fortunate enough to start *Canadian Literature* just before the beginning of the 1960s, when Canadian cultural nationalism emerged as a force in the country and literature took on an unanticipated vitality. From the start, I found to my pleasure and astonishment, there was never any lack of interesting subjects or of new books worth discussing, and soon I had to abandon the promise I made to review every new literary work, for from about 1964 onwards the number of books being published was far more than any quarterly could hope to notice in detail.

To find writers was initially more difficult, and there were several early issues I had difficulty filling with work whose quality satisfied me. The problem was solved in two ways.

I began to encourage practicing writers — poets, novelists and dramatists who were largely outside the academies — to write for me, either about their own work or, more often, the work of others. This approach became so successful that in 1974, when I collected for Oxford University Press an anthology (*Poets and Critics*) of seventeen of the best critical essays in *Canadian Literature*, ten of them were actually written by practicing poets.

At the same time, the growing movement towards cultural nationalism helped to increase interest in Canadian writing. Courses in Canadian literature began to proliferate, and every year more criticism that was well-written and imaginative began to reach me from the universities. Two of the younger critics, Don Stephens and Bill New, became associated with the magazine and I valued their advice and help and the friendship that came from working together.

I am not suggesting that *Canadian Literature* was responsible for this wave of new criticism and critics. Such a development would have come about through the maturing of the literature. But the fact that journal existed and was ready to consider any new work of potential interest, was perhaps the kind of guarantee that kept younger critics working so that very soon I wondered how I could make use of all the interesting essays that arrived. When Canada Council help materialized, I was able to expand the journal, but I never had the financial support or the kind of staff that would allow me to turn it from a quarterly into a monthly.

I found the 1960s and 1970s fruitful and exciting decades in which the stream of literature in Canada became diversified and deepened in ways none of us foresaw. One had the sense of being in the flow of history, and in some degree of even making it. And if *Canadian Literature* became steadily more interesting to read — as it certainly did to edit — this was because of the entirely new relationship that developed between criticism and other fields of writing, so that only a few old-fashioned romantics like Morley Callaghan kept up the traditional creative-critical feud. Most of the poets and many of the novelists in the younger generation were also critics.

Inevitably I have my regrets. There are essays I took for the early issues that now embarrass me because their acceptance shows that I was still fumbling towards a clearer definition of where Canadian writing was going; but soon I had read so much that I began to plan and choose with authority. I also regret the failure of my attempt to make *Canadian Literature* a bilingual journal that would see the English and the French traditions within an unifying context. I tried hard to gain the collaboration of Québec writers, but I soon learnt that their compasses were mostly set towards Paris and there was little chance of deflecting them out of that course. This had little to do with rising separatist sentiment. It sprang rather from an indifference on the part of Québec intellectuals towards the English Canadian culture that was even greater than the classic indifference of the English towards the French culture. On the level of literature Hugh MacLennan's "two solitudes" evidently still existed. Never did the French contributions amount to more than a tenth of any issue, and in the end I had to drop the pretence of bilingualism, and resign myself to presenting Québec writers mostly through the eyes of English-speaking scholars. The only consolation I could draw from the experience was that I was not alone in my failure; there never has been a successful bilingual journal of any kind in Canada. And perhaps we should derive a lesson from this and accept the essential plurality of our cultures and not strive to bring together what history has set apart. Equality in separated proximity, which is what Québec has now virtually achieved, may indeed be the proper destiny of Canadians as it is of the Swiss.

Canadian Literature has always been regarded as an idiosyncratic and even eccentric exception in the ranks of university journals, but there are certainly no apologies to be made for this. From that first issue I edited it to make a magazine as much a work of creative design, even if on a different level, as a poem. A literary journal really succeeds only in so far as it develops a presence that is more than the sum of its contents. In developing its own direction and impetus it takes its place among the literary *oeuvres* of its age. I believe that was the case with *Canadian Literature*, which developed a continuity that made it as much a running history of the development of the Canadian literary tradition as a mere magazine. For the next eighteen years editing *Canadian Literature* became the constant element in my own life. It released me progressively from teaching, without making the demands on my creative energies that the classroom had done; editing seemed to augment writing rather than diminish it, as teaching had done. It also provided a basic income. On other levels it gave me a special position, and eventually an influential one, in the Canadian literary world, and it brought me many interesting human contacts and some lasting friendships.

It seems to me strange, now that I look back over those years, that I did not make such friendships with my fellow teachers, who resented my independent attitude and my eventual success in making my own terms with the academy. But that, I suppose, is a matter of members of one species or tribe recognizing one another and rejecting the outsider. I belonged to the tribe of writers. I did not belong to the tribe of academics, and those with whom I remained friendly have been, like me, natural artists conscious of being at least slightly out of place in their setting.

But always, above this kind of ground bass that my editing work provided, my life was weaving other patterns as old interests continued and new ones emerged.

X

AT HOME IN A HAUNTED HOUSE

B Y THE END OF 1958 the desire to find a permanent home after
the moves and wanderings of the past nine years became a preoccupation. We started searching, and one day Inge met me at the
University with the news that she had found a house I must absolutely
see. It was in an obscure little two-block street in Kerrisdale, where the
escarpment begins to break down towards the Fraser River flats.

The house itself was the oldest in the district; it had once been a hired
man's cottage for the old McCleery Farm which antedated the foundation of Vancouver by twenty years, though it was not as old as the
farmhouse itself. The original cottage had probably been put up round
about the time of the Great War, which made it old by Vancouver standards; a flat-roofed addition had been built at the back. We first saw it as
slightly forbidding, for someone had painted its shingled walls battleship
grey and the garage, approached by a pitted earth driveway, was tumbling down. The inside was not much better. Upstairs was a warren of
small bedrooms in which big families had once been reared. But on the
ground floor, at the back looking out over the garden, there was a large
room lined with book shelves, and though the paper was peeling off the
one clear wall, I recognized it as an ideal study. The house was cheap;
and it would involve much work to put it in order, but not so much as
we had undertaken at Sooke. In fact, we rather looked forward to a bit
of manual toil once again.

So we bought the house, got a garrulous old Cockney painter in to put
the ground floor in shape for living, and moved in early in April. On the
day we did so a great cherry tree at the back of the house, fifty years old
and the last of a former orchard after which the street was once named,
was blooming in a great surge of white blossom against a clear blue sky.
It seemed like a blessing.

We were drawn by the setting more than the house, for the latter we could adapt with white paint and some carpentry, whereas the former was given. We were in a city — ten minutes' drive from the University and fifteen minutes from the centre of Vancouver — yet the street was so "secretive", as Bert Binning called it, that we might have been in the country, for only local traffic passed through. We were near to the golf courses and horse farms of the Fraser River flats — excellent walking space — and to the big wealthy houses along Southwest Marine Drive with their large wooded lots, so that the wild fauna was abundant.

Every morning in the spring and summer of our first years there we were awakened early by choruses of robins like avian sound barrages; there were garter snakes among the rocks at the bottom of the garden which kept down the slugs and snails and which our new kitten Greypuss (for Tim had died while we were in France) brought writhing into the house; native red squirrels came into our cherry tree and chattered angrily as we worked in the garden. Soon we became aware of nocturnal visitors — the raccoons coming over from the forested lots on Marine Drive.

Those links with wild nature have remained part of our lives over the years. There have indeed been changes in the pattern of animal presence. Because of the excessive spraying with pesticides in the neighbourhood during the 1960s, the snakes disappeared and have never returned. The robins also, by the end of the decade, declined drastically in numbers, but since then their population has increased. The red squirrels vanished because the last patch of wild woodland in the area was felled a year or two after we arrived.

But though the snakes did not come back, little green treefrogs sing every summer in the garden. And the raccoons have increased, so that some evenings eleven or twelve of them will come, in families and singly, to eat the day-old bread, broken biscuits, and throwout grapes we provide every night; many of them have become old friends who eat from our hands, and whom we remember when they no longer appear with a poignant sense of generations passing beneath our eyes. The red squirrels appear rarely, but black and grey squirrels, which were formerly restricted to Stanley Park, have moved into Kerrisdale, and this morning, looking out of the bedroom, I saw five of them — three black and two grey, chasing each other with improbable acrobatics through the bushes and over the fruit trees, scampering over the snowy ground, and voraciously nibbling the sunflower seeds I had put out in little heaps. I hear of foxes in the neighbourhood, but have never seen one of them, though one early morning, returning from a party, we saw loping before us down Cherry Street the unmistakeable silhouette of a coyote.

And, even if the robins have never again been so many, other birds now appear. Today four varied thrushes arrived, accompanied by a small flock of darting juncos and chickadees to take the grain from the feeding box hanging from the old apple tree in the centre of the garden, a starling sat in a bush by the backdoor waiting for the breadcrumbs he preferred, and later two flickers came, flashing their salmon-pink under-wings and then climbing like parrots up the oak by the lane which in twenty-five years has grown from a sapling into a giant, fed by our compost heap over its roots.

At acorn time a flock of heavy grey band-tailed pigeons arrives, just as the vine maple outside my study window draws its annual autumn gros-beaks. Steller's jays scream and flaunt their Prussian blue plumage in the garden at all seasons, and many small finches, warblers, vireos, tits and tree creepers appear, mostly attracted by the feeding possibilities pro-vided by the rough bark of the great old cherry tree; my favourite among them is the house finch for his marvellously intricate melody. Sometimes a heron flaps overhead, gaunt and prehistoric, on his way from the Fraser River to another waterway, occasionally a bald eagle from the woodlands near the university circles high with the sun flashing on his white head, and every now and again a raven flies over and I recognize his coming from afar by the deep bell tone that distinguishes his call from the raucous and petulant cawing of the local crows.

From the beginning we cultivated the garden more to attract birds than to grow produce. I did put in some fruit trees, but as the shade increased few vegetables would grow, and only flowers that flourished in semi-sunlight. In the first three years we employed a diminutive old Chinese gardener who had come over in the coolie ships and answered only to the name of Georgie. Georgie hated lawns, loved rockeries, and was perpetually telling me: "You no want-em glass! You want-em lock!" Because we could not curb his passion for stone instead of greenness we parted company with him.

That summer of 1959 we worked hard giving our character to the house. The Cockney painter introduced us to a Cornish carpenter and handyman, taciturn and capable, and we worked with him, tearing down partitions to open out the upper floor, rebuilding the porches, refitting the bathroom, changing dog-chewed doors, laying sisal carpeting every-where, and at the same time, by awakening it with good bone white paint, reviving the touch of late Georgian elegance which the original carpenter-builder had given to the interior.

The house had inhabitants as well as us. It was haunted. The manifes-tations were not visual, but aural and olfactory. We would hear a crack in the air, close to us, as if someone were snapping his fingers near our ears, and sometimes the clear light ringing of a silver bell, again elusively unplaceable but always high in the air. As soon as I started teaching, I developed the habit of writing far into the night, when I had finished preparing next day's classes and the telephone was silent, and Inge would often sit up doing her own work until we had decided it was time, at three or four in the morning, to go to bed. Then we were most often aware of the olfactory haunting, which took the form of both of us, often in separate rooms, suddenly noticing smells for which there was no immediate physical cause. The odours were in a restricted spectrum: cakes baking; bacon frying; fresh violets (in all seasons); and the ammoniacal sweetness of horse urine. The domestic associations of cakes and bacon were obvious; there were clumps of white violets in the garden, so that some former owner must have had a liking for that flower; the smell of horse urine puzzled me until, reconstructing the basement, I found a crawlhole dense with cobwebs under the back porch in which there were chains and bits of harness; at some time, perhaps while the cottage still belonged to the McCleery farm, someone who worked with cart horses had lived here. The hauntings never went beyond sound and smell. No spectre appeared, no voices spoke, and no identifying clue was offered. All we knew was that the ghosts were benevolent, and we felt happy when they manifested themselves, saying to each other, as if we were spying on flesh-and-blood neighbours: "They're baking cakes tonight", or, "The horse has just been pissing."

After a while the hauntings diminished. The sounds ceased first, and then the smells came less frequently, though even now, late at night, my nose will sometimes be tantalized with the smell of well-cured bacon. We often wonder about this quiescence. Is it because the presences are pleased with the way we have treated their house and no longer need to draw anxious attention to themselves? Or is it perhaps because, over the years, our introduction of more and more religious images, masks, and paintings from India and Tibet and from various animist cultures has created a spiritual barrier which they are shy to penetrate?

XI

ANARCHIST EXORCISMS

I N THE AUTUMN OF 1959 I received a letter from Aaron Asher of the U.S. publishing house, Meridian Books, inviting me to write a history of anarchism. At that time the literature on the subject was scanty; my books on Godwin, Kropotkin and Proudhon, written before I left England to return to Canada in 1949, had been the first serious and substantial works to be published for many years on the anarchist thinkers, at least in the English-speaking world, and no adequate general history of the movement and the development of its ideas existed. I was eager to write one and I foresaw that it would be important to me as a means of clarifying my own ideas and redefining where I stood in relation to a movement to whose service I had once dedicated myself.

That winter I devoted to the basic research for the book. I had much information at hand, and since I had trained myself to retain clues to the sources of facts rather than burdening my memory with the facts themselves, I was able to find my way to other necessary material. But there remained much, especially archival material, that was unavailable in North America, and to find it I had to visit Europe in the spring and summer of 1960. By this time Herbert Read of Routledge and Kegan Paul had agreed that his firm would publish the English edition, and the advances from the two publishers paid for the trip.

We first went to Paris, where I researched at the Institute of International Documentation, and thence to Amsterdam, where we spent our days at the Institute of Social History, sitting in damp rooms overlooking one of the canals and generating rheumatic pains as we mined the mass of notes and documents accumulated by Max Nettlau, the best early historian of anarchism and its most assiduous archivist. Nettlau had known many of the classic anarchists, and his German scholarship provided a hoard of useful information.

From Amsterdam we went to Frankfurt, a hideous journey, since I had contracted food poisoning and spent most of my time in the toilet, paralysed by vomiting and diarrhoea; fortunately the train was not full, and the attack passed quickly. From unsympathetic Frankfurt, we continued to Innsbruck and crossed the Brenner Pass into the South Tyrol, where we met Inge's parents in an old wooden hotel, its floors scarred by the boots of generations of mountaineers, in the remote little Alpine village, Italian by name but Austrian in feeling, of Dobbiacco. And from there, after a few days of mountain walking, we took a coach through the Dolomites and down to Venice.

We fell instantly in love with it. Like all who have remembered it, from Ruskin and Proust to Mary McCarthy, we responded to its fragile grandeur which the mirroring waters made seem more than half illusion. We wandered in the galleries and academies, and I learnt for the first time the power of Tintoretto's painting, was confirmed in my admiration for Tiepolo and Veronese, and looked with uneasy awe on the great Christ Pantocrator at Torcello. Yet I remember façades of neglected palaces looming spectrally over the dirty canals more clearly than I recall the detail of any painting, and my most poignant memory of Venice is of sound rather than sight: footsteps in a city virtually spared the curse of the wheel, mingling with the slap of water against the quays in the wake of the vaporetti.

WE WERE BACK IN VANCOUVER at the beginning of August. *Canadian Literature* was already showing itself notably successful. Writers welcomed it as a critical journal which was neither superficial, in the manner of the newspaper review, nor academically arid, and typical of many letters that came to me that autumn was one from Hugh MacLennan, remarking: "This has become an absolutely splendid magazine, no doubt of that."

By this time, I was paying my own critical attention more closely to Canadian writing, and MacLennan wrote me again shortly afterwards when A.J.M. Smith published in his anthology, *Masks of Fiction*, my essay, "A Nation's Odyssey: the novels of Hugh MacLennan," in which I explored for the first time the Odysseus theme that runs through MacLennan's books. The letter was characteristic of MacLennan, cordial, showing both his openness to criticism and the manner he saw images and analogies moving through his unconscious towards the revelation that writing offers.

"Until I read your essay, it had never consciously occurred to me that I was following the Odyssey-myth in these books. The choice of the name Penelope in BAROMETER RISING may have been subconsciously prompted, but the passage at the end where it seemed most obvious that I was rubbing the symbol in was not much more than a device, and rather a corny one at that, used by an inexperienced author to conclude his book. As for the others, it never occurred to me consciously that the events were paralleling the Odyssey, least of all the smash-up scene at the end of EACH MAN'S SON. I was bothered by the Enoch Arden aspect of Martell in the last novel, but it never occurred to me that once again this was Odysseus returning.

"This is all the more curious because I once was a classical scholar and have read the Odyssey several times in the original Greek. . . . I write much more out of the subconscious than I appear to many to do, including myself. That is probably why in some of the books the wires have been crossed. But I think it may be damaging to a writer to worry too much about wire-crossing. The thing is to get the stuff out."

The year from mid summer 1960 to June 1961 was exceptionally productive, owing partly to a cluster of favourable circumstances. I was teaching only two courses, my European Literature in Translation course, and a survey course in English literature from Chaucer to the Victorians, and since I had already constructed them, I could now carry them on with ease and much pleasure. Besides, I had been allocated a reader for my survey course; I rejoiced to find that it was Phyllis Webb. Since I could rely completely on her taste and judgment, Phyllis virtually relieved me of the burden of marking the papers for half my students, and was altogether a congenial, stimulating colleague. By now, I had also established a routine for *Canadian Literature*, and already good material was beginning to flow in without urging.

So I was able to devote much time to writing, and especially to *Anarchism*, and I was fortunate in finding an excellent assistant when Catherine Easto came to work for me as a part-time secretary, mainly typing my books; she proved so efficient and intelligent — and often excellently critical — in interpreting typescripts that were often tortuous and difficult in their alterations and insertions, that our association became a collaboration which lasted for a decade, and which I was sad to see ending round about 1970 when Catherine got married a second time and decided to abandon what must have been a taxing employment, but which she endured with much loyal irony. Indeed, she was so excellent a secretary that after she left I never found anyone to replace her adequately, and after three years decided that I would save myself frustration, if not time, by typing all my own work, which I have done ever since.

The writing of *Anarchism* went with splendid impetus. I had finished it by early June. It reflected my changing views. I had come to see anarchist ideas, no longer as offering a reliable program for a revolutionary society, but rather as a touchstone by which existing societies could be judged and their creative elements be identified and fostered. I saw not a utopia of complete anarchy in the future, but partial anarchy in the present, quietly changing society by encouraging the existing tendencies that directed themselves towards mutual aid.

When *Anarchism* was completed, there was a piece of publishing chicanery that distressed me but worked out in my favour. Meridian Books had contracted to start with a hardcover edition, but instead published its paperback edition immediately. Routledge and Kegan Paul angrily withdrew as the English publishers, because they felt that clandestine imports of the American paperback edition would undercut their hardcover sales. Almost immediately my agent, John Smith, sold the English rights to Penguin Books, who brought out a big first edition and have kept the book in print for more than twenty years, so that it has been easily the most popular and the best-selling of all my books, and also the most influential. It has also been the most translated, having appeared in Italian, Spanish, Swedish, Japanese, and Portuguese.

While writing *Anarchism* I began to develop the habit of tandem writing, working in two major directions at once, which I have done ever since. The other direction I followed in 1960 was that of drama.

About two years previously, I had a call from Gerald Newman who had just been appointed a drama and music producer for the CBC in Vancouver. He asked if I would be interested in developing some Miracle Plays for a Christmas program. I agreed, found interesting the problems of transforming something written to be seen into something to be heard, and over the next couple of years continued with adaptations of dramatic classics — *The Shoemaker's Holiday, Venice Preserved, The Beaux Stratagem, Riders to the Sea,* and *The Playboy of the Western World.*

Out of this activity developed one of those exceptional creative relationships encountered too rarely. Gerald Newman is the kind of man whom all his friends think of as a character, an original, and speak of with an affectionate amusement that conceals a deep respect for his knowledge and his skills: a shortish, fattish man with a sharp wit and excellent dramatic sense who prowled like a caged feline with tension, walking up and down the production booth, when a play was being recorded. His were austere but direct and evocative productions. He was also inclined — rare among producers — to trust the writer and to see his own role as interpreting the work given to him, and bringing out nuance and implication by orchestrating his actors. So with Gerald there was rarely any quibbling over one's script. He carefully picked the writers with whom he worked, and used them to the utmost. He was fortunate — and so was I — that the years from 1958 to about 1967 were an exceptional and experimental period in radio: there were many spaces for drama, and Robert Weaver — then a key figure in Toronto — encouraged the local producers to seek out good writers and persuade them to write radio plays.

Neither I nor Gerald was content for long with adaptations. He kept urging me to write original plays, and in the summer of 1960 I came home with a scenario building into my head which I turned into a cynical little verse play, a tragi-comedy called *Maskerman*. I wanted to write something out of the imagination rather than out of research or direct experience, and also to start writing poetry again. I had written no lyric verse, except a few nature poems in 1950, since I left England for Canada in 1949, and I have always attributed that abrupt interruption of my creative activity to the death of my friend Marie-Louise Berneri in 1949 and my failure to find a way of poetically expressing my grief. Now the lyric voice was still frozen, and I had to project my identity as a poet dramatically.

The plot of *Maskerman* had emerged in my mind as we were travelling to Venice. I had been hearing of the troubles of a friend who kept on picking the same kind of wrong woman, and getting himself involved in repetitive emotional and financial difficulties. He lived in the Rhineland, and it struck me that this was a classic case of haunting by the Lorelei. But the man himself was too pleasant to be the real stuff of drama; suddenly I realized that if I were to take merely the circumstances of his life, and adapt them to the bounderly character of a young (now dead) actor, Ian Thorne, who was then performing brilliantly in Vancouver on radio and on the resurgent stage, I would have not only a character to give life to this situation of amorous folly, but also — in the very studios where Gerald and I worked — an actor almost destined for my purpose. Gerald immediately recognized, when he read the script, what I had done. "Ian's the man for Maskerman," he said. "Perhaps you wrote it for him?" "No," I answered, "he wrote himself for me."

Maskerman was a success, but as a kind of extended poem rather than as a play. But radio plays, because they are directed towards neither the theatre nor print, usually have only a precarious afterlife. *Maskerman* was produced three times by the CBC, and even that was unusual for a radio play. If Jan de Bruyn had not decided to publish it in *Prism* in 1962, it would have been forgotten or perhaps even destroyed in the labyrinthine archives of the CBC where thousands of radio plays by first-rate writers, many of them obviously minor masterpieces, await a Last Trump that may never be sounded.

The desperation of a poet in distress over his words that echoes through *Maskerman* caught the attention of another poet. A couple of weeks after the first performance a postcard arrived, whose address, "Woodcock, British Columbia" intrigued me. The writer told me he had been camping beside the Skeena and on his portable radio had listened to *Maskerman*, whose "decadent" tone had attracted him. He was Al Purdy, whom I knew as one of the interesting newer poets whose books were coming in to *Canadian Literature* for review. Al had spent part of World War II at an RCAF station in the tiny village of Woodcock, and had just returned there on a sentimental journey. I was interested to receive his card, since a desire to explore how far the attitudes and methods of the Decadents might be valid in a world three quarters of a century later had indeed been one of my aims in writing *Maskerman*. The loyalties I had developed in writing *The Paradox of Oscar Wilde* had not died away, nor have they done so even today when I recognize how much so many of our self-styled literary prophets like Northrop Frye in fact owe to Baudelaire, Pater, Wilde, and the other great figures of the Decadence.

A few weeks later, Purdy came down from the North, and we met. He was tall, gangling, and reminded me of Lee Marvin, whose ironically plebeian acting I have always admired. Purdy and I were at once on common ground, as autodidacts, men without any university training, isolated except for a few similar figures like Alden Nowlan and Milton Acorn in the academically dominated world of Canadian writing. I recognized immediately the vast erudition and experience he had accumulated in much the same way as I had, and how similar we were despite our dissimilarities, as poets, as persons. Al must have had a similar recognition at that first meeting, for we have remained firm friends ever since, and have carried on voluminous correspondence even when circumstances have made our meetings rare. Nobody among my Canadian fellow writers except perhaps P.K. Page understands me more than Purdy does, and I hope I understand him as well. The most gratifying result of writing *Maskerman* was the establishment of that friendship.

Happy with the way both the actors and the audience had received *Maskerman*, I decided in the late fall of 1960 to attempt another verse play, and this time departed entirely from the autobiographical. I wrote a play deliberately using — because I felt I could make it my own — a Canadian tale that has always been a favourite with poets, that of Marguerite de la Roque who with her lover was marooned in the sixteenth century by her wicked uncle, the Sieur de Roberval on the Island of Demons in the estuary of the St. Lawrence. I made *The Island of Demons* into a drama of alienation and spiritual conflict, and had much fun turning the demons into the voices of Freudian complexes. Also, at roughly the same time, I embarked on my first major translation work, a version of Racine's *Phèdre*, which Gerald also produced. Those were extraordinary times at the CBC in Vancouver, particularly when one compares them with the increasingly barren era through which the Corporation and its programs have gone in recent years. I found it a stimulating period when I was never short of ideas, and rarely was one of them wasted.

XII

PASSAGES IN INDIA

URING THIS PERIOD, WHEN I was simultaneously teaching, editing, writing my book on anarchism and my radio plays and adaptations, I developed a routine that often meant working sixteen hours in a day; Inge at the same time was hard work at making ceramic jewellery, and we stimulated each other. With my radio earnings and Inge's ceramics we were able to pay off our debts and the mortgages on our house. But we were thinking beyond security. Our journeys in South America had given us an appetite for travel, and me an increased interest in the travel book as a literary form, and this would not be assuaged by trips to Europe. So we began to look towards Asia, and first of all towards India.

Both of us had reasons to be attracted. Inge had long been interested in Tibet, and the exodus to India in 1959 of the Dalai Lama and thousands of followers suddenly gave that country a special fascination. My attractions to India were more complex, beginning perhaps in the astonishment and pride with which every English boy in the 1920s accepted the fact that his tiny island controlled an empire that was larger than the Romans or the Persians had governed. A great hero of the British Raj, Robert Clive, had been born and raised near Market Drayton, my own family town in Shropshire; his legend flourished in my childhood, and when I went fishing for undersized perch and roach in the great pond below the house at Styche where he was born I would wonder if I might ever follow him, less heroically, to India; I had been told only of Clive's glory in India and not of his agony. Later, when I went to Sir William Borlase's School in Marlow on the Thames, which turned out boys fitted for minor posts in the imperial service, the possibility of one day going to India loomed. I was prevented from pursuing it when the Depression rolled in to destroy opportunities for young men in distant places of the empire.

But by this time I had become involved with India in other ways. In Britain, India became a focus of political contention during the 1920s and the 1930s, and as I grew more radical in my attitudes, it was natural that, among all other leftist dogmas, I should begin to support the cause of Indian independence. As my personal politics during the 1930s edged towards pacifism, it was even more natural that I should admire Gandhi's great experiments in civil disobedience which were shaking the fabric of the apparently indestructible British Raj. My interest in Indian events continued passionately until the country became independent in 1947, and then such unexpected events as the great massacres of the partitian period, and the murder of Gandhi by one of his own people, revealed a complexity about India which I had not anticipated when I sat in Soho pubs with Moslem and Hindu students whom I regarded indiscriminately as Indians and puzzled about the new word, *Pakistan*, which they were beginning to hurl at each other.

Some of the young writers from India I then met, like Mulk Raj Anand, Narayana Menon, Bhalchandra Rajan, and Tambimuttu, became my friends, and with independence they returned home to the new free India. I received fragments of news about them; Mulk, I learnt, was editing an art magazine in Bombay; Rajan was at the University of Delhi; Narayana Menon was with All-India Radio. With so many friends there, I believed, India could not be entirely alien.

Once *Canadian Literature* was established, I planned a journey to India over the winter of 1961-1962. Alan Pringle commissioned a book, but that was the least problem, for Fabers always gave meagre advances and I should have to seek real funding elsewhere. Roy Daniells managed to arrange that I was allowed a year's leave from U.B.C. with 60% of my salary. At the recently established Canada Council, Peter Dwyer came up with a travel grant of $3,500 which would pay for our fares. Robert Weaver and Robert Patchell persuaded the CBC to commission from me a documentary on the standing of Gandhi's thought and reputation in India fourteen years after his death. By mid-summer of 1960 everything had fitted into shape, we found an excellent person to sit our house, and in August we set off, crossing Canada by train to Toronto, going on to Hamilton, where I foolishly took part in a summer seminar (I was quick to learn the time-wasting folly of such occasions), and in Montreal only just catching the little Dutch liner *Rijndam*.

We landed at Rotterdam in mid-September and went to Offenbach, where Inge stayed with her parents while I flew to London. By now our journey had begun to assume almost imperial dimensions, for we were to approach India by P. & O. liner through the Suez Canal and the Red Sea, visiting Egypt and Aden on our way there and Ceylon on our way back. Though we would be joining the boat at only Port Said, it seemed appropriate that I should start off from London, where I had not been for the past twelve years.

There I had to talk to my agent John Smith and meet Alan Pringle, to discuss articles for *History Today*, to interview people like Fenner Brockway, V.S. Pritchett, Hugh Thomas, John Davenport, and Salvador Madiaraga for CBC television programs on the Spanish Civil War and on Malcolm Lowry, to see old friends like Herbert Read, Julian Symons, Roy Fuller, and Elizabeth Early, and to tramp central London, observing —and generally disliking — what had been done to restore the parts of the city I had known so well before the war and had even cherished in their bomb-shattered decrepitude. I began to develop a distaste for postwar London which I have never lost, and I was glad to meet Inge in Frankfurt, and travel through Paris to Venice, where we embarked at the end of September on a slow steamer down the Adriatic, going ashore at Brindisi to savour its Levantine atmosphere, and sailing through the Ionian islands and past Crete until, at the end of three days, we reached Alexandria.

Nineteen sixty-one was the paranoiac height of the Nasser regime, a time when foreigners were still hostilely regarded by officials, though not, as we soon realized, by most others. At Alexandria we were herded by armed guards into a queue that stood on deck in the burning sunlight as its members vanished one or two at a time into the first-class lounge where the Egyptian immigration officers had established themselves. Spread out before them they had ten enormous leather-bound black books, like great ledgers, and though the books were arranged alphabetically, there was no index, so that each passport had to be handed on down until it could be cleared by the official with the last book. Once that was completed, the old Egyptian ways took over and a kind of dragoman appeared who for a few Egyptian pounds collected our luggage, organized porters, hectored the officials in the crowded old customs house and put us in a taxi to the railway station.

During our ten days in Egypt we were tourists. In Cairo we visited the Pyramids and the Sphinx, went to Memphis and to Saqqara, where I thought I would die of claustrophobic fear crawling through the low passages deep into the underground chambers of the tombs. We picked our way through the dusty chaos of the Cairo Museum, but we went as well to the splendid Islamic Museum, which was almost deserted, and to the even finer Coptic Museum in Old Cairo, which was completely so. In old churches nearby, we admired icons and descended into waterlogged crypts, and outside one of them, as we walked up the path between the date palms, we found the black-robed priest sitting and sunning himself.

Father Cyril rose to greet us in excellent English, his face young-ish and olive-skinned, long hair jet-black, eyes large and deep like those of a Fayyum coffin painting under his priestly stove-pipe of a hat. He showed us knowledgeably around the church. Remarking that we must be tired, he gave us coffee in the parsonage, serving it with earthy tasting glasses of well water, which we drank out of politeness we afterwards had reason to regret. We talked about antiquities, for he had lived in Luxor and the Fayyum, and was something of a collector, his study filled with bric-à-brac, which he began to bring out, demon-strating some tests that we might use to authenticate antiquities which might be offered to us when we got to Luxor. The spittle test deter-mined whether pottery was a recent fake. If the spittle were absorbed quickly, it meant the pottery was still porous and probably new. "And stone?" he asked us rhetorically. "How can I tell the age of stone?" A piece of carved limestone was lying on the floor, and he dramatic-ally knelt down and prostrated himself to lick it noisily. Then he rose, smacked his lips, and declared: "Salt! I taste salt! Not more than six hundred years old! Recent limestone exudes salt! Only very old lime-stone is tasteless!"

I could not imagine myself going around the antiquarians' shops of Luxor licking stone-carvings, but I thanked Father Cyril, and put a cou-ple of pounds into the poor box on his desk. Beaming with pleasure, he remarked that we could not leave without a souvenir. He selected a small Roman lamp of red pottery and thrust it on me. Not wishing to be outdone, I popped another pound into the box. Father Cyril now of-fered an Islamic panel of wood delicately inlaid with lighter woods and with scraps of ivory. It seemed too good to accept, Inge protested, as I slipped in another couple of pounds. Thereupon Father Cyril said that we must have his own handiwork, and offered a neatly done little stained glass panel of a Coptic cross. It was a gift from the heart, he declared. He could accept nothing for it — no (gently pushing back my automatically offering hand), not even for his beloved poor. So, we de-parted, and though the other items somehow vanished, I retained Father Cyril's cross, which shines before me as the rays of the setting sun strike my study window where it hangs, its arms golden among the surround-ing stars of green, red, and azure glass.

We travelled by train to Luxor, through the great Nile flood, unaware that we were among the last to see that phenomenon which had created a whole religion, a whole philosophy and civilization, and which was about to vanish from the history it had occupied for six millenia — thanks to a few ingenious engineers working on the great dam at Aswan, virtually unaware of the destructive ecological consequences.

As we travelled south through the valley, on the railway high-embanked to keep us above the level of the blue waters that stretched on each side to the tawny escarpments which marked the start of the desert, we looked with wonder over this shimmering plain of water, out of which the villages rose on the mounds of ancient settlements, with their gleaming white mosques and the pierced towers of the dovecotes from which the white birds flew out over the waters.

After this, the human wonders of Luxor took on a rigid, postcard-like quality. The great processional ways and the vast colonnades of Karnak, with their population of pink hawks, and the tombs of the pharaohs in their arid little gullies across the river, projected an expected grandeur, a replica of the vision one had built. I found the monumental conservatism of ancient Egypt stiff and stifling, but my disappointment, I realize now, was not so much with Egypt itself as with my own response to it. As we sailed down from Port Said through the Suez Canal and the Red Sea, appreciating the arid passions of the Koran as I read it in view of the desert coast of Yemen, I began to fear that we might react as negatively to India. Certainly Aden, that outpost of the Raj with its shark-infested harbour and the dismal crater that sheltered its apology for a city, was no promising introduction. But on the bright moonlit night after leaving Aden we stood on the deck watching the tropical constellations, and as the schools of flying fish broke the waters with glittering impact, I felt my expectations restored.

TWO NIGHTS LATER OUR BOAT docked and we got up at dawn to look at Bombay harbour; Inge, who had been most doubtful about our journey, felt immediately, like a revelation, the combined appeal of the familiar and unexpected which India holds for Europeans. At that moment of recognition we knew that our association with India would be long and complicated.

As soon as we navigated through the chaos of the Bombay customs house, things seemed to come together. My old friend, Mulk Raj Anand, was in Bombay the day we arrived; a letter of introduction from Bill Holland, editor of *Pacific Affairs*, brought us to the house of Patwant Singh — the Sikh editor of *Design* — and Keeni Kessler, the handsome Dutch woman to whom he was then married; both would become our longtime friends. Mulk took us behind Bombay, to the region of ancient Buddhist caves, and set us on our way to Ajanta and the even greater site of Ellora with its Kailasa temple that is not built but is cut deep out of the living rock. Patwant lavishly entertained us in both Bombay and Delhi, giving us access to what Mulk called the "Brown Sahibdom" of Indian officials and politicans who succeeded the British and socially imitated them by taking over the clubs of the Raj and applying new but still exclusive standards of admission. Patwant and Mulk introduced us to literati and artists, among them the shy, ironic figure of R.K. Narayan, finest of all the Indian writers who have honoured the English language by using it. At a Delhi celebration of the centenary of Rabindranath Tagore, a writer I have always regarded as both pretentious and banal, I met Aldous Huxley for the first and only time, and was troubled by the tired nimbleness of his wit, constantly playing brilliant variations on old themes. As well, I encountered another Indian friend from London days, the novelist and critic Bhalchandra Rajan, who had retired from the Foreign Service and was acting as Dean of Arts at the University of Delhi. Rajan would later become a scholarly ornament at the University of Western Ontario, a world-recognized authority on Milton and Eliot.

The CBC had arranged for All India-Radio to help me make my recordings about Gandhi's heritage, and one day, when Inge and I were walking through the broadcasting building with the producer who had been assigned to us, we saw a door with a notice announcing Tibetan programs. While I taught at the University of Washington, Inge had been taking the rudimentary classes in Tibetan, which taught her the written language but left her incapable of speaking it since nobody in Seattle knew the true pronunciation. In the back of her mind she had thought of finding a teacher in India, and now our companion offered to introduce us to the director of the Tibetan section of All India-Radio.

Lobsang Lhalungpa was a small, soft-spoken man, with the slightly ruddy complexion of people from Lhasa. He had left Tibet several years before the exodus, and had spent the first years in Kalimpong and Darjeeling, where he learnt English. The western scholars who gathered there relied on his knowledge of Tibetan religions, acquired in youth when his father was the state oracle at Nechung and later when he worked in the offices of the Potala. When the Chinese invasion of Tibet made links with the peoples on their northern borders important to the Indians, he was given charge of Tibetan broadcasts from Delhi.

When he learnt of our interest in Tibet, Lobsang was helpful and hospitable. He and Deki, his beautiful young Bhutanese wife, entertained us in one of the dismal concrete apartment blocks provided for Indian civil servants, and we established an enduring friendship. Lobsang also located a young man, Ngawang Lungtok, whose name meant "Castle of Meditation", and who gave Inge her first lessons in spoken Tibetan. Ngawang introduced us to Kundeling, one of the Dalai Lama's ministers who happened to be in Delhi, and Kundeling urged us to see the condition of the Tibetan refugees and suggested we go to the old hill station of Mussoorie, where Jigme and Rinchen Dolma Taring, two Lhasa aristocrats, had established a residential school for Tibetan children.

We went to Mussoorie, intending to go on from there to Le Corbusier's new city of Chandigarh, then to the Golden Temple at Amritsar, and afterwards to imperial Simla. But all these plans were thrown over after we reached Mussoorie and found the old British bungalow around which the Tibetan residential school had been organized.

Mrs. Taring, a sad gentle Tibetan woman dressed to suit the voluntary simplicity she and her husband had accepted, came on to the verandah as we approached and invited us in for tea. The Tarings, whose friendliness to foreigners in Lhasa had become proverbial, received us with a hospitality that concealed their straitened circumstances. There were other guests, one of them a vivacious Tibetan girl of about sixteen who spoke excellent English. The more we asked about Tibetan refugees, and the more Inge showed her knowledge of Tibetan culture, the more excited the girl became, until finally she said, "You absolutely must come and see Uncle! He will love to talk to you." Mystified, I whispered to an American missionary woman sitting beside me, "But who is Uncle?" "Don't you know?" she answered. "She is Khando Yapshi, the Dalai Lama's niece."

We abandoned our original plans and, after a few days with the Tarings, observig the wretched conditions in which they were trying to educate and feed hundreds of children, we went on by train to Pathankot on the Kashmir border. Khando had kept her word: a car was waiting to take us up into the Himalayan foothills to Dharamsala, where the Dalai Lama was now living. And there we met that modest and gentle young man, with his vast sense of humour, who insisted on his role as a "mere monk", and talked long about Buddhism and about the fate of his people. Seeing even more suffering than at Mussoorie among the younger children whom his sister, Tsering Dolma, had gathered into a makeshift orphanage, we promised the Dalai Lama that when we got back to Canada we would do what we could to help them.

But before we did return, we wandered, by bus, by car, by air, by river boat, in a vast sweep through India, from the Kashmir border to Darjeeling in the north, and southward as far as to Ceylon (as it then was) at Adam's Bridge.

Re-reading the book I wrote from that journey, *Faces of India*, what strikes me first is a vividness and clarity of visual perception and description, and next a quality of innocence. On that earliest trip to India I had the advantage that our travels in Mexico and Peru had inoculated me against the culture shock that often comes from the first encounter with deep poverty; the writer's block which I had suffered in Mexico I did not experience here. Also, the fact that I had come with a specific project required that I find and interview many people and gave me a kind of access to the peoples' lives that would have been much more difficult for the mere wanderer. Though Nehru resolutely evaded letting me draw him out about Gandhi, I did encounter such political leaders as the former governor-general Rajagopalachari, a waspish saint, on the right, and the benign intellectual of the Praja Socialists, Ashoka Mehta, on the left, and discovered in the interstices of the new India a surprising number of Gandhi's less political disciples striving to give shape to his social message. As well, the Dalai Lama's introductions and messages led to encounters with Tibetans along the Himalayan foothills from Dharamsala to Kalimpong.

But it is still the innocent quality that now, two decades later, impresses me in *Faces of India*. The effect was partly due to a desire to find a country not irrevocably committed to the paths of centralized industrialism and nationalism which appeared to be destroying Western societies, and partly due to the fact that India did impress me as containing possibilities lost already in the West. In the quest for Gandhi's influence, I hoped to find, fourteen years after the country's liberation, the evidence that Gandhi's plan of a decentralized society based on village regeneration was still alive.

India in 1961 was still that country of immense variety which the British had nurtured, perhaps unintentionally, by preserving the double system of directly administered territories and native states. The native princes had been unseated and their realms incorporated into larger units, but still enough remained of traditional differences to give India the exotic diversity which it has since slowly lost. Perhaps we went there at the best time, when the old tyrannies, both British and native, had come to an end, but the ancient local ways of life that had managed to survive were largely untouched by alien and homogenizing influences. One encountered such an immense variety of custom, landscape, and physical types that one could predict, on going to bed at night, that the next day one would see at least one thing entirely new and strange, and this constant unexpectedness was exciting. And yet, thanks to India's history, one was never at a loss to communicate. It was a foreign setting in which one's language was always understood by someone nearby, and in which to speak with an English accent meant that one was seen as a kind of cousin bred out of the odd, temporary marriage of two peoples into which love and hate entered with equal intensity.

But even then, events were beginning that would irrevocably transform the country. Nehru had already rejected Gandhi's vision of a village-based society in favour of an industrialized and militaristic state that would imitate the discredited old nation states of Europe. One day, trying to get from Agra to Delhi, we found that all trains had been cancelled, and we had to hire a car at an exorbitant price. The railways were being used for the invasion of Goa. This was not Nehru's first military adventure; he had sent his troops into Hyderabad when the Nizam was talking about making it a sovereign state in the middle of India, and he had done the same in Kashmir when Pakistani irregulars came over the border. One of these could be interpreted as an internal policing operation and the second as an act of self-defence in disputed territory. But the attack on Goa, whatever its moral aspects, was politically an aggression against the possessions of a foreign power and its possible repercussions were different. A few weeks later we were in south India, attending a dinner at the Maharaja's College in Mysore, and as we sat afterwards on the moonlit lawn, the conversation turned to the Goa incident which, as South Indians, most of the professors there treated with detachment as an adventure of the "Men of Delhi", as they called Nehru and his ministers. One professor was concerned about the danger of a chain reaction that might run through all of Asia. Smaller nations like Indonesia might use India's example to justify their own attempt to take by force what they could not get by quick negotiation. "And perhaps it will not be only the smaller nations," he said. "One never knows where such a process may end. I fear that Nehru and Krishna Menon have set something in motion whose consequences they may soon be regretting." Within a year his fears were confirmed when Chinese armies marched over the mountains into Assam.

One factor has remained constant in all the years we have been visiting India: the irreducible poverty of most of the population. I have never been able to forget how, travelling through Bihar on our way from Darjeeling to Calcutta, we saw an old woman fighting with pariah dogs for the scraps of food the passengers threw from the train windows; the stubborn memory of that episode has been largely responsible for my continuing desire to help the people of India.

On the last day of that visit to India, we travelled slowly by train from the temple city of Madurai to the seacoast, where we crossed a long bridge beneath which the tide rushed between the teeth of the enormous flat slabs of greenish rock, the stepping stones of Adam's Bridge. I noted the skeletal thinness of many old people, the breasts of old women often flat loose flaps of skin. Starvation seemed more evident in this extreme south-east even than in the cities, and more tragic because it occurred in a setting that appeared to offer such richness, and showed such waste. Straw was burnt to fire kilns, dung for house fires. Needed were vast teams of dedicated educators in farming, birth control, simple hygiene. But, apart from the Gandhians, few then responded. The educators were concerned either with making money, or obsessed by their own insecurity, or dominated by some kind of Brahminical snobbery. Only a minority showed a practical interest in the submerged 400,000,000.

That anger over the insensitivity of the Indian upper and middle classes, finding a dubious justification for themselves in Hindu doctrines of Karma that seemed to predestine a being's condition, has recurred in my long relationship with India, which perhaps has been a Karmic relationship of its own kind; Asians would believe so. A little earlier, in Dharamsala, I had sat a whole afternoon with an old Tibetan aristocrat named Phala who was a member of the *Kashag* or Tibetan cabinet, during which, though neither spoke the other's language, we had constantly anticipated the interpreter, so that in the end Phala remarked: "There is only one possible explanation for the way we have understood each other; we were friends in a past incarnation." A few weeks later, at a party in Madras, a young Brahmin woman concentrated her attention on Inge, declaring they were sisters in a previous life. Two days later, after she and her brother had generously entertained us, we bade farewell to them as we stepped on the night train to Bangalore, and she brushed aside our thanks with the remark: "Why not? After all, we've known each other for so long!"

THE STRENGTH OF OUR relationship with India was emphasized in a negative way by our experience in Ceylon. In the early 1960s, before the period of the Bandaranaikes and their Buddhist Trotskyite radicalism, and before the recently intensified feud between Singhalese and Tamils, Ceylon seemed tranquil and prosperous. We were aware of this the moment we landed at Talaimenar Pier, slipped suavely through customs and immigration procedures, and settled for the night in a comfortable mahogany and silver-plated sleeping compartment on a train that had no barred windows and no Indian-style notices warning us about thieves and people who might offer us drugged food. The countryside we awoke to as we neared Colombo was fertile and the settlements unimpoverished. We found pleasant people, whether they were the Ceylonese who took us to the ancient centres of Anuradhapura, Pollonaruwa, Sigiriya, and Kandy, or the foreigners we met, or Jim George, the Canadian High Commissioner to Ceylon and his wife, Carol, with whom in our last afternoon in Colombo we began a long friendship. The rain-forested mountain landscapes were luxuriant and beautiful. Standing beside the serene reclining Buddha at Pollonarawa, climbing the shaking metal stairs to see the sensuous painted nymphs under the cliff overhangs of the massive rock of Sigirya, going of an evening to the Temple of the

Sacred Bo Tree in Anuradhapura, with the drummers beating and the *hautbois* playing at the door and air within the temple heavy with the scent of the flowers piled on the altar and all the statues flickering as the wind blew the little sheets of gold leaf gently attached to them, we were moved as deeply as we had been anywhere in India.

In every way Ceylon should have seemed relaxing after our rigours; we should have seen in its relative prosperity an Asian alternative to the travails of India, and have detected in the serene greatness of its monuments the signs of a past under the Buddhist kings in which — as in the realm of Ashoka — power was tempered with compassion and with the search for truth in ways rarely encountered before.

Yet, perversely, we found Ceylon too bland and predictable. We missed the Indian variety; the constant challenges to our consciences and sensibilities; the tang of Indian smells and dust; the changes in custom every hundred miles of the route and the oddities of personality produced by such a mingled heritage; we even irrationally missed the daily frustrations of travel and the nightly hardships of wretched hotels. We missed the unforeseeable adventures of a land we had immediately accepted as our own. And so, when our ten days in Ceylon came to an end, we departed only with gratitude for the pleasure and rest it had given us.

The ship sailed at night, and we passed the last low palm-crowned tropical islands of Ceylon at lunch time. Two days later we saw the inhospitable dunes of desert islands in the morning, the outliers of Arabia, yellow dunes piling up to grey steep cliffs, and then, early in the afternoon, the dry desert coast of Somaliland to the south, pale tan and grey in the haze that hangs over it. Then the next day Aden. With this knotting of the loop the journey seemed virtually complete, familiarity — Port Said and Europe — ahead, a winter having been consumed in strange lands.

XIII

FAREWELL TO CLASSROOMS

W E RETURNED TO VANCOUVER in the spring of 1962, deeply affected by our experiences in India. My first task was to write *Faces of India* and to prepare my radio program on Gandhi, but though the latter was produced in the summer of 1962, it took me a year to finish my book. The delay was partly due to the fact that the journey to India, unlike earlier travels, inspired us to do something practical in response to what we had seen.

We had taken our promise to the Dalai Lama seriously enough to write to associates at the university about the Tibetans' situation, and we found that John Conway, a professor of history whom I then hardly knew, had been inspired by one of my letters to persuade the student members of World University Service to put on a fundraising drive. They organized an election for "the ugliest man on campus", and by charging a few cents a vote they raised $700, which Conway had waiting for us when we returned. I never met the ugliest man.

This concrete example of goodwill led us to do more than we had first intended, and in April, with the help of Roy Daniells, Bill Holland of *Pacific Affairs* and John Conway, we called a small meeting and founded the Tibetan Refugee Aid Society. Norman Mackenzie, then president of U.B.C., became its chairman, which was virtually an honorary post. I became vice-chairman and carried on most of the correspondence, but most importantly, Inge became an energetic and resourceful fund-raiser. The $700 we owed to the ugliest man paid for roofing a new building Inge and I had seen being constructed at Mussoorie.

We spent almost a year building the society up by small newspaper and radio campaigns and speeches to whatever groups would hear us, and established contacts with trustworthy people in India. Mrs. Taring wisely used our money at her Mussoorie school and at the Tibetan

Homes Foundation she shortly established, modelled after the Pestalozzi Village in Switzerland, a series of "families" of 25 orphan children, each supervised by a house mother and father. For less than $10,000 we bought a large deserted British summer mansion that accommodated two of these groups — 50 children in all. At Kangra we found a Canadian Anglican medical missionary, Florence Haslam, who organized the provision of clothing and food supplements for the six hundred children at Dharamsala for whom the Dalai Lama's sister was caring and did the same for a refugee school in Kangra itself where a Canadian girl, Judy Pullen, was working as a CUSO volunteer. At Campbelltown, near Dehra Dun, we got in touch with a retired Indian army officer, Bill Davinson, who was working for the British Ockenden Venture, and he built a Tibetan school there for us, with refugee volunteer labour, at the minute cost of $4,000; we would continue to work with him on projects in India until his death in 1985. By April, 1963 we organized a Tibetan week in Vancouver. There was a gala ball, a show of paintings donated by local artists, there were concerts, and Arthur Erickson designed the setting for a Tibetan Fair, a kind of megalomaniac rummage sale, in the Scottish baronial fortress of the Seaforth Armouries. By this time we had attracted a group of British people in Vancouver who had links of some kind with India, and these volunteers formed a long-time nucleus of helpers, many of whom became personal friends. Indeed, the friendships we gained were a more than adequate reward for the long hours of work that we put into the Tibetan Refugee Aid Society over the next decade.

Yet I had felt ambivalent from the beginning, not about what we were doing, but about my role in it. In my anarchist past I had believed that philanthropy merely diverted attention from the fact that society's injustices could only be ended by a radical change in the political and economic order. But after encountering the deep poverty of Mexico, Peru and India, I began to feel that any improvement, no matter how slight, or temporary, was worthwhile so long as even a few people were raised a little out of their misery. My study of Gandhi's teachings and my contact in India with people who had worked with him led me to accept his advocacy of working from the roots, of permeating rather than destroying, and I saw the wisdom of the slogan, "One step enough for me", that he eclectically plucked from John Henry Newman's hymn. I saw the wisdom of proceeding gradually once one had recognized that society contained within its structure the mutual aid of which the anarchists had spoken, and which was prevented from flowering only by the state, whether in its repressive or its benevolent "welfare" form.

Thus I saw nothing wrong with collecting money from those who could afford it, and working with Tibetan refugees and with trustworthy people in India to spend it. Still, I had never seen myself as a philanthropist, but rather as a teacher and propagandist, trying to show people how to bring about their own freedom, and salvation from oppression and want. Dispensing what I still saw as charity made me uneasy, and my misgivings were brought to a head by an unpleasant encounter with a rich man. Up to this point — some time in the late summer of 1962, our gifts had almost all come from people who were not well off, and had no desire that their donations should be made known. This sense of poor people aiding poorer people helped reconcile me to our activity, though I still felt uneasy in the role of public benefactor.

Then a situation arose in which we could have made good use of a modestly large sum of money if we could raise it immediately. One highlight of our visit to the Dalai Lama had been a special performance of a Tibetan play enacted traditionally by players and musicians who had followed him from Lhasa. It was an exotic entertainment that might appeal to Western audiences, but we needed an assessment from a Western expert in the performing arts before we would be able to contact agents and gather funds for the group's tour expenses. We were eager to present Tibetan culture to people in the West, and we realized that the attendant publicity would help us with our own fundraising.

At that time the conductor, Nicholas Goldschmidt, was running the Vancouver Festival. We had become friends, and Nicky agreed to go to India and assess the troupe, provided we could raise his travel expenses. I was averse to taking the money from the funds for direct aid to the refugees, and I hit on the idea of approaching a rich man for a loan that could be repaid from the tour's proceeds.

The man I picked on was a lumber baron known in Vancouver for his ostentatious gifts, which he seemed to believe would guarantee that posterity remembered him well. The sum I asked him to loan was a little more than a thousandth of his latest well-publicized donation. It would not even be an outright gift, yet it might have benefitted many people. But nobody would know about it. W. not only refused me, but did so in an insulting letter, preaching about the need to restrain frivolous expenditures at this time of national crisis. (It was the period when Diefenbaker's government, which W. fervently supported, was foundering.)

Had I asked for myself, I would have shrugged off the incident; plenty of writers have tried to touch a rich man for money and have failed. But I had asked on behalf of others, whose need had been amply documented, and the way he refused had rankled. So I wrote a play, *The Benefactor*; it was performed on a CBC Wednesday Night and published years afterwards by Oolichon Press. In baring the motives of the ostentatious benefactor, I could not help doing the same for his unostentatious counterpart. They are both there in the play, and Simon Mercator, the Benefactor, is as much me as the Vancouver tycoon it took me so long to forgive. Confession and exorcism combined, the play enabled me to carry on philanthropy with fewer personal misgivings. Having acknowledged the corrupting nature of charity — at times to the receiver as much as to the giver — I have been able to carry on helping other people with a minimum of avoidable self-righteousness.

Meanwhile, if working for the Tibetan refugees was involving me in moral situations that called for a solution through literature, it also confirmed the views I had developed on the kind of man who becomes a politician. I had always believed that, like a good actor, a successful politician must be a blank soul, lacking any core of conviction and of morality. The actor's inner neutrality enables him to receive the impress of characters that are not his own and to project them to an audience as their creator conceived them. According to the requirements of his profession he can go from one character to another, from Hamlet to Iago, and render them, good and bad, with equal felicity. The politician too can assume any role. I received confimation of this conveniently Protean nature of the political mind when, against my better judgment, I was persuaded to approach Canadian political leaders for help to the Tibetans.

From John Diefenbaker, then Prime Minister, I received a letter telling me that he had written to the Dalai Lama commiserating with him and his people in their misfortunes; financial stringencies and diplomatic complications prevented him from doing more. From Lester Pearson, then leader of the Opposition, I received an encouraging letter deploring the lack of action on the part of the Conservative government, and hinting that if he were in power something different would happen. In the spring of 1963, the Tories went out of office and the Liberals came in, with Lester Pearson as Prime Minister. I wrote reminding him of our correspondence, and suggesting that now he could give the help he had criticized his predecessor for withholding. But, as I might have expected, Tibetans — who had no votes in Canada — were now far from Pearson's mind. The letter I received from him was virtually a carbon copy of Diefenbaker's, expressing the same facile concern and making the same excuses for inaction. Clearly the same permanent official had written both letters, and the two leaders, whatever their apparent differences, were responding to bureaucratically developed lines of action rather than to human feelings or even to political conviction. I was confirmed in my view that the main aim of the politician is to gain and hold power; the ideology that takes him to his goal is secondary, and the housekeeping of the nation is mainly left in the hands of civil servants who provide the stultifying continuity from which even apparently radical leaders seem unable to escape.

PARALLEL WITH OUR WORK for the Tibetans, and with my writing, the tasks of editing and teaching were continuing. By 1963 *Canadian Literature* had proved its usefulness and viability. The writers whose books provided its justification were increasingly present as the 1960s went on, and critics — some very good ones — were more frequently appearing to discuss their work, so that *Canadian Literature* became much more than a mere critical journal; it became almost a continuing manifesto for the literary movement which was gaining impetus in the 1960s, so much so that I was occasionally foolishly credited with having "created Canadian literature".

But if editing was going well, my academic career ran into shoaly waters and was finally wrecked by the spring of 1963. I had been appointed Associate Professor on the eve of my departure on sabbatical leave in 1961, and when I returned to teaching in 1962 it must have seemed that I was well set for a successful academic career, with a full professorship in another few years and from then on an easy time teaching graduate seminars until retirement.

The prospect did not entirely please me. I had come to like teaching far more than I had expected, established good relationships with my classes, enjoyed the questing minds of my better students — so different from the closed minds of many professors. With brilliant exceptions, most of the North American university teachers I have encountered have exemplified the levelling effect of academic democratization. Far too many teachers are needed to deal with the masses of students for the minds of many of them to be filled, as Wyndham Lewis remarked in the last paragraph of *Self-Condemned*, with "anything more than a little academic stuffing". Universities are notable forcing grounds for inferiority complexes, and an unpleasantly large proportion of the teachers with whom I worked tended to compensate for their lack of ability, their dullness in the classroom, the pettiness of their research, the dim understanding of the material they were teaching, with shallow arrogance and a hollow pomposity which the students did not fail to detect and to recognize as symptoms of inadequacy. One main reason for the student "revolt" of the later 1960s and the early 1970s was the sense of having been defrauded. I could not see myself as a permanent member of such a community.

Still, teaching offered a secure income, and having struggled to live from freelance work in Canada made me reluctant to abandon a guaranteed living. Yet the possibility of liberating myself was always in my mind, as it had been when I had held regular jobs before, and when the challenge came to break free, arising from an unexpected conflict between my teaching career and my other interests, I was not reluctant to accept it.

By the beginning of 1963, Inge and I began to feel drawn back to Asia. India had given a first pungent taste of the continent, and we wanted a whole meal of oriental places and cultures. Alan Pringle of Fabers tempted me to write a book on a sweep of territory that would stretch from West Pakistan to Japan, and he was also interested in an idea I had of a history of the Greeks in India. Furthermore, the Tibetan Refugee Aid Society was spreading its aid to more groups of refugees, and it seemed imperative that someone should go there to meet our contacts in India and see just what was going on; since nobody else had the time or was likely to be able to lay out the cash for such a trip, the obligation fell on Inge and me. And if we were going to India, we had no intention of attempting to travel there during the hot early summer months or during the monsoon. This meant that we would have to make our journey in the autumn and winter, the first half of the university year. We calculated that since we had paid for our house we could probably keep ourselves for a year with our savings and what Inge earned from pottery and I from freelance writing. So I went to Roy Daniells and applied for a year's unpaid leave.

Roy raised no problem and the Dean of Arts was equally accommodating. Unfortunately, this was the first year of a new President, a dentist, whose principal aim seemed to be the establishment of a Faculty of Dentistry, and who little understood the peculiar needs of people involved in teaching the arts. As part of the rising tide of pseudo-democracy, he had delegated decisions about leave to an academic committee dominated by scientists. To them my reasons for applying for leave, even if it were unpaid, seemed frivolous. Not wishing to admit his new system was faulty, the President turned down my application.

I faced a decision of whether my prospective academic career was more important than my life as a writer. Security lay with academic obedience; my needs as a writer made me recalcitrant, and I declared that I would resign if my request were not granted. Four months of largely subterranean negotiations followed, until, at the end of May, the President agreed to recommend my change of status to a part-time Special Lecturer whose duties would be understood to extend not beyond the editing of *Canadian Literature*.

This compromise provided me with a far better situation than I had anticipated — better even than if my plea for a year's leave had been accepted. I was relieved of teaching, and returned to it only for one brief and disastrous period. For the next fourteen years, I would be a titular Lecturer who gave no lectures; the university hierarchy had no title of "editor" that could be applied to me. My sole duties would be the editing of *Canadian Literature* and whatever writing might go with it, and so long as the four issues a year appeared on time, I could travel where and when I wished. I had virtual freedom of movement, plenty of time for my writing, and a basic income — half my existing salary with increases each year as if half of me were climbing the ladder of academic promotion, so that, with what I earned from writing and Inge from pottery we could live reasonably well and afford to travel as we wished. The academic grove became a kind of lair in which I found refuge yet out of which I could range where I wanted. For a writer it was the ideal position, particularly since the one task that I agreed to do consisted of the activity I enjoyed next to writing, editing. I was grateful, even to the President whose obstinacy had made me threaten to resign.

XIV

A DIVIDED SUBCONTINENT

HAVING VIRTUALLY TERMINATED my brief academic career, I set to work arranging and financing our trip to Asia. It was again the jigsaw puzzle of fitting together sources of subsidy. Faber & Faber had commissioned two books, the travel narrative of Asia from the Khyber Pass to Tokyo, and the history of the Greeks in India, but their advances were rather stingy. The Canada Council came up with a small grant towards our travel costs, and the CBC commissioned me to write a documentary on modern Pakistan. Peter Quennell encouraged me to develop articles for *History Today* on themes that might occur to me on our travels. I had recently been appointed a contributing editor of *Arts* in New York, and Hilton Kramer, who was editor, invited me to write pieces for him on museums and sites of artistic interest we might encounter.

But many of these commitments involved payment on delivery, and we found ourselves still underfinanced. However, one evening at dinner in the spring of 1963 Gerald Newman asked me whether I had thought of writing detective stories or mystery plays. He said that he would shortly have a new spot available for half-hour plays. Although I had never written a detective story, this seemed an opportunity to earn the money we needed for our trip. When Gerald had gone home that evening I mentioned it to Inge, and we decided there might be a great bonus in amusement if we were to create a burlesque of the fashionable action thriller while somehow writing a serious message into the parody.

We had recently arranged our time in a way that soon became habitual. We would work hard six days of the week and devote each Monday to relaxation. We would either drive up Howe Sound to Squamish and its nearby valleys and perhaps over the coast mountains to Pemberton, or, more often, up the Fraser Valley to Hope or to Harrison or Cultus

Lake, and sometimes even as far as the crest of the Cascades in Manning Park. People who pass through the Valley on the freeway heading east have little idea of the network of backroads it contains, leading into clusters of pastoral hills or stretches of woodland, and often opening out into surprising mountain vistas. In recent years much of the valley has been spoilt by housing developments, but there are still parts comparatively uninvaded, and even now we take trips to tune us for the rest of the week. The weekly "greening" seems to restore me since the mere colour of grass and leaves causes a regenerative effect on my mind. But even in winter, I delight in the architecture of the bare trees, the quiet colours of moss and lichen on branch and trunk, and subtle browns and tans of dead grasses and reeds.

On the Monday after my conversation with Gerald we sat on the shores of Harrison Lake and invented a pair of airport detectives — a Don Quixote-Sancho Panza partnership named Moon and Short — and involved them in adventures with a conspiracy called the Servants of Light, centred in South Africa and dedicated to creating a racialist pattern of world domination. Gerald gave us a contract for seven plays, and we called them *The Luck of the Just*. We had a great deal of fun, with Inge inventing most of fantastic situations, I embellishing the dialogue, and both of us drawing freely on our travel experiences in India and Latin America, until we had the kind of play which the naive might take at face value and enjoy for its exotic settings and exaggerated action, while those who read their mysteries with a little more sophistication would recognize the burlesque element and enjoy the plays for their parody; a minority we were sure would also catch the undercurrent of anarchist argument that ran through the plays.

To our surprise, the series was an immediate success, with a public response which led to an episode unique in the history of the CBC. When the listeners in the Northern region — the Arctic and sub-Arctic areas, served by a station in Yellowknife — heard the first program they rang in by the scores, saying they could not wait to hear the remaining episodes, which they knew existed on tape because the rest of the country had already heard them. The station manager cancelled all other programs for the next three hours and played the whole series.

A second series of a further six plays was commissioned; we started on them before leaving and finished them on the train across Canada and on liners crossing the Atlantic and going down the Red Sea, so that I was able to post the scripts from Karachi. Later, after we returned, the series was rebroadcast, and out of our experience in the Far East we wrote two more plays, *The Electric Tree* and *The Carrier Pigeon*, each an hour long, in which our detectives displayed their powers of deduction and their ability to get into trouble in Malaysia and Hong Kong.

By then we had spent nearly two years in the company of our creatures, and had grown impatient with their limitations. They were inevitably fixed types, not evolving characters, and we decided not to extend their adventures further. In fact, I did not even turn the plays into a novel, as Alan Pringle had suggested I do. But they served us well in helping to subsidize our journey through Asia.

WHEN WE ARRIVED IN France, we took a train to Zurich, intending to sail from Genoa to Karachi. The next morning, as we walked down the Bahnhofstrasse after breakfast, I saw a newspaper poster: KENNEDY ERMORDET.

It is difficult, now so much time has passed and so much has been revealed about Kennedy's personal and political failings and now that political violence has become so frequent, for young people to understand the extraordinary consternation we felt on hearing the news of his death. I was antagonistic to Kennedy, first because he was so unmistakably a political animal, and then because I saw how his policies on Cuba brought the world nearer to destruction than anything the old soldier Eisenhower had done. Yet when I saw that Zurich poster the shock was almost visceral; I was appalled by this abrupt severing of a life in its prime, and I also knew it would mean a return in American politics to unthinking reaction, as it did with the accession to the presidency of the quintessential Texan, Lyndon Johnson. Yet, despite my opposition to the use of violence, I felt a strange joy, mingling with my gloomier thoughts, at the way the episode showed — despite all the advances in security — the vulnerability in political power systems and those who operate them.

FOR THE TOURIST West Pakistan, as it was then called before East Pakistan became the independent state of Bangladesh, was a dull place of uninteresting deserts in the south and arid mountains in the north, with ugly sprawling modern towns built on to ugly Victorian British cantonments. Because of its Islamic homogeneity it lacked the bizarre variety of custom and character we found in India, and it was subjected to authoritarian military rule; the dictator was Ayub Khan. Even the archaeological sites were of limited appeal unless one had special interests. Fortunately I did have them, and they took us to Taxila and Peshawar and into the country of the Khyber Pass to see the regions where the Greeks had once ruled and their influence had lingered for centuries.

The Greeks of Bactria — army units settled there by Alexander and encouraged to intermarry with Iranian women — had revolted against the Macedonian rule of Seleucus in the middle of the third century B.C. Early in the second century Greek princes crossed the Hindu Kush and annexed the Punjab. Somewhere about mid-century King Menander marched down the Ganges valley and captured the Mauryan capital of Pataliputra or Patna. Menander, who figures in Indian legend as King Milinda, appears to have been converted to Buddhism, and the interconnection between Greek rule and the rise of the Mahayanist form of that religion seems very close. The last Greek king of the region, Hermaeus, appears to have died in the latter part of the 1st century B.C., when his realm was overwhelmed by the Parthians. But, ironically, the Parthians themselves, and the later Kushana rulers of the region, became Hellenized, and it was during their reigns that the extraordinary Greco-Buddhist art of Gandhara evolved in a hybrid culture that was finally destroyed in the 5th century A.D. when the White Huns came over the mountains and put an end to both Buddhism and the Greek influence.

The story of the Bactrian Greek kings had been told already, but the full narrative of Greek penetration into India, including the Gandhara school of art, the spread of Greeks over India after the dissolution of their kingdoms in the Punjab, and the independent link through Greek trading ships sailing from Alexandria down the Red Sea and across the Arabian Sea to the Malabar Coast, had never been told entirely. The researching of it took us from Karachi to Rawal Pindi, which became our base. From there I was able to visit Taxila and other important sites, to talk to local archaeologists, to see many sculptures and other artifacts connected with the Greek period in local museums and collections that were largely unknown outside Pakistan, and get a physical feel of the setting. It was when I set about gathering material for my radio documentary on Pakistan that I ran into difficulties.

I had good contacts with Radio Pakistan, and a few academic links, and I had no difficulty in meeting public figures, scholars, writers, mullahs, tribal chiefs, etc. in sufficient numbers to give us a good cross-sectional idea of Pakistan society, both in the West and East. But although in India I had found most people willing to speak into a microphone the thoughts they expressed in conversation, this was far from the case in Pakistan. People would talk quite frankly face to face, so that I came away with an excellent personal knowledge of social and political circumstances. But the tapes I took home with me were a miserable tissue of half-truths and evasions.

To give one example, a political scientist in Dacca with a Columbia Ph.D. and some experience teaching in the United States, gave me a frank, thorough analysis of Ayub Khan's "Basic Democracy", a system of indirect suffrage that was being introduced, showing all its flaws and errors; but he spoke into the microphone as if he were a devoted Basic Democrat. Two honest men actually said to me, in conversation: "Do not expect me to say this into your microphone." The only man in all Pakistan who spoke his mind on tape as well as privately was an old blind *ulema* or Koranic teacher named Abul Hashim, and he had such a reputation for sanctity that even the dictator would not dare touch him. And Hashim, talking of the philosophic freedom he felt to be implicit in true Islam, as opposed to its sectarian manifestations, was raising his comments to a philosophic plane above the strife of politics.

I had the feeling of living in two landscapes, and not being sure which was the real one. Undoubtedly Khan's dictatorship was more genial and less oppressive than Zia's is today, and much trust and openness continued in private contacts, yet nobody dared to speak publicly. During the time we were in Pakistan a newspaper editor and some student leaders were arrested and imprisoned indefinitely for having criticized the regime. Yet nobody actually refused to do a recording with me. They preferred being misleading to being silent, and I could never make out whether this came from vanity, from a feeling that if it became known that they had refused to speak it would be assumed by the authorities that they had some guilty opinion to conceal. Whatever the reason, it left me with a program that was strong on background but weak in opinion, and when I got home to Canada I had to seek out expatriate Pakistanis who did not fear to fill in the gaps with honest views about their country. In Pakistan I began to feel guilty towards my interviewees for putting them in a difficult situation, and I began to understand what it must be like to live as a journalist under an aggressively authoritarian regime.

ALL OF INDIA lay between the two halves of Pakistan. Relations between the two countries were fairly hostile; a war had been fought recently and another would come fairly soon, but the planes were flying between Lahore and Delhi, and we were able to relax awhile in India before we went on to East Pakistan. We reached Delhi two days before Christmas, which is celebrated with great spirit in the Indian capital by peoples of all religions. We attended lavish and extravagant parties with our Delhi friends — Patwant and Keeni Singh, Bhalchandra Rajan, Mulk Raj Anand, Lobsang and Deki Lhalungpa, and at one of them I met the poet Octavio Paz, then Mexican ambassador in Delhi; he was enraptured by the beauty and spirit of the Delhi women and muttered darkly, "Why are they so delectable, and the men so . . . ?" Delectable the women were, and some of them, in festive mood, were challengingly free in their behaviour.

Our serious moments in Delhi were spent mainly with Tibetan and Indian officials, discussing the problems of the refugees, and this led us to meet Sir Olaf Caroe, who was there representing the Tibet Society of the United Kingdom. Caroe, who had been the last British governor of the North-West Provinces, was an example of the servants of the Raj at their best. Gentle-mannered, courteous, scholarly, he had written a first-rate book on the Pathans. For tribal and martial peoples of the old India he harboured, like many other British administrators, deep affection, and I noticed that, while he treated the Sikh factotum the Indian government had allocated to him with consideration, he appeared not to have much respect for the Hindu officials, and this they sensed, to his own and our ultimate disadvantage.

From Delhi we intended to tour Tibetan refugee settlements, and to travel into Sikkim, where we had recently gained the friendship of a Gangtok nobleman whose daughters we befriended when they arrived at the University of British Columbia. The early part of our mountain trip went well. We celebrated the New Year with the Tarings at Mussoorie. Like Indians, Tibetans are ready to adopt any excuse for a celebration, and, though their own year, like that of the Chinese, begins in February, they zestfully celebrated what they called "international New Year". We gathered on the bare mountainside with a thousand children and a cluster of maroon-robed monks. The monks burned juniper on open-air altars, chanted rumbling sutras, and handed us handfuls of barley meal which we threw into the air, whitening each other's heads and shouting a cry meaning "Victory to the Gods", after which the children performed intricate Tibetan dances to the tune of flute and drum. A few days later we were in Dharamsala, talking long and seriously to an older and sadder Dalai Lama whose thoughts had now taken a political turn, for he defended the encouragement of nationalist feelings among his followers in the hope that one day the Communist regime in China would crumble and it would be possible for the Tibetans to repossess their own country.

We reached Darjeeling and Kalimpong, but never got to Sikkim. We had applied for the permit needed to enter the little principality, and had been told that it would have to be approved by the foreign office and the army. When there was a delay, we went through the usual Indian procedure of lobbying as high as possible. We remembered that a man we had known as Indian High Commissioner in Canada had returned to Delhi so we went to the foreign office to see him, finding our way through corridors so piled with bundles of yellowed chits that there was only room to walk single file; out of the little niches left among these walls of paper, uniformed peons would leap up from kitchen chairs and salute us as we went by. Over the inevitable cup of tea, our acquaintance assured us that the difficulties would be removed and the permit issued. "No problem at all!" But the evening before our departure from Delhi we received a message from the ministry of home affairs telling us not to rely on receiving the permit. We wired from Darjeeling to our man in the foreign office; no permit came.

Only later did we get an explanation – from a friend in the Indian civil service who saw the file. Apparently Caroe too wished to go to Sikkim, but Lord Mountbatten was due in Gangtok to advise the Indians on their northern defences; the Indian army did not want Sir Olaf to be there in case these two former pillars of the Raj encountered each other. And because Caroe also had asked for a permit, and had to be refused, we too must be denied, since if he got to know we had gone to Sikkim, he would undoubtedly complain to the British High Commissioner and create an embarrassing inter-Commonwealth tiff. I had the impression that Mountbatten was going there through a private arrangement with Nehru and without the knowledge of the British government, which obviously complicated matters.

So we came down from Darjeeling to Calcutta, where there had been much Communist agitation, and some violence. The tourists were scared, and those who had to pass through the city were staying in their hotels. I did not take the warnings I received seriously. In the streets I saw some small processions of young men carrying the red flag and shouting slogans, but they were not interested in stray white men, and I was able to turn the situation to our advantage, for the timidity of the tourists meant that the merchants who sold Indian crafts had greatly lowered their prices, and with brisk bargaining we bought a large painted Rajasthan wall hanging, and a large folk figure of the god Jagganath, a splendid piece of Orissa village brazier's work, for a few dollars each; together with the fine Tibetan thankas (religious scroll paintings) which on this trip were presented to us by the Dalai Lama and by Sonam Thobten, our Sikkimese friend who came to Darjeeling when he heard we could not get into Gangtok, they are among the best Asian pieces we possess.

EXCEPT FOR SOME WARM human contacts, our visit to East Pakistan was universally depressing. We had the same difficulty in recording frank opinions as in West Pakistan, and it became all the more frustrating when we realized that a vast gulf of resentment and distrust existed between the two parts of the country because the martial races of the west – the Pathans, Punjabis and Baluchis – got favourable treatment, and the Bengalis of the east felt even more oppressed and deprived than under the British. Rebellion was in the air, and we were not surprised when, a few years later, the people revolted and, with some aid from

India, gained independence, to become perhaps the world's least viable country, Bangladesh.

The poverty and the squalor of Dacca were bad enough; only in the villages of Bihar and the remote southwest of Talminad two years before had we seen anything so bad, and that on a smaller scale. But when we travelled down the eastern shore of the Bay of Bengal and arrived at Chittagong, we found that its dereliction exceeded even Dacca's. It was the most dejected, hideous, poverty-stricken city I had ever seen, and I have not since seen anything else so bad. It consisted of miles of dusty grey slums with a hopeless, filthy population of whom vast numbers had been forced into mendicancy, so that the beggars penetrated like bedbugs into the wretched hotel where we had to stay. And what we saw in Chittagong was only the consequence of what we had seen travelling through the countryside from Dacca — the deceptively neat little villages of bamboo huts so close together that from the train one could usually see at least three at once, situated on land so overcrowded that it could not support the relentlessly growing population; Dacca and Chittagong received the overflow, but the meagre urban economies of East Pakistan, largely dependent on the dying jute industry, provided little means for millions of rural immigrants to make a living.

WE INTENDED TO GO on to Burma, but found that all tourist travel had abruptly been cancelled, and the visas we had obtained with difficulty in Delhi, by persuading the consul that I was a writer on art and not on politics, were useless. We had to fly back to Calcutta, and there we learnt the real reason for our exclusion. A Thai Airways plane landed as we were waiting for the Qantas flight that would take us over forbidden Burma to Bangkok. Out of it came a dejected procession of people with bedrolls and bundles of umbrellas; they were all Indians and were refugees. We managed to talk to the pilot, and he told us they were merchants who had lived in Rangoon for many years; under a new Burma-for-the-Burmese program of the dictator Ne Win they were being expelled after their homes and businesses had been expropriated. As night fell and we flew on, the rivers of Burma shone pale below us in the last light and the fires glistened as the peasants burned over the rice paddies.

From Bangkok onwards, apart from parts of Malaya, we were in the Buddhist rather than the Moslem East. The ferocities of life were less obvious, for Buddhism encourages a behaviour that is at least publicly gentle and urbane, and rarely east of the Bay of Bengal did we encounter anything even close to the abysmal poverty we had seen in India and East Pakistan. I watched everything with a delighted detachment, from the gaudy Thai temples, through the grandeurs of Angkor Wat and the remoter temples in the Cambodian jungle, to the homely pragmatism of the old Chinese shrines in Malacca and Macao and the environmental subtleties and ceremonial predictabilities of Japanese traditional life. Perhaps I was getting near to the Buddhist secret by which the very absence of attachment allows one to enjoy every moment of this physical life, as it happens and for what it is.

Not that this part of the journey lacked difficulties. When we went into northern Thailand, I had a tooth infection which rampaged in the tropical heat so that my face swelled suddenly until I was unable to drink without spilling my coffee and could hardly speak, but luckily we discovered behind a furniture store in Chieng Mai a young woman dentist who had just returned from training in the United States.

In Bangkok I became interested in the Mekong River Project, a now forgotten but then highly promising scheme that was being developed under United Nations auspices. Romen Basu, Patwant Singh's brother-in-law, was working on it and through him I met the international group of Americans, Indians, and Thais directing the project. History, manifested in the ravaging of Vietnam and Cambodia by the rival power urges of the Communists and the Americans, eventually ruined this excellent project, which involved tapping the immense volume of the Mekong at flood periods to transform the agrarian economies of Thailand, Laos, Cambodia, and much of Vietnam by enabling the peasants to grow three crops a year instead of one and thus eliminating the long periods of dry weather idleness that nurtured discontent and provided many recruits for the Viet Cong. An economic instead of a military solution to the problems of South-East Asia could have been achieved if it had been completed. I saw the potentialities, and began to gather material, hoping that I could inform North Americans of the promise of this scheme as a means of avoiding the threat of a major war that was already evident.

The first dams on some of the Mekong's tributaries were being constructed in Cambodia. Thailand and Cambodia, which have had a traditional enmity since the middle ages, had gone into one of their phases of non-communication, and, though both were involved in the Mekong River project, they had closed their common frontier and withdrawn diplomatic and consular missions. The Thai and the Cambodian airlines were respecting the break in relations, and at first it looked as though we would be unable to make our journey. But South-East Asians have always been adept at providing means to evade official restrictions, and we found that communications were being sustained unobtrusively by the Vietnamese airline, which put down at Pnom Penh on its way from Bangkok to Saigon.

When we reached Pnom Penh, everything seemed at first to be going well. We were welcomed by local representatives of the Mekong River Project, and on our first evening an official came to our hotel to make arrangements for us to visit a dam being built under the supervision of Australian engineers. We were taken to other sites where dams were planned, and were promised that after we came back from Angkor Wat we would have an interview with the minister himself. But when we returned to Pnom Penh we were told that the minister had suddenly been taken ill. The assistant minister was involved in pressing family problems. And when the local United Nations representative arranged an interview with another high official, the man was not even there when I kept our appointment.

At this point, I realized that there must have been some sudden change of policy, and abandoned my efforts. Shortly afterwards, in Penang, we heard that Prince Sihanouk had made a speech denouncing the western democracies and spurning their help, and an obedient crowd had spontaneously attacked the British and American embassies in Pnom Penh. I never wrote about the Mekong River, and the project itself shortly became a casualty of the Vietnam war, killed by national leaders who had no desire for a peaceful solution.

We were pursued almost to the end of our journey by political uncertainties. We had intended to visit Borneo, but when we reached Singapore the hostility between Malaysia and Indonesia resulted in all the planes to the island being filled with British soldiers and Ghurkas sent out to defend the frontier of Sarawak. After waiting a week in the hope of getting a flight, we embarked on a Dutch freighter crossing the South China Sea to Hong Kong, then we continued our journey on a British freighter through the North China Sea to Japan.

In Japan the only hardships we experienced were caused by a chronic shortage of hotel rooms. The search for a place to sleep drove us from booked-up Kyoto to ancient Nara, and introduced us to the most delightful of Japanese cities, with its great deer parks and ancient temples. It also condemned us to endure the old station hotel in Tokyo, with its cockroaches and the stench of coal smoke percolating through the primitive air conditioning system. Yet we enjoyed the cultural rituals of Japan. Kabuki, Noh, and Bunraku theatre, the pilgrimages to spring landscapes around Mount Fuji and the spring dances of the geisha — the Miyako Odori — in Kyoto, though the season was so capricious that they tied plastic flowers on to the cherry trees to make sure of a blossoming.

In the oldest temples of Nara and Kyoto, among the serene millenium-old wooden statues of gods and bodhisattvas, we recognized that Japanese awareness of the organic world of growth and decay where even stone and water have their place in the infinite interdependencies of consciousness. We found it hard in Japan to take Buddhism seriously for there it is imbued with the same latent animism as Shinto, and expresses a culture linked to those ephemeral aspects of existence that in a wing's flash reveal its true essence.

By the middle of April we were back in Vancouver. In all its streets the trees were flowering in abundance: no need for plastic blossoms here. But it seemed an empty place after the teeming towns of Asia, and its folk pallid beings after the oriental peoples.

XV

TAPPING THE ENERGY

A FTER WE RETURNED TO CANADA, we remained in Vancouver for more than a year and a half. In this period I found myself tapping immense sources of energy, and I pushed myself to the limits of those sources.

I had by now developed the skills of writing quickly and certainly, with a minimum need for revision, and of remembering material so that what notes I made seemed to become imprinted on my mind by the act of notation. Once my research was complete I could write easily without much need to refer to my sources; it was all there in the mind, and the shape of a book seemed to evolve in the writing, so that I gave up making outlines. More important, I had a confidence in my prose that carried it forward, often with exhilaration and rarely with any of the sense of toiling which I had often in earlier years been forced to overcome.

Finally, I began now to realize how much I had gained, both in time and energy, from having abandoned teaching. My time was now entirely my own, and I began to evolve new living patterns. I would sleep till eleven o'clock, and spend the early afternoon writing letters and doing literary chores such as reading proofs and editing copy for *Canadian Literature*. I worked later than ever, and I would sometimes not finish until four or five in the morning. I often worked a fifteen hour or sixteen-hour day, and I was able to do it because my work was, after all, my play. Inge is also a night hawk by nature, and we had no difficulty arranging our common pattern.

I wrote three books during this period. Two of them, *Asia, Gods and Cities* and *The Greeks in India*, emerged from our last journey, but the third was a book I had been considering a long time — my study of George Orwell, *The Crystal Spirit*. The idea, which was an obvious one given my fairly long friendship with Orwell and my general sympathy with his literary aims, had occurred to me in the 1950s after John Sutherland invited me to do a reminiscent essay for one of the last issues of *Northern Review*. Orwell had asked in his will that no life of him should be written, but this did not disturb me, since I felt too close to him personally to be able to write an objective biography; what concerned me was to give a clear critical view of his work, a view illuminated but not dominated by my personal knowledge of him and his intentions. I intended to preface it by a memoir of George as I had known him, an extended version of the *Northern Review* essay, which might be useful to anyone who later attempted a life. Still, out of courtesy, I approached his widow, Sonia, whom I had known when she was Cyril Connolly's editorial assistant at *Horizon*; even for a critical work I would need her permission if I were to make lengthy quotations from George's writings. So I wrote to her, and she surprised me by answering that she had received so many requests to authorize a biography that she had finally decided to pick the best possible writer and had given Malcolm Muggeridge permission to write a life. She asked me if I would wait with my book until Malcolm's had appeared.

I knew Muggeridge, whom I had met with Orwell, and regarded him as a bright and superficial man who had a flair for making himself seem interesting in public, but little insight into people or problems, and none of the staying power needed for a serious book. Orwell got on with him, but George had odd areas of tolerance and befriended some very strange people. However, I agreed to postpone my book until we had seen what Muggeridge produced. I still have notes written by Malcolm, from *Punch*, which he was then editing, thanking me for bits of information.

Muggeridge's book did not appear, and after I had waited several years and my agent John Smith had told me that he could certainly find publishers for the book I had in mind, I wrote to Sonia in Paris. When I reached Delhi at Christmas 1963, there was a letter from her which shed light on what had actually happened. She explained that she had been "bombarded on every side" by requests for permission to write a biography, and even Orwell's publishers were impressing on her the "*necessity of a biography*", "so I asked Malcolm to announce he was doing a biography, knowing full well that he would never do it and the manoeuvre seems to have worked since I don't get so many requests for permission to do a biography these days and they seem easier to refuse." But there was a favourable change in her attitude, for she added at the end "I shall do everything in my power to stop a biography being written, but would never and could never want to inhibit any critical writing on George."

I took this as assent, and as my ideas had already been formed, I found the book developing easily and the writing quick and sure. In the end

Sonia, whom other people often found difficult, was as good as her word, and when she saw the manuscript, she not only gave me permission to use many quotations, but also specified that I should not be charged. Unavoidably, given the autobiographical character of much of Orwell's writing, I had been forced at times to the verge of biography, and perhaps the book can be regarded as an intellectual biography, since it deals with the development of Orwell's ideas and his prose until the climactic point of *Nineteen Eighty-Four*.

When *The Crystal Spirit* appeared, Orwell's old friends, like Cyril Connolly, Richard Rees, and Julian Symons, praised it in print, and Bernard Crick, himself a political scientist, said years later that it contained the best discussion of Orwell's political thinking. *The Crystal Spirit* went into a Penguin mass edition, it won the Governor-General's Award for non-fiction literature in 1966, and in 1984 it was reprinted in Britain and the United States; at the same time a German translation was published in Switzerland.

WHILE WORKING ON THESE BOOKS, I continued to write articles and radio talks. I also translated Molière's *Tartuffe* for production on the CBC, and I wrote *The Empire of Shadows*, a historical tragedy on the reign and death of the Emperor Maximilian of Mexico.

Ever since we visited Mexico in 1953 and I saw the pathetic relics of Maximilian's last days in a dusty little museum at Queretaro, I had been haunted by his tragic life. He was a good nineteenth-century liberal-minded Victorian prince, the best of the Hapsburgs, who rashly allowed himself to be set on the throne of Mexico by that ignoble schemer, Napoleon III. He found himself at the head of a government of discredited conservatives who were not interested in his liberal reforms. He was dependent on the French occupation force for maintaining his power against the rebel armies headed by Juarez. When Napoleon withdrew his troops, Maximilian's realm shrank as the rebel armies moved in. He led a desperate expedition to Queretaro, an old colonial town on the plateau, and there his army was surrounded and starved into surrender. The implacable Juarez insisted on executing him, and Maximilian died with admirable sangfroid. In the meantime his young wife Carlotta, a cousin of the Prince Consort, had gone to Europe to seek help and in her despair had drifted into insanity. It seemed to me a tragedy of Shakespearian proportions, and the more I read it, the more I found myself in the paradoxical situation of an anarchist entering into the predicament of an emperor, which is not so strange as it may first seem, since Maximilian and Carlotta were victims of the power that slipped from their hands when they tried to grasp it: enlightened, well-intentioned, but too innocent for a land like Mexico where political force has always been brutal.

When Gerald Newman urged me to write another play for CBC radio, the idea came powerfully back to me. But I was confused about Gerald's production dates, assuming that the play had been scheduled for October instead of August. When Gerald rang up to ask about the delivery of the manuscript, I had not even begun the play, and I found that instead of two months there was less than a week in which to write it. At first I said this was impossible, and Gerald grumpily agreed that he would have to pick some other play from his backlist. But as soon as I rang off, the theme of the play came into my mind with all its pathos; the obligation I felt was to Maximilian as much as to myself.

So I worked almost day and night for four days, taking naps of an hour or so whenever I felt too tired to continue. By noon on the fifth day I had completed a play that would last an hour and a half, with prose dialogue and connecting narratives in verse to evoke the physical setting and act as verbal backdrops. It is my favourite among my own plays. Occasionally, even now, one of the performers who had a part in it will mention it when we meet. This pleases me, for a playwright's first and best audience consists of the actors.

Another radio work was a literary documentary to commemorate T.S. Eliot, who had died early in 1965. It brought me an appreciative letter from P.K. Page, who had recently come to live on Vancouver Island after wandering over the world as a diplomat's wife. In this way began a friendship I have treasured with a poet whose work I have always found admirable and sympathetic.

As well, I undertook a series of lectures for the CBC Ideas program which Phyllis Webb had started towards the end of 1964. The Civil Rights movement in the United States was now at its dramatic height, and Phyllis asked me to do seven talks on the history of civil disobedience. It was a timely opportunity to reaffirm my faith in pacifist action. The Ideas format, with lectures of almost an hour each, gave me plenty of time to develop my material, and I wrote and recorded them during the autumn. They were broadcast early the next year and the CBC published them as a book. *Civil Disobedience* was actually the first of my books whose publication originated in Canada.

THAT IT SHOULD HAVE TAKEN so long — seventeen years after my return to Canada — for one of my books actually to be printed and issued here, may have been partly caused by my pattern of writing, for the books I wrote were not of the kind that Canadian publishers could then release. But it still speaks of a failure to recognize talents in their midst.

Canadian publishing was cautious and unenterprising, supported by an agency system for the sale of foreign books that subsidized the publication of a few Canadian titles in which the demand for local content was pushed so far that even the novels were expected to have Canadian settings and the poetry to have recognizably Canadian themes.

When a publisher did approach me towards the end of 1964, he was the editorial director of one of the excessively maligned "branch plants" of foreign publishers and not a representative of one of the few native houses which existed at the time. During that year a Vancouver journalist, Simma Holt, had published a superficial and unfair book on the Doukhobors, *Terror in the Name of God*, which gained a wide repute. I wrote a sharply critical notice in the *Tamarack Review*, and this attracted Bill Toye of the Oxford University Press, who asked me whether I was interested in the idea of writing a definitive history of the Doukhobors.

I was indeed interested, for I had followed up my original contacts, and early in the 1960s I had written the scripts for two TV documentaries on the sect, which Alex Pratt produced at CBC in Vancouver, and a subsequent radio documentary on relations between Doukhobors and their neighbours in the British Columbian interior. These tasks had brought me into contact with many orthodox Doukhobors as well as the Sons of Freedom whom I had encountered in 1949-50, and I had met not only John Verigin, leader of the orthodox Union of the Spritual Communities of Christ, and great-grandson of Peter the Lordly, but also members of the sect who had reacted against the anti-literary traditions of the Doukhobors. Notable among them was Peter Legebokoff, the editor of the Doukhobor journal *Iskra*, a self-taught scholar and a man of rare religious feeling who was gathering psalms and hymns before the old people who remembered them had died out.

I realized that my ignorance of the Russian language made it impossible for me to write unassisted a definitive history. Fortunately by this time Ivan Avakumovic, who had collaborated with me in researching and writing *The Anarchist Prince*, our biography of Peter Kropotkin, after a spell at the University of Manitoba was now at U.B.C., teaching political science.

For Ivan the Doukhobors fitted in with his own interests in Russian dissidents — both political and religious — and we agreed to write the book for Oxford. We started our research in 1965, building on the information I had already gathered in my earlier forays into Doukhobor history.

Meanwhile Alan Pringle had written to say that Richard de la Mare, who was then chairman of Faber & Faber, had recently made a trip to India and the Far East, and had come back with the idea that an interesting book could be written on Kerala. What we had seen of the place on our first trip to India had left me with a feeling that this tiny southwestern state, with its varied religions and its political turbulence, was a bizarre epitome of India yet also unique. The mixture of ancient Syrian and Chaldean churches and Jewish communities, of Moslems whose ancestors had arrived by sea long before the Moghuls invaded North India and of matriarchal castes of Hindus, made its society a fascinating pattern of religious and social contrasts; the land of lagoons and mountains was beautiful and quite unIndian; the historical associations, going back to Greek contacts in the distant Dravidian past, were intriguing; the people were the best educated in India and the women the most emancipated; Kerala, finally, had acquired notoriety by becoming the first region in the world where a Communist government had been freely elected — albeit a Communist government dominated by the leader of one of the most exclusive castes in India, the Nambudiri Brahmins.

Presented with the prospect of writing a book on such a fascinating region so soon after I had been invited to write on one of Canada's most interesting minority communities, I felt tempted by two equally appetizing choices.

Fortunately by this time I had almost finished *Asia, Gods and Cities*, and *The Crystal Spirit* would be finished in October. I decided there was no need to make a choice. I would write both books in 1966.

I told Alan Pringle that I would do the book on Kerala if I could get modest support to pay for my journey. The Canada Council promised a travel grant; the Institute of Pacific Affairs in Vancouver offered a smaller amount on condition that I write a brief monograph on some aspect of Keralan culture; Fabers for once gave a relatively generous advance, and several magazines commissioned articles. We decided to leave for Kerala in November. Two other approaches were made to me in 1965, both of which I welcomed. I was moving on the impetus of a hubristic confidence which made me feel I could undertake anything, provided the time was there — and time I was inclined to measure in sixteen-hour days with Monday off.

The first was another suggestion from Pringle, that I should act as General Editor for a Faber series of books entitled Great Travellers. They would be biographies of neglected travellers and adventurers, people with whom, after my own travels, I felt a special sympathy. Though I realized it would involve much hard and often dull work, finding writers, and getting their manuscripts into shape, I knew that Catherine Easto, still my secretary, would help, and for the next seven years I added it to my other tasks and brought out a total of eleven volumes.

My search for authors and subjects that could be combined brought me to interesting writers as well as fascinating half-forgotten travellers. The authors ranged from Edouard Roditi, the cosmopolitan poet and art critic who one day arrived unexpectedly on our Vancouver doorstep and agreed to produce what turned out a good book on Magellan, to General James Lunt, an Old India Hand with much experience of the Northwest frontier country who wrote an excellent narrative on Bokhara Burns. Michael Edwardes wrote on Ralph Fitch, the first Englishman to bring back an account of India, and Geoffrey Dutton on the Australian explorer, Ernest Giles. There were books on the papal envoys to the Mongol courts and on the early Portuguese explorers of Africa who had preceded Vasco da Gama, on Alexander Mackenzie and on Thomas Gage, the English Jesuit and early traveller in Central America. Two of the volumes I wrote myself. One, called *Into Tibet*, was on the early British travellers to that country, George Bogle, Samuel Turner and Thomas Manning. The other was a biography of Henry Walter Bates, the Victorian entomologist whose *The Naturalist on the River Amazons* had done so much to shape the imaginary landscape of my childhood.

The work on the series was sometimes easy and sometimes onerous, and my relations with the authors I dealt with ranged from genial to acrimonious. The professional soldier among them produced the most serviceable, clearly written of all the books. The most self-consciously literary author was the most difficult; what had seemed like a promising friendship was virtually destroyed by the attacks I made on his prose. But at least his book turned out well in the end. One book by a reputable Canadian historian I had to reject because of its irremediable obscurity, and another book I had to rewrite completely, which I did in three summer weeks, but in this case the author, whose scholarship was excellent and original, recognized the deficiencies of his prose and was so happy that he insisted on my name appearing with his on the title page. Faber ended the series after seven years because other publishers were beginning to compete with books on little known travellers; by this time my own interest was waning. But in the process I learnt a great deal about the history of exploration, though I did not learn much more regarding the idiosyncracies of writers than editing *Canadian Literature* had already taught me.

The other approach involved a retrogression to a stage in my life I had already abandoned and should have left safely in the past. The Department of English at U.B.C. had never quite accepted that my career as a teacher had ended. Ever since I resigned in 1963 suggestions were made that, even if I did not want to teach full time again, I might return for the occasional year to teach European Literature in Translation. In the autumn of 1965, Bill Holland, who headed the Department of Asian Studies as well as editing *Pacific Affairs*, suggested that I might combine my English course with a course in Indian literature in translation. I remembered how I had enjoyed teaching the European Literature course, and liked the idea of demonstrating how many good books in English had been written by Indians. The two departments combined to make me a fair financial offer, but it was the thought of being back among young people and seeing how the minds of another generation were working that most tempted me. I agreed; at the same time I did not drop any of my writing projects. I calculated that the most demanding of them would be out of the way by the time I started teaching almost a year later.

Somehow, both of us battling against influenza, Inge and I managed to get everything cleared in time for our journey to Kerala: *The Crystal Spirit* was finished, an issue of *Canadian Literature* ready to go to the printers in my absence, the affairs of the Tibetan Refugee Society in sure hands. Two Malayali students at the University of British Columbia gave me the addresses of relatives and friends in Kerala, and a travel agent offered an invaluable hint when she mentioned the head of the government travel agency in Trivandrum, Captain Hariharusubramony. Otherwise, we had no contacts, and had made no plan we would follow once we got to Kerala. We relied on the country itself to offer the right opportunities and shape our experience.

XVI

ON THE MALABAR COAST

O N REACHING DELHI we had to reckon with the parochialisms
of India. One of our friends there, who had pull in the political
world of north India, had offered to make all the arrangements
to ensure our welcome in Kerala. But as soon as we arrived we realized
not only that he knew even less than we did about southern India, never
having himself been beyond Bombay, but also that whatever influence
he might have in the capital carried little weight outside it. He had done
nothing, and was blusteringly embarrassed to say so.

So we had to rely on our introductions. We sent Captain Hariharusubramony a telegram, never a certain method of communication in India,
booked our flight and set off on trust, spending a night in a beach hotel
outside Bombay, and then flying down over the Konkan coast until the
vast areas of Kerala's coconut groves waved beneath us like a green sea,
with the crags of the western Ghats rising like a shore to the east and the
white towers of the great old Syrian churches standing up like icebergs
out of the verdure.

At Trivandrum a tall, thin, soft-spoken man in a faded silk suit stepped
forward as we came off the plane. He was Captain Hari, as he insisted
we call him instead of trying always to use his tongue-twister of a name,
and the warm, courtly welcome he gave us seemed a fine omen. He had
booked us a room in the government-run Mascot Hotel in Trivandrum,
and as we drove there in his car he told us the story of his life: how he
was a Brahmin of Tamil descent (not a member of the exclusive Nambudiri caste of Kerala), and how as a young men he had followed a
peaceful military career in the tiny army of the native state of Travancore, and had eventually become aide-de-camp to the Maharajah, a post
at which he had remained until the ruler had given up his princely
privileges in 1956. Then he had been appointed head of the tourist

bureau, and had found that this position, which involved welcoming special visitors, was not greatly different from his courtly duties.

Captain Hari arranged for a government car and driver to be at our disposal for a nominal fee as long as we chose to stay in Kerala, and fixed up our stays in government guest houses where there were no hotels. He also introduced us to a great range of people, beginning with the Maharaja; all of them received us cheerfully and were willing to talk with great candour. To the Malayalis, a highly literate and inquisitive people with a good opinion of themselves and a poor opinion of other Indians, it seemed understandable that one should wish to write a book about them. Our curiosity was never resented.

We found our other contacts as helpful as Captain Hari. Dr. Bhuleyan, a relative of one of the Vancouver students, was a professor of surgery at the excellent medical college in Trivandrum; he specialized in the disfiguring disease of elephantiasis and his friend Paramaswaran Nair was a professor of Political Science at the University of Kerala. Both were of the Nair, or warrior caste, and in knowing them and their wives we quickly understood how different the status of women was in matrilineal Kerala compared with the rest of India. Here marriages were equal partnerships: the women ran their own affairs.

Nair was particularly helpful in guiding me to the political leaders, like E.M.S. Nambudiripad, head of the world's first freely elected Communist government. Nambudiripad was out of office in 1965, and Kerala was being administered by the state governor under what in India is called president's rule. A stuttering intellectual in a plain shirt and a white cotton *mundu* (or kilt) sitting on the verandah of a decaying house, Nambudiripad talked proudly of the incorrigible individualism of Keralans. He seemed a strange man to lead what at times had been a militant, authoritarian, and even violent Communist Party, but, as we found, nobody and no movement in Kerala defers to norms established elsewhere.

One Vancouver student friend, Savitri Shankar, had told us to call on her sister. Meeting her, we were received into the warm, large heart of a Keralan joint family, where the grandmother was the revered matriarch, the father was a guest, and the maternal uncles the real powers. Genial and generous uncles they were, pressing meals upon us, getting us tipsy on palm toddy, discoursing endlessly on mundane and spiritual topics, carrying us off to meet their favourite guru (a grinning man naked except for an orange loincloth who never spoke but opened an enormous chest out of which he offered us a bunch of bananas), introducing us to the Trivandrum sights we might otherwise have missed, like the state archives, its cellars filled with brittle bundles of palm leaves on which the public records were scratched with a stylus as late as 1878, and taking us on Sunday afternoon picnics to the beaches at Kovalam or the old fishing villages along the coast.

Another good Trivandrum friend was an old scholar named Poduval to whom Captain Hari introduced us. Poduval was by caste an Ambalavasi, or temple-servant, but he once confided to me that his actual father had been a Brahmin, under an old Keralan custom by which the young sons of a Brahmin household would enter into morganatic relationships with women of lower caste. We spent many hours with Poduval in his old house near the big temple in Trivandrum, talking of Keralan traditions, of the primitive religions that had been incorporated into Hinduism, and of a past Kerala, before the recent explosion of population, when life had been more spacious and less anxious. Poduval, like many other old Malayalis, felt that the independence of India, at least for people in Kerala, was a mixed blessing. The rule of the maharajahs of Travancore had been enlightened, with a great stress on education, and the British had kept their proper distance, while now the Delhi government interfered constantly and did nothing constructive to remedy the economic problems that were driving the Keralan young into the arms of the Communists.

We talked to people of all kinds; I wrote diaries and read the books which Nair got for me out of the university library or which I picked up in the bookstores. Occasionally, we would go out of the city to watch the fishermen from Vijinjam sailing out in their flotillas of big black wallams, a kind of canoe made of planks sewn together with coir fibres, and encircling the fish in circles of nets as they beat loudly on the sides of their boats to frighten them; or to wander through the old palace of Padmanabhapuram, a confection of carved wood and stone within massive Cyclopean walls. Once we went down through the temple town of Suchindram to Cape Komorin — Kanyakumari — the end of India, where a young man on the beach — a fisher of men — enticed us to an ashram where a lady guru, as fat and swollen as a queen bee, lay on an ornate couch and poured tea for us, surrounded by her followers.

ONE NIGHT WE SAT IN THE yard of a temple for a performance of *Kathakali*, the typical dance drama of the Malayalis. The Keralans are stricter even than other Indians in keeping non-Hindus out of their temples. Indeed, it was only after long civil disobedience struggles in which Gandhi played a part that people of lower castes were allowed to enter. But the *Kathakali* performance took place in a courtyard outside the sacred area, and when we arrived we were ushered on to the stone platform on which the dancers would perform, like the notables at an Elizabethan play.

A great brass lamp blazed there whose several tiers were awash with coconut oil. It would be the only light during the whole long night of drama, which enacted one of the episodes from the *Ramayana*. Its flickering and flaring flame added to the mystery of the performance and accentuated with its shadows the grandeur of the mythical characters; as we waited, it shone on the front ranks of the audience ranged below on the sandy ground; the back rows were lost in shadow. The white-clad men sat on the left, the women in their brilliant skirts and blouses on the right, and the children in front, prepared to watch the slow impressive unfolding of the drama through the night that was perfumed with the scent of the frangipani trees growing in the temple yard.

Kathakali is a dance drama in which the performers are silent. The tale is told by two singers who stand at the back of the stage, bare-torsoed and clad in white mundus draped in elaborate folds. The leading singer, the *Ponnani*, is the most important person in *Kathakali*; he is the virtual producer, assigning parts to the various dancers, regulating the pace of the performance by his chanting of the narrative (often composed centuries ago by some local kinglet or noble), and keeping pace by beating a thick gong of bell-metal. Another singer supports the rhythm with small brass cymbals and relieves the *Ponnani* by repeating the verses when the dancer lags behind.

Equally important are the two drummers. One plays the *Chenda*, a cylindrical wooden drum beaten with curved sticks. The other plays the *Maddhalam*, a small-headed drum which bellies at the centre like an elongated keg and is beaten at both ends with the fingers protected by hard tips of glue-bound cloth. Its softer tone comes into prominence during the performance of the female characters, who are played by men.

Shortly after we arrived, the drums began to beat, first the *Maddhalam* and then the deeper *Chenda*, joining in a duet in which the performers gave the audience a foretaste of their virtuosity. Then, in a high pitched and rather nasal tone, the singers chanted the prelude to the play. Next appeared two men as ordinary as the scene shifters in a Chinese opera and held up between them an embroidered curtain of brilliant silk, with a blazing golden sun as its central motif.

Now was the time for the *Nayaka*, or central character of the play to appear — in this case Rama. At first all we could see above the curtain was his towering, carved and painted wooden headdress, encrusted with tiny coloured mirrors and iridescent beetle wings glimmering in the lamplight, and below the curtain his prehensile-looking feet, bent over so that he balanced on their sides, and his belled ankles. Still concealed in his improvised sanctum, he performed the ceremonial dance with

which every Indian dancer propitiates the tutelary deity, and then, facing
the audience, he gradually lowered the curtain with his hands until he
stood fully revealed in the fantasy of his costume and makeup, with his
long-sleeved tunic and jewelled breastplate, his pleated crinoline-like
skirt and dangling stoles ending in mirrors, and the beard-like frame
built around his features out of lime and rice-flour — an adaptation of
the mask which as one dance teacher remarked to me, has the advantage
that "it makes the face into a stage to display the changing emotions."

Facial expressions and hand gestures dominate in *Kathakali*. The
movements of the eyes, mouth and neck are conventionalized to express
the nine emotions or *rasas* of Indian drama — desire, valour and pathos,
wonder, wrath and ridicule, fear, loathing and tranquillity. There are
ninety-five manual gestures, made with one or both hands, and, according to an old dance connoisseur who sat beside me that evening, they
can be made to represent no less than five hundred different images,
enough to tell any tale.

The singers sang, the dancer mimed and so the tale unfolded, and
grew more complex as other characters appeared, in this case Rama's
consort Sita and the monkey god Hanuman. The high points were the
soliloquies, when narration ceased, and the dancer improvised through
gestures, seeking to arouse in his audience the emotions he portrayed, by
dance postures but above all in the intricate play of eye and hand movement, while the drummers accompanied him, so that it became a double
show of virtuosity.

It was the pure artistry to which Inge and I responded. I received a
running summary of the action from the old connoisseur, in an English
difficult to follow by the fact that he retained only two shaky front teeth,
but neither Inge nor I understood the intricacies of gesture any more
than, I suspect, did the people in the audience, many of whom sat too
far away from the stage to have any idea what the dancer was doing with
his eyes even if they saw what he did with his hands. But, like us, they
were bemused by the magic of the occasion in which, strange beings
sitting on the stage behind the dancers, we undoubtedly played minor
roles.

IN THAT FIRST MONTH in Trivandrum we had an old shrewd man
for a driver, a Christian almost inevitably named Joseph who intimately
knew the state of Travancore and its people. When we left for the north,
the man who replaced him knew no English, he seemed familiar with
neither the country nor anyone on the road, and he had none of the
sharpness of mind that characterizes the Malayali. We found ourselves
asking people we met casually to act as interpreters between him and us,

until we were forced to make every arrangement for ourselves and in this way found out many things of which we would otherwise have been ignorant.

We travelled up the coast road through Quilon and Allepey to Cochin, diverging from our path to visit the little eighteenth century palace of Krishapuram with its mural painting of Vishnu, and the stark ruins of the East India fort of Anjengo where Laurence Sterne's Eliza Draper was born. We travelled through endless miles of palm groves interlaced by canals, where the settlements merged into one continuous village. Most of the people lived under the trees in palm-leaf huts that merged in the setting, so that it was only in the morning, when the roads were filled with hordes of neatly dressed children setting off to school, and in the evening when they were filled with equal hordes of neatly dressed adults returning from work that we realized how dense the population was; in these coastal regions it often exceeded 2,000 per square mile.

At Cochin we settled into the old Malabar Hotel looking over the harbour towards the sandy palm-fringed islands that mask it from the sea. We spent three weeks there. Cochin is an even more scattered place than most of the loosely planned cities of South India, consisting of a number of distinct, virtually autonomous communities, between which we travelled by the shabby little ferries that ply regularly across the harbour.

The Malabar Hotel stood on the tip of Willingdon Island, which is largely reclaimed salt marsh and gives space for the airport, the modern docks, the factories. Across a wide inlet from the hotel lay Fort Cochin, from which the Portuguese, the Dutch, and finally the British had exercised their suzerainty over the Malabar coast. Vasco da Gama's first grave was in the old cathedral there; from another church, now vanished, St. Francis Xavier had set out to convert the poor low-caste fishermen. It was still a place where rich traders lived, and the narrow land that ran parallel to the inlet down to Mattancherri was lined with old Dutch-style tiled warehouses, and the country craft that brought in produce — spices and copra and coir — by canal from the hinterland were moored several deep against the quays.

At Mattancherri itself was the old palace of the Maharajas of Cochin, called the Dutch Palace but built by the Portuguese for one of the reigning princes — a European building on the outside decorated on the inside with epic frescoes painted in the vivid and crowded Malayali style, of conflicts between gods and evil beings; in the rooms that had once been the *zenana* the murals were bawdily erotic.

A lane away was Jewtown, the old centre of the Sephardic Jews of Cochin, with its beautiful little seventeenth century Paradesi Synagogue.

Just as the Christians of Kerala were divided into several churches that corresponded in rank to the Hindu castes of the first converts, with the Roman Catholics at the bottom because their forefathers were converted untouchables, so the Jews were divided into the White Jews and the Black Jews, who had separate synagogues, did not intermarry, and in death were parted by a wall that ran down the centre of the Jewish cemetery. The White Jews had come from Persia and Babylon; the Black Jews were native low-caste Malayalis who in earlier centuries had been bought as slaves by the White Jews and then converted and liberated according to Judaic law. But making them Jews did not make them equal. The Jewish community was much diminished. Most of the Black Jews had left for Israel, where they would obviously have a better life than if they stayed on as menials in Jewtown. Most of the White Jews had stayed in India, since they had property they could not take out of the country, but many of them had left Cochin for Bombay, the home of the other historic Indian Jewish community, the B'nai Israel.

Eastward across the harbour lay the other main community of Cochin, the thriving commercial and administrative centre, Ernakulum. Ernakulum had the biggest native bazaar in the area and most of the European shops, including some excellent bookstores. The lawyers and most of the doctors lived there, and so did many leading Keralan politicians, so that it was a focus of influence that rivalled Trivandrum in the same way as the former native state of Cochin had rivalled Travancore. Both states were much more progressive than most of the other principalities the British had allowed to survive as part of the Raj; they made great progress in education and also in constitutional government, but Cochin was always a little in advance of Travancore, and it was the first native state in India to have an elective assembly. I was rarely left in doubt of the rivalry between the states, though their language and their culture were identical and their royal houses both claimed descent from the ancient Chera kings.

In Cochin we met Samuel Koder, a leading member of the Jewish community. He ran a small chain of miniature department stores in the large towns of Kerala and lived in a spacious merchant's house filled with books and massive Goanese furniture, overlooking the harbour at Fort Cochin. A man of cosmopolitan taste and culture, Koder had been a prosperous wine merchant until the imposition of prohibition at Fort Cochin forced him into general trade. His lavish and lengthy Sunday lunches were an institution. He did a little historical writing, and was an invaluable source of information about the Jewish community and the role it had played in mediaeval Kerala when its leaders held the rank of local chieftains and were famed for their skills in arbitration, while the ships of its merchants sailed regularly with Keralan products to Canton and Malacca.

Through Koder we met William Bandey, a melancholy Englishman and the last of the European managers who had run the coir industry at Allepey. Only twelve years before, there had been seventy of them and a flourishing English club; all had departed and Bandey was not expecting to stay much longer. He asked us out to Allepey to see his house and factory, both of them monuments to the age when British merchants controlled the ancient export trade on which, since the days of the Ptolemies, Kerala had depended. Bandey's house was an early colonial structure, built in the 1830s by the first English missionaries in Allepey. The upper floor, where Bandey lived, had fine arched balconies and enormous lofty rooms, built for coolness. On the lower floor his servants lived, and Bandey kept a menagerie of dogs, rabbits, budgerigars, guinea fowl, turkeys, geese, and ducks. We lunched on one of the ducks, served in piquant mango sauce.

Bandey believed that his animals and servants were not the only beings who shared his house with him. He had often heard light footsteps on the creaking old wooden floors of the corridors, and sometimes when they halted outside his bedroom door the handle was turned and the door opened yet nobody stood there. Once he had entertained an English family and the children had come in to say that they had played in the garden with other children; they were not Indian children, but were very peculiarly dressed; it turned out that they were wearing the pantaloons which young English girls in the early nineteenth century wore beneath their skirts. The haunting of Bandey's house was a subject of much discussion in the Cochin community, and one day Koder, who was a great sceptic on such matters, went out to spend the night in Bandey's room. He returned convinced, for the light steps had come unerringly to his door and it had opened; there was no one to be seen in the corridor. In the Church Missionary Society graveyard in Allepey the three small daughters of the first missionary lay in a single grave among the invading weeds; they had all died from cholera on the same night.

The factory Bandey managed, with its thick fortress-like walls and its inner courtyard, looked like something from the East India Company's days. In the courtyard, coir yarn spun by cottagers was weighed on great old steelyards, and bought largely for export unwoven. But some was still used on the clumsy wooden hand looms that had been devised generations ago for coir matting and stood in a cloister around the courtyard; the sound of their dry clatter took the place of the noise of machinery, of which there was none. A factory system had been developed without the help of the industrial revolution.

Another encounter took us into the traditional Keralan past. Rama-chandra Menon was a young lawyer whose family ran a private bank in Ernakulum. He was a municipal councillor, deeply involved in local causes. But he still lived — albeit without the sword and shield of the ancient Nair — the traditional life of his caste, and one day, realizing our curiosity about that life, he invited us to the *tarwad*, or joint family home, where he lived.

It was a large compound with a big carved gateway through which one entered a green garden of pomelo and breadfruit trees, coconut and areca palms, trellises loaded with betel and pepper vines. Four children of one generation lived there in four separate houses, two of them sons, and two of them daughters with their husbands who ranked as guests. In the corner of the compound was a private cremation ground, with a concrete slab where the mother of the family had been burnt after she died; a sacred lamp illuminated a photograph of her above the slab. A central building, over a century old, was used for entertaining guests. It had a roof opening to the sky and a well beneath it to drain away the rain, and here we were fed South Indian delicacies, sweet and savoury, made mainly of rice, before we went into the *puja* room or private chapel where the family Brahmin, with his scalplock like a Blackfoot brave, sat among the gaudy oleographs of the gods. We went on into a room that, in terms of Nair matriarchy, was even more sacred; for the mother had lived and died there. (The father, a member of another *tarwad*, was hardly ever mentioned.) The wooden death bed had been turned into a shrine, decorated with strings of coloured lights and with peacock fans; where the head must have lain a miniature altar had been constructed. Nowhere else in India — and rarely anywhere else in the world — had I ever seen such reverence shown by men to a woman; I found it just as oppressive as any reverence I had seen paid by women to men. The fact that the Nairs had inverted the authoritarian structure of the family by making it matriarchal rather than partriarchal did not seem to make it any more acceptable.

The next morning Menon and a brother-in-law, who lived in the *tarwad* and was a member of the Cochin royal family, took us to see the palace at Tripunithura, which the former Maharaja had abandoned to end his life as a religious recluse. Only the old servants were there in the building, wizened bare-torsoed men with white waistcloths and gold-and-ruby earrings, looking after the great rooms that had been designed by some wandering European architect and filled with the bric-à-brac that maharajas all over India gathered around them: English steel en-gravings, French bronzes of fighting animals, photographs of the Prince of Wales (later Edward VIII) on his trip to India, and here and there, unexpectedly, a wall painted in fierce colours and with demoniac energy by a traditional Malayali artist. A sacred pool lay at the bottom of a deep shaft in the rock on which the palace stood, and down its many steps the rheumatic old maharaja had laboured daily for his ritual ablutions. It was not surprising that he finally left the palace for a simpler dwelling.

On our last day in Cochin Koder invited us to Sabbath dinner, at which he entertained the half-dozen Jewish women of the neighbourhood who had no men that day to say the prayers, which he rendered in an old Sephardic Hebrew whose pronunciation he assured me would not be recognized in Israel. They sang rather lively Hebrew hymns before settling down to their cosmopolitan conversation over the good food and illicit wine one could always rely on in Koder's house.

In the morning we set off in a long rambling journey that would take us eventually over the mountains into Mysore. We went first to Kottayam, the Keralan Rome, seat of the Catholicos of the East, head of the Syrian faith; he was away on a visit to the Patriarch of Antioch and we had to be content with meeting a suave and intellectual young bishop who talked knowledgeably of ancient Buddhist communities on the Malabar coast as he led us through Kottayam's great mediaeval churches which, with their murals of the Passion, are among the unknown master buildings of Christendom.

We went on into the High Ranges of the Western Ghats, visiting Canadians who were building dams there, and lingering among the tea planters of Munnar, who in their club and their English summer gardens preserved one of the last visible remnants of the Raj. In the hills above the plantations we saw the survivors of another vanishing species, the Indian elephants, dusty creatures the colour of the earth in which they rolled after bathing in the mountain pools. On the way down to Trichur we found the remains of the Keralan megalithic culture, represented by "mushroom stones" that looked like Cornish cromlechs and underground chambers dug out of the soft laterite rock of the region. In southern India the megalith builders were still at work at the beginning of the Christian era. And in Trichur we took part in the services of the Chaldean church, a Nestorian community which holds itself apart from the Syrian church, claiming the most authentic descent from St. Thomas, the apostle to India.

In Trichur we also became alarmingly involved in the food politics of India. There was a shortage of rice in Kerala, and the people had begun to hold demonstrations. Much wheat had been imported, often as *macroni*, which consisted of fake rice grains made from wheat flour. But the Malayalis would have none of this. Wheat was the food of despised North Indians. Rice was their own traditional food, and it would be

demeaning to eat anything else. All the way north from Trivandrum we
had driven past the demonstrations, which consisted largely of high
school boys, but though they shouted at us cheerfully, there was nothing
menacing about them.

At Trichur, however, we were staying in an old palace that had been
turned into a Tourist Bungalow, and one of our fellow guests was the
federal Minister of Food who had come to Kerala to investigate the
situation. He too had been given a Kerala government car exactly like
our own, and when we returned at noon we were surrounded by a
crowd of students who had been there to take on the minister, had
found him absent, and had smashed a lot of flower pots and a few
windows. Obviously they mistook us for him, and even when they saw
their mistake, they charged at us and began rocking the car. Our driver, a
very black man, turned pale grey from fear, and we found our own
upper lips began to lose their stiffness as the shouts became more
menacing, until a group of taller youths suddenly spearheaded their way
towards us, shouting: "These are foreigners! It is not their quarrel!" Suddenly all the rage dissolved into boyish laughter, and the students went
off to burn a grandstand.

We wandered on through Calicut and Tellicherry to Cannanore in the
far north of Kerala, interviewing in every town on the way, visiting farms
and factories, weddings, even lecturing at colleges. Then it was time to
leave. In Calicut, the officials of the Central Bank invited us to a party
they were giving, a very wet party in a dry town well supplied by smug-
glers from Goa, and there we encountered the violet-robed Italian Bishop
of Calicut, who delegated his secretary to accompany us into the jungle
of Wynad on our way to Mysore so that the missionairies there could
introduce us to the local tribes.

At the the mission, high on the mountain barrier, we were welcomed
by two Indian Jesuit priests. One wore a khaki military cap that seemed
of Great War vintage and the other a black knitted balaklava; both wore
grimy white soutanes. Their hospitality was warm, though the lunch they
provided was one of the most extraordinary I have eaten.

The dining room was also a granary; rats were rustling among the rice
sacks and occasionally scampering across the room, pursued by the ill-
fed mission cats. Lunch began with a dark, sour soup that Inge was
convinced had been made with blood. Next came a dry-fleshed river
fish, boobytrapped with tiny triangular bones, and then a chicken so
tough that the presiding priest finally brought a cleaver to chop it
apart. Then it was revealed that the bird had never been cleaned, for
when he split it apart, the foul-smelling entrails sprayed out over the
table. We had little stomach for the last course, which consisted —

with seeming appropriateness — of a large custard apple locally called "bull's heart."

But afterwards the missionaries' arrangements worked out admirably, for the tribes appeared. Some danced in a shuffling circle as the men beat monkey-skin drums and the women howled like wolves. Others showed their prowess with longbows and steel-headed arrows which they claimed would kill tigers. An old chief gave a confused talk on tribal theology from which I gathered that they were sun-worshippers of a kind and that their dead were buried on a mountainside among large stones, by which he seemed to mean the lines of megalithic menhirs some of the teaplanters had described to us.

Our last place in Kerala was Sultan's Battery, where the leading Moslem merchant, Hajji Moussa, completed the pattern of Keralan hospitality. He sought us out and feasted us on his plantation, giving us graphic accounts of the catching and taming of elephants he sold to zoos abroad. On the morning of our departure for Mysore the Hajji appeared with a gift of pepper grown on his own plantation. And so we left the strange sweet land of Kerala.

XVII

LANDS ONCE PEACEFUL

W E WENT ON TO IRAN and Lebanon. We had no idea how events would later change both these countries, and I treated them as pleasant and peaceful places where we would be able to relax from the ardours of our months in Kerala, to sight-see and pass aimlessly through the land.

In Iran we divided our time between Teheran, where the Elburz mountains were still snow-covered and the trees were bare, Isfahan, and Shiraz, where the spring had begun but the famous roses were not yet blooming. The impression we acquired of Iran and of the Iranians was so different from anything one might gather from reports of Khomeini's Iran that I often wonder whether the Iran we knew does not still survive under the grim surface, waiting to emerge as the true France re-emerged after the dark days of the French Revolution.

At that time, in the streets of Teheran we were struck by the generally European look of the people we encountered, whether they were red-cheeked, blue-eyed peasants selling flowers or early radishes, or the sophisticated young women in French and American fashions whom we encountered everywhere in the capital. In the other towns, one did sense that another Iran existed. In Isfahan, more of a manufacturing town than I had anticipated, I noticed the hordes of poor working men in suits of cheap drab serge who filled the streets at certain hours, surging past the blue-tiled ancient mosques. I thought of them as Wellsian Morlocks compared with the effete Eloi who patronized the Shah Abbas Hotel, a hostelry rivalled in Asia only by the Peninsular in Hong Kong. But I never really imagined that people like these would rise from underground at Khomeini's call and overturn not only the Shah's rule but also the pleasing way of life we observed and enjoyed. In Shiraz it was the more colourful tribal people, coming in on buses which used the ancient, deserted caravanserais, and especially their brightly clad, jewelled and unveiled women, who impressed us with a different and more ancient way of life that linked the present with the past which the vast ruins of Persepolis so magnificently represented.

In Iran, more even than in other Asian countries, the lack of manifest hostility to infidel strangers was striking. There seemed an unusual anxiety to help them and make them feel welcome. In Isfahan a grey-eyed schoolboy named Ali came up to us in one of the gardens, speaking excellent English, and offered to show us the old city behind the spectacular monuments. We spent an afternoon with him wandering through the tortuous miles of the bazaars and into the disused mediaeval caravanserais, where the chambers in the arched tiers of cloisters had been transformed into workshops of every kind, making metalware, pottery, clothing, sweetmeats, and above all carpets, which were largely woven by children, some of them aged four or five. At the end of this long ramble, at times delightful and at times heart-rending, Ali would accept no payment, and it was only with difficulty that we persuaded him to come to a shop with us and take a bag of the pistachio nut candies he liked.

In Shiraz we were stopped in the street by a dark stocky man — a Shirazi who worked as foreman in the oilfields of Abadan, and he insisted on taking us through the bazaar and to all the old buildings he could think of, explaining them in excellent English and with a notable grasp of the history of his town. He not only refused to accept anything from us, but insisted on treating us to hot pancake-like breads just out of the great clay oven which we ate wrapped around pungent local cheese.

Iran was sophisticated and comfortable in comparison with India, but Lebanon — or at least Beirut — was at the peak of Asian Westernization, as an accident I suffered in Teheran seemed to epitomize. I slipped in the hotel bath, gashed my brow, and immediately began bleeding profusely. The hotel clerk called in a doctor, a friendly little man who came with his assistant, and out of his bag produced a tin box of instruments and a spirit lamp. The rusting lid of the box, filled with water and held in a pair of tweezers over the lamp, served to sterilize his instruments before the doctor gave me a local anesthetic and stitched up my brow. The wound healed well but I had to wait until I reached Beirut before I could have the stitches taken out. At the American Hospital there the Lebanese doctor examined my wound and then said: "Where on earth did you get those stitches?" "In Iran. Why do you ask?" "They're back in the dark ages," he laughed. "Still using cotton! We use only nylon."

Fortunately the Lebanon of that period was far from being only a nylon culture. Beirut seemed to combine the best of many worlds:

French, Arabic, Ottomon, Armenian, Greco-Levantine, with a large dash of American. The cafés in the main streets were as pleasant as those of the grand boulevards of Paris or the Via Veneto in Rome, and their customers reflected the best of transplanted European elegance. The corniche drives along the seashore were lined with handsome villas. The banks were temples. Every kind of appetite for food, drink, and other pleasures could be satisfied. At day and at night one walked the streets without fear.

At that time the various communities — Christians of several kinds, Sunni and Shia Muslims, and Druzes who did not fit in neatly anywhere — were living together in relative harmony, and the threats seemed to come from outside — the constant threat of Israel and the intermittent threat of Syria. With our Maronite taxi driver Joseph, whom we had hired at a sharply bargained price for our five days of wandering, we could travel freely over the country except for Tyre in the far south; to get there we had to deposit our passports at a guard post to the north of the city to prevent us from crossing into Israel. To judge from Joseph, the Lebanese were unenthusiastic members of the anti-Israeli alliance. He assured us persistently that they had nothing against the Jews and were merely anxious to get justice for their fellow Arabs, the Palestinians. It struck me as strange that he called himself an Arab, since with his strong face and great prow of a nose he fitted in perfectly with one's image of a Phoenician sea captain, and I am sure he was of Punic, not Arab descent.

The Israeli frontier was quiet, but we had an ominous foretaste of Syrian intentions. We had planned to cross the border into Syria to visit Palmyra, which was easily reachable on a day trip from Beirut, but as we set off we heard on the radio that the frontier had been closed because of some threat from Damascus. We still decided to go north-east, to visit the temples of Baalbek, just inside the Lebanese border; and we found the whole frontier area alive with tanks and armoured cars, though I doubt if the Lebanese army even then would have been strong enough to hold a serious Syrian push. But no push came.

Of the ancient Lebanese cities we visited, Baalbek with its gigantesque architecture was the most impressive, Tyre with its sickle beach the most beautiful, and Byblos, with its layered cultures going back through Ottoman and Saracen, Crusader and Roman, Hellenistic Greek and Phoenician, to the Neolithic of the 4th millenium B.C., the most fascinating in exemplifying the changing continuity of Mediterranean civilizations. It was the Lebanese spring, with drifts of crimson anemone flooding through the maquis on its limestone hills and drifts of mauve cyclamen blooming where the flowers of Adonis did not predominate. Nowhere did we encounter hostility.

Undoubtedly our encounter with Joseph had much to do with our attitude towards his country. He was not only a good driver and a resourceful guide, but a genial companion. On the last day of our travels he invited us to dinner at his home, and there his wife, Maria, cooked a Lebanese meal which offered all the native delicacies Joseph told her we had missed on the road; as it was a Christian household, the dryish local wine and the strong arrack flowed freely. The conversation was excellent, for Joseph had brought in not only his Maronite friends, including a young priest who talked illuminatingly on Camus, but also some of the Armenian Christians who found a refuge in Beirut and had adopted the cosmopolitan culture of the Levant. I lost touch with Joseph, for he did not answer the letter of thanks I sent him after we returned, and I have often wondered what happened to him and his young children after we left what seemed one of the most truly civilized places on earth.

XVIII

MISSING THE FERRY

THE SHROPSHIRE PEASANT SOCIETY in which I grew up took a poor view of people who did well and gloried in it, and they had a whole anthology of sayings to deal with such situations. Someone in the community would suddenly make a great deal of money and spend it ostentatiously. "Put a beggar on horseback and he'll ride to the devil," the wiseacres would say, and time and again the consequences in humiliating bankruptcy would prove them right.

When I was young I never had the kind of fortune that would qualify me as a "beggar on horseback", but I was no less threatened, for another saying much favoured by my mother and aunts would greet me whenever I boasted about my modest achievements: "Pride cometh before a fall!" "Don't tempt Providence" they would sententiously add.

Some of these sayings came back to me during the months of 1966 after we returned from our journey to Kerala. For by that spring and summer I was beginning to believe that there was no limit to my capacity to triumph in anything I undertook. On the way back from Kerala, for example, I had written the libretto for an opera, to be produced by the CBC's Gerald Newman as part of the 1967 centenary celebrations of Confederation. *The Brideship*'s subject was the fate of a shipload of young women sent out by Baroness Burdett-Coutts, a friend of Dickens, to provide wives for some of the many bachelor farmers who had immigrated to Canada.

I knew nothing of the craft of libretto-writing but made it a rule, when composing recitatives and arias, that they were singable. This I did during a week in the South Tirol by intoning them to tunes from Mozart. As it happened, the composer, Robert Turner, found the words acceptable and they were performed as written, though once only.

Back in Vancouver, I justified my salary demands for the forthcoming year of guest-teaching by boasting of my triumphs. In 1966, I said, I would have five books coming off the press, and had been invited by Penguin to edit Cobbett's *Rural Rides* for their new English library. James Cochrane of Penguin Books had indeed written to me while I was in India suggesting I might edit Cobbett, and over several years, as well as *Rural Rides*, I prepared editions, for Penguin with massive introductory essays, of *A Tale of Two Cities*, *The Egoist*, *The Return of the Native* and *Typee*. In Teheran I also heard from Peter Quennell, for whom I had already written many articles, inviting me to undertake, as part of the Social History of the British Empire he was then editing, a book on *The British in the Far East*. I agreed to do this book as well, scheduling delivery some time in 1967.

This meant that I had three books to write when I returned. As well, I had to carry on my editing of *Canadian Literature*, to keep up my work for the Tibetan refugees, and to continue seeking out and editing new volumes for Faber & Faber's Great Travellers series. I added to my burden by writing essays for *Saturday Night* and other magazines on our recent travels, and I did not abandon my links with the CBC for I prepared a documentary — *Death Stalked the Olive Trees* commemorating the thirtieth anniversary of the Spanish civil war.

The Crystal Spirit, my book on Orwell, came out at the end of the summer, and it drew good reviews. But most of all I valued a letter Herbert Read wrote me from Zurich. He was already suffering from the cancer that would soon kill him; it was the last time I would hear from this old friend who had meant so much to me in my early years as a writer. Though Read's opinion of my book was gratifying because it came from a man who was one of my masters in prose, I valued the letter as much for what Read said of Orwell. It established a link and a resemblance between the two men that I had always sensed but never sharply defined.

It is criticism of a high order, perfectly controlled, perfectly in command of its subject, enlightening & comprehensive, and leaving one with a sense of complete & final understanding of its subject. I haven't re-read any of Orwell's books recently, but they have always remained in my mind, and his personality, which remains so vivid after all these years, often rises like some ghost to admonish me. I suppose I have felt nearer to him than to any other English writer of our time, and though there were some aspects of his character that irritated me — his proletarian pose in dress, &c., his insensibility to his physical environment, his comparatively narrow range of interests — yet who was, in general, nearer in ideals & even in eccentricities? You bring out these contradictions very well, & justify them. They didn't trouble me much, except when it came to the war —

but by then he was a sick man & I saw little of him. I think you are right to call him essentially a moralist — he was too big a man to be merely a politician or even merely an artist, though I think towards the end — & this too you admit — he was beginning to realize that a writer only survives by virtue of his style & form. If only he had lived a little longer he would have got rid of those "monumental" imperfections & would have become as great as any of the authors of the past he admired so much.

I rode on the crest of this wave of activity and success until I came near to putting an end to activity and success alike. I was already living the classic life of the self-doomed man. I was so over-weight that my old friend Alex Comfort, arriving to lecture in Vancouver, did not at first recognize the fat man who greeted him. My exercise consisted of no more than walking from office to classroom on the campus. I was smoking heavily, by now pungent Dutch and German cigars at the rate of fifteen to twenty a day. I drank increasingly frequent and potent martinis to fuel my activity. I was working up to 14 hours a day even before I started teaching in the latter half of September, when the day automatically stretched to 16 hours. But the precipitant factor was the inner tension that built up because I had worked myself into a situation in which I was no longer in control of everything I did.

I was sure of myself in editing and writing, and though I changed my European literature course radically by opening with the *Odyssey* and *Don Quixote* as background works to modern fiction, I knew that I had this course under control, and I had no fear of appearing at anything less than my best.

It was the course in Asian studies that led me into difficulties. I should have limited it to modern Indian literature in English — the works of twentieth century Indian writers which I knew well. But, because of my interest in Buddhism, I decided to include English translations of classic Sanskrit and Pali texts, like the *Ramayana*, the *Jataka Tales* and the plays of Kalidasa. And here I found that my students, a bright small group including some Indians, were already well informed, so that I was constantly hurrying in the little time I could spare from my other activities to keep a day ahead of them in my reading. Some of them knew Sanskrit and Pali, which I did not, and this created anxious moments from which I extricated myself in unconvincing ways. In the past I had been able to master similar situations by learning as I went, but now I did not have time for this and I wondered how I would ever bluff my way through it. By the end of the second week I was blaming myself for my presumption.

If I had been an ancient Greek, I would have said the gods were quick to detect and punish my sin of *hubris*. As it is, I am content to say that my body was wise enough to find a decisive if drastic way to extricate me. I had given six lectures on Homer which I am convinced were the best in my teaching career. During the last of them I had two slight spells of dizziness as I stood talking at the podium, but they passed and I thought no more about them until, at three in the morning, I felt a hard pain searing up my arm and into my jaw and gripping my chest in a relentless vice. I knew what was happening, and I felt detached as I told Inge and she went to call our doctor. I then lay wondering, for I had always thought myself a coward and had imagined that faced with a threat of death, I would be paralyzed with fear. Instead, I felt an equanimity, somewhat troubled by the thought of the difficulties for others my death might cause, and an immense curiosity. "Here it comes — and what afterwards?"

I was taken to the Vancouver General Hospital and that night, after I had been dosed with morphine and put in an oxygen tent, I had a dream that remains vividly with me. I was on a train rather like the old-fashioned trains surviving from the Empire that we had travelled on in Malaya and Ceylon; it was running beside a wide river I knew to be the Mekong. I got up from the bunk, dressed and began to pack an overnight bag, since I knew I was reaching my destination. There seemed to be no one else on the train; evidently it was running for me only. By the time I had dressed, the train began to slow and I saw it was approaching a wharf beside which a large white steamboat was moored. Even before the train stopped I was leaping down, but as my foot struck the platform the boat gave a single mournful hoot, swung away from the wharf and began to steam across the river to the town of white pagodas and pinnacles on the other shore. I felt both relieved and bitterly disappointed as I got back into the train, which immediately sped into the fading of the dream.

The dream, of course, was telling me that it was not yet time for the release from life that is implied in the Buddhist symbolism of the Other Shore. Though there were still anxious days when I was kept in my oxygen tent under sedatives, enjoying the strange geometrical hallucinations induced by barbiturates, I at least knew that this time I was walking safely through the valley of the shadow, and I feared no evil.

Not entirely perversely I enjoyed my month in hospital, which still stays as a strange quiet island in my memory. I was forced out of the obsessive pattern of work I had developed. I read books unconnected with my work. I listened to music a great deal on a radio Inge had brought in. I valued the visits of my friends.

I even liked the hospital routine, ascetic and sybaritic at once, for although I was kept on a meagre diet I was otherwise spoilt by a group of pleasant young nurses who had decided I was what they called "a good patient". There was a Québec girl who would come in to talk about French novels after she saw me reading Simone de Beauvoir, and a Chinese girl from Borneo with whom I had long conversations about Malaysia, and a girl from New Brunswick who had a fund of tales about the Maritimes.

I also thought a great deal about my future. I did not intend to play the role of the "cardiac cripple", but I realized that I would have to make radical changes in my way of life. Some were simple, like going on the proper diet, cutting out smoking (for which I had lost the desire while in hospital), and taking more exercise. But I had also to reduce tensions, and I realized these had little to do with either writing or hard work. I suspected — and later proved — that I would be able eventually to work hard and even exhaustingly without causing a repetition of my illness if I stuck to writing and editing, which I did with assurance and ease. On the other hand, I had always found that teaching and public lecturing made me tense, and I expended much histrionic energy in masking this condition and appearing the easy, untroubled teacher. Writing was my true vocation. And now, when the decision had been made, I opted for the written word. Since making that decision at the height of my illness I have never taught a class, nor addressed a hall full of people.

After I came out of hospital, it took time to recover my strength. For the next month, I spent most of my time in bed, but I insisted on having the bed made up in my study so that I would be among my bookshelves, and could begin the reading that would set my own books in motion again. I was resolved to begin writing as soon as I could, and though I was so weak that to lift a book weighing three pounds from the ground set the pain working in my chest again, each day I spent some time at my typewriter. The first day, a week after coming out of hospital, I was exhausted after a quarter of an hour of work, but I made sure to do each day whatever my slowly growing strength would allow, and by Christmas I was back working on the last pages of *Kerala*.

What I remember most vividly from those weeks of convalescence is the sensual delight with which I tottered out on my first walks, the beginning of the program of exercise and simpler living. At first I walked only about a hundred yards before my strength ran out and I leaned against a power pole while Inge went back to fetch the car. But I saw everything with a new intensity, irradiated as if the world, too, had come back renewed from the verge of death. The colours of flowers, as they began to emerge in that mild winter turning into an early spring, assumed a preternatural intensity that was shared by the subtle shades of bark and lichen and the texture of rock walls and old wooden fences. I took new delight in the harmonious shapes of natural things, the marvellous spiky green rosettes that thistles form when they first emerge from the ground, the architecture of bare trees. My renewed interest in wild birds dates from those weeks when Inge would drive me around Stanley Park and, barely capable of moving, I would delight vicariously in the flight of gulls and eagles and the easy aquatics of grebes and goldeneyes. Though no evangelical preacher worth his offertory would count me among the born again, I did feel as if I was living in a world sparkling with the dew of a first dawn. It stayed with me for months and has never completely faded.

XIX

SEEING THE EARTH ANEW

THIS SENSE OF SEEING the earth anew was most important to me as the year 1967 unfolded and we began the travels for *Canada and the Canadians*, a book that Alan Pringle had suggested to me; I intended this to be a portrait of the country, with history and commentary on present-day life, but I also wanted to give the book a personal authenticity.

The first months I was still working hard at clearing the various commitments that had been held up owing to my illness. *Kerala* was completed in January and scheduled for publication in the autumn. *The Doukhobors* was finished in the early summer, and mid-July I had got level with the delays caused by my illness. After that I began the research on the other two books to which I had commited myself, *The British in the Far East* and *Henry Walter Bates*.

At the same time as *Kerala* there appeared another book that was more personally important to me, the *Selected Poems* which John Robert Colombo had persuaded Clarke, Irwin to publish. It was twenty years since I had brought out a book of verse, and although there were less than a dozen new poems from that interval to add to those I had chosen from earlier books, I was glad to remind Canadian readers that I had been first a poet and only afterwards became a prose writer. The result was often pleasing, as when P. K. Page told me that the book "gave me a curious sombre pleasure reading it &a great — &additional regard for your skill."

I had hoped that its publication would release my lyric gift from its almost complete silence since the late 1940s, but not until the early 1970s would I be writing poetry of this kind again. However, during the summer of 1967 I wrote dramatic verse again, for I composed a series of six verbal tableaus, each an hour in length, based on incidents in

Canadian history, which Gerald Newman produced as part of the CBC's contribution to the Canadian Centennial during his last year at the CBC. The best plays of the group concerned the death of Isaac Brock in the War of 1812 and the failure of the Northwest Rebellion of 1885; the latter, somewhat adapted under the title of *Six Dry Cakes for the Hunted*, was the only one that even reached print; it appeared in the volume of *Two Plays*, in company with *The Island of Demons*, which Talonbooks published a decade later.

I also compiled a documentary on the Indian Mutiny for Gerald to produce, and that was the last work in our creative collaboration, for before the end of the year Gerald gave up radio work to teach English literature at Simon Fraser University. His departure coincided with — in part was caused by — a constriction in regional radio production by the CBC, and henceforward broadcast writing was to occupy much less of my time. Though I would later denounce the increasing centralization of the Corporation and the diminished quality of its programming, I was personally glad to concentrate on writing for print. Yet I never regarded as lost the time spent during my radio writing period on acquiring new literary skills.

Already by the end of January I had recovered sufficiently from my heart attack for us to plan our travels over the coming year. We had arranged for Inge's parents to come from Germany and stay with us in the beginning of May, when we would take them on a tour of British Columbia and the Alberta foothills of the Rockies. By early March I was able to arrange meetings in London in October with editors, agents, and friends, and by the month's end I was fit enough to join Peter Dwyer, then the director of the Canada Council, and a group of literati whom he had gathered in Vancouver to talk about writers' problems. They included Al Purdy, Gwendolyn MacEwen, Phyllis Webb, Robin Skelton and Austin Clarke, most of them friends I was anxious to see again. Peter Dwyer was the best person who ever headed the Canada Council, doubtless because he was not an Ottawa bureaucrat. Like Graham Greene and Malcolm Muggeridge, he had been in MI5. He had good taste and wisdom, and the ability to establish genuine as well as spurious human relationships. He gave a human face to the Canada Council that after his death faded away. For about four years, until the illness that in 1971 took him away from the Council, I encountered Peter quite often, argued with him and even fought him until I won Canada Council funding for *Canadian Literature*, yet, like many other artists and writers, I found him a sympathetic, understanding man. I remember how pleased he was in early 1967, to tell me that *The Crystal Spirit* had won me the Governor General's Award for literature.

INGE'S PARENTS ARRIVED FROM Offenbach at the start of May. Otto was a retired civil servant, a small, stubborn, generous man who had fled from Weimar into the West zone of Germany because he found the Communists as detestable as he had earlier found the Nazis. His ancestors had been Austrian barons who actively sympathized with the peasants in their sixteenth century revolts, and one at least of the family had been executed by the Hapsburgs in a little town of Upper Austria; the anti-authoritarian strain ran strong in Otto, and Inge inherited it.

Gertrud came from Koenigsberg in East Prussia and her partly Polish descent showed in the shape of her high-cheeked face. She was — until she died at the age of 94 — a woman of sharply ironic humour, and she and I sustained a jesting affectionate relationship that enabled us to get on very well in our macaronic language, half-German and half-English.

Otto had been a mountaineer and hunter when young, and though he was now too old for the peaks and no longer enjoyed killing wild animals, he still felt close to the natural world and loved to go among the mountains of Austria and Switzerland. The idea of coming to a land that was still largely wilderness and the hope of seeing some of the large game animals that still survived there excited him. His curiosity was as intense as mine and he was a trained observer so that there was not much that missed him. He and I competed in keeping elaborate diaries and his was eventually published in a German newspaper while mine was absorbed into *Canada and the Canadians*.

We started off by exploring Vancouver Island, still at the height of its spring blossoming. Returning to the mainland, we set off into the British Columbian interior, heading up the Fraser River into the beautiful country of pinewoods, their floors blue with delphinium, around Lillooet and Pavilion. We continued to Williams Lake and the Chilcotin ranching country and northward to Barkerville and the remnants of the Cariboo goldfields, which had been reclaimed from dereliction and reconstructed in a way that was authentic enough to please those with a historical turn of mind, so that we were not ashamed to show the old town, as a late snow fell in its streets, as a fair example of a mid-Victorian mining settlement without, of course, its teeming crowds of fortune-seekers.

From Barkerville we took the long road to the Skeena and its Indian villages, a kind of spiritual focus to which we had been drawn back several times since our first visit there. Then we drove down through the Thompson River country into the Okanagan valley and over Anarchist Mountain to Grand Forks, up the Arrow Lakes to Revelstoke, and across the Rogers Pass to Golden and Banff.

By now it was time for me to go to Ottawa to receive the Governor General's Award, and I flew there from Calgary. At Rideau Hall the winners went up to the little dais on which Roland Michener sat in a gilded chair and gave each of us a leather-bound copy of her or his book which he — the Governor General — had signed. I was in pleasant company, for Margaret Laurence, already my friend, and Margaret Atwood, soon to become one, were receiving awards at the same time. The hall was filled with cultural bureaucrats and writers invited for the occasion; the breach in the solemnity came as I went up to Michener, and Kildare Dobbs pointed up the occasion's irony by shouting from the audience, "Up the Anarchists!" Michener laughed, for we had already met in India, and whispered to me, "I want to talk to you about the Tibetans," which he did a little while later at the reception, and we quietly plotted strategy for getting Canadian government aid for the refugees; it eventually came to fruition.

We went on to the Canada Council's celebration, where we dined well and received our cheques. That night I got mildly drunk for the first time since my illness in the company of good friends — Al Purdy, Bob Weaver, Kildare Dobbs, and Henry Kreisel. There were no ill effects.

I REJOINED MY COMPANIONS AND WE WENT on the high mountain highway from Banff to Jasper. The thaw had been recent, the wild animals were grazing on the fresh pastures below the receding snow line, and I was able to show Otto mountain goat white and fleecy on the high slopes and mountain sheep on the lower meadows, moose and elk in the mountain marshes, coyotes cadging for food by the roadside, wolves loping through the trees, black bears on the garbage heaps outside the mountain hotels and even a distant grizzly.

We returned by way of the Crow's Nest Pass to Vancouver. We had travelled some five thousand miles over the roads of western Canada.

In September Inge and I set off again, travelling through the parklands along the North Saskatchewan River, through Batoche and the country of the Northwest Rebellion, where the poplar woods were already tinged with autumn gold; through Verigin, with its beautiful little meeting hall of fretted wood in the old Russian style, built in the days of Peter Verigin and still a centre of Doukhobor activity, and through Neepawa, where the people were in two minds about Margaret Laurence's novels, in which she had turned their town into the fictional community of Manawaka. We went along the shore of Lake Superior and through the dreary woodlands of the Shield to Toronto, where there were publishers and editors to be seen, and literary parties to remind one that though Canadian writers live scattered over vast territories, there is a tribal solidarity that joins them together.

We left Toronto as soon as we could, since I was intent on visiting the old Loyalist towns along the shores of Lake Ontario from Port Hope to Cornwall, on our way to Montreal, through which we passed quickly, taking the road along the north shore of the St. Lawrence to Québec City and crossing the river so that we could continue into New Brunswick and Nova Scotia. Now we seemed to be getting into the marches of Europe, as if the Atlantic were a frontier rather than an ocean, for there was a sense of tradition and age in many eastern communities, both in Québec and in the Maritimes, that had not yet developed in Canada anywhere west of Sault Ste. Marie, and I remember, especially on the red-earth terrain of Prince Edward Island, a feeling of European smallness in the buildings and trees and of particularity in the landscape that contrasted strikingly with the largeness of nature and the broadly scattered way of human life one experiences in British Columbia.

My fresh impressions of that journey are recorded in *Canada and the Canadians*, in which I evoked much that was pleasant and charming. Now, after two decades, the dominant memory is starker, of the poverty-stricken farms along the southern shore of the St. Lawrence as we travelled east of Gaspé on our return from the Maritimes. Their land had never been anything but barren, and the stones that had risen up through the ungrateful soil had been built up, like great man-made moraines, to divide the starveling holdings. After seeing this rural poverty even the slums of Montreal, to which so many people from the depressed farms of Québec had gone, seemed islands of good living and opportunity.

We found it hard to rent a room on returning to Montreal, and we ended up in a nightclub in the northern part of the city, which had a few bedrooms, doubtless in normal times at the disposal of the tarts who frequented the place, but now being let at inflated prices to Expo visitors. We could never even think of sleeping before about half-past three in the morning when the obsessive beat of the music, entirely Parisian in tone, would die down. The people who ran the club were among the few immigrants from France I have encountered in Canada. Without exception they disliked and despised the Québecois, and were not backward in expressing their opinions to English-speaking Canadians, whom they professed to prefer.

As for our actual experience of Expo 67, or perhaps rather our lack of experience of it, it took us two and a half hours to get through the traffic jams — the result of a transport strike — and when we did arrive the holiday weekend crowds were so enormous that both of us found all our anti-social hackles rising, decided that we were solitaries by nature, and fled for some clear air on the top of Mount Royal. No doubt there were treasures buried in all this jimcrackery, but a quick walk through the plaster filmset landscape of Expo convinced me that I would prefer to seek them in their native habitat and enjoy them in peace. We decided to spend the rest of our time visiting the villages of the Laurentians and exploring unfamiliar corners of Montreal. This we did.

XX

LANDS WHERE THE
LEMON TREE BLOOMS

T HE YEAR 1968 SAW the virtual end of the Atlantic crossings by
the great ocean liners. Services had been steadily reduced, but we
were still surprised when we got on board the *Sylvania* and were
abruptly told this would be the ship's last voyage; the Cunard Line had
suddenly decided to abandon its crossings.

The great Cunard tradition was vanishing with a whimper. We had
booked first class, but the food was bad and the stewards were slack
and grudging because the crew, like the passengers, had just been told
that this would be the last voyage and their jobs would end with it.
The ship was so dirty that an epidemic of enteritis ran through the First
and Tourist classes alike, and Inge was a victim, sick for most of the
voyage. The final indignity came when the doctor presented a bill
for his services; he at least must have cleared a tidy profit from the last
voyage, for he was busy from early morning until late at night with
the hundreds of patients. For more than twenty years we had enjoyed
the Atlantic voyages, treating them as recuperation between bouts of
hard work or travel, but this time we were angrily glad to leave the boat at
Le Havre.

We drove westward through Rouen and Rheims, and into the stark
countryside of Lorraine, with its depressed and colourless villages as the
night settled down over the ugly landscape. We drove into the sombre,
stone-paved streets of French steel towns and the moonless darkness was
broken by bursts of magenta sheet lightning. The monstrous vases of
blast furnaces loomed in the middle distance. Our ears were filled with
thunders and clankings, and cascades of sparks burst out of dark buildings. A tall blond man gestured indifferently from a frontier post, and
we entered Luxembourg's share of the industrial inferno. For a few miles
more, the lightning flashed, the sparks cascaded, the mills clanked and

thundered to remind us that despite its smallness — just 999 square miles — Luxembourg is one of the great metal producers of Europe.

Luxembourg is also the largest of the five minicountries of Europe, large enough to contain Andorra, San Marino, Liechtenstein and Monaco with room to spare, but it shares with them the prosperity which the little states have acquired as a bonus added to survival. Such countries have always fascinated me with their promise that perhaps after all the meek shall inherit the earth.

The whole grand duchy measures 35 miles from east to west and 50 from north to south, and it took us less than an hour to get from the border to the heart of the capital — modestly affluent buildings, well-lit streets, beer signs everywhere, but an air of nocturnal sobriety. The hotels varied from expensively modern to well-preserved Victorian. Ours had once been the great hotel of the country; the walls were covered with gold-framed mirrors ten feet high, the parquet creaked like the whispering floors of Japanese palaces, and in the corridors discarded armoires kept watch like lines of sentinels. We walked in the neat empty quadrilaterals of the streets, found an opera house with no opera, a crowded *discothéque* in a back street, an empty restaurant where we ate trout from the Ardennes.

In the light of next day we saw Luxembourg as a small neat city, set on low hills which a knot of rivers had sliced with deep narrow valleys. The streets were inclined to end in winding dizzy corniches or to plunge into wooded ravines in which squatted early Victorian mills and factories. The old town had market squares, gateways with clocktowers, bits of town wall, authentically mediaeval but unconsciously stagey. In the new town another backdrop fell abruptly into place. Vistas, parks and boulevards, magnificent plane trees, English clothes shops, solid public buildings. Here the theatricality was conscious. Unlike the towns of the smaller mini-states, this was undeniably a capital city, built in miniature but to impress. The vintage was that of Ottawa, for Luxembourg, after centuries of subjection to many invaders, finally gained national being in 1867.

Next to the blast furnaces of the south, the banks of Luxembourg city, with their multichromatic displays of foreign bank notes in the windows, were the most impressive buildings, and gave the streets the look of a northern Zurich. During the 1960s laws were devised to allow foreign companies incorporated in Luxembourg to pay dividends abroad without withholding taxes and to transfer funds without disclosure. Multinationals set up holding companies to tap the millions of dollars then floating free in Europe and use them for operations abroad. The state benefitted by collecting registration fees, and the local lawyers and financiers made small fortunes by arranging deals. Most Luxembourgers were neither steel workers nor bankers. They remained dairymen, wine-growers, and small townsmen, speaking a German dialect which they insisted was a separate language, eating and drinking well.

We drove out of the grand duchy down the Moselle Valley, eating in Trier, sleeping in one of the little castled towns beside the river, and drinking the cloudy new wine in the cellar of a Piesporter wine-grower, who sang the praises of Moselle culture which, he declared, was superior because here the Romans had brought the benefits of classical civilization. All the troubles of Germany he blamed on the Prussians, who had never benefitted from the Pax Romana. The natural regionalisms of Germany were as much alive as they ever were in the days before the Hohenzollerns united the country into an artificially centralized Reich.

After reaching Frankfurt, I flew to London and stayed in a decrepit Bloomsbury hotel, holding conferences with Alan Pringle and his colleagues and with John Smith. We talked of various books as well as those to which I was committed: a book on Aldous Huxley and one on Herbert Read, an account of East India men in Tibet for the Great Travellers series, and, at some future time, another travel narrative. All these books would be written and eventually published by Faber & Faber. In 1968 it seemed as if the connection would last my life out, and I returned to Germany confident that at last I would be able to live by my writing, and that now, if I continued to edit *Canadian Literature*, it would be out of pleasure rather than necessity.

In late October we started southward, driving down German roads lined with fruit laden apple trees and through Rothenberg and Dinkels-buhl, those mediaeval Bavarian towns whose beauty saddens one with the thought that they are mere relics of a tradition of architecture whose best examples did not survive the Second World War. We were heading now for eastern Switzerland, since after seeing Luxembourg I was anxious to visit a different political survival, one of the last havens of the direct democracy that the Athenians had practiced, the canton of Appenzell.

We came down to the autumn-orange vineyards along the northern shore of Lake Constance, through whose pale and shifting haze we could see a green shoreline that was the Swiss canton of Thurgau. We took the ferry at the little walled town of Meersburg and entered Switzerland at Kreuzlingen. We drove eastward to St. Gallen and then south into Appenzell. These cantons are rarely visited by tourists. The small towns are not as spectacular as Berne and Basel, and lack the literary associations of places of western Switzerland like Joyce's and Lenin's Zurich, Gibbon's Lausanne, Madame de Stael's Coppet, Bakunin's Locarno and the

Geneva of Rousseau and Calvin. But a vivid and verdant fertility coloured the landscape as we followed the narrow roads behind whose spidery wooden fences thousands of dun cattle grazed in fields where the high, dark green grass was fed with meals of liquid dung sprayed out of tank carts. After Emmenthal, this is a great cheese region of Switzerland, and Appenzeller has a smell as robust as Limburger and a fine sharp flavour.

The road from Kreuzlingen ran through modest hills like a more pastoral Laurentians. But between St. Gallen and Appenzell the true Alps began, as we drove beside the little cogged railway through upland villages of wide-eaved wooden houses whose size suggested a fertility among the people as generous as that of the land. Thick-legged women walked the roads in blue-flowered aprons, with huge conical baskets of firewood and rabbit-greens on their backs. The country plunged and rolled; people say of Appenzell that there is not a level hundred yards in the whole canton, and the apple orchards clambered to steep meadows on which the distant cattle seemed to hang as prehensile as flies, with the pale limestone crags walling them at sunset with glowing amethyst. The mountains of Appenzell are dwarfs beside the Matterhorn, but the valley bottoms are low, and so they appear immense.

Appenzell, the *hauptort* or chief place (nobody thinks of talking of a city or even a town in such a peasant world) consists of a winding main street, with a couple of squares, on one of which stands the deeply-arcaded *Rathaus*, and on the other a massive wooden hotel called The Santis after the mountain which towers over the town. The air smelt richly of dung; herds of dun cows parted grudgingly before us. The tall wooden fronts of the buildings with their tottering storeys shone like mosaics with painted geometric and floral patterns; a gallery of medicinal herbs adorned the apothecary's establishment; the guild hall bore the symbols of crafts. Intricately welded iron signs swung and glittered with gold leaf; eagles, lions, carps. The cinema opened three nights a week. Stuffed pike was the dish of the day at the inn near the *Rathaus*. The clouds settled into the town as darkness fell.

That day an Appenzeller peasant was marrying off his daughter and the feast took place in The Santis, where we stayed. We were served at one end of the banquet room, behind a latticed screen. Tables were laid in the rest of the room for the two hundred guests. The musicians came first, dark, gipsy-faced youths, dressed in the local costume of crimson waistcoats, embroidered braces, brown breeches; each wore a single gold earring, shaped like the dangling bowl of a coffee spoon. Slowly the guests appeared; stoop-backed craggy peasants, young women with mountain-red cheeks which looked painted. "Ten years ago they would all have come in *tracht*," commented the innkeeper as he put a carafe of straw-coloured Valais wine on our table. Now only a few of the women did so, with the Appenzeller head-dress whose doubled upright wings resemble a gigantic butterfly in repose. But the music was traditional, playing in the couple with a march on fiddle, zither, and accordion, and interrupting with lilting dances the long speeches in Swiss German rhyming couplets, spoken by children and schoolteachers and the master of ceremonies until, two hours later, the rattling, shoe-beating peasant dances began. Far into the morning they stomped, and raced around the corridors, and bottom-pinched the squawking women, and shouted in throat-clearing dialect.

These were the democrats, stolid and silent men on anything but a feast day, who govern themselves literally, as we unfortunate parliamentarians can never do. Like three other Swiss cantons, Appenzell is still ruled by the *landesgemeinde*, the folk-moot to which all men come, carrying the dagger that is the symbol of their status as free men with the right to bear arms. We did not witness the *landesgemeinde*, which takes place on the last Sunday in each April, but the innkeeper came into the square outside, and showed us the ancient lime-tree around which thousands of men gathered with vivid banners of the canton and the communes which give an air of mediaeval brilliance to Swiss public events. There, by show of hands, two fingers raised upward as in a blessing, they made their laws. The council and the officials they elected could only administer these laws, not change them, and further legislation waited until the citizens gathered a year later. Women did not vote, a mediaevalism which then applied in most Swiss cantons. To allow his wife a share in ruling him would seem to an Appenzeller peasant the gravest danger to the liberties for which his ancestors fought when the first *landesgemeinde* met in the fields to plot its resistance to Hapsburg autocracy five hundred years ago.

WE CONTINUED SOUTHWARD through Schwyz and Uri, two of the three cantons of herdsmen whose rebellion against Austrian rule in the thirteenth century was the beginning of Switzerland; more roads looped over vast green alps and ran through chestnut woods turning golden, and dipped into hollows where villages clustered around onion-dome church towers. Then came the narrowing valley that led beside a sombre limb of Lake Lucerne into the St. Gothard pass; halfway up it the first snow was falling in big succulent flakes, and at Goschenen we ran our car on to a flat-bed wagon and were taken, a long snake of cars swaying in the darkness, through the railway tunnel to Airolo, and from there went down the parched valleys of the Ticino to Bellinzona and Lugano, lying beside the cobalt of its three-legged lake, between its little sugar-loaf mountains. There were massive white Victorian hotels along the shoreline; behind them the stone arcades of the old town. It was a high bourgeois resort, delightful only in winter when the visitors are away and the accidents of topography dispel the snows in an almost endless succession of sunlit days.

We spent our first night in a lofty frowsy room in an old hotel. The next day we found an apartment in a Victorian house in the quarter of Massagno, on a hillside behind the town. We had the whole ground-floor to ourselves: a big living room opening on to a patio that overlooked the terraced garden and the lake; a bedroom; a kitchen with a breakfast nook that caught the morning sun; a little room like a monk's cell with a single bed and a desk which suited me admirably. Our hosts were not native Ticinese. Signor Defilla came from the Grisons and spoke Switzerland's fourth language, Romansch; he was a retired engineer with a love for water-colour painting and had some skill in it; his wife was German Swiss and was addicted to English detective novels, which spilled over shelves in all the corridors, so that we were never at a loss for light reading.

The climate came up to our expectations. Just after Christmas there were two or three days of snow, which melted quickly. The last raspberries still hung on the vines late in November; the first wild snowdrops started blooming in the woods in January. Lugano's own lake was naturally at the centre of our excursions, and quite often we went to the lake of Como; indeed, Como itself became our Italian metropolis. We also explored the hill country on the southern side of the Alps, with its austere villages of rusty-coloured fieldstone houses and its little Lombard towered churches, and went often to the other Ticinese towns, Locarno, Bellinzona, and Ascona. But until late January we made only one excursion out of the lake region and that an abortive one.

The San Bernardino tunnel, which led from Bellinzona into the Grisons, had just been opened, and in mid-December we drove between Bellinzona's three castles which span the valley with their saw-toothed crenellations and north-east into the Val Messolcino, where the people spoke an Italian dialect different from that of the Ticinese. The valley ran north and south, and even in winter was full of sunlight, glowing on the dwarf oak trees which covered the mountainsides and would keep their dead leaves until spring. At Mesocco a giant castle, ruined and ivy-green, with a Romanesque tower, guarded the hairpin road that leapt into the high pinewoods and up towards the pass. Villages were gaudy with banners — the ibex flag of the Grisons, the flags of the various communes, rarely the Swiss confederal flag, to celebrate the opening of the tunnel, which provided the first allegedly all-weather road across the Alps.

Up in the pass, near the entrance to the tunnel, peasants from one of the Romansch-speaking valleys had come to rejoice, with their band and choir. They crowded around the little windswept hotel where we stopped, drinking wine out of flowered crocks. The girls, in long maroon gowns and white headdresses, sang in Italian, Romansch and Swiss German, and then — spotting us — struck up *John Brown's Body* in English. The men played their brass instruments out of tune, red-faced and long-nosed, silk flags streaming in the wind.

We went on, through the new white tunnel, into the rime-grey country beyond the Alpine chain. Fir woods and stony river beds; it reminded me of the northern Rockies until we passed villages of vast shabby houses, half shuttered up and silent in the snow. In one place where we stopped, sixty-seven people were left — mostly the old — compared with several hundred twenty years before. They hoped the opening of the road would wake things up and bring back some of the young men who had gone away. Whole regions of upland Switzerland were dying in this way in the 1960s. Their life was too harsh to compete with the temptations of the lowland cities where work was plentiful and life was comfortable. By the time we reached Splügen, a blizzard began. The all-weather road was blotted out of sight, and we edged back nervously to the tunnel and the sunlight of Ticino at the far end.

We had few visitors. As for the local people, we found them even less outgoing than the people of Menton had seemed. In Lugano we would go to certain stores two or three times a week without a sign of recognition from the shopgirls — and this continued for more than four months. We struck up an acquaintance with the women who ran one of the bookshops, but they were German Swiss and so was the girl in the post office at Massagno who would sometimes chat with me about Canada. It was strange to think that these aloof Luganesi spoke the same language and came from the same stock as the open and friendly Lombards and Ligurians at the Italian ends of the lakes. The Defillas, neither of them Ticinese, served as our only interpreters of the introverted little culture.

Yet I found myself accepting as sufficient the pleasure of wandering in the Ticino's valleys and along its lakeshore, and of uninterrupted work. I immersed myself in Bates's letters and in his diaries of the Amazons in the 1840s, and in ten weeks of concentrated writing I finished my life of him, and gained satisfaction from having repaid the debt of inspiration I had incurred when I first read *The Naturalist on the River Amazons* as a boy more than forty years before.

On New Year's Day the Luganesi held the first of a series of celebrations that made me feel more sympathetic to these dour people. That morning we were down in the town, walking towards the lake to feed the swans, when we heard the sound of music echoing from the courtyard of the town hall. Inside, rank upon rank, we found the Luganesi standing, dressed as their distant ancestors, in uniforms and eighteenth-century, three-cornered hats and shouldering long-bayonetted muskets that had belonged to the Ticino's cantonal army in the Napoleonic age. The struggles against the tyrants to the south in Milan were remembered as the band played Lugano's own anthem, and the city's banner, an oriflamme of crimson and white silk, was unfurled and carried ahead of the little army out of the past as it marched off into the stench of gasoline in the twentieth century streets.

At least in their liking for festivals, the Luganesi resembled both the real Italians and also the rest of the Swiss. There were processions at Carnival with fisher kings and other allegorical figures in grotesque and gigantic masks, and priapic battles with water pistols and confetti and obscenely shaped balloons, and on Shrove Tuesday a great public feast, when savoury steam wafted along the arcades from a battery of field kitchens, tended by white hatted cooks, which filled the main square. At the expense of the city, every person who came, rich or poor, citizen or stranger like ourselves, received his plate of saffron-yellow rice and sausages, and his glass of wine, and ate and drank under the plane trees in the fountained gardens by the lake. It was the first and only occasion we felt accepted among the Luganesi.

BEFORE WE LEFT WE made one long expedition. Our landlord was concerned that we should observe Swiss laws by leaving the country briefly before the end of our first three months there and then returning, and we decided to drive down to Sicily, which for us was untrodden ground. There had recently been an earthquake, but we felt the dangers were over. And indeed the only evidence we saw of disruption in the life of the island was a tent encampment for homeless people in one of the parks of Palermo, while the earthquake had frightened most of the winter tourists away.

I was in poor shape when we started off, having had a bad influenza followed by severe conjunctivitis, worsened by the attentions of a local oculist, who gave me drops that turned the whites of my eyes an alarming blood-red. Two days before setting off for Sicily I went desperately to an apothecary, who shook his head at the follies of the medical profession, and gave me a soothing wash, which was all I needed. By our second day of travel, when we left Pisa, my eyes were already recovered and the sun was working wonders on my general condition.

On that second day we drove south, reaching Salerno just before night-fall. We should have stayed there, but we were tempted by the thought of getting farther on our journey before stopping, and a brand-new autostrada, plunging into the mountains, lured us on. The road, broad and empty, ran straight into the wild heart of the Apennines. The land became parched and lifeless, a great rock skeleton, its outcrops tufted with stunted oaks and olives. No cultivation. No houses. No villages. Not a person or an animal to be seen. The country had drained away to the hilltops, invisible in the gathering darkness, where the villages are perched throughout this harsh land.

After cleaving its way through many miles of rugged emptiness, the autostrada petered out, and we bumped on to an old road that clambered and coiled among the mountains, clinging to the contour lines and suddenly plunging headlong into valleys with trickles of green vegetation. On this road there were villages, many miles apart and monotonously alike — a main street in each of them with a few ugly stucco buildings, and on each side a jigsaw of wretched alleys lined with hovels that served as houses and stables. There were always heaps of garbage; as in the middle ages, pigs served as scavengers. There was not a touch of architectural grace; not even a garden. It was another world from the soft landscapes of Tuscany and Umbria.

We saw nothing that resembled a hotel, though once, about two in the morning, we came to a rough café, open all night for the truck-drivers, where a sleepy peasant boy in a white monkey jacket was serving coffee laced with brandy. Twice we pulled in to the roadside and dozed. The first time we were awakened by two *carabinieri* who warned us of the dangers of sleeping in this region where poverty tempted people into banditry. The second time it was the cold before dawn that awakened us. We climbed a steep hill into a town called Marmanno and as we drove through it the sun began to show over the mountain crests to the east, and the light spread over the bare hillsides, scarred by the tree-felling of two thousand years, the soil stripped by the rare rains and parched by the drought of a climate ruined by deforestation. Shepherds were afoot, driving their flocks out from the folds where they had been kept to protect them from the wolves, and wild-looking horsemen appeared on the road, wrapped to the eyes in heavy cloaks.

When we came at breakfast time to Castrovillari, the biggest town since Salerno, we felt we were in another continent, for it reminded us less of any Italian town we had seen before than of one in Persia. The people were dark and short. Women were few, and those one did see were dingy creatures who wore black shawls which they drew closely over their faces so that they acted like veils. Pack mules and battered little donkey carts were more common than cars, Vespas, or even bicycles. The houses were grilled and secretive. Outside the butchers' shops hung scraggy fragments of fly-infested mutton. The air was sharp and invigorating. And there was the rawness — heaps of rubble left around half-complete buildings — that characterizes Asian cities struggling towards modernity. Like every town in southern Italy, Castrovillari was growing, not because it was prosperous, but because the Calabrians were deserting the villages. Not that all of them found work in the towns. Having experienced the depression in Wales, I found the look of the men who stood around at all hours of the day in the plazas sadly familiar. One needs a developed sense of the romance of desolation to like Calabria.

Sicily was different and more perplexing. At moments it was hauntingly beautiful, and at others heartbreakingly squalid. In the end I found myself remembering the island with a sense of hopelessness, although there was much to bemuse the eye. The rocky islanded coastline was celebrated by Homer, and some of it is heroic enough for the world of Odysseus. The Greek city of Agrigento (Acragas to the ancients) disposed of its temples of honey-coloured stone with a magnificent sense of landscape along a ridge with on one side a valley filled with blossoming almonds and on the other a sea at times literally wine-dark. We found the finest of all Roman mosaics in the imperial villa at Piazza Amarina, yet even better were the golden mosaics with which Byzantine artists had covered the jewelbox interior of the Capella Palatina in Palermo and the vast walls of the abbey which the Norman kings of Sicily built in the hills at Monreale. We travelled through landscapes with olive gardens and orange groves, and along wild mountain roads bordered by blue irises, and into small, charming uncelebrated towns like Nicosia, where Lombards from north Italy built a community of houses clinging like limpets to dome-shaped rocks, and Noto, which was destroyed in a seventeenth century earthquake and rebuilt as a perfectly unified baroque city in miniature. We saw it all under ideal conditions. The climate was perfect, the light clear and lucent, and the island uncrowded. There was every reason to enjoy it and often we did. But always there was a shadow of reservation.

In terms of positive human suffering Sicily was far less appalling than Mexico and India. There were streets in Palermo of a positively oriental squalor, but people do not die in them of hunger as they did in Calcutta. The ugliest and most decrepit Sicilian village was far less frightful than the worst villages of Bihar. Much of the land had been worn out by senseless exploitation, but it was still a less dramatic devastation than in the eroded highlands of Mexico. We saw towns in Sicily, prosperous in the days of the Greeks and even in the eighteenth century, where the streets were now dustbaths, the buildings shored against ruin, the children ragged and shoeless, and where water was hawked in the streets by men with tank wagons, but even these places were one step above the abyss compared with sinks of Asian poverty like Chittagong and Dacca.

Yet one felt that here, in Europe, the European dream of liberty and progress had been completely negated. The Greeks and the Carthaginians oppressed Sicily's aboriginal inhabitants; the Romans, Arabs, Normans, French, Spaniards, and mainland Italians came after them. From the beginning the pattern was exploitation. Sicily was a great wheat-growing land of the ancient world, but at the expense of its fertility. It provided timber for the fleets of Greece and Rome, and became deforested. In the middle ages the Sicilians fell under the rule of absentee landlords, until by the nineteenth century four-fifths of the land was in the hands of a hundred and forty princes and two thousand three hundred dukes, marquises and counts, most of whom lived away. Even the movement that arose to defend the people against the impositions of the landlords turned into the Mafia. Small wonder the Sicilians lost hope.

The Sicilians long wanted to be left to themselves. Now they have given up even that hope. More and more they want to escape from their poverty, even if that means escaping from home. The interior of the island was becoming depopulated. The marginal lands were falling out of cultivation. The peasants were coming down to the coastal towns, and travelling on, to northern Italy, to Germany, if they were lucky to Canada or Australia.

What happened in Cefalu, a pleasant-looking little town with a cathedral containing famous mosaics, epitomized for me the Sicilian situation. We had stopped there on our way to Palermo, hoping to see the mosaics, but the cathedral was locked and we could find no sacristan. We drove on, and on our way back stopped again. The cathedral was still locked, but a man in the square told us to return next morning. The only hotel that looked possible had a decor combining gloom and gaudiness: heavy black furniture and crimson curtains. We went up to the reception desk. It was obvious from the number of keys hanging there that plenty of rooms were free. But instead of taking a key or looking in his register, the clerk scurried off to a table where four men in dark expensive suits were sitting with their hats on. He approached the largest and most powerful-looking, who glared at us and then shook his head.

It did not need much insight to recognize that we had chanced on a local Mafia haunt and that it was the *capo*, not the hotel proprietor, who did not want us in the hotel. Giving up the idea of staying in Cefalu, we went into a restaurant, and when he heard us speaking English, the cook came out to greet us; he had been a prisoner of war in Devonshire, and it had been the happiest time of his life. He felt far more confined in his native island.

WE LEFT SICILY WITH darkness shadowing our minds like the smoke of Etna that was hanging over its landscape, but this was dispelled when we travelled up the mainland coast and reached the old Greek city Podisonia, now called Paestum. The three temples there are close to two thousand five hundred years old, and the accident of malaria driving out the population preserved their structures of yellowish limestone. The site was almost deserted; the stones of the sacred way stood in a sea of fresh green grass starred with big yellow oxalis flowers, and in the bright early February sunlight the temples glowed with a grandeur and a serenity that filled our minds with light. Nowhere have I seen ruins that more faithfully seemed to preserve the spirit of archaic antiquity.

Another month in Lugano enabled me to make a start on the book I was doing for Peter Quennell, *The British in the Far East*, in which I expressed the fascination with the Empire — amounting almost to identification — which my long dedication to anti-imperialism had paradoxically bred in me. Then, in early March, we started our long journey back with a great looping trip through France and Spain.

It was my first visit to Spain. I had kept away because I was unable to dissociate the country from the memory of its civil war. Spain, for me, was Orwell's Barcelona. It was the blood-stained olive groves beside the Ebro. It was the deep gorge at Ronda, into which the Left and the Right in turn threw their living enemies. It was the dictatorship in which the cruel conflict ended. Those events of my youth, though I knew them only from the reports of others, had implanted themselves sharply on my mind. So strong is the power of the remembered word. So conservative is memory.

What we found when we drove round the brown parched headland that separates France from Catalonia was nothing like this mental construction. The only stormy weather we ran into was actual not metaphorical, a bitter, violent wind that blew stones down from the slopes above us, almost lifted the car from the road, and covered the jade sea far below us with silver veils of spray. But the customs officers merely jested at our Spanish, whose pronunciation had been acquired in Mexico, and let us pass without even looking into our car.

As we travelled on towards Malaga and Alicante and on around the perimeter of Spain, we realized that historical events which had become frozen in the minds of non-Spaniards who were young in the Thirties had in Spain passed on. Half the people of Spain in 1968 had not been born when the civil war took place. Rarely did we find ourselves talking to anyone about the war. An old man in the silence of the caves of Altamira neutrally mentioned how the Republican soldiers had sheltered there a generation ago. The prehistoric men who painted the bison on the cave walls, and the ragged soldiers who slept beneath them, defending a losing cause, seemed equally submerged.

On the other hand, nowhere else in Europe were we so conscious of the continuity of tradition. In this way Spain felt like the Asian countries. It had always seemed rather outside Europe and its concerns, and had remained aloof from the continent's recent experiences. It had kept out of the Second World War and the Cold War that followed it; the trump card in Franco's propaganda in the late 1960s was a single phrase: Thirty Years of Peace. Remaining a right-wing dictatorship, Spain had also been slower than the states east of the Pyrenees to become absorbed into post-war currents of progress and prosperity. Except on the Costa Brava, its old towns had not yet been besieged by residential and industrial suburbs. And Spaniards were palpably poorer than Frenchmen or Germans, or anyone I had seen in postwar Europe except the Calabrians. We felt as if we were visiting in a decayed mansion whose inhabitants did not have the money to live in the style that became them.

Everywhere were the solidly visible relics of power and prosperity. The palaces and mosques of Seville, Granada, and Cordoba recalled the civilized Moorish kingdoms of Andalucia; the great Gothic churches of Salamanca, Burgos, and Valladolid celebrated the eventual triumph of Christianity. And then, by the end of the seventeenth century, the decline of Spain began, the power and the glory and the wealth were dissipated, and Spaniards settled down to live among the grandeurs of their past, a few men rich, and most men poor but proud.

The poverty was still there, though less dramatically past. Tourism had brought raised standards in the coastal areas. Andalucia, the absentee landlord province of the south, the Ireland of Spain, used to be notorious for the extreme poverty of its landworkers, but even here now we saw settlements of new cottages built on the estates, and lines of motor bikes standing by the fields where labourers were working in gangs.

It was in the arid centre, in Old Castile and Extremadura, that classic Spanish poverty survived. Extremadura is a wild and beautiful province, its hillsides covered with forests of cork oaks, and in the spring blossoming with wild blue iris and white and magenta rock roses. But it has always been a meagre land, where ragged herdsmen tended other men's sheep and swine in the arid and rocky wastes that teemed with vipers. In its decayed towns, like Caceres, many people were blind from ophthalmia. Extremadura was the only part of the country where beggars accosted us, proudly, as if demanding tribute rather than asking for alms. The villages were tumbledown, the peasants gaunt and bitter. Some of them lived in caves like paleolithic men. Women stood by the roadsides trying to sell bunches of thin wild asparagus.

Yet everything in Spain was changing. The police were fewer and less flamboyant and offensive than in democratic Italy. We bought liberal English newspapers and saw the works of Marx and Engels openly for sale in Spanish translations. The dictatorship was loosening its grip, for the Spaniard, even when he is not a political democrat, is often an aristocratic egalitarian. Servility is outside his nature, and if he behaves with affability and courtesy it is because he regards one as his equal.

We sensed change in Spain, but we did not sense as surely the forces at work in France during that spring of 1968. We left Spain through Biarritz, cut across Gascony and through Albi to the Rhone valley, thence to Annecy in the Savoy, from which we went on to Besançon and by the foothills of the Vosges to Frankfurt. After a few days, we crossed Lorraine in a snowstorm and continued through Champagne into Normandy. Our last day we wandered through the Norman lanes to Honfleur and back, passing through apple orchards heavy with blossom and meadows golden with cowslips, of which we picked large bunches to decorate our cabin on the voyage to Canada.

Our impressions were of a fat and golden land, smug in its prosperity. But a few weeks after our return to Canada, student unrest at Nanterre ended in the Paris riots and the general strike which accompanied them; it seemed as though the days of the Commune were about to be re-enacted. Newspapers were filled with reports of a France different from that of provincial towns and villages, of cautious shopkeepers and peasant farmers.

As we read of the dramatic rebellion, we began to feel our impressions must have been wrong. But the great, slowly aroused conservatism of the French provinces had not really vanished, though this was not observed by correspondents who reported from Paris hotel rooms. When the dust settled, and the Left was routed in the next French elections, it was clear that the provinces wanted to keep what they had gained under De Gaulle, and were deeply opposed to revolutionary solutions. Our impressions during the weeks before the uprising had been correct, but only of the France we saw. The news media in their turn had made the mistake of assuming that the metropolis was France.

XXI

THE GREAT NORTHERN SHORE

F OR MORE THAN A YEAR to come I would be mainly involved in writing and travels that helped me to define my attitude to Canada. In the process I wandered in regions that were as strange and as interesting as any foreign country I had visited.

The proofs for our book on the Doukhobors were waiting for me and Avakumovic to check when I got back, and I had to prepare the special issue of *Canadian Literature* that would celebrate the tenth anniversary of the journal in 1969. It was a symposium on the writing of the 1960s, for which I got contributions from Margaret Laurence, P.K. Page, Mordecai Richler, Hugh MacLennan, Dorothy Livesay, Norman Levine, James Reaney, Al Purdy, Louis Dudek and Alan Crawley. Their presence confirmed the acceptance of the magazine not merely by academics, but by the Canadian writing community.

Before they passed out of my mind, I distilled the impressions of our winter in Europe into articles for *Saturday Night* and talks for CBC radio. Although I was no longer so deeply involved in dramatic writing for radio, I did translate Albert Camus' play *Les Justes*, and I was happy when Madame Camus wrote to express her pleasure at reading my English version which Norman Newton produced for the CBC.

Meanwhile the University of Victoria had offered me my first honorary doctorate, and in May I went over to Vancouver Island to be decked out in violet and crimson robes in that pseudo-mediaeval ceremonial. It was the first of five doctorates that over the years I would accept: from Sir George Williams because it was the first college in eastern Canada to recognize me; from the Université d'Ottawa because it was a French-speaking institution that offered an exotic Gallic insignia of gold thread and white silk and fur; from the University of Winnipeg because it was situated in the town of my birth; and from the University of British

Columbia because I had been so long associated with it. After that I declined the invitations of other universities. It would be tactless to name them or to express more than amused astonishment at those academic scalp-hunters who are not content until twenty or thirty bright hoods hang from their belts.

I worked hard now on *The British in the Far East*, finishing it by the end of June. At the same time I was busy making arrangements for the journeys into the Canadian North which I had postponed from 1967. In May I heard from an American publisher who wanted a concise history of the Hudson's Bay Company, and this task seemed to fit in admirably with my plans. It gave me an advance I could use towards expenses and enabled me to approach the Company itself for assistance. In June I heard that it would provide transport and accommodation for a trip up the west of Hudson's Bay to Rankin Inlet and Baker Lake. At the same time I got a small grant from the Canada Council that would pay our plane fares to Yellowknife and the Yukon.

While making these arrangements, I had a letter from Robin Skelton, asking me to write a piece for a special issue of *Malahat Review* to commemorate Herbert Read. It was a shock; Read had died a few days before and I had missed the news. I remembered he had been suffering from a throat cancer three years before, but I had thought it cleared up. I felt an immense sadness. I had known and liked him for thirty years, and I owed him many debts of the kind no younger person can repay to an older.

A few days later a letter came from Alan Pringle asking whether I had any ideas about a book on Read we had already vaguely discussed. I said that, having books on Canada and Aldous Huxley to complete, I could not make a start until 1971, "which would probably be to the good, since it would give a few years for the perspectives to settle into position." As well, given Herbert's own excellent autobiographical writings, recently brought together in *The Contrary Experience*, it did not seem the time for an ordinary biography. I wanted instead to trace the development and interaction of ideas in the fields which Read explored. His case was of peculiar interest, since we are so often told nowadays that the Renaissance man, the creative polymath, can no longer exist. Read's case disproved this; he did, even in an age of specialists, manage to encompass an amazing range of the important knowledge of our time, and his example was important, since it was vital to preserve and to reinvigorate the synthesizing approach.

To me such a book, like the books on Orwell and Huxley, was a means of exploring the origins of my own intellectual development. Most books of any interest are partly autobiography, and biographies of other people are especially so.

In August we finally set off on our trip to the North. We drove from Vancouver to Winnipeg, where the summer had been damp and cool and I found my native city uncharacteristically green. The Hudson's Bay Company's representatives entertained us with fur-trade lavishness before we flew to Churchill, a sketch of a town at the southern end of Hudson's Bay — which is the entry point for the central Arctic. By 1968 Churchill had abandoned its wartime role of a key military post, and the port, which only operated three months a year, did not seem active, though they were unloading Volkswagen Beetles from a German ship and there was another small vessel there flying the Swiss flag, which had come down the Rhine from Basel and crossed the Atlantic to pick up a cargo of wheat.

Churchill was a town of ghettoes: a civil servants' enclave served by utilidors (heated conduits containing sewage pipes, water supply, electricity, telephone connections); an Indian village kept going by welfare cheques; a tiny settlement of Inuit brought down from the north to be educated in the white man's ways; a terrible slum of métis who, unlike the Indians, were not guaranteed government aid because they still lacked the status of native people. In every way, the town seemed to demonstrate the tragedy of the white man's intrusion into a world where the native peoples had lived in a condition of precarious equilibrium with the natural world. The problem was not one of death by starvation; it was the pointlessness of being kept alive without meaning.

Much as the town depressed us, we felt the appeal of the worn rocky coastline of the Bay. There were ice-sculptured Henry Moore rocks, pools white with water crowsfoot, and dwarf tart-fruited wild gooseberries hugging the crevices. It was a botanical frontier; the avens Arctic, but the fireweed the narrow-leaved southern species. We stood on the low summit at Cape Merry, looking across the estuary to the stone star of Prince of Wales fort. The beluga whales were rolling in the heavy currents, their backs dazzlingly white above the cold blue of the water. At evening the Indians hunted them from canoes with harpoon and rifle. They sold them to the cannery, $1 a foot length for whales up to 10 feet, $1.25 a foot above that length; the skin would be canned as muktuk, the flesh sold to feed mink. We did not stay to see the evening butchery, for the small whales were beautiful gleaming creatures. That wild men might take them for food seemed part of the inevitable pattern of nature; that tamed men killed them for sale seemed a violation.

RANKIN INLET AND BAKER LAKE were equal violations of the natural order. They were settlements created during the 1950s when the great herds of caribou seemed to be vanishing and the nomadic groups of Inuit roving the Barren Land were beginning to starve to death. Under the orders of the federal government, the RCMP herded the wandering families together and brought them in to spots along the coast. Hitherto these had been sites of Hudson's Bay posts to which the hunters would come periodically with furs to exchange for the ammunition, tea, and other simple items they needed, and of missionary compounds from which priests would go out on to the Barren Land to work among the hunters, giving them a little education and medical aid. Now these places became quickly transformed into settlements of several hundred Inuit living largely on welfare and with several dozen white people to minister to them.

Travelling in a small Transair plane we flew to Rankin Inlet mostly over the Bay, and landed on a long airstrip, so rough that at one point as it taxied in the plane tilted and I saw sparks splashing from the tip of the wing when it touched the large stones on the runway. The manager of the Hudson's Bay post met us with his tractor and trailer, on which we bumped a mile over the tundra into the settlement with the mail and replenishments for the store. He and his wife were generous hosts, putting us up in the Bay staffhouse, where the young English clerks lived, but giving us meals in their home.

On low rocky hills was a bare scanty growth of lichen, dwarf bushes, and minuscule flowers. In ten minutes I could pick the vivid flowers of a dozen different arctic plants still blooming in mid-August. On the hillside were the squat cylinders for the oil that kept this community of 500 Eskimos and 50 whites alive during winter and during summer for that matter, since the temperature was less than 10° and we were glad of parkas. Above the oil tanks, on the crest of a hill, was a man-shaped Eskimo cairn: how old nobody knew. Stark and decaying, its corrugated iron rotting in the salt air, the tower of the nickel mine, now abandoned, still dominated the settlement. Below it gaudy pyramids of red and orange oildrums gave Rankin Inlet its only colour. Out in the inlet the Inuit in powered canoes raced around the little vermilion ships of the Ministry of Transport and a barge chugged in from Whale Cove down the coast, carrying muktuk for the cannery which a German immigrant operates — the only private industrial plant on the western shore of Hudson's Bay. The annual HBC boat had been delayed through running ashore elsewhere in the Arctic, and the warehouse in the store echoed with emptiness. This was no longer the catastrophe it would have been in the days before the planes began to fly regularly into the Arctic, but air freight made goods expensive, and this was a burden particularly on the Eskimo community, since most of the whites are government employees whose stores were brought in by the Department of Transport.

Rankin Inlet was a relatively fortunate place in the Arctic. There was plenty of work: construction in summer, in winter the crafts centre; some Inuit worked in the HB store, some in the government offices as clerks and interpreters. A few men fished, but though many were caribou hunters (and teenagers remembered the life of the camps as part of their childhood) there were only half a dozen older men in the settlement who still lived off the Barren Land. It was also older men who remembered the traditions, and, in the crafts centre, stopped their work and sang songs for me to record. They were their own songs, personal property, inherited from their fathers. Okoktuk sang the song of the Hungry Camp; Erkuti sang the song of Caching the Meat.

Among the Inuit, there was no tribal structure, since the People never banded together in more than extended family groups, but in Rankin, where people from coastal settlements and inland camps were united, an undefined stratification arose, with the coast people who were more practiced in the white man's ways forming an upper stratum.

The Inuit had their own community council and housing committee, which assessed rents for the government-built houses, and here men rose by intelligence and oratory. But there were other men who, if not exactly powerful, are feared. These were the men still reputed to be shamans, who either practiced in the past or have received the "gift" by descent. A young woman said there were three in Rankin Inlet but refused to name them. The white men said they no longer practice. The Inuit evaded answering. A missionary insisted that the Inuit no longer *believe* in the powers of the shaman, but fear him in a precautionary way.

We became acquainted with some of the Inuit. Sadie, 16, a girl from Rankin, said of Churchill: "What a big place! Once I got lost there!" One man had been to Montreal. "There were four of us, among all those people," he said. "We might have died, and nobody would have known!"

Tiktak the carver was a man with a deep-lined mobile face who seemed to be in his fifties but was unsure of his age; he was partly crippled by a fall, so that, though he did some hunting still, he could not go far from the settlement. He had a great humour, so that sometimes one felt a life of laughter had creased his face. He giggled shyly and made oriental protestations of inadequacy when we praised his work. "I am a bad carver!" He had been carving only five years, and maintained that he still worked without premeditation, taking the stone and letting the shape that is in it emerge. He thought the old life of the Barren Land was better than the new life. Caribou meat was better than costly store food, which he and his wife agreed was "too sweet".

Caribou was still eaten raw in Rankin; so was polar bear. One bear, whose skin we saw drying, had been killed a few days ago. Outside the

Eskimo houses the flesh of arctic char turned mahogany brown as it air-dried as food for the sleighdogs.

As elsewhere, the white fox was the principal source of fur income. It ran in a four-year cycle linked to that of the lemmings. This was a low year; no more than $8,000 worth was expected to be stacked in the cool attic above the HB store.

The Inuit families all talked of children dead, suggesting high death rates in the past. They never knew offhand the exact number of children they had, but counted slowly, turning down a top finger joint for each child. Was this bad memory? Or a lingering difficulty with numbers? Or perhaps some superstitious fear of being too exact? Half the families we met had children adopted according to Inuit custom.

We flew on to Baker Lake over the tundra, a scape so dotted with small pools that there seemed barely more land than water: a jigsaw of blues, buffs, and browns with little rock visible on the smooth undulations of the Barren Land. Suddenly some grey dun specks fanned out beside a lake like a small explosion; it was a little herd of caribou, smaller than flies, scared by the plane. Finally we saw the spread of Baker Lake and the broad waving band of the Thelon River, cutting its silvery course through the tundra to the west. The first sight of the settlement was of the white, red-roofed buildings of missions and stores along the lakeshore, and then, behind them, the lines of prefabricated huts where the Inuit lived, and finally the buff specks of tents on the slope above the village. The Hudson's Bay trader met the plane, with Father Choque, a stocky Frenchman in beret and mackinaw. It was Father Choque who put us up in his mission, and I learnt more from him than from anyone else about the Arctic, and learnt to respect, even if I did not agree with them, the Oblate fathers who have devoted their lives to the people of the north and who know them far better than the government officials who come and go so frequently.

The Oblate mission was a one-man establishment: tiny church, guest rooms, the Father's apartment, all under the same roof. Father Choque conducted services, kept the house tidy, cooked, made bread, cut and hauled ice for water from the lake in winter, helped with the problems of the many who come to see him (not all of them from his own flock), scanned the shore with binoculars to identify arriving planes, and maintained communication through shortwave radio with missions in the rest of the North. He had been there since 1944, longer than any other man. When he first came, no Inuit lived here. There were the Anglican and Oblate missions, the HBC and the RCMP, and the Inuit came only to trade. They lived on the Barren Land, in little groups or one or two related families, staying put in igloos during the winter. It was only in the start of the 1950s that some of them began to stay permanently at Baker Lake. In the past Father Choque would visit those outside it by dog team. In summer they would be on the move, in their skin tents, and hard to find. "Those were good days," he said sadly. In Baker Lake there was only one family which still lived on the land, and five or six families — out of 600 people — camped during the summer.

I talked with Scotty, an old hunter and trapper, who carried sewn on his coat the number by which Inuit were recognized — like convicts — by the non-Inuktituk speaking officials who lorded over them. He was 60, and this was his first summer off the land; his legs were letting him down, and there was work to be got from the Department of Transport. Normally he would go in September to kill and cache the caribou that would feed him and his dogs for the winter of trapping. He would take only tea and sugar (Inuit seemed to feel no need of salt); tea and caribou would sustain him through the winter. Often the caribou would be eaten raw, though when willows were available for fuel he would try to cook once a day. If he ran out of tea, he would drink caribou broth. Scotty trapped mainly white fox, with some wolf and wolverine; the best trapper of Baker Lake, he never went short even in the famine years, for he was ready to go far on his own in search of game, relying on his knowledge of the land and a good rifle. He believed in having the best of both old and new worlds, and boasted of possessing a dog team and *two* Skidoos.

Scotty didn't have much use for the missionairies or for the new administrators, but he thought there was good in the coming of "the law". Before the law came, he said, the Inuit hunters killed without discrimination, for excitement, slaying from kayaks with spears and later guns when the caribou crossed the rivers, and keeping pace with the herds by laying their paddles on the backs of the swimming animals. Thus many beasts not needed for food were killed each season. Like most Inuit and some white old-timers, Scotty did not accept the view of the wild-life bureaucrats that it was a vast reduction of the herds that led to the great famine of the late 1940s and early 1950s. He believed that caribou merely showed their intelligence by not returning to the places where their relatives had been killed indiscriminately, and by changing their migration routes; he firmly believed vast herds still roamed the remoter parts of the Barren Land. In the same way many Indians long refused to acknowledge the virtual destruction of the buffalo herds. But Scotty would not like to be compared with the Indians; like most Inuit, he despised them.

On walks I heard the large grey and white gulls wail. The arctic terns hovered like kestrels, dropped rapidly, and flew with sickle-winged grace. Small greyish birds flitted over the tundra with undulating flight. One morning a gyrfalcon sat for an hour on an old sleigh near the shore. The tundra was like a great dry sponge, or, even more, like a landscape of loofah: the tall lichens (pale grey and dull green) matting with alpine heather, blueberry, bearberry, and a few ferns; the tiny leaves of the miniature scrubs already turning bright red and orange. In some places were purple splashes of arctic fireweed, yellow of Arctic poppy and arnica. In the gullies going down to the lake were aged willows, two feet high, gnarled and twisted like bonsai trees.

From the mission we could just see the white cross of the cemetery up on the hilltop behind the settlement. On the way there, climbing up from the beach, we passed the one-room plywood boxes which the government first put up as Eskimo houses; the doors were open to give ventilation. Around them water stinking of sewage stood in deep puddles, where the children played. Beyond this slum of modernization, the tents — widely spaced over the tundra — seemed healthier and more appropriate to Inuit life; outside them the dogs, large, shaggy and dirty white, lay about at the end of their chains. Higher up we picked our way through bogs white with cotton grass, sometimes jumping from one spongy tussock to the next. There were berries on the minute blueberry bushes, rather tasteless, and little mauvish mushrooms and puffballs; on higher levels, pink bearberry flowers and large-cupped white heather, also cushions of minuscule pinks. The cemetery lay on a rock platform to which one climbed through defiles between piled cubical rocks. The rocks were bright with green and orange map lichens. Above us rose the tall white cross. The graves were stones piled over rough wooden boxes, with a small white wooden cross at the head of each, bearing the names of the occupants in English and Inuit syllabics — and dates of birth and death. Many small stone piles suggested the high child mortality rate of the recent past. The RC's and the more numerous Anglicans were separated even in death by a no man's land of bare rock, empty except for two uncrossed graves, said to be those of shamans who refused conversion.

Whites were called Kabluna, which meant eyebrows. Sometimes this was applied also to Inuit who had become more or less acculturated through government employment. Thus there are three Inuit groups at Baker Lake, the few acculturated and usually privileged ones, the equally few and mostly elderly ones who tried to sustain the old hunting life, and the majority who adopted much of the white way of life but without direction; a people on the way to alienation, but still a generation behind the Indians, and so not so hopeless and potentially explosive. At present they accepted too easily, with a smiling helplessness, what was done to and for them. This was obviously more pleasant for everyone than the resentful sullenness of many Indians. But was it more healthy? One got the impression that, in relation to their numbers, the government was doing far more for the Inuit than for the Indians — perhaps trying to assuage our general guilt for having neglected the Indians — but without much imagination or foresight. The creativity and imaginativness of the Inuit were being only slightly employed, and then often wrongly. This was true of much Inuit art, mechanically produced under dreary working conditions in government craft centres.

On Sunday Father Choque rang the mission bell in the morning, and with the single monotonous toll I was taken back fifty years, to the village church of my childhood. The whites gathered in little sitting room, with the geraniums blossoming in the window: the administrator's and school principal's families, some French Canadian and Irish summer workers, the nurse from Hong Kong, wearing a mantilla of black lace. We trooped into the chapel to join the Inuit. Altogether there were less than fifty of us, but the small church was full. Father Choque, in green vestments that contrasted with his daily mackinaw, conducted mass in Latin, preached in Inuktituk and English. An elderly Inuit played the harmonium, the children alternately cried and slept, a woman in front of me suckled her child.

One would have thought this simple but colourful ceremony not as alien to the Inuit as the Low Anglican service at the other end of the village, but such matters seemed to have been determined in the Arctic almost entirely by what church happened to arrive and build up loyalties first. In Baker Lake it was to the Anglican church that the people flocked at evening along the insect-ridden lakeshore, and we had difficulty squeezing into the seat at the back of the church, which held at least 200 people. Women and girls were on one side of the aisle and the men and boys on the other, while the singing was unaccompanied. Appropriately the first hymn was "From Greenland's icy mountains to India's coral shore", sung lustily and unhesitatingly, like all the other hymns. Much of the service was conducted by the old Inuit catechist, who wore a medallion on a red ribbon over his surplice. The missionary, who came direct from England four years ago with virtually no orientation, preached in halting Inuktituk, to the accompaniment of much coughing and crying, while the elder children played in the aisle with their plastic cars and airplanes, and adults assumed a look of seemly and impenetrable boredom.

On our last night in Baker Lake the phone rang at 11 pm in the HBC house, where we were drinking with the trader. The drum dance was on, the people gathering, and we went along the dark sandy road to the

I.O.D.E. hall — the hall of the Inuit community. A hundred people were seated around the great bare room. Most were Inuit; the HBC people were there, and some of the French Canadian construction workers, but none of the government people. Three old women, sitting on one of the benches, were chanting shrilly as we entered; one was a shrivelled dwarf, and the other two were enormous, but all wore shapeless berets and sealskin kamiks. The drum, about three feet across, lay in the middle of the floor; it was a single hoop of willow branch from the treeline down the Thelon River, on which stretched a caribou skin, damped with water to keep it taut. The five dancers, all middle-aged men wearing gum boots, sat on another side of the hall from the women. After a few minutes one sat up and began his performance. He held the drum in his left hand by a short handle, and beat the rim with a short stick wrapped round with a caribou skin, which gave a sharp resonant thud. He always beat upward, keeping the drum in constant motion and striking alternate edges as they came lowermost. At first he stood, bending his knees to the first slow and tentative beats. Then the speed and the rhythmic vigour of the drumming increased, the women sang more loudly, the man began to stamp and to utter loud hoarse cries. Suddenly, it was over, the drum was dropped, the man returned to his place, and we waited until the next man was ready. Even in this dingy hall, some of the magic remained to remind one of the days when this was a dance connected with the hunt; one dancer did a kind of pacing Russian dance, squatting low in his haunches, and then advancing on the audience with growls and menacing threat, suggesting the anger of the hunted bear.

When we returned to the mission, along the cold starlit track at half past one, Father Choque was still up. As we drank a nightcap, he shook his head reminiscently. The drum dance, he remarked, would never be what it was in the old days, held in mid-winter, in an igloo twenty feet across, with the beating and chanting echoing in the dome until it seemed as if the sky would fall.

The next morning Father Choque came with us to the airstrip. We were grateful for his hospitality, and for his way of slowly opening to us a mind full of knowledge and recollection. We left some money for the poor; and quietly abandoned the rest of the case of *Vat* 69 with which we had set out, as all travellers then did, to the dry Arctic; we remained indebted, but at least, as we got on the plane, we realized that Father Choque accepted us as serious inquirers instead of looking on us with the sceptical eye that had greeted us when we arrived. I remember him with the vivid respect that true men, known for however short a time, imprint on one's mind.

The other parts of the North were not lacking in human interest or in enjoyment of the natural environment. Places like Yellowknife and Whitehorse and Dawson City at the end of the 1960s formed the last edge of the Canadian frontier, harbouring the remnants of the ephemeral gold mining age, and largely populated by engaging eccentrics. The Yukon, with its deep river valleys and its blue-hazed autumn mountains, was romantically splendid. I learnt much there which I was able to use effectively in my book. Yet in the eye of memory it has quickly faded into an atmospheric background to the central human drama of that journey, which was the witnessing of a people — The People, as the Inuit called themselves — coming out of a unique way of life built on a highly specialized adaptation to the world's most rigorous environment, and forced to create a new way of living in a wholly alien setting governed by the white man's norms. Nowhere else in the world, up to this time, had I seen past and present in so stark, sad, and sudden a confrontation.

XXII

OLD AND NEW LEFTISM

B Y THE TIME WE RETURNED from our northern journey we had
travelled, since May of 1967, some twenty-five thousand miles in
Canada, apart from our travels in Europe. We were ready to settle
down for a time of undisturbed work, and that fall I immediately started
on *Canada and the Canadians*.

It was to be an exceptionally hard winter for Vancouver. By late January we had had a month of snow in a town totally unprepared for it. The
one advantage was that snow also tended to insulate me from people so
that I was less disturbed than I would normally be at this time of the
year. I was able to write quickly and with concentration, and by early
February I had sent the completed manuscript to Alan Pringle. It was a
book written with deep feeling for I was engaged in much more than
preparing a book to inform foreigners about Canada and Canadians
about their country. I was also defining my own attitudes to the land and
its people.

In twenty years I had developed feelings regarding Canada, which
were markedly different from those of the newcomer who in 1950 had
gone on the journeys that produced *Ravens and Prophets*. I found myself
involved in the troubling distinctions between nationalism and patriotism. I have never been a nationalist, and because of my criticism of the
nationalist standpoint I have incurred considerable hostility. But I found
that I had developed a feeling for Canada as a land and a culture that
bound me to it, one that implied no agression towards other lands or
other peoples, and this I recognized as patriotism and admitted it.

My patriotism has changed its emphasis over the succeeding years, as
the influence of the *genius loci* grew strong and I came to declare that I
was a British Columbian first and a Canadian second. This has not made
me less a Canadian, any more than an Appenzeller is made any less a

loyal Swiss by his deep attachment to his canton and its peculiar political traditions, but it has made me realize, more clearly than when I wrote *Canada and the Canadians*, that Canada's history and its geography predispose it to regionalism, and that the attempt to deny these deep regional urges on the part of centralist leaders has been the greatest danger to the country's unity.

I also suspect that, if I wrote a similar book today, its tone would be much less confident than that of *Canada and the Canadians*. I was writing at the end of the Pearson era, when we still believed that Canada was a potent influence for peace in world affairs, and at the time of the Centennial of Confederation and of Expo, when Canadians were pleased with themselves and exhibited a collective creativity they have not shown before or since.

The rest of 1969 was occupied with small miscellaneous projects. Pringle had been trying to urge me to write the book on Herbert Read quickly, but I felt it would be better to wait a little longer. In any case, much of 1970 would have to be devoted to my study of Aldous Huxley, so I proposed to visit England towards the end of 1969 to see Herbert's widow, Ludo, and his children, but not to complete the book on him until 1971, which would give me a chance to go through the personal papers that Herbert had sold before his death to the University of Victoria. I was now beginning to conceive a long-term view of my writing career. Over the next five or six years I planned to supplement books on Orwell, Read, Huxley and Forster with my memories of the Thirties and onwards and the book on the French novel in the twentieth century, all of them coming together to produce a panorama of the kind of influences that played on the literary world from the Thirties to the 1950s, at least as seen through the eyes of one man of letters.

These plans did not mature quite as I anticipated. I never wrote on Forster, since in the end I found myself too little in empathy with him. The book on the French novel is still half-finished, but will take final shape one of these days. But the rest have been written, and the present book largely completes the pattern I envisaged then.

The small miscellaneous projects included finishing the book on the Hudson's Bay Company, a potboiler of which I have never been proud. Because of my deep personal interest in the Himalayan regions I took much more seriously my book on the East India men in that region, *Into Tibet: The Early British Explorers*, which I wrote for the Great Travellers series. Here I was involved in the past of Tibet, but Inge and I were still deeply concerned over the present of its people, continuing to run the Tibetan Refugee Aid Society. We were distressed over the way the Left, with which in so many matters I naturally aligned myself, had refused to speak out about Chinese activities in Tibet as they were willing to do about U.S. intervention in Vietnam.

Indeed, there were many ways in which, by 1969, the acts and attitudes of the New Left were beginning to disturb me. I had started off in general sympathy with the social and political liberation that was taking place during the 1960s. My anarchism, pacifism, the environmentalism I had already adopted, predisposed me towards the counter culture, in most of its manifestations, and particularly in its call for a more simplified, natural, and freer life. I had admired the students of Paris when they broke into rebellion in 1968, with the black flag flying on the Bourse, and the skeletons of the Thirties rattling their bones in every direction. But as the months went on I began to sense a lack of positive direction in student radicalism.

I distrusted the academic system enough to agree with student criticisms of its structure and of the way it turned students into second-class members of the scholarly community, but I found nothing constructive in the alternatives they offered. I applauded their resistance to the Vietnam War, but I was appalled by the blindness with which they failed to see that the Viet Cong were cruel authoritarians. I found that their own knowledge of political traditions was so scanty that they were capable of mouthing sentences from Bakunin and Marx in the same paragraph — if they were politically educated enough to have read either. But what disturbed me most was the growing arrogance and authoritarianism of some student activists, whose tactics I often found insensitive and brutal. Their harrying of good and often radically-minded scholars reminded me of the actions of the Red Guards in China or of fascist youth in Europe during the 1930s. I began to fear that if such elements gained control of the New Left it would fall into the hands of dictatorially minded Marxists, and I wrote an article expressing my misgivings, entitled "The Ominous Politics of the Student Left", for *Saturday Night*. It involved me in arguments with Anthony West and Robert Rae, then a moderate student activist and now New Democratic Party leader in Ontario. On the other hand, I gained unexpected support from the poet Walter Bauer, a long-term leftist who himself had suffered persecution under the Nazis and whose knowledge of political movements was broad and direct.

The New Left, and student radicalism in general, faded away as important movements almost as quickly as they had emerged, since, as Bauer suggested to me, they had too little foundation in reality. They were products of middle class frustrations in the western world, to which the Vietnam War gave a focus. But as soon as the war ended, and an enduring recession began to bring a little risk once again into middle class expectations, the students mostly became conformists as they had been in the 1950s, intent on securing jobs and acquiring material trappings. Particularly in Germany and Italy, a few of the more convinced militants turned to authoritarian terrorism like that of the Red Brigades and the Baader-Meinhof groups, but, sensational as their acts may have been, they had few followers. The best of the surviving radicalism of the 1960s became diffused in anti-nuclear protest, which can still draw many people out to demonstrate against the suicidal military policies of our rulers, in feminism, and in the environmental movement. Where these trends have combined with a drive towards a greater degree of participatory democracy, as in the case of the Green Party in Germany, the best elements of 1960s radicalism have survived and found a new expression. Even the Green Party, of course, is not perfect. Its members too aim, like any other party, at gaining power, and whether its leaders if successful would be resistant to the inherent corruption of authority remains to be tested.

I took no active part in the movement of the 1960s, because it seemed so much a movement of the young that an ageing Old Leftist would have been out of place. I was willing to stand aside and watch with interest. But while I criticized as well as praised the movement, I did harbour the hope that its call to participatory democracy, which resulted in widespread and often successful civil disobedience actions on some issues, would help to halt the general progress towards centralization and the growing interference of the state in the lives of people. The 1970s were to show that hope quixotic; if anything the entrenched establishment gained added strength from the technological changes that had been proceeding through the years of protest.

Was all the enthusiasm of the 1960s then wasted? I do not think so, for what happened then showed that society is in its nature more volcanic than monolithic, and that however heavy a lid the rulers may try to impose on people's desire to live and rule their own lives, protest will always find a way to express itself and change will become inevitable even in the most rigid society, as afterwards was shown by the Solidarity movement in Poland.

XXIII

A YORKSHIRE KNIGHT

T HE WINTER JOURNEY of 1969-70 to Europe and then to India was as arduous as any we had undertaken in the past, and just as eventful. We went first to Frankfurt, and there we hired a car and set off with Inge's parents on a holiday to Spain. We went into Alsace and across the Massif Central to Bordeaux, and through the pine forests of the Landes to Bayonne. In Spain the changes that characterized the last years of Franco's regime were evident. The old towns were being surrounded by rings of new buildings, and it seemed as though more attention was being paid to housing for the working people than in some democratically governed regions of Europe, notably southern Italy. People one met in shops and restaurants were speaking more freely, and often critically of the situation in Spain, though we heard no personal criticism of Franco. A little while before we arrived in Spain I had heard from my English agent that a Spanish publisher had bought the translation rights of my book *Anarchism*, and though he was not to bring it out until after Franco's death, the very fact that he should even have contemplated the publication in 1969 was a sign how the situation in Spain had changed.

At Ciudad Rodrigo in Extremadura we crossed briefly into Portugal; it was our first and, I imagine, our last visit, for we found it, in comparison even with latter-day Francoist Spain, a depressingly poor and repressed country. Salazar had resigned the year before, but Marcello Caetano was continuing his style of government, which did not end until 1977. Unlike the tourists who at this time were flying in to Lisbon and enjoying the inexpensive resorts of the country's southern coastline, we entered from the rear, into the province of Douro. Punning aside, it was dour indeed, for the frontier officials, even compared with those of Spain, were unwelcoming; they were obviously suspicious of anyone who entered Portugal by land. Perhaps they were ashamed of what we would see.

For nowhere in Spain, even in destitute Extremadura, had we come across people still so poor that they had not footwear; even the shepherds standing in the rain of La Mancha, protected only by ragged blankets, had at least rope-soled sandals on their feet. But in this back country of Portugal there were many people, particularly women, who went barefoot. And while in Spain the Guardia Civil were now keeping a very low profile, as if they sensed the changes coming near as the Caudillo grew older, their Portuguese equivalents were still visibly active in the areas where tourists rarely came, harrying the peasants who took their oxcarts of produce into the towns.

Even to the traveller with his privileges, internal Portugal was still an uncomfortable place. Not wishing to travel through the coastal resort towns, we found even passable hotels hard to discover, for the few posadas, the equivalent of the Spanish paradors, were all full while the food everywhere was edible only as an alternative to starvation. After three days we became involved in a noisy scene with a traffic policeman in Evora, the most arrogant man I had encountered for a decade in Europe, and decided to leave Portugal. At Badajoz across the border we were relieved to be back among Spaniards whose pride demanded that they be courteous to the stranger even if at times they were inhuman to each other.

THERE WERE SO MANY people to see and so much work to do in preparation for my book on Herbert Read when we arrived in England in late October, that apart from our journey to Stonegrave we undertook no more than a day's trip to Marlow, to walk through my old school like an unrecognized ghost, to show Inge my name in gold letters on the honours board in the cloisters, and look for what I am sure was a last time on the wretched terrace house where I had spent so much of my childhood; its early Victorian brickwork, more than a century old by now, was so palpably crumbling that it was surprising the building still stood.

Read's family, when we made our journey to Stonegrave, were hospitable and co-operative. Inge and I had known Ludo Read, who was Herbert's second wife, from the occasions when we would go to their reed-thatched and whitewashed house, built to Read's own design, at Seer Green in Buckinghamshire, and then also we had met his two sons, Piers Paul the novelist and Benedict, the art historian, when they were still children. Now Ben had become Read's literary executor, and I had corresponded with him since the spring.

There were sides to Herbert Read which I, a fellow anarchist, had found incomprehensible, or at least difficult to understand. One was the curious and apparently inconsistent conformism that had led him to accept a knighthood, an honour which many English writers who were far from being anarchists had refused, for the simple reason that it placed them, as artists, on the same level as merchants or manufacturers who were being honoured because of the partisan funds they had contributed. When Herbert accepted the knighthood, he was assailed by anarchists of every kind and the little sectarian magazines hummed with righteous indignation. Only Augustus John and I refused to attack him, and even we only defended, according to the basic principles of anarchism, his right to choose; we did not defend his choice, because we did not know why it had been made.

I recognized that my friendship with Read, which extended over more than the last third of his life, but had taken place — except for a few days in Vancouver and a few days in Venice — only in the south of England which both he and I as men from north of the Trent regarded as an alien land, had not revealed to me all I should know about this withdrawn and elfin man who had been my friend as a writer and radical, but still had become by some incomprehensible alchemy Sir Herbert. I hoped to find the clues in his homeland where we had never been together, for I had left England before Herbert decided to return to Yorkshire; I knew that the clues to what many people have regarded as my own inconsistencies could only be found in my ancestral Shropshire.

We travelled north with Ben Read, the nearest in temperament among his children to the Herbert I had known. Neither Inge nor I had ever been in Yorkshire, and we were delighted with the austere grey-stone beauty of York and with the pastoral abundance of the Vale as we drove through the gold-stubbled fields to Stonegrave; I had never imagined that natural sufficiency, even abundance, extended so far north. From this point we were in the heartland of Read's inimitable account of childhood perceptions, *The Innocent Eye*. Rievaulx Abbey was a few miles from Stonegrave, and in an afternoon we travelled with Ben and Piers Paul, who had come the day after our arrival, up the dales on to the moors which in his book Read had presented as a world of the vast distances of childhood. Crumbling in a copse of blackberry vines, we saw Moon's Farm, to which near the end of his life Read had devoted a series of poems; a single window had been broken, so few were the people who came this far even to vandalize, and the stone had left a seven-pointed star of darkness. We saw the mills that Read's uncles had owned up the dales, easily accessible by car on a modern road, but at the turn of the century days of travel away. I was astonished by the excellence of their stonework, though a generation of Yorkshire weather had done more damage to them than two millenia of sunlight at Paestum. Up on the moors, where the trees had ended or sought refuge in gullies rain-scored through the peaty soil, I got out to walk over the close-packed heather, and the springy solidity of the earth-clinging mantle reminded my feet of the Canadian tundra.

All these impressions were in a sense confirmations. Ravaged though they might be by time, the abbey and the well-built mills, the dales and the moors were what I would have expected from Read's descriptions in *The Innocent Eye*. But Stonegrave itself was not even mentioned there, perhaps because it lay a little westward of the infant territory of that early book, and I found it hard at first to fit into the pattern of Read's recollections.

It was an old rectory, one of the immense structures of gold-grey stone, almost manor houses in size and style, that were built for those among the younger sons of the aristocracy who chose the church rather than the army. Under a massive archway with some crumbling escutcheon, certainly not that of the Reads who had been yeoman farmers, we entered a great flagged courtyard with deserted stable buildings on one side, their walls hairy with autumn-dull pellitory and wallflower. There were also decaying barns where, as he had told me in his letters, Herbert had tried and failed to rear pigs profitably when he first moved to Stonegrave and re-entered the rural life.

The rectory itself was a monument to the grandiosity and the physical toughness of the north country gentry in the eighteenth century when most of it was built and in the nineteenth century when it was inhabited by a succession of gentlemen clergy with enormous Victorian families. On a sunny day it was squirely to sit with the Read family, augmented by some Yorkshire cousins who volunteered the revealing information that "the Reads were always looked on as snobs in the neighbourhood", and drink our gin and eat our lunch of tender moorland lamb and look out from a room hung with Herbert's Paul Nashes and Ben Nicolsons over the flagged terrace and the great lawn with the season's last dahlias wilting in its beds and the golden vistas of the Vale of York, richly treed in comparison with the moors a few miles away. But once the sun went down in the early evenings of a northern autumn, we would cluster in small rooms, for the heating bills were becoming impossibly high by the end of the 1960s, and huddle over the diaries, letters, and uncompleted works that Herbert had not sold in Canada to pay for his gentlemanly ambitions.

Why had he felt forced to return to Yorkshire, in such grand and expensive style? Why, when his friends remonstrated that he was starving his creative work of time and energy, did he ignore us all and continue to devote himself, in paying for this great white elephant of Yorkshire stone, to pot-boiling and self-repetitive books on painting, to ephemeral but profitable lectures, and to the endless travels as the emissary of the arts that continued almost up to his death and prompted T.S. Eliot in 1963 to remark, "Nothing will ever stop your ceaseless movement over the world, I suppose?"

I began to understand when, at the end of our trip through the dales to the old mills and the outlying farms, we finally came to the original Read holdings at Muscoates, which was the setting of Herbert's childhood. When I saw it I was surprised at its meagreness. It was not a matter that the day was dull and the landscape dank and autumnal; that the present farmer had neglected the place and turned it into a jungle of tottering planks and chicken wire. It was the scale of the place, the fact that it could never have been, even in a child's eye, as it had been in Read's transfiguring imagination. He gave his early years a nobility they may never have possessed, and perhaps this was because his world collapsed so quickly when his father died and he was taken off to a depressing school for orphans in one of the drearier Yorkshire towns.

But it was not merely a matter of the need to compensate by balancing a gold infancy against a leaden boyhood. The cousin's remark about the Reads being "looked on as snobs" made me recall Herbert's accounts of his father breeding hunters and riding regularly after the fox with the local gentry, though a farmhouse like the one I was looking at would never have qualified him for the title of "gentleman farmer". Yet a gentleman he aspired to be, and so, later, did Herbert in his own romantic way. He always showed a special feeling for the age of chivalry; he was particularly attracted to Froissart, whose pages he described as "vivid with the personal radiance of men who achieve glory".

The final understanding came when, at the end of our day, we reached the church at Kirkdale which Saxon monks had built twelve centuries before. Here Herbert had gone to worship through the happier years of his childhood, and here, at the end, he wished to be buried under the shade of the slow-growing northern fir trees. I stood there and read the inscription on the gravestone: a name, and dates, and then merely the words: "Knight, Poet, Anarchist." The extraneous aspects of his life, the work to maintain his family and his pride, the journalism and the lectures, the books that popularized modern art, had all been ignored. But the central dialectic of the life was there.

I did not ask his sons who had decided on the wording of the stone, though I suspected it was Ludo, who had chosen not to accompany us. But I felt that here, in the sharp chisel lines of the grey Yorkshire stone, the whole story of my friend's life was told in three true words: if by knight we mean a man imbued with the sense of glory, and by anarchist a man imbued with the sense of freedom. The poet was central, for it was this that Read saw himself always, and where the poetic sensibility continues to operate, no matter how few the works that may technically be called poems, the sense of vocation wields an incalculable influence over a man's manner of living. It was, as I found increasingly when I finally came to write *Herbert Read: The Stream and the Source*, the poetry that for him reconciled the apparent contradiction of anarchism and knighthood.

But for him only, striving to complete his father's hopes of gentility, to justify his heritage as well as his adolescent visions of chivalry. I learnt from Read's example that my own heritage and hence the acts I could do with poetic and personal validity were different from his, however much our ideas might coincide, and when later on I was offered the Order of Canada, our local equivalent of knighthood, Read's choice helped me realize that my choice must be different. The blood of old Henry Lewis, my Baptist and radical and peasant grandfather, ran too hotly in my veins for me to contemplate with more than laughter the vision of Sir George or even George Woodcock, Companion of Canada. Yet Sir Herbert I continued to regard with affection and undiminished esteem. The anarchist he most admired, Peter Kropotkin, had after all been born a prince.

What I conceived for my book on him was the pattern of the stream in his novel, *The Green Child*, that eventually flows backward to its source. I recognized it as in keeping with his anarchism that progressive patterns did not work in considering his career or his writings; he was always in one way or another going back to the heart of the mandala. These musings also taught me much about the essential conservatism of the anarchist as a type who strives to preserve what is good and natural in human relations, and it taught me how my advance from childhood Toryism through adolescent socialism to manhood anarchism had been an upward spiral rather than an ascending plane. I had liberated myself from a conservatism of convention to emerge again at a conservatism of insight, which selected the values it wished to protect with a regard to man's due place in the natural world. Here anarchism and environmentalism coalesced as the true conservative teachings of the twentieth century.

At the same time, I was more immediately concerned with my book on Huxley, and here again I came across aspects that enabled me better to understand myself. The examination of Huxley's spiritual evolution had set me thinking about my own, and especially about the profound changes that had come to me after my heart attack in 1966. I am not in the conventional sense a religious man and am never likely to be, for the devotional inclination is not part of my nature, nor, though I have been granted epiphanies of a kind, and have experienced fleeting moments of second sight, have I ever undergone anything that might be described as a genuine mystical experience, even if at times I have envied those to whom such experiences are vouchsafed. But there are many roads to light, and the road I found myself taking was inevitably one of rational insight, leading me towards deism rather than theism. I expressed my views in a letter I wrote from England to Eve Galitzine, who was living in our house and with whom I had engaged for years in often heated discussions about the frontier at which belief becomes credulousness. Since Eve is still my cherished friend, it must have aroused her tolerance if not her respect.

"Experience, particularly at the time of my illness four years ago, taught me that man is *not* alone, and reasoning has brought me to the conclusion, given the extent of patterning in the universe that, even if believing in the existence of God (as a moving intelligence) presents certain logical difficulties, believing in His (if one must use that pronoun) non-existence poses even greater difficulties and absurdities. If nothing else, such a conclusion simplifies and serenifies life."

XXIV

TRIBULATIONS OF TIBETANS

T HE TASKS THAT FACED US in India were very different from those in England. This time we were not going to gather material for another travel book, but to deal with the practical results of that first journey in 1961, when we had become involved in the problems of the Tibetan refugees.

The situation of these exiles had reached a turning point. It was impossible to find room for all of them in the land-poor Indian foothills of the Himalayas, where most of them had been surviving in wretched conditions since their flight in 1959.

The plan now was to resettle those who could not take care of themselves into scantily inhabited areas of scrub jungle which could easily be cleared in the state of Karnataka, where a pioneer settlement had already been established at Bylakuppe. A European committee under Prince Bernhard of the Netherlands was co-ordinating an international project for this operation, which would basically solve the refugee problem, and we in the Tibetan Refugee Aid Society (TRAS) were anxious to play our part.

Our mission in India was a triple one — to take a look at the various smaller projects TRAS was already sponsoring in the Himalayan region and to confer there with the Dalai Lama, to go south and see the progress being made by the Mysore Resettlement and Development Agency, which had been created to carry out the actual work in Karnataka, and then in Delhi to try and work out a participation that might tempt the Canadian government to make a contribution.

On the way to India, we broke our journey in Athens and Istanbul. Istanbul we found a melancholy, dust grey town, the dead end of Europe rather than the beginning of Asia. Athens, on the other hand, was a much alive and in those days a sympathetic city. The great veil of pollution that now shrouds it most of the time was barely evident even as late as 1969, and though the cement works were already whitening the air at Eleusis and the refineries were starting up at Delphi, one could see far into the hills from the Acropolis and the light at evening still had that marvellously jewel-like luminosity which used to justify the title of the city of the violet crown.

I felt, as I had not done in Rome, the sense of being at the heart of an ancient tradition to which I belonged. The modern Greeks are a mixed people, very few of whom look or behave like the men and women who peopled the world of Homer and Aeschylus and Alexander. Christianity and the Turks between them eliminated the classic Greek civilization which the Romans, to their credit, had never tried to destroy even when they incorporated the Greek communities into their empire. But, in a superb revenge for its death on Hellenic soil, the Greek tradition, preserved among the Arabs and revived by the Renaissance humanists, has entered so much into European and by inheritance into North American cultures, moulding our ideas of freedom into something concrete and immediate, that for me to go to Athens is to visit one of the holy springs that have fed my faith. I climbed the Acropolis, and looked on the tall broken monuments and out beyond them to the wooded slopes of Hymettos with an intensity of feeling that was almost like the pietistic emotion of a pilgrim.

Crete I found almost wholly alien. The reconstruction of the great Palace at Knossos had given it the appearance of a giant public urinal, but I had a suspicion that Arthur Evans, who supervised this massive work of piecing together a past before writing, had not been entirely to blame. Everything I saw of the ancient Cretan civilization struck me as florid and vulgar, a kind of antique circus world, and contemporary Crete, represented by Heraklion, where they were busily pulling down the fine Venetian buildings of the old Candia and replacing them by rawly jerrybuilt apartments, repelled me even more.

Autumnal Delphi, on the other hand, empty of tourists, projected a sense of great spiritual potency, as if it were a true power centre, and perhaps some of the power clung, for I dipped my tired feet in the clear trickle of the Castalian Spring, and not many months afterwards I began to write poetry again. But Mycenae seemed to the most potent place of all, as we listened to the living silence that followed the echoes in the great darkness of the Treasury of Atreus and stood on the citadel walls, guessing we were near the spot where Agamemnon was slaughtered and, looking south, recognized the break in the hills through which he must have come up from Argos on the day of that fateful homecoming.

WHEN WE FLEW INTO DELHI, the dung fires were being lit for the evening meals and their blue smoke lay flat over the landscape. There were camel carts on the roads and a couple of elephants padding along. Then, moving through the wide streets and around the traffic circuses of New Delhi, we were back in the bland green ambiance which the British had created when they took over the city of the Moslem dynasties.

We had hardly settled in than James George, whom we had first met in Colombo almost a decade before, came round to our hotel. We had kept in touch over the years, and now he was Canada's High Commissioner in India, where his interest in Buddhism had led him to develop strong ties with the Tibetan community and to take their interests as much to heart as we had done. He and Carol insisted that we move into the High Commission and make it our headquarters for the time we would be staying in India and, after the three conventional refusals of Asian good manners, we accepted gladly.

The High Commission was then situated in an old imperial mansion in the expansive British Indian style on Aurangzebe Road, which is now merely the residence of the High Commissioner. In those days a green padded door divided the domestic from the official part of the High Commission and also divided our life there. On the domestic side of the door there was a shady flagstoned courtyard around which the guest quarters were arranged: a series of small apartments, each with a bedroom, sitting room and a bathroom, furnished with the artifacts the Georges had gathered in their long peregrinations over Asia; we could be as solitary or as social as we wished, for the Georges were the easiest of hosts.

We always met for breakfast, where there would usually be two or three Tibetan lamas with whom the Georges had been going through meditational exercises on the roof, from which we quietly absented ourselves, but the evenings were the most pleasant times, when we met on the lawn under the great old jacaranda and peepul trees into which, as the light intensified and the colours grew more luminous just before sunset, the parakeets would come in like flights of green arrows from the countryside where they had been feeding and settle noisily to roost for the night. There, over our drinks and later at dinner, we would talk. The Georges were interested in mystical religion, from Sufism to the more esoteric forms of Mahayanist Buddhism, and towards the end of our stay they tried to persuade us to enter their meditational circles and become pupils of their favourite lamaist gurus. But both of us have always shied away instinctively from that kind of mental subordination as we have from drugs, sensing a similar abdication of personality, and we politely evaded involvement, though we have continued to be assiduous students of Buddhism as we believe it to have been preached and practiced by the Buddha himself.

The discussions about Canadian involvement in Tibetan aid took place beyond the green door, in Jim's big ambassadorial office, and there it was extraordinary how not only the atmosphere but also the personalities seemed to change. East of the door, in the residence, Jim was a relaxed and open person, informally clad and talking with great humour and ease on a vast variety of subjects. But beyond the door he became what I have always imagined the perfect diplomat to be, impeccably dressed for the Delhi winter, watching everyone carefully through eyes that had become strangely hooded, and speaking with a neatly fused mixture of candour, courtesy, and circumspection.

Part of the time the two of us negotiated with a Dutchman named Brouwer, a tough former resistance fighter who was the representative of Prince Bernhard's committee in Europe, and with Bill Davinson, the Anglo-Indian retired army officer whom we had encountered some years before working among the Tibetan settlements near Dehra Dun and who was now the director in India of the Mysore Resettlement and Development Agency. Brouwer and Davinson had realized that in settling the Tibetans in the jungle of South India, a situation might emerge in which tribesmen and other poor Indians would be worse off than the resettled Tibetans and regard them as unwelcome intruders. Brouwer tried to push me into agreeing that any Canadian contribution would be entirely devoted to programs for Indians in the region. I refused to consider this, since I represented a society whose very title showed that it was devoted to helping Tibetans, and it was agreed to leave the detailed breakdown of the Canadian contribution until we had actually visited the settlements. Meanwhile, concocting cables on the domestic side of the High Commission which he then despatched from the official side of the green door in his diplomatic persona, Jim George and I managed to convince Maurice Strong, who was then director of the Canadian International Development Agency (CIDA), that the Mysore settlements represented the most important step to date towards a resolution of the Tibetan refugee problem.

We were already starting our visits to existing Tibetan settlements. An Englishwoman was on her way to Mussoorie in a battered army surplus truck in which she moved from one Tibetan group to the other spreading sensational stories of widespread sickness and starvation which never turned out to be true. Ernest Wiederkehr, the head of Schweizer Tibethilfe was also on his way to the Hills, and the four of us crammed into the uncomfortable front seat of the vehicle, in which the Englishwoman was transporting supplies for the Tibetan Homes Foundation. It was a tiring, sometimes hazardous journey, for there were unexpected torrential rains between Meerut and Dehra Dun, and the roads were covered with a kind of slippery gumbo; the tires of the truck were worn completely smooth, and for several miles we slithered from side to side of the road, expecting every moment that the truck would either overturn or slide — unstoppable — into an approaching vehicle or, worse, into a herd of cows and involve us in the one unforgiveable Indian crime, the killing of a sacred animal. But somehow our driver succeeded in riding out all her skids and in coaxing her ancient vehicle up the steep lacets from Dehra Dun to Mussoorie and to the guest cottage in Happy Valley which Mrs. Taring has ready for us.

There was little to trouble us at Mussoorie, where the Tarings ran an efficient operation on little money, and when we remembered the sad waifs we had seen in 1961, we were pleased to see healthy and happy children. With students from the residential school, orphans in the Pestalozzi style small homes, house parents, a group of old people, and all the indeterminate poor relations and other hangers-on who gather around any Asian situation of this kind, the population was almost two thousand. The centre, the bright omphalos, was the temple Jigme Taring had designed and built, with the help of old exiled craftsman, according to the canons of traditional Tibetan religious architecture. It was alive with all the strong colouring of painted carved wood, brilliant religious scrolls, and gleaming gilt and silver that meant so much to the Tibetans in their austere mountain landscapes.

On the hillsides around the temple were scattered the many buildings where the Tibetans lived and especially the old British villas that had been transformed into 25 homes for children. Our own society had by now provided three homes for 75 children and was sponsoring 120 children as a contribution to running costs. We had also built a dispensary and a home for old people, and in all this we had accumulated a store of merit in Tibetan eyes that must be repaid, remotely by Karmic benefits, but directly by hospitality, which at times seemed more a punishment than a reward. One afternoon we visited a dozen homes, and at each politeness demanded we accept a bowl of buttered tea, a greasy concoction prepared with soda and salt which is more like a soup than a beverage. I felt dyspeptic for days afterwards and wondered how Tibetan livers could stand up to it.

Our aid in this sub-Himalayan area was not restricted to Mussoorie. Down the hill at Rajpur we were building classrooms for a group of Sakya monks who were educating the local children, and at a settlement at Campbelltown near Dehra Dun we were involved in developing a vocational training centre.

But our interests spread into more isolated places, like Puruwala, in the foothills about forty miles from Dehra Dun, where the Sakya Lama, one of the five great hierarchs of Tibet, had set up his headquarters in an old zamindar's grange. Because there was no highway to Puruwala, we travelled there by jeep. It was a rough drive, over humpy jungle tracks where the branches lashed at us as the jeep drove between the trees, and for about three miles over the gravel of a dry river bed; the road, we gathered, was impassable during the monsoon rains.

The Sakya Lama himself came out of his grange to greet us, a much more exotic figure than the Dalai Lama. He was a fat man with a coarse intelligent face, his hair plaited around his head and big jade earrings hanging from his long lobes; he wore a robe of gold brocade and embroidered felt boots in the old Tibetan manner. At the lunch of chicken and pork and vast mounds of rice and vegetables that was served immediately he ate copiously; it was evident that he had no intention of missing the good things of the world. He told us that, according to the traditions of the Sakyas, and unlike the Dalai Lama and the leaders of the other major sects, he was not a monk. He was a layman credited with spiritual powers and learned in the lore of Buddhism, a sacred king rather than a pontiff. His position was hereditary, passing alternately through two related lines, so that not his son but his grandson would eventually succeed him after an intervening incumbent from the other lineage. Keeping the succession going meant that he would shortly have to marry, a prospect he did not seem to relish. Since coming out of Tibet he had learnt to speak English fluently and, he confided to me, he greatly admired the works of Lewis Carroll. It seemed strange to be discussing the March Hare and the Mad Hatter with this mediaeval Asian potentate within view of the snow peaks of the Himalayas, but there is no doubt that the Sakya Lama had capably grasped the realities of the western world, and was using them to do the best he could for the thousand or so lay followers and monks who had gathered around him. He put forward a well-thought out scheme for buying a little more land and starting a dairy herd, and eventually we helped him with it.

The Sakya Lama's settlement in Puruwala was typical of the relatively small groups of devotees who gathered around respected religious leaders where land could be found in the northern foothills. Such groups were usually well-run, for the monasteries of Tibet — like the abbeys of mediaeval Europe — had been efficient economic units and some of the expertise acquired in the past had been transplanted to India. But there was not much room in the north for such settlements to be either large or numerous.

The settlements in Karnataka were different. They were planned to include Tibetans of all kinds and from all areas, brought together in groups of five or six thousand people each. The construction of the settlements was to be financed by various foreign agencies co-ordinated by Brouwer, and supervised by Davinson and his Indian staff at the Mysore Resettlement and Development Agency, and their operations directed by the Dalai Lama's delegates until co-operatives could take them over.

Bangalore was the centre of operations, and it was there we went after we returned to Delhi. Bangalore is — as Indian cities go — my favourite. It has not the disadvantages of size, overpopulation, and widespread poverty that mar Calcutta and Bombay; it is not a soulless bureaucratic capital like Delhi; or perpetually humid like Madras. It lies high enough on the edge of the Deccan for the winter climate to be dry, sunny, and relatively cool, it is green with parks and gardens, and has harmonized the European and the Asian.

Davinson was there when we arrived to arrange for our journey to the Tibetan settlements, of which one was settled, at Bylakuppe, and two others, in the Kauvery valley and at Mundgod, were being organized. One of Davinson's Christian clerks accompanied us on what turned out to be a difficult journey. Our car was so decrepit that by night, after we had looked at Bylakuppe and arrived at the Kauvery valley, it was incapable of being coaxed any further by its dour old Moslem driver. However, there was a young contractor at the Kauvery valley camp who had managed to buy an English car from some departing consul, and he offered to take us the rest of our journey, to Mundgod, which was a good way north and then back to Bangalore. But his car proved little more reliable than the Moslem's old wreck. In a village region far from any town, where the roads were dense with herds of cattle moving towards a local fair, we had a flat tire. We took the spare wheel out of the trunk, and found it was also flat. All the village could produce was a bicycle pump with no tube, and it was only the luck of a pilgrimage bus driving through the village that enabled us to get at least one tire into shape to carry on to the nearest tourist bungalow.

Apart from these mishaps, our journey revealed to us an extraordinary act of mass adaptation to alien circumstances. Nothing could have been less like either the fertile high valleys or the bald steppes of Tibet than the hot scrubby jungles of the Mysore hills, where the most profitable crops were not the barley and apricots of high altitudes but maize and — if there were water enough — rice. More difficult even to deal with than unfamiliar crops was unfamiliar wildlife. Wild pig were common, and had to be fenced out, since the Buddhist Tibetans were disinclined to hunt and kill them. Even worse were the wild elephants, whom the Tibetans had no idea how to handle. In the early days they would surround them with flaming torches and beating drums, which meant that the animals would become angry and break destructively out of the fiery and noisy circle. Quite a few settlers were killed before they learnt that it was much less costly in lives to employ the local tribesmen who had their own tried and tested ways of discouragement.

But the Tibetans are active, surprisingly flexible, and receptive to new ways of living, particularly when one considers the conservatism of their society which had continued for centuries virtually unchanged within its mountain barriers. Some were nomads from the high plateaus who had never done anything but herd yaks and cattle. There was a whole encampment of them in the settlement of Mundgod, heavy-chested and bright-cheeked mountain people who still clung to traditional woolen garb in the southern climate and who lived in a group of rough grass-covered huts with prayer flags fluttering raggedly among them. But these rough untutored people perhaps adapted best, for since they were completely ignorant of farming, they were willing to listen and to learn from instruction, while the former barley and wheat farmers from the southern valleys of Tibet first had to unlearn their old methods. In the early days it was the rapidly adapting nomads who raised the best crops of maize.

There was a strange symbiosis between the settlers and those who settled them, for Davinson gathered around him the people he knew he could trust most of all, fellow Christians and army and navy officers, most of them Anglo-Indians like himself. Often they were throwbacks to the Raj. The head of one settlement was a former brigadier, a prime caricature of everything military. He would pace in a starched khaki suit like the uniform he had once worn, a swagger stick under his arm and enormous moustaches jutting out each side of his face below his monocled eye as he delivered barking British orders and equally barking comments on the shortcomings of his charges. But, comic as they sometimes seemed, Davinson's recruits were dedicated men and they were inspired by that tradition of incorruptibility which the Indian army inherited from its British predecessor, and which in India, if one has a chance of dealing with an army man or a civil servant, led one always to pick the army man. I always found it an anomaly that in Gandhi's country a pacifist like me should feel more confidence in dealing with soldiers than with civilians.

We ended our tour of the southern settlements confident that we had seen the start of a scheme that in a few years would end the problem of the Tibetan refugees. After our return to Bangalore we sat down with

Davinson and worked out a plan for our participation in a further settlement, a plan whose magnitude seemed astonishing when we remembered our initial gift of $700 to put the roof on the Mussoorie school.
Now we were planning to raise and spend about $650,000, for which we
would be able to build the settlement's school and hospital (leaving
other agencies to equip them), put up 160 double housing units (a third
of those that would be needed) and provide their water supply. We
would then have enough left over to spend $100,000 on agricultural
equipment, $70,000 on subsidiary industries, and to satisfy Brouwer by
contributing $150,000 as a quarter of the cost of Davinson's scheme for
providing tube wells and tractor pools for neighbouring underprivileged
Indian communities.

HAVING SETTLED ALL THIS, we flew via Madras, which was unsea-
sonably flooded and insect-ridden, and Calcutta, where Communist
bands were harmlessly roaming the streets, to Katmandu, where we
wanted to assess the possibility of helping Tibetan refugees in Nepal.
Katmandu at that time was an unsettling place because of the exaggerated importance which the world powers then attached to it. All the
major countries had embassies there, which were mainly listening posts,
and the listening seemed to go on everywhere, so that if one were talking
in a hotel lobby one would always be aware of the open ears of girls in
travel desks, lounging porters, or nondescript little men (most Nepalis
are nondescript to alien eyes because of the drab darkness of their dress)
who would hang around in every place where Europeans were to be
seen. I realized how far this situation had gone when the Pakistani representative of the United Nations High Commissioner, whom we con-
sulted about the Tibetans there, insisted that we meet neither in our
hotel room nor in his office, both of which were bugged, but in his car,
which he drove around himself, having sent his chauffeur home for the
day.

The Chinese were especially noticeable in Katmandu, always dressed
in the drab utility suits they wore in those days in imitation of Mao
Tse-tung. We would even encounter them on the sacred hilltop of
Swayambu, with its multitude of Hindu shrines and its big Tibetan temple where twelve-foot long horns boomed and the bells and gongs
clashed in a service that was being held by the red-robed and red-hatted
monks to celebrate the arrival in Katmandu of Karmapa, the leader of
their sect.

The Chinese had built a paved highway from Katmandu to the border, and one day a young Swiss who was working at his country's refugee
rehabilitation centre in Katmandu offered to drive us along it. Hofer

came in his Beetle with a dreamily beautiful blonde called Ida, a Swiss nurse who had been working her way across Asia and whose languor, as she freely proclaimed, was due to the hashish she could buy so freely in Nepal.

Hofer too must have been partaking before he joined us, and this probably explained a bizarre mishap. We had climbed out of the valley of Katmandu and over the masking foothills, so that now we saw before us the line of the Himalayan peaks. It was in this region of terraced hillsides and far snowy ranges that we came on one of those groups of rocks which drivers in India and Nepal will place around a stalled truck to divert the traffic. The truck in this case had gone, but the stones were still there, and Hofer, evidently unconscious of their presence, drove straight ahead. There was an ominous thud beneath the car. We took no notice of it until we stopped to look at a view and noticed that the oil was dripping steadily away. A passing motorist suggested we drive on to a road camp where he was sure we would get help.

We soon got to the road camp, which was Chinese. Inside we could see drably uniformed men sitting at tables and talking under vast portraits of Mao and Stalin. There was a Chinese soldier with a submachine gun outside the gate; Hofer stopped the car and asked him a question in Nepali. The soldier, who did not understand, put on an expression of suitable ferocity for dealing with red-haired foreign devils, pointed his gun at us, and with an imperious gesture threatened to sweep us away.

I realized that this must be the camp where a few months earlier James George had been stoned; where my old journalistic acquaintance Frank Moraes, then editor of the *Times of India*, had been roughed up by the Chinese workers, who smashed his photographer's camera. We hurriedly turned back to Khatmandu, not knowing what we would do when the oil ran out. Luckily we passed a potter with a great net of terra-cotta crocks on his back. We bought one for a few pence and contrived to hang it under the oil tank, stopping every now and then to pour the drippings back. In this way we got to Bhatgaon, one of Katmandu's two sister towns in the valley. It was then I learnt the power of advertising even in a small country like Nepal. The attendant at the gas station told us he had no oil. There was a poster for Mobiloil and I pointed this out. He grinned; "Ah, but you asked for oil, not Mobiloil," and happily filled up.

Katmandu was too spoiled a town for my liking, shoddily half-westernized and full of the Europeans I do not admire — diplomats and spies, bureaucratic representatives of relief agencies, and a horde of parasitic hippies, who went there for cheap dope and were prepared to beg even from Nelapis, who were a degree worse off than Indians. We were not even successful in arranging aid for the Tibetans. Those around

Khatmandu were not badly off, for they were attached to craft centres that also exported carpets for good prices to Switzerland. The people who really needed help were nomads in the hinterland, inaccessible except by treks that would have taken us weeks to complete. In any case the Nepali government insisted that all aid go through official channels, which meant that it would be vulnerable to pilfering by a notoriously corrupt bureaucracy, and we found no one we could trust to make sure our funds were well spent — or spent at all — on the refugees.

We much preferred Bhatgaon and Patan, which had the same warm red brick buildings and temples with carved wooden gatehouses but were almost entirely unvisited by the tourists, so that one could wander solitarily — or sometimes guided by friendly children — through mazes of courtyards filled with the workshops of smiths, weavers, cabinet makers, and a multitude of Buddhist or Hindu shrines. Some of the latter were gruesome little places, hung with the entrails of freshly sacrificed animals from which the flies rose in buzzing swarms.

What we failed to see was the mountain hinterland between the valley of Katmandu and the Tibetan border, of which we heard much from Peter Aufschnaiter. Aufschnaiter was Heinrich Harrer's companion on the escape from a British prison camp in northern India which Harrer described in *Seven Years in Tibet*. But while Harrer chose a career in the west, where he profited from the romance attached to old Tibet and the tragedy of its downfall, Aufschnaiter elected to stay in the mountains he had learnt to love, and settled in Nepal. He resembled an old Alpine guide, white-haired, fresh-complexioned, a look of candour in clear blue eyes that seemed habituated to the stare of vast distances. We sat with him one afternoon on the terrace of an apartment he had in the Swiss Centre outside the capital, and birds of bright colours fidgeted in the trees.

Aufschnaiter remained a mountaineer, transferring his loyalties from the Alps to the Himalayas. He had earned his living doing surveys for the Nepalese government in the high ranges; now that he had abandoned such work, he still went each summer for his own satisfaction into the remoter regions which, as a Nepalese citizen, he was allowed to visit, taking with him an entourage of three porters and a cook and wandering into the areas where the people still maintain the ancient Tibetan shamanist religion known as Bon. Though he was in his sixties, he regularly travelled at between 15,000 and 16,000 feet above sea level and found no difficulty going to 18,500 feet; kept near earth by my bad heart, I deeply envied him. He seemed a free and happy man, and though he enjoyed talking with us about his native Austria, he obviously had no desire to return to live in his homeland, where the highest mountains would seem mere hills to him.

BACK IN DELHI JIM GEORGE and I put the finishing touches to our project for Canadian aid to the Tibetans, which was substantially accepted by Maurice Strong at CIDA. A few days later, at six in the morning, Inge and I set off to northwestern India, to visit the Dalai Lama and the smaller settlements located in the foothill regions of Himachal Pradesh. Delhi was still sleeping — it is one of the world's latest rising great cities — when our Sikh driver took us out into the Haryana countryside over which the dawn was breaking, dimly revealing the villages of mud-walled houses that seemed to grow out of an earth the same colour.

We drove through the Punjab, winter drab between crops and monotonously flat, like a featureless part of the prairies. About mid-day we got our first distant view of the Himalayas. Everything went well until we began to enter the mountainous country, going up from Pathankot into the Kangra hills towards Dharamsala. There our driver, a man of Delhi and the plains, began to seem anxious. By Macleodganj, the little bazaar before the steep hillsides where the Dalai Lama and his entourage live, he was in such a funk that we had to halt and send a messenger to get one of the Dalai Lama's drivers to fetch us.

The Dalai Lama had moved out of the old British bungalow with its leaking tin roof, where we had paid our earlier visits to him, into a new building which the Tibetans called the Palace, though it was really a large villa with some offices attached, surrounded by a high barbed-wire fence with a guard post at the entrance gate where a policeman who could hardly speak English laboriously took down the particulars from our passports. As we went in there was a changing of the guard, and twenty Himachal Pradesh police in khaki uniforms filed in to relieve their colleagues around the perimeter. Plain-clothed guards wandered about on the paths. Clearly the Indian government regarded the Dalai Lama as a high risk guest.

His Holiness, who had clearly been watching out for us, came halfway down the verandah to greet us, a signal honour in terms of Tibetan protocol, which he extended by speaking the whole time in English although both his secretary and his interpreter were present. He had just come out of a month's retreat, and had emerged, to our surprise, in fighting political mood. Indeed, we were conscious of a perceptible diminution of the spiritual intensity that he had seemed to emanate as recently as six years ago: it was as if coming to his thirties had made him more sharply aware of the temporal aspects of his role, an evolution which had taken place in his predecessor, the Great Thirteenth, when he made his decisive break with the Chinese in the 1920s.

Since as early as 1969 there were already rumours of tentative negotiations going on with the Chinese government relating to the Dalai Lama's return to Lhasa, I was impressed to hear him declare that the national traditions and also the skeleton of a political organization, with the necessary political symbols, must be kept alive outside Tibet because the Tibetans within their own country had not accepted communism. Not a single Tibetan had become a leading Communist and the young had shown themselves even more opposed that the old people who remembered the pre-Chinese past; there had been new attacks in recent months on Chinese posts and columns.

For this reason he believed immigration to Canada and Switzerland was important for the future of Tibet and the Tibetan people. "A tree with one root is never secure; a tree with three roots is better equipped to survive the storms." By this he meant that if the Tibetan exiles were confined to India, their traditions would be at the mercy of that country's uncertain future; in Canada and Switzerland they might be subject to social influences, but not nearly as much to political pressures. He seemed pessimistic about India's future, and even more so about that of Nepal, where he thought the people foolishly accepted Communist promises at face value. He thought that China would soon either invade Nepal or gain hidden power there. But in the long term he was not pessimistic. He believed that "the human mind is stronger than steel," a remark which reminded me that though the Buddhists do not believe in the existence of a human soul, they set great store in the mind, to such an extent that "mindfulness" can perhaps be regarded as the principal Buddhist virtue.

And mindfulness was certainly much in the Dalai Lama's thoughts as he asked our help in a new direction. "After the belly is full," he remarked, "it is time to look after the head." When the physical needs of the Tibetan refugees had been met — as he was sure they would be by the resettlement projects — we should begin to think of their cultural needs.

As Jim George had warned me to expect something of this kind, I had my answer ready. I agreed with him, but I also remarked that westerners also had cultural needs, and that the wisdom of all peoples should be available for common enlightenment. I had already suggested to him in 1964 the possibility of creating a college where scholars from Tibet and the west could study together. It was time not merely to preserve what important texts had survived the destruction of the Tibetan past, not merely to ensure that young Tibetans were kept aware of their great tradition, but also to make those treasures available to the world by translation, publication, and illustration, and to reveal the wisdom that had long been secreted in remote monasteries. There might be times when knowledge should be hidden, but every kind of knowledge was ultimately of benefit to mankind and other suffering beings and had its time for revelation. The Dalai Lama agreed, and from the friendship, rather than mere friendliness, with which he gave us as we parted a little thanka of the preaching Buddha, I think he meant it.

But nothing came of the suggestion, since the powerful lamas among his entourage were interested only in reassembling a replica of their ceremonial past. They did not intend to share their wisdom with the world, though they recognized the advantages — often pecuniary — of acquiring western disciples. They believed, like their predecessors, that knowledge is power, and must not be given up easily. I was not surprised. The Dalai Lama I had long recognized as a man of unusual insight and intellectual courage marooned among people who had learnt little from Tibet's misfortune. This was why in the minds of many ordinary Tibetans we met, and even of westerners who had long associated with them, we would find a sharp distinction between the entity called "Dharamsala", by which was meant the ecclesiastical and political power structure that had reconstructed itself in exile, and the Dalai Lama himself, whom they called "Kunden" (the presence) and who represented the best aspects of Mahayanist Buddhism.

The return to Delhi was uneventful except for one of those incidents of Indian travel which then I thought of as a quaint archaicism, though recent events in the Punjab have made me see differently. We drove through the industrial towns of Jullundar and Ludhiana with their bustle of small industry, and across the farmlands we noticed how modernized farming had become compared with the rest of India; then, on the road to Ambala, there came a strange irruption from the past.

A company of horsemen came clattering down the road, with blue and gold banners, lances raised up, their turbans bright blue and gold and decorated with silver emblems, wearing long embroidered mediaeval coats, carrying swords on their sides, round shields of shining iron on their backs, their faces often covered with orange or blue scarves. Some were old men with white beards, others beardless boys, but all had a look of deliberate ferocity, perhaps induced by the *bhang* to which they were addicted.

These were the Nihangs, last remnants of the suicide squads of the Sikh armies, religious fanatics who now spent their lives on perpetual pilgrimage from one *gurudwara* to the next. For miles afterwards the stragglers followed, old men riding sedately on horses less spirited than the wild ponies which the leaders rode, some men too poor for horses who rode on bicycles, but still with spear, sword and shield, and bringing up the rear as of a small army, the bullock wagons, attended by walking spearmen, which bore the baggage and stores of the pilgrims. It was like an incursion from the world of the Moghul artists, except for the bicycles totally mediaeval, and undoubtedly the Nihangs aroused feelings of nostalgia and guilt in the hearts of their co-religionists, for our Sirdarji, a Delhi man whose car had replaced the horses of his warrior ancestors, looked at them rather sadly as they passed by, and remarked, "Those are *real* Sikhs!" More than a decade later, when the Punjabi troubles began that culminated in the invasion of the Golden Temple and the assassination of Mrs. Gandhi, I remembered this strange procession.

XXV

MEMORIES LOST AND FOUND

THE WINTER OF 1970 was one of those idyllic Pacific Coast seasons that occur occasionally and so impress one that they are seen as typical of Vancouver, whereas most winters there have their weeks of snow, and sometimes of hard, bitter frost. But in 1970 the spring did come early with the daffodils blooming in February. The propitious mood continued when in April the Canada Council granted me a Killam Award of $10,500 to write my book on Herbert Read. I therefore decided to concentrate on Huxley and Read. My urge to write something new on India was satisfied when Frank Kermode invited me to do a volume on Gandhi for the Modern Masters series of small monographs which he was editing for joint publication in England and the United States.

Not only did I find the Huxley book complicated, but one that involved me deeply, though in a different way from my books on Orwell and Read. They had both been close friends, while Huxley I had encountered only once in the flesh. But his early intellectual influence on me had been enormous, and in considering the evolution of his thought I found that I was perpetually challenging myself. For it was more difficult to write on someone whose shifts in perspective had once struck me with dismay, than on writers like Orwell and Read with whose ideas and even whose ways of expressing them I had remained in basic sympathy.

Essentially, in facing Huxley, I was dealing with the Lost Leader syndrome. For me he had once appeared the intellectual liberator. I even found myself politically on the same side; like him I elected for a militant anarcho-pacifism rather than for the more fashionable Marxist doctrines of the 1930s.

And then had come, in 1936, the novel — *Eyeless in Gaza* — in which Huxley seemed to abandon all the broad intellectual questing of his earlier years and narrow his perspective to an investigation of man's relation with God. For years, noting the steady decline in his artistic powers that seemed linked to his "conversion" (as had happened also with Tolstoy) I felt betrayed by the light-bearer of my youth. But by the time I began to write *Dawn and the Darkest Hour* my ideas had evolved enough for me to undertake that wrestling with the angel which the book in fact became. In the process of reassessing Huxley's intellectual development I noted that the changes which had taken place in his attitude to the spiritual quest had in no way made him a social or a political reactionary. Rather they were accompanied by remarkable pre-visions regarding world problems. Huxley accepted the transforming power of non-violent revolution long before the Civil Rights movement, by the skilful use of mass disobedience, changed the shape of American society in the 1960s. When they were still unrecognized as acute world problems, Huxley was warning about population growth, the coming exhaustion of our non-renewable resources, the destruction of the environment. As early as the late 1930s he had provided a bridge between the anarchists of the past and the radicals of the post-World War II generation by sketching out ideas of a decentralist society where the perils of monolithic industry and monolithic government might both be avoided.

As earlier in my books on Proudhon and Orwell — and later in my book on Herbert Read — I was discovering how much an autobiographical element enters any biography, even if it is mainly concerned with tracing the subject's ideas and his artistic development. One chooses one's subjects, like one's friends, because of intellectual or temperamental affinities, and half-consciously the images of them that emerge become mirrors in which one's own nature is partially revealed, so that in them one can recognize one's hidden motives and masked failings. One proceeds in self-knowledge by knowing others; one clarifies one's ideas by trying them against those of others. There may even be a healing function, as I remarked in a letter to James George during the summer, when I had once again moved into a period of excessive work and I was feeling the strain.

By November I finished *Dawn and the Darkest Hour* and sent it off to Faber. I had not been working wholly on Huxley, for my usual need for variation had led me into writing a dramatic adaptation of Zamiatin's dystopian novel *We*, which Robert Chesterman produced on CBC radio. I had also been writing regular reviews for *The Toronto Star* since the beginning of the year, and in the autumn Emile Capouya invited me to become a reviewer for the *Nation* in New York; I continued this assignment for several years, since Capouya gave me as much space as I wanted, so that often I was writing essays rather than reviews.

LATE IN THE YEAR Inge and I took a brief interlude from writing and pottery and went to Ottawa and Montreal on various missions. In Ottawa I was involved with Northrop Frye and Malcolm Ross in jurying applications to the Canada Council for literary grants, a task I did not relish because as I sat there pondering imponderables I realized how far, as three elderly critics, we were removed in spirit from many of the younger poets and novelists whom we were judging. I felt this so strongly that later I refused to serve on any more juries of this kind, since I believed that with the best will in the world they could not choose effectively among the writers who most needed grants; afterwards, when I was invited to participate, I replied that I preferred to leave my place on the jury to a younger writer.

When we arrived in Montreal, where I was to receive my D.Litt. from Sir George Williams University, the city was still under the shadow of the October Crisis of 1970, that tragic, appalling occasion when the Canadian government allowed itself to be scared by a couple of cells of terrorist fanatics — who had imagined they could strike a blow for the freedom of Québec by depriving others of their freedom — into a massive abrogation of civil liberties under the War Measures Act. The soldiers standing fully armed at the street corners and at the entrances to public buildings gave Montreal the appearance of a city ruled by a frightened dictator, which Pierre Trudeau had at that time allowed himself to become. Though I had no sympathy with the shabby terrorists who had provoked the situation, I felt at one with the ordinary Québecois who bitterly resented what amounted to a military occupation of their cities by the foreign power that Canada had temporarily become, an occupation whose enormity was aggravated by the arrest of hundreds of the province's citizens, against whom no specific charges were ever laid, merely because they had been outspoken advocates of separation from Canada. The situation was made more ironical by the fact that in his radical youth, Trudeau had admitted that a true federalism implied the right to secede. Theoretically, of course, Trudeau's measures were taken in response to specific terrorist acts, but they were so exaggerated that they became a Draconian attack on the legitimate aspirations of Québeckers who six years later elected a separatist government under René Lévesque, which would probably never have happened if Trudeau had not reacted so extremely in 1970.

Thus the Sir George Williams convocation ceremonies became something different from the usual display of pageantry and pomposity. Bryce Mackasey, a member of the federal cabinet which had approved the invocation of the War Measures Act, was among the other people being honoured, and this seemed to confer a special vulnerability on all of us.

The ceremonies took place in a large, shabby theatre, and Mackasey was placed beside me on the platform. He was a typical North American Irish politician, full of bluster, blarney, and bad jokes, but also alertly defensive in the manner of insecure men who go into politics as a way of proving themselves. On that day the defensiveness was especially evident and, sitting next to Mackasey, I was aware how nervously his eyes flickered over the theatre's galleries, excellent vantage points for taking a pot shot at the stage. Naturally, I was as apprehensive as he. What if an assassin did appear and he turned out to be a bad shot? I would be next to the bull's eye. I decided on the first sign of trouble to forget all dignity and flop to the ground behind the podium. Not a word of such fears was said on the platform, but the tension was evident as we watched student after student coming up to the platform, and wondered what might be hidden under the academic gowns. Nothing happened of course, but for the first time in Canada I had a real sense of social evil.

I HAD BEEN GLAD to finish the book on Huxley, partly because it had taken so long to get into shape, but also because I had been struggling with my own depressions, and using my work on the book to dissipate them. I felt a sudden release, and went on with alacrity to the long introduction to the edition of Melville's *Typee* which I was preparing for Penguin, and to the book on Gandhi, which I wrote quickly and with much zest.

So much of my attitude to life and to politics had been shaped by Gandhi's influence, as it still is, that I wrote with a confident intimacy, while the restrictions of space forced me to write concisely and sharply. The comparison of Gandhi's India to the India I had known forced me to consider Gandhi in a double relation, towards India and towards the world. The conclusions I reached were two: that ever since independence successive Congress Party governments of India have systematically moved away from Gandhi's vision of an agrarian, non-militaristic and loosely governed confederation based on the villages; and that at the same time Gandhi's ideals had found an expression outside India in the civil rights movements in the United States and elsewhere, and in the counter culture, with its ideals of a simplified and agrarian life and its non-militarist and decentralist politics.

I still hold to the first conclusion; while I love India as a country, I detest it as a state. At the same time, with the general retreat of the movements of the 1960s, I am aware that Gandhi's influence in the west is far less than it was two decades ago, and has become once again, as it is now in India, a matter of ideals sustained by small minority groups and individuals. However, I console myself by the knowledge that such impulses never die out. The gains they make are never entirely lost, and even when some extraordinary social catastrophe, like the coming of the Nazis to power or the establishment of the Stalinist terror during the 1930s seems to obliterate them, they re-emerge, perhaps slightly changed in form but as vigorous as ever.

In March 1971 we went to London, to see old friends and publishers and combined our visit with a return to Provence, flying to Geneva and hiring a car to drive down the Route Napoléon to Nice and Menton. The coastline, which we had found so liveable when we stayed more than a decade before, had become overbuilt, and Menton had turned into a winter haven for the French petit bourgeoisie, while the valleys of the Alpes Maritimes which we had so loved had been ravaged, whole hilltops and ridges scored away to provide building material for the expansion of the resort towns. We eventually found a relatively unspoilt refuge on the tall rock of Èzes from which we could visit the remoter and less ruined countryside. It was a strange season, with snow falling on the coast at the beginning of March and settling a foot deep over the spring flower beds at Cannes.

Once we had returned to Vancouver in April, my work on Herbert Read dominated my time until almost the end of the year, involving me in a number of trips to Victoria during its beautiful spring season. My visits to the Read Archive gave us an opportunity to see our friends who had settled there, notably P.K. Page and her husband Arthur Irwin, and also two other local poets whom I found especially congenial, Robin Skelton, a bard bearded and haired like an Ainu who had just started the excellently international *Malahat Review*, and Mike Doyle, already an established poet in New Zealand before he moved to Canada. Eve and Nikita Galitzine had also by now moved to Vancouver Island and found a cottage outside Victoria.

Inevitably, I undertook other tasks that helped to vary the rhythm of work. Dave Godfrey, who had recently founded New Press, asked me for a book, and I put together a collection of published and unpublished essays on literary and social themes which I called *The Rejection of Politics*; it came out, like *Herbert Read, The Stream and the Source*, in 1972.

Once more I became active in broadcast writing. I had once discussed with Gerald Newman the possibility of a documentary on the career of Mozart's best librettist, Lorenzo da Ponte. I had no time to follow up the idea, but I remained curious about successful partnerships in the arts. Few had been more successful than that between Mozart and Da Ponte, but Da Ponte himself, with his Jewish background and his tortuous connections with the Catholic church, was a fascinating figure in his own right, and as I uncovered his links with Mozart's musical rivals I began to

realize that here was the material for an even more interesting program than Gerald and I had first envisaged.

Now that Gerald had left the CBC, I took the idea to Robert Chesterman, whose interests as a producer spanned music and drama. Rob
persuaded Bob Weaver to commission it as a major production, with
enough funds for Hugh McLean to carry out intensive musical research
and to hire instrumentalists and singers so that we could resurrect at
least parts of the largely forgotten operas we had disinterred.

I called the program *Mozart's Moon*, though afterwards I felt the title
did less than justice to Da Ponte, for he shone with much more than
Mozart's reflected glory: he had a light of his own, and Mozart and he
inspired each other, so that the works on which they collaborated were
not only Mozart's best operas; they were also Da Ponte's most inspired
libretti, and never were words and music in more perfect accord. Thanks
to my excellent collaborators, *Mozart's Moon* turned out to be a music-
ally rich and humanly interesting programme in which Mozart stood, as
he has so rarely done in the concert hall, among his contemporaries and
rivals, themselves no insignificant composers.

I also delivered some long radio talks on offbeat subjects. In one of
them, "A Plea for the Anti-Nation", I suggested that Canada, with its
vast geography, its loose organization of communities and its many cultures was the ideal place in which to discard the outworn nation-state
and replace it with a confederal structure, so that, proceeding upwards
from autonomous individuals through autonomous communities and
districts, the base of the pyramid of authority would be broad, with little
power left to be wielded from the narrowing tip. The talk aroused unusual attention and among the many letters I received I most valued one
from Phyllis Webb, who had been led into anarchistic thinking and towards her own *Kropotkin Poems* by reading my book, *The Anarchist
Prince*.

"I have just heard your talk on the "Anti-Nation", and, though
there was nothing new in it for me, since I've read your books on the
subject, I was thankful to you for making this statement again. . . . I
wish there were more of "us". You probably know if there are. Are
we more than two? I am so unable to be rational in argument, and
anyhow avoid argument to the point of total withdrawal, I feel I am
a pretty useless propounder of the faith. And then I suppose I really
do think it is a dream. Yet your point tonight about Canada being
an ideal potential federal state made me think. And I get so sick of
hearing anarchy and anarchist mis-used as grab-bag-bugaboos I feel
the need to clarify, educate. Yet you are the only one who does this."

This kind of response made me decide to reprint the talk, and I sent it to Abe Rotstein, who was then editing the *Canadian Forum*. Though his nationalism led him to disagree with much I had written, Rotstein saw I had hit on a vital weakness in the nationalist approach; its advocates had never really applied themselves to considering what kind of a society might be the objective if efforts to make Canada both politically and economically independent should succeed. He decided to make it the basis of a symposium, which occupied a whole issue of the *Forum* and was eventually published by New Press, *Nationalism or Local Control*. It may well have been the first time that what Abe Rotstein called "the anarchist postulate of radical decentralization" was seriously discussed in Canada. Not that I encountered much agreement among other writers who contributed to the symposium. Ironically, the most sympathetic was a young M.P. named Ed Broadbent, who of course later came to lead the mildly socialist New Democratic Party.

An even more interesting CBC project had developed in an elephantine way during 1971. Before we left for England in March, Gordon Babineau, a TV producer with whom I had worked on a small project a couple of years before, had unfolded a plan for a series of television films on the South Sea islands. Gordon is an enthusiast by nature, and as he talked of Tonga, New Caledonia, the Solomons, and the Gilberts, he trapped our interest. Inge and I had never visited the region but it had fascinated me in boyhood and only recently my interest had revived when I was editing Herman Melville's *Typee*. Gordon wanted me to write the scripts for the films, which would involve about five months of research and travel among the islands, with all expenses paid by CBC, a good fee, and the material for a new book as a bonus.

It was high time I had a break of this kind, for I had got myself back into the pattern of 15-hour days. Once again, the body gave me its warning. Once Sunday morning at the end of August, Inge went out for the day. I remember seeing her off and taking the garbage cans into the lane. I remember the dew on the grass and the feeling of a hot day stoking up as I came in and closed the basement door. The next thing I remember is Inge returning about eight hours later. I went to the door and said, "I've lost my memory". I knew Inge; I also knew Catherine Easto, who had been with her for the day. But for about eight years back my memory was *tabula rasa*. I had no idea that I was writing a book on Herbert Read, or what had happened yesterday or a year or five years ago.

The doctor — a young locum — arrived, looked into my eyes, felt my pulse, tapped my knees with his hammer, pronounced that I did not appear to have suffered a stroke, and gave a sensible prescription of three days of absolute rest with a shot of whisky every two hours; then, when my memory had returned, which he assured me it would, I should take a brief holiday, and perhaps review my schedule to see if there were some tasks I could shed.

My memory did return, at times muzzied by the whisky, over about twenty-four hours. It was a fascinating process. I first remembered vividly the encounter with the Nihangs on our last trip to India, nine months before, and then an incident five years before that, and around these first two memories, by association, other memories began to coalesce. It became like a great jigsaw puzzle: whole areas complete and other linking areas blank, until in the end it was all filled in and I had recovered the power to wander through my past at will — except for that eight hours between Inge's departure from the house and her return. That remained a blank in my life; I could never reconstruct what I may have thought or done in that fragment of lost time.

We went off for a week into the Okanagan valley, where the rich autumn light strengthened and revived me. And then, when we returned, I performed a very similar surgery to that I carried out after my heart attack six years before. I gave up my work for the Tibetans. It was a good time to give up. The Tibetan Refugee Society had established its role in the resettlement program, and everything was going well, with the prospect of further CIDA involvement. Thus I could hand on the chairmanship to someone who would be happier than I expected to be in dealing with government departments and bureaucrats. John Conway took over.

Otherwise things worked out so well that the only casualty of my illness was the entry on Anarchism in the *Encyclopedia Britannica* on which I was working at the time; even that was delayed only a fortnight, and I spent the last three months of the year slowly putting the final touches to my book on Herbert Read, handing over Tibetan affairs to Conway, preparing the two issues of *Canadian Literature* that would go to press while we were in the antipodes, and reading widely on the South Pacific. We even found time for a trip to Victoria in late November to see Pat Page and the Galitzines before the bad weather closed in. It turned out, in fact, to be a hard winter on the Pacific coast, and when we left in mid-January for Suva, the Vancouver airport was weatherbound, and we were taken by coach down to Seattle where we boarded the plane to Fiji on the first stage of our journey to the southern islands.

XXVI

IN THE SOUTH SEAS

TRAVEL WRITERS TELL WHITE LIES to make their books appear shapely and convincing, and so the account of our visit to the Oceanic islands reads differently in my book *South Sea Journey*, than it does in this autobiography, which has different truths. In the travel book I showed us travelling to the airport of Nadi on Fiji and then, after a time in the rain and sunlight of the early morning, taking a plane to Samoa. We did in fact take a plane from Nadi to Samoa, but two weeks later; in the meantime we had travelled to New Zealand and spent a fortnight there. But the experience of that bland and civilized little country was so different from anything we encountered in the island groups to the north that it seemed to have no place in the book. It was only several years later, when I went for a second time to New Zealand, that I wrote my impressions of the country in an article I contributed to *Saturday Night*.

Even on our second visit when we spent more than a month there, I never found anything that was tangible and distinctive enough about the place to induce me to write about it at length. Which is surprising, since we had only to get off the plane and find our way into the heart of Auckland to recognize we were entering a society of unusual virtues. New Zealand was a small state with no pretentions to power but a great feeling that a minor country could wield its own moral authority, as indeed it has shown recently in its opposition to nuclear adventures. One can travel the world and not find a pleasanter, more decent or friendlier people than the inhabitants of these islands. Far more than Canada or even Australia, New Zealand is an egalitarian society in which everyone is accessible to the appeal of his neighbours. I never smelt there anything like the sickly stench of old money and snobbery I have smelt in Westmount or in Melbourne. Once I asked a woman in the

Government Travel Bureau some question about Mount Cook which she could not answer immediately; she promised to find out. Next day, when I looked in, she had the information I'd asked for, clearly presented. I asked her how she'd got it so quickly. "Very simple," she said. "I saw Sir Edmund walking by, so I just nipped out and asked him." Sir Edmund was Hillary, to the world the famous conqueror of Everest, but to Auckland people one of their own, to be treated with a familiarity that did not preclude respect. One "nipped out" to ask him a small question, but one did not forget the title he had earned.

And yet there was an inertia about the society of this beautiful and often bizarre land: much physical energy and little intellectual impetus to complement it. And this may be because one is in an English culture; not an imitation one, but perhaps the last vestige of England in its distant heyday. New Zealand was always nearer to English roots than the other imperial dominions, perhaps because its immigration was so completely English, Welsh and Scottish. So faithful to roots is it that one often finds places where all the original families came from one English county or even one town; there was never any disturbing admixture of Afrikaners or of Québecois or of Australian Irish or other breeds outside the imperial mainstream. It is a far-flung country still intensely loyal to the traditions of its people, and it has deeply resented abandonment by a homeland that listened to the siren song of the European Common Market and in the process almost ruined the antipodean economies.

The links with neglectful England are still numerous and often pathetic. The food is English, with little variety and not much taste. The songbirds are English backbirds and finches imported to replace the native song-birds destroyed by the stoats and weasels brought in to combat the rabbits introduced by Acclimatization Societies that aimed to reconstruct the English countryside in these southern islands where mammals had never evolved. Sometimes, in the farmlands, one would see an English hedgehog quietly crossing the road; sometimes in the mountain forests an Exmoor red deer.

Most of the North Island has been converted into pasture land where one sees endlessly repeated replicas of English downs bitten by grotesque numbers of English-looking sheep. Even the wilderness is being reshaped. Around Rotarua, the ancient forests of Kauri pines have been felled and the land is being replanted with regimental groves of foreign trees — Douglas firs from the northwest coasts of North America and Ponderosa pines from California, both of which have matured far more quickly in New Zealand than in their native habitats.

The South Island saw the most ambitious attempt to transport English society to the antipodes, with the settling of the Canterbury Plains and the foundation of Christchurch under the auspices of the Church of England. There was even a thought of replicating the rural society that was already dying out in England by establishing a hierarchy of squire, tenant farmer and labourer. Fortunately that hope never worked out, since the ordinary settlers regarded their immigration as a sign of liberation from the rural class system, but there is still the flavour of a colonial Barchester about Christchurch, with its plausible imitations of English public schools and its cathedral designed by Sir Giles Gilbert Scott.

This setting of pleasant human relations and fine scenery, with nothing novel that called loudly to be understood, was just what we needed. We wandered north to Rotarua with its volcanic curiosities and the subtropical Bay of Islands, and then south to Wellington and across Cook Strait to the South Island, where we travelled to the mountains and the hill ranges on a bus mostly filled with Australian tourists, a different breed from the New Zealanders, more self-assertive, less secure. For the time being we were not travellers, but vacationing tourists, and floated willingly on the stream.

ONCE LANDED IN SAMOA, we were among peoples who had never raised themselves to the complexity of major civilizations, but had absorbed and adapted elements — notably religious creeds — from the Europeans who had been interfering with their lives ever since the first Dutchmen and Spaniards reached the area in the sixteenth and seventeenth centuries. Nevertheless, they possessed intricate and distinctive cultures.

Using Fiji as our base, we travelled in an area of ocean two thousand miles in diameter — and even then we did not cover the whole of the classic South Seas, for we left out the Marquesas as too far, Tahiti as too spoilt, and the Cook Islands because we already had excellent examples of Polynesian cultures in Tonga and Samoa. The total land area of the islands we visited was about 40,000 square miles, a thousandth the area of ocean in which they were scattered, for though the largest, New Caledonia, was 6,000 square miles in area, some of the others were mere coral atolls with no more than a few hundred acres of real land. We went by air and where we could by water, travelling through the Gilberts on a copra ship and through the Solomons on a police launch.

There were five of us in the team. Gordon Babineau was leading producer, and Mike Poole, a red-haired Viking with a gentleness that belied his looks, associate producer, and it was mainly with them that Inge and I travelled. I had little to do with the cameraman and the sound man, since most of the shooting was done after Inge and I had left, and I wrote the scripts the following winter when I had the footage before my eyes. We travelled with Mike in the New Hebrides and New Caledonia, and with Gordon in Fiji and the Gilberts, but in Tonga and the Solomons and most of the time in Samoa we were on our own. At the end Inge and I went on to New Guinea but, like New Zealand, this was not part of the film project.

Samoa impressed us immediately with the way in which the South Sea Islanders were often able to use elements that had entered their culture from outside to support its essential structure. The Samoans indeed accepted a drastic change in their lives when they became converted to Christianity. If there were any pagans left in the country, I did not hear of them, and the villages were dominated by large churches, sometimes in English Gothic styles but often in a baroque manner the Samoans had borrowed from the Germans during their occupation of the islands. In contrast to these great ornate buildings into which the people had poured their labour and their money, most of the people of the villages lived daily lives according to *"fa'a Samoa"* — the Samoan way — in *fales* consisting of poles supporting a roof thatched with palm leaves. Life was lived openly in the *fales*, for they had no walls, and the rolled mats which took their places were let down only for coolness; normally one looked in and saw all the family's possessions — the sleeping mats on the floor, the chests where they kept their belongings, and in the middle of any self-respecting *fale*, a large unused bed with German down quilts piled upon it. The German occupation had left its mark in a few customs like this — the women made excellent *Berliner pfannkuchen* — and in the names of some of the families; German merchants frequently married local women, and then their children, as often as not, would become absorbed into village life, often indistinguishable, except for paler skins and occasionally astonishing clear blue eyes, from the rest of the Samoans and carrying on the traditional life of gathering sea food and cultivating coconuts, taro and fruit in their plantations which stand away from the villages where the *fales* are grouped on grassy greens around the churches.

The villages, still tied to a subsistence economy, dominated even Samoan political life. Apia, the only town in Samoa, is a straggling beach community with stores and, right at the end of it, Aggie Grey's hotel, perhaps the most celebrated hostelry in the South Seas. The parliament house is in Apia, and the government offices, but the fragile western life that goes on there has not yet proved a sufficient magnet to draw many people from the villages, and a political life proceeds that is a surprisingly effective combination of the traditional and modern, with relatively efficient bureaucracies and a good educational system, but a form of government that is mixture of democracy and feudalism.

Theoretically the system is an indirect democracy, since, except for a couple of seats in Apia, the members of parliament are not elected by universal suffrage but by the *matais*, who are the heads of land-holding lineages, groups consisting of anything from a dozen to fifty people. The *matais* themselves are elected by the lineages, and at this level democracy is complete, since the assemblage at which the *matai* is chosen includes not only women but also the children, who are encouraged to express their views in the process of reaching a decision by consensus. The *matai* system, based on land-owning laws which prevent land being alienated from the lineages, ensures that the basic interests of the villages are always kept in mind. But the real power is controlled by the old chiefly lineages called the Four Royal Sons. When we arrived the head of one such lineage, descended from a hero who had driven the Tongan invaders from Samoa long ago, was the elective king or Ao-o-le-Malo, whose palace was the mansion which Robert Louis Stevenson built for himself at Vailima; another was Prime Minister, and the other two held key posts in the government. Besides keeping their hands on executive power, the noble families influenced the way the *matais* elected members of parliament from the rural fiefs where they had traditionally held power, so that in fact the old Polynesian chiefly system had been re-enacted in modern form, and for Samoa it seemed to work. Politically it was the most stable of all the places we visited in the South Seas.

"Custom" was a word we were hearing constantly in the South Seas. Thorough-going custom people, who retained their pagan beliefs, lived in the bush and refused commerce with the modern world, survived only on the Melanesian islands, in parts of the Solomons and the New Hebrides. Among the Polynesians there seemed to be no such extreme traditionalists, but in some ways the compromises they made tended to strengthen rather than weaken the traditional forms, and made them less vulnerable than the real custom people because they provided a *modus vivendi* with the modern world. The mass conversion of the Polynesians to various forms of Christianity was an example. The church gave the community an emotional focus whose power was evident when one entered a Samoan church on Sunday morning, listened to the fervent and beautiful singing of the congregation and to the pastor haranguing his flock from the vast two-tiered pulpit, with the deacons ranged below him. The Congregationalists of Samoa and the Wesleyans of Tonga were able to preserve what was valuable to them in traditional life while feeling united with the world outside.

We learnt much about ambiguous Polynesian attitudes when we went to Apolima. Tupuola Epi, a chief who later became Prime Minister, had insisted that we go to this outlying island because it was the most traditional community, and because it had a place in history as the island fortress to which the intransigent retreated during the Tonganese invasion of Samoa, later emerging to sweep the invaders away. We had to go there with a man of noble ancestry. A school inspector of the right lineage, named Afamasaga, was recruited, and we chugged across the lagoon of the main island of Upolu in a rickety whaleboat with an outboard motor and a crew of Apolima men who knew the way through the perilous reef.

The cone of Apolima was visible ahead of us by the time we left the Upolu lagoon and entered the choppy stretch of open sea between the islands. As we drew near, Afamasaga explained that the name Apolima meant "Held in the palm of your hand", and as we swung around the island we saw that one side of the volcano had broken down to sea level, into an amphitheatre of rock walls surrounding on three sides the verdant floor of the crater.

Afamasaga remarked that it would help if he could give us a touch of nobility in his introductory speech. Inge offered her descent from an Austrian baronial line. "I'm merely a writer," I said. "Excellent," he answered. "That means I can call you Tusitala, the teller of tales, which is the title we gave to Stevenson, whom all Samoans revere."

But before we could meet the chiefs, the reef had to be negotiated. A boat had capsized last week, Afamasaga remarked; the local school teacher had been in it and, though he survived, he had lost all his books. When we saw the reef, we were not reassured; it consisted of what was left of the rocky rim of the volcano, and was penetrated by an L-shaped passage through the lava rock. At first we were unable even to see the passage, as the waves broke over the barrier and the water returned in a seething white race; Afamasaga pointed to a spot where the flow, though no less powerful, seemed at least less white and broken. "They always wait for the seventh wave," he said, as the boat moved into position and the crew shifted into their posts, one in the bow where he stood poised with a pole in his hands, one seated on the awning and watching the water with his hands dangling so that the steersman in the stern could see the signs he made. The man in the bow gestured, the engine sprang into life, and suddenly we were moving full speed with the green wave towards the gap. In a few seconds we were between the brown rock masses that loomed in the tumbling water. The passage ahead seemed hardly wider than the boat. The man on the awning gestured frantically, left hand and then right. We wavered slightly, and then we were in the passage, forging ahead and curving as we went, with the poleman fending off the rock on the port side as we swung round through the L-shaped kink and out with the last rush of the wave into the bay, the calm water, and the sudden release of fear.

A tall, sturdy man with a strong angular face, clad in a flowered *lava-lava*, came striding down the beach from the *fales*. The crew leapt into the shallow water as the boat beached, and carried us ashore, forming chairs with their clasped hands. The man who welcomed us was Tautai, the *tulefale* or orator of Apolima. He expressed ritual astonishment at our arrival, though we knew a message had been sent by a boat that reached the island the previous day. He led us up to the beach on to the green where the *fales* of Apolima were laid out. The actual area of the village was small, for the ground sloped quickly to the walls of the crater, whose lower levels were a pattern of palms, bread-fruit trees and banana groves. The slopes around us, dense with intricate vegetation, and the grey combs of rock above; everywhere the brilliance of flame trees and hibiscus and the scent of frangipani; and no mechanical sound to disturb the natural harmonies of insect and bird.

Tautai walked before us to a large oval *fale* which stood on a natural platform overlooking the bay, its wooden columns outlined against the sea like some primitive Sounion. It was the *fale* of the village *fono* or council, and two men were waiting there for us, one thin and the other fat. The thin man was the *ali'i*, or hereditary head chief of Apolima; the fat man was the pastor. The *fale* was laid out with pandanus mats on which we took carefully designated places, supporting our backs against the posts: Afamasaga opposite the *ali'i*, I opposite the *tulefale*, Inge to my left, and the pastor to Afamasaga's right, for since he was not a native of the village he could not sit with the chiefs.

Two girls brought green coconuts of welcome; by sipping their clear sweet water we accepted the welcome. Samoan protocol is complex and oblique. It would have been impolite for the chiefs to ask about us. It would have been undignified for me to identify myself. Only a third party could resolve the impasse, and this Afamasaga did.

The pastor made the first welcoming speech, thanking the Lord Jesus Christ who had brought such important visitors through the perilous waters to their tiny land. Afamasaga replied briefly, having told me to reserve my own speech until later, and then Tautai remarked that, unexpected though our visit might be, Apolima knew its duty to honourable guests. The two chiefs disappeared, and returned, each bearing a woody, bleached stem about four feet long, with a gnarled sprout of root at the end; holding them in his open palms, Tautai explained that they were the roots of kava, the sacred plant of Polynesian peoples. When such roots passed from one man to another, there must be peace between them. He begged me to accept the roots as tokens of goodwill. I took them.

Now began the kava ceremony, conducted with a mixture of ritual and earthy matter-of-factness. A girl and two young men appeared, carrying a tin bucket, a shallow bowl of carved wood about four feet in diameter which stood on squat legs, and a coil of fibres that looked like raffia. The girl seated herself beside the *tulefale*, with the kava bowl before her. One of the young men sat beside her. The bowl, and a cup made from the polished half of a coconut shell, were rinsed. Then more water was poured into the bowl, and the girl dipped the coil of fibres, dipping and wringing. "They are hibiscus fibres," Afamasaga explained. "The shredded kava is inside them."

After many rinsings and wringings, the water took on a cigar-brown colour, and was ready to serve. The young man beside the mixer set up a high-pitched shouting chant, which we accompanied with rhythmic clapping. "He is celebrating the drinking of kava as a symbol of peace and friendship between the chiefs of Apolima and their guests." The second young man filled the cup with kava and, approaching with flexed knees, presented it first to the *ali'i*, then to Afamasaga as the titled Samoan guest, then to me as the visiting *tusitala*, then to the *tulefale*, then to the pastor, and finally to Inge, which surprised her, since women do not usually partake of the holy drink. Each carefully spilt a few drops on the grass as a libation to the community's ancestors, and then drained the cup in a single draught as our companions clapped three times and shouted "*Malo!*"

I had expected an atrocious flavour from a brew that looked so unappetizing, but the kava was distinguished only by a slightly disagreeable flatness. It is said to sharpen the perceptions, but after the cup had gone round three times mine remained unchanged. The only physical effect I felt was a slight tingling numbness at the back of the mouth.

After the triple drinking of Kava, Tautai embarked on his speech. It was long, punctuated at the end of each flowing period by grunting exclamations from the listeners. I was grateful for the metaphoric verbosity acquired in childhood from listening to Welsh revivalist preachers; when it was my turn to speak of the great history of Apolima, its place in Samoan legend, its role in the great war against Tonga, I declared unashamedly that its fame had reached Europe and North America; I lavishly praised the welcome we had received; I called sanctimoniously for the protection of God to extend itself to this jewel island of incomparable beauty. As Afamasaga translated, fragment by fragment, I was reassured; the chiefs grunted regularly and loudly. I had started on a course of flamboyant speechmaking that would not end until we left the South Seas.

No sooner had my speech ended than a long file of young men and girls appeared, weaving over the village paths. Each bore a coconut frond mat with a banana leaf laid on it as a cloth and plate. The island feast included roast bread-fruit, boiled taro and steamed yam; baked reef fish, octopus stewed in its ink, and fragments of muscular chicken; seaweeds, eggs and cooked plaintains; thick coconut cream was the sauce into which everything could be dipped. Bowls of water were brought, with towels, and we washed our hands before and after eating with our fingers. The girls sat cross-legged before us with fans, driving away the flies and offering choice tidbits. The food was bland, with no herbal seasoning and little salt. We washed it down with strong sweet milkless tea.

Afterwards we settled into a conversation that became a ritual contest; I was anxious to learn how the native system of village government worked, while the chiefs were intent on finding what advantage might be reaped from this windfall visit of a *palangi* (white man or — literally — sky-breaker) whose power, thanks to Afamasaga's flowery introduction, they imagined to be great and far-reaching.

Tautai was eager to answer my questions about village organizations. The clan chiefs formed the *fono* or council of the village, or *aiga*. The *fono* acted as both municipal council and customary court. It administered village finances, raised levies for specific purposes, and supervised such communal activities as the building and maintenance of church, manse, school and roads. It passed village by-laws, which often included curfews for children and even adults; it policed the locality effectively because its members knew everything that went on in the open *fales*; it imposed fines on those who broke the village laws, and in extreme cases it wielded the penalty of expulsion from the village, which meant that a man lost his rights to a share of the land's produce.

But Tautai had more on his mind. Not every *matai* was the leader of a land-holding clan. A village could adopt a stranger as a *matai*. "And now we have a guest among us who is worthy of our regard. Should we not make him also a *matai*?" The *ali'i* and the pastor grunted approval. Then, slyly jocose, Tautai asked me what I would think if it were suggested that I become an honorary clan chief. Afamasaga translated. "If you say no, it will be acceptable," he explained. "But if you say yes or show hesitation, the *tulefale* will make a ceremonial speech offering you the mataiship; then it will be offensive to refuse." He smile quizzically. I had been forewarned that if I accepted I would have to give a large feast and lavish presents to all the real *matais*, and I would never afterwards be free of requests for aid. I expressed appreciation and gently indicated my probable refusal of an honour so manifestly undeserved. "Nevertheless," Tautai remarked, "this is your village and this is your clan. You will always be welcome among us."

Suddenly, children shouted from the beach, and we all rose and went to look down into the bay. A high wave had come sweeping in over the reef and lifted our boat, so that it lay broadside and tilting on the beach. It was soon righted, but the leading boatman came to tell us that we should not be too late in leaving, for the wind was blowing up in the channel.

Nevertheless custom and courtesy came before safety in Tautai's mind, and we had to sit down, drink more green coconuts and deliver final speeches. I made the customary presents to the chiefs and the pastor — two Australian silver dollars each as Afamasaga instructed me. The coins were touched to the brow in thanks, Tautai remarking that next time a big tin of corned beef would also be appreciated.

The pastor went with us, and we all climbed into the boat, while Tautai and the young men waded into the bay to bid us farewell. We shot the reef in great style, going out on the receding wave, but it was an alarming voyage back. The swell rose high, and the boat rolled, sometimes shuddering through its fragile timbers on the impact of a wave, and sometimes rising before a crest, then scudding down sickeningly into the trough. Many times we shipped water, and the boatmen bailed steadily most of the way. I felt that any moment we would be swamped or capsized, and so did Inge. Afamasaga looked grave, which perturbed me in a man who knew these waters. The only people who seemed unmoved were the three young boatmen who brought us skilfully through the entrance to the Upolu reef, and who regarded the feat as so unexceptional that they were astonished when I made them a small gift after we landed.

THE ISLAND SOCIETIES DIFFERED greatly from each other. Samoa and Tonga were highly divergent societies, though both had sought to re-establish Polynesian chief-dominated traditions. Samoa felt like an open and emotionally stable society; Tonga felt an enclosed and an emotionally explosive one.

While Samoa had developed a surprisingly successful indirect democracy based on everyone belonging to a land-holding group and therefore enjoying economic security, Tonga was a monarchy that had opened up a tiny window of direct democracy but whose population was economically insecure. The king was an almost absolute ruler in a Christian kingdom where Wesleyan Methodism had incongruously become an established church. It was a strict and sabbatarian place. No craft could leave the harbour of Nuku'alofa between midnight on Saturday and midnight on Sunday, nor could any automobile move on the roads during those hours, except for the king's limousine taking him to and from the church where he asserted his majesty by sweating in a pew raised even above the level of the pulpit.

The king, Taufa'ahau Toupou IV, received us in audience one day, a massive figure whose three hundred pounds was regarded, according to Polynesian traditions, as symbolizing the prosperity of the kingdom. He was a shy and likeable man, who had travelled around the world with his eyes open and had many interesting ideas. As a shrewd old woman retainer said to me, "He's a dreamer, but he's an active dreamer." And he was obviously doing what he could to improve life in a place much more crowded and constricted by traditional attitudes and privileges than Samoa.

The question of land reverberated through most of the little island groups. Tonga was in fact, if not in theory, a surviving feudal kingdom. Two-thirds of the tiny parliament consisted of noblemen appointed by the king or elected by about thirty magnate families; a third was elected by universal suffrage. Though the constitution guaranteed every adult male a plot of eight acres, most of the land lay in the fiefs of the nobles, who were reluctant to divide it among commoners, so that a man might wait until his late forties before he acquired a diminished plot of four acres or less. Hence there were many landless men, often without employment. Some went to work in New Zealand and Australia; the rest had to depend on the king's ineffectual attempts to develop labour intensive industries.

When we talked to him, his mind was full of such schemes: growing rock melons for export to Australia, exporting sunhats made locally from pandanus leaves, producing hibiscus-flower honey. But the country's life, like that of Samoa, was based on subsistence farming and fishing, so that the unavailability of land created an increasingly difficult situation which helped to explain the touch of xenophobia we were aware of in Tonga. Though Cook called their group the Friendly Islands, we found the Tongans withdrawn and notably less hospitable than other peoples in the South Seas. As one sat on a beach of Tongatapu and looked over the vast lagoon to the palm clad islands that enclosed it, there was always the sense of a lost rather than a living paradise.

THOUGH FIJI WAS THE CENTRE of our travels because plane routes radiated from it to most of the other island groups, and we returned there to hold conferences, pick up mail and enjoy the attenuated city life of Suva, we saw little of its hinterland. Yet we liked the Fijians. They were Melanesians by descent and language, but they had interacted for centuries with Tongan Polynesians, who had interfered in their tribal politics. They were tall and powerfully built people with amiably craggy features: the *beaux laids* and *belles laides* of the South Pacific. The amiability permeated their characters, and it was hard to imagine the anthrophagous feasts that in earlier generations had given Fiji the name of the Cannibal Isles. They were always friendly and courteous.

This applied not only to the people of the mountainous interior, where a traditional life went on and an old chief we visited insisted on calling his musicians so that the slit drums could be beaten to summon the menfolk and we could be asked the ritual question, "Do you come in war or in peace?" It applied also to the people of Suva.

I shall never forget the kindness of the staff in that colonial hostelry, the Grand Pacific Hotel. Inge had to have an emergency operation in the hospital at Suva; it was a dingy place, and the surgeon, who was a capable Indian, suggested I get her out as quickly as possible. I was apprehensive; sickbed cases are not usually welcome in grand hotels. But no sooner did our taxi draw up than the porter — a giant even by Fijian standards — lifted Inge in his arms like a child and carried her upstairs to the room that was waiting. Immediately the maids were there to make her comfortable, and the housekeeper with flowers and fruit, and with this goodwill and attention she recovered amazingly quickly. The Fijians took us to their hearts in our misfortune, and when we left the clerk said to me, "However full we are, there will always be a room for *you*," — and he kept his word.

Apart from New Caledonia, Fiji was the only place in the South Pacific with a genuine racial problem that accentuated the land problem it shared with many of the other small countries in the region. During the nineteenth century many Indians came as indentured labourers to work in the sugar plantations. Most of them remained after their contracts came to an end, and they bred fast, so that when we reached Fiji the Indian population was already beginning to exceed the native Fijians. Suva was largely an Indian town, because the Indians had taken up the shopkeeping the Fijians despised. But there were also many Indian farmers, and this varied the pattern of the thatched Fijian villages with gaudily little painted temples, covered with figures of the deities in the South Indian style. Once we went out to such a tiny rural temple to see the Indian fire-walkers. From a few feet away, before the actual ceremony took place, we saw the priest inserting sharp steel skewers into the temples and cheeks of the devotees without either blood or any perceptible pain. And when we returned to the temple, the dancers repeatedly crossed with bare feet a bed of glowing embers forty feet across and so hot that we felt like swooning as we sat on benches six feet away. Yet they suffered no burns of any kind.

Except for the plantations which had been set up in the nineteenth century, land ownership had long been restricted to the Fijian clans, who held it communally. An Indian farmer had either to acquire a plot in a plantation when it were broken up, or lease from a native group land they did not want to cultivate.

Politically, too, the Indians were kept as second-class citizens. Representation in the parliament was balanced equally between Indians and Fijians, with the comparatively few Europeans controlling a key group of seats whose incumbents regularly voted with the Fijians.

The national leaders were always Fijians of old chiefly lineage. The police seemed to be entirely Fijian, as was the small army. Politics were polarized on racial lines, but though the Indians were discontented they were powerless to effect change, since they controlled no real lever of power. But we sensed strongly the potential for widespread trouble. And if Fiji has not disintegrated into the same disorder as has recently overtaken New Caledonia, it is probably because of the precarious prosperity that tourism has brought to the islands thanks to their central position.

THE GILBERTS WERE ON the far periphery, and our journey to Tarawa revealed to us how vast and empty are the oceans in which the small nations of the South Seas are scattered. We went 1,365 miles, flying in a slow propellor plane, and for the first four hours we saw no land. Then the atolls of the Ellices, now Tuvalu, came into sight. Hours on from Funafuti, the village capital of the Ellices, we reached the Gilberts, now Kirapati.

These were the coral islands of legend, true atolls consisting of islets where a little soil had built up on the reefs, and within a necklace of them a lagoon came into being. The lagoon at Tarawa was so large that its farthest end was lost over the horizon when I looked for it from the beach outside the little hotel where we stayed, and the farthest islands I could see were a mere furry line of palms; the great stretch of water seemed as much a fluid microcosm, a world caught in its own distances, as the great lakes of Canada. Yet the fragment on which I stood, watching the frigate birds gliding and the phalaropes running on the beach, was so narrow that I had only to turn and walk a few yards through a coconut grove and I would stand on the ocean shore, with the Pacific breakers beating up the white sand and throwing a veil of spray over the outcropping coral rocks. The nearest other island, even of the Gilberts, was far out of sight.

In the Gilberts we were fortunate enough to find a copra boat that took us on a voyage round the remoter islands, Nikunau, Tabiteuea and Abemama, where Stevenson had lived. We watched the loading of copra, went ashore and were invited into the great *maneabas*, or thatched meeting halls, always to be entertained with the green coconut of welcome and questioned about the village we came from. We were called

Imatangs, for the Gilbertese believed that white men came from Matang, the earthly paradise from which their forebears were long ago expelled. On Tabiteuea we were given a feast in the great *maneaba*, where the men danced their limbering-up-for-battle dances, and their chronicle dances, celebrating historical events like the coming of the first whalers, and the bare-breasted girls performed the Gilbertese sitting dance, the *bino*, with its eloquent hand and head movements. The next morning the elders of the village gave us breakfast in the *maneaba*, talked of their problems, and crowned us with little chaplets of seashells.

Water was a major problem on the Gilbertese atolls; apart from rain, there was only the brackish water that seeped through the coral rock, and the only useful plants that throve on this were coconut palms, pandanus trees and the babai plant, a larger and coarser relative of taro that was grown in pits dug deep into the rock to catch the seepage. The pandanus provides a coarse fruit, and both pandanus and palm provide building materials. Except for the products of these plants, everything that kept life going had to be taken from the lagoons or the ocean; it varied from the sharks with which the fishermen duel in the open sea to the white sandworms the women and children gathered in abundance on the beaches.

Not only were the Gilbertese resourceful in making use of every possible source of food. They also developed a technology, not only in building their great *maneabas*, often 40 or 50 feet tall, from coconut trunks lashed together with coconut fibre rope and thickly pelted with palm-leaf thatch, but also in making the slim fast outrigger canoes on which they would often undertake considerable voyages, steering by the stars at night and using charts made from sticks and seashells.

That ingenious native subsistence culture we still found flourishing because there was no alternative; the Gilberts had no exportable resources like minerals. Yet they did not reject the advantages of western living. Most of them were by now Christians, and they valued the education which the churches provided, for they nurtured the illusion that somehow by acquiring knowledge of western ways their children could have a better life than they had endured.

At the same time the Gilbertese seemed to retain much of their largely animist beliefs. They believed in spirits of all kinds, particularly the *antis*, or whistling ghosts. We were warned of these and we were also warned never to talk to a stranger we met walking northward on the road up the atoll. He might be a dead person making his way to the abode of the Lord of Death beyond the farthest island.

LIFE WAS DIFFERENT IN the high islands where we encountered the Melanesian peoples. The soil was volcanically rich, water was abundant, and land problems were not caused by population stresses but by the presence of alien exploiters.

The three Melanesian groups where we visited were the New Hebrides, New Caledonia and the Solomon Islands. The Solomon Islands was nominally a British protectorate, but when we arrived it was being ruled as a colony. New Caledonia was a French colony with a large white *colon* population. The New Hebrides, a product of competing imperialisms, was a condominium — an uneasy dual rule established by the British and the French in 1886 to keep out the Germans who had already established themselves in New Guinea and Samoa.

The moment we arrived at the airport of Vila, the capital, we encountered the oddities of what in pidgin the local Melanesians called *Two Pella Gubment*. Actually, it was Three Fellow Government. There were two immigration queues. Commonwealth citizens went to the British desk and French citizens went to the French; native New Hebrideans picked their desk according to the language they learned in mission school; Americans were fair game for either side. But once one's passport had been stamped, the customs counter presented another political entity, the Condominium itself; the two powers had set up a common administration in customs and communications and a joint court whose impartiality was guaranteed by its being presided over by a deaf Spanish judge who had never spoken either French or English, let alone a native language. In Vila itself the tripartitism was symbolized by the fact that the British Commission stood on top of one hill and the French on top of another, while the grotesquely modernistic headquarters building of the Condominium squatted in the middle of Vila's untidy downtown.

To add to the complexity of New Hebridean life before the rush to independence in 1980 when the islands emerged as the new country of Vanuatu, the heart of political and social life in Vila was a Corsican establishment, Rossi's Hotel, run by a formidable clan consisting of Madame Rossi and her stalwart sons. The hotel rooms were shabby, noisy, and usually full, and we chose to stay in a beach hotel a few miles out of the city, but every day we went to Rossi's and ate the best meals in the South Pacific. There we would meet everyone who was anyone in Vila: British and French officials, doctors, nurses and anthropologists who had come in from the islands, and the native civil servants who had been educated either in Australia or in France. We found these men of future power dull company. To search out more interesting Melanesians we had to go to the outlying islands, and fortunately there was an excellent service of small planes, eccentrically operated by young Qantas apprentices and elderly drunken Frenchmen, that linked the islands.

Malekula, where we went in the hope of encountering the Big Nambas and the Small Nambas I had read about in Tom Harrisson's *Savage Civilization* in the 1930s, turned out the most disappointing place. We failed to reach the village where the Small Nambas came out of the bush to trade, because a flood had made the fords impassable. As for the Big Nambas, named for the enormous and ornate penis wrappers that were the men's principal garments, our single encounter with them occurred when two decrepit men in shabby castoff suits who were sitting outside the District Officer's bungalow rushed up obsequiously to give us flabby handshakes. "You've met your Big Nambas," remarked the D.O., explaining that most of the tribe had become dismally acculturated, though a remnant kept up the old ways and supplemented their jungle cultivation by coming to the coast and charging tourists high prices to photograph them in their codpieces.

Tanna and Santo were more rewarding, for there at least we encountered native movements that were claiming land back from the planters and seeking to re-establish traditional ways of life. Tanna interested me because in childhood I had read the memoirs of John G. Paton, the Scottish missionary who had converted Tanna to Presbyterianism. Tanna remained faithful to the Kirk until the American forces began to arrive with their vast dumps of stores during World War II: then the people began to think of earthly rather than heavenly rewards, and the rise of a cargo movement called Jon Frum decimated the faithful.

We flew to Tanna on one of the small planes, crossing low over the sea until the volcanic crest of Mount Vanua came into view and we descended between the lines of coconut palms to an airstrip located in a fold of the ground so that the plane landed on the top of a slope, taxied down it and then up the opposing slope to come to a halt at a sign that announced Burton Field. The airport building was a rubble of broken planks among which two white toilet pans glistened in the sunlight; it had been demolished in a recent hurricane. A tall young man with long yellow hair and piercing blue eyes got down from a Land-Rover and came towards us. "I'm Russell Paul," he said. "Bob Paul's my father." Bob Paul was the main trader of Tanna, an Australian who had come in 1946, and he owned the beachside cabins that were the nearest thing to a hotel.

Tanna has no roads — merely tracks that wind over the hills and through the groves and jungle, turning at the slightest rain into red, slippery mud. Tough vehicles with four-wheel drives like Russell's are the only possible transport. He drove us first to the big white house behind the trading store where his family lived. It had large airy rooms and great shutters kept open with white poles, so that the breeze came in and the sunlight kept out. Shortly afterwards, Bob Paul himself came in, a large, slightly shambling man in whom an essential toughness was combined with gentleness. Bob Paul had been one of the early air pilots in the New Hebrides, and now he was the most important trader and the largest planter on Tanna. He was a member of the Advisory Council that was the nearest approach to democratic institutions the New Hebrides had yet attained. He was sometimes called the King of Tanna, but it was a title he neither invited nor relished, since he had learnt the danger of authoritarian stances. He tried to live at guarded peace with all men, including the militants of Jon Frum.

We were given coffee grown on the plantation and fresh rolls baked in the Paul store; Bob Paul and his family had recognized that a measure of self-sufficiency was essential to the civilized way of life they sustained. Then we drove to the cabins, native-style huts of bamboo and palm-leaf standing on the shores of a rocky cove. Beside each door a padlock hung on a hook with its key. "There's no need to use it," Bob Paul remarked. "Taboo still counts on Tanna, and a padlock beside a door is now a taboo sign. You can leave everything you have without worrying. Nobody will step past that padlock." During our days on Tanna we left the cabin open with cameras and money and other usually tempting items lying about inside it, but nothing was ever touched.

We lunched in the cabin on charcuterie and Alsatian wine, wondering what John G. Paton would have said to the enjoyment of Gallic luxuries. After lunch, Russell Paul drove us through palm groves and we found Father Sacco in his parsonage that looked over a sloping lawn towards the sea. Sacco looked Italian, but his accent was not; into its indefinable Europeanness would break now and then a mystifying twang of the English north country. "A good guess," he laughed when I told him my impression. "I'm Maltese, and I spent many years in Middlesbrough before the Marist mission decided to send me here. It's not so far from Durham miners to Tannese villagers as you'd think. They both live close to the elemental. They both live close to death."

We were standing on his verandah, and he pointed across the lawn. "Why do you think I have such a good view of the sea? Because ten years ago the church above the beach was swept away by a tidal wave. And in the last hurricane the school building collapsed and the roof fell flat on to the ground. I was all right in my parsonage because I braced it properly. The Tannese women and children squatted down in the centre of the houses, and the men and youths stood in a circle around them, clinging to the roof timbers to prevent everything flying away. Three-quarters of the houses collapsed, and some of the roofs were blown three miles before they came to earth."

Father Sacco took us around his compound, to show us the new prop-erly braced school he had built and the never-failing pump he had installed that ensured a supply of water for him and the villagers. And then, back on the verandah, he began to talk of Jon Frum.

"It started up when a man began to go around saying that one night he had seen the devil on the beach, and that by magic he had been able to catch him and use his powers. Whether the original Jon Frum was the devil or the man who caught him is not certain any more even in the minds of the Tannese, but Jon Frum, however he was, began to meet people in the dark and pretend to inject them, which in itself is a pecul-iar thing, since he appeared before the great campaign of penicillin that virtually eliminated yaws. After the Americans came, the idea of cargo cropped up. Whether it came from New Guinea or was generated here spontaneously I cannot say, but now Jon Frum became the being who would bring cargo, and his prophets multiplied.

"A former teacher named Nambas appeared and organized Jon Frum into a movement with himself as its leader, invented the bloody cross as its symbol, and made it openly anti-Christian. He created a village at Sulphur Bay which became the Jon Frum mecca. He drilled his storm-troopers who marched up and down on special days with wooden imita-tion rifles and the letters U.S.A. painted on their chests in white clay. They still do it! He sent the kava stick over the islands to call for the abandonment of Christianity, and when the people in the villages re-ceived it, they drank kava openly — which the missionaries had forbid-den — to signify that they renounced their conversion. Nambas died. Then came a leader called Milas. He went to Vila, and came back with the story that he had been transported to America in what he called a 'thing', and there he met two soldiers who told him that they were waiting for the Eagle to take off any moment, after which the cargo would arrive in Tanna. Milas made his people clear airstrips in the jungle and build dummy planes to act as decoys for the real planes that would bring the cargo. Now Milas has gone, and his dummy planes have van-ished, and all you will see in the jungle are the bloody crosses of Nambas. But the headquarters is still at Sulphur Bay, and the leaders come and go. Frankly, I cannot tell you whom you will find in power now."

The next morning Mike Poole and I set off with Russell for the Jon Frum village of Sulphur Bay. We travelled by old horse-tracks — for-merly the foot-tracks of trade — that took us up over the interior spine of the island. Beside the track, every two or three miles, we passed a big tramped clearing with a single great banyan tree under which rough benches had been made out of tree trunks. This was the *nakamel*, the meeting centre for a village whose houses were scattered in the bush. In most of these upland settlements the hurricane had destroyed the crops, and the men had gone to New Caledonia to earn a little money while the women kept alive eating coconuts. In one village Russell stopped to talk to a man with one hand; the other had been blown off fishing with dynamite. He told us that apart from himself there were only two old men and two youths in the village, though there were thirty women.

Not far beyond this village Jon Frum showed its first sign. Within a little red wooden fence like the surround of a grave and about the same size, stood a tall cross, also painted red. "It's just to show us," Russell remarked. "Defiance, not taboo. They wouldn't try that! After all, they still trade with us!"

The road climbed higher, through dense woods inhabited by large black-and-bronze winged pigeons. We went into cloud and rain, at times slithering perilously down hills that showers had turned into slopes of red mud, and then, above the cloud, drove along the edges of precipices that fell into the shifting vapours. As we approached Mount Vanua the roads turned into dark grey ash, porous and firm, and then the volcano came into sight, a grey heap of ashes towering over wooded hills, with a wisp of smoke blowing from its crest. The land around its base — the Ash Plain — was bare and black, but as firm as the finest ocean beach, so that Russell could drive over it at top speed. It was a grim impressive scene: the black ash field with a few gaunt pandanus trees its only vegetation; the rusty red field of lava that cropped out of it; the grey lake inhabited — we were told — with black fish imported from Africa; and the black cone of the mountain in which thunder growled and reverberated until a columnar puff of smoke rose suddenly into the sky.

Skirting the mountain on the coastal side, we came to a barrier of stakes. It was Sulphur Bay. Beyond the barrier lay a square green of well-grazed grass; the houses of the village were on two sides of the green. A young man in shorts was standing near the barrier, and when Russell talked to him in pidgin, he waved us on over the green. Sulphur Bay was a planned community, much larger than the other villages we had seen. The houses were arranged in orderly rows, some of them built traditionally with curved roofs like Nissen huts that came right down to the ground and were densely thatched; the wooden frames of these houses were well carpentered, so that they were sturdy and gave little purchase to the wind. All the other houses had cane walls, woven neatly into herringbone or chequered patterns, with roofs of palm or pandanus thatch. Four Jon Frum crosses within their little fences were spaced over the green; another stood in the hollow of an old banyan. A second and larger banyan, with benches under it, was a meeting place and a few women sat there gossiping. The young man followed us and pointed out another rectangular fence on the edge of the green. It was the grave of Nambas, the first leader of the village; some plastic wreaths lay fading on a pile of lava rubble.

Most of the men were up on the hillsides, working in their gardens. A second young man, in a blue *lavalava*, was walking about with a baby in his arms, and he led us towards the beach, where a line of outrigger canoes was beached and a score of village boys were riding and tossing on the surf that broke in the reefless bay. Seated on a log watching them was an old man with a broad greying beard who looked like a black Charles Darwin. "He's one of Nambas's successors," said Russell, and we went up to the old man. He shook hands and smiled benignly, but as soon as Russell began to talk in pidgin he turned and slipped away as silently as a ghost among the huts. The young man in shorts laughed and went into a long gabble of pidgin. It turned out that the old man had been recognized as a prophet and leader until a few months ago, but then there were disputes, and he was forced to share his power with two of his rivals. The old man did not wish to say anything to strangers out of their presence.

The clatter of bamboo drums sounded on the edge of the village, and then up in the hills. "Calling pigs home," said the young man in shorts. The clouds began to drift over the sun, and it seemed wise to begin making our way back. We walked to the row of stakes. A toothless old woman in a dirty, shapeless cotton dress came up and spoke affectionately to Russell. "This is Marguerite," he said. "She was my nanny!" Marguerite spoke something nearer to English than the local pidgin and when Russell told her we were waiting for the leaders, she laughed. "You hear them drums?" "Calling the pigs," said Russell. She laughed again. "No calling pigs. Telling big men stay away!" And though we waited for another half hour, anxiously eyeing the sky, the leaders failed to appear.

At last we gave up, Mount Vanua celebrating our passing by clanking its bowels and puffing up an even taller column of smoke that hung in the air and shaped itself into a miniature mushroom cloud. About half-way back to the rain began to fall heavily and we all felt the end of the journey had come when the Land-Rover went out of control and slid sideways down one of the hills. It did not topple over, but then there was the opposing hill, equally slippery to ascend; only after six runs at it did Russell reach the top. Ours, we learnt next day, was the last car to make the journey over the island; the others were left on the road and their passengers had to sleep in native huts.

When we got back to the cabins, Inge told us that Bob Paul and his wife had been to call and had invited us to what the Australians call "tea" that evening. Tea was the one thing missing from that repast, and

Bob and his tall wife, a handsome Australian blonde, were fine hosts. The evening gave us a glimpse of planter life at its best — the life of those who refuse to let go into pseudo-native squalor and in compensation hold more deliberately to the urbane aspects of life than most people in Europe or North America.

Bob Paul was not surprised by our reception — or lack of it — at Sulphur Bay. "The movement's in flux," he told us. "There isn't a dynamic leader any more and the militant phase is over. You could go back a dozen times, and until there's a real leader again they'll just fade into the bush. But Jimmy Stevens up on Santo — that's another matter altogether! You'll have no trouble seeing Jimmy and his men!"

Bob Paul was right about Jimmy Stevens. Jimmy was the leader of Nagriamel, the native movement which had started in the bush on Santo (or Australia del Espiritu Santo to give it the full name conferred by the Spanish voyager Quiros in 1606) and had spread into the other northern islands. When we arrived at Jimmy's headquarters at Vanofo, strategically placed in the foothills between the bush and the coast and well guarded by young men armed with weapons ranging from old American carbines to longbows, he welcomed us as emissaries from the great world.

Nagriamel was a traditionalist "custom" movement but not a cargo one. Jimmy's aim was to get back for the people the vast areas which land sharks had bought for derisory payments in the nineteenth century and which the plantation owners had not put to any productive use. He was a typical example of the "big man" who among the Melanesians takes the place of the hereditary chiefs of the Polynesians. The "big man" had to show, by accumulated wealth, by magical powers, by political skills, that other men gained by giving him their support. Jimmy had the political skills. He was a man of mixed blood; his mother had been Tongan, his paternal grandmother Melanesian and his paternal grandfather an English mariner. Jimmy had worked a bulldozer for the Americans, operated a trading schooner, and run a store in Luganville, the rough little capital of Santo. White men regarded him as shiftless and sly, but the bush people and the landless men of the coast saw him as the outsider who had made their problems his own.

Jimmy realized that his chance lay in uniting what he called "the men of the mission and the men of the fire", meaning the partly acculturated people of the coast and the pagan villagers of the bush. He had established at Vanofo a utopian community of about 250 people that seemed to operate to a highly regimented rhythm. The discipline Jimmy created he meant to use in the clash he foresaw; the idea of destruction was much on his mind, and he often used the vivid pidgin phrase for it —

"baggerap pinis!" Just before we arrived an envoy had come from the Jon Frum community we had visited at Sulphur Bay, proposing an alliance with Nagriamel. Jimmy had turned them down. "I no waiting for steamer," he said to me. "I rather have black cargo than white cargo. Land my cargo."

Stevens was the only leader of a custom movement in the South Sea whom we succeeded in meeting, and that was doubtless because he liked to impress white men with his reasonableness. For this reason he was taken more seriously by the authorities, and perhaps justifiably, for a few years after, when the New Hebrides became independent as Vanuatu, he led an uprising aimed at establishing an independent "custom realm" on Santo. The new government had to call in troops from New Guinea to help quell the revolt, and for Jimmy, as a political force at least, it was "baggerap pinis."

Everywhere in the Melanesian islands movements devoted to restoring custom and regaining land were stronger than in Polynesia and Micronesia. They looked back to autochthonous ancestors, who had appeared, apparently by spontaneous generation, on the lands the clans possessed. They perceived a symbiotic link between the clan and the land, which to them belonged as much to the lineage as the ancestors themselves did. Thus, when the white men arrived seeking land, there were two views of ownership that were in fact irreconcilable, and land was "acquired" by white speculators from "chiefs" who had no authority to dispose of it, under the misapprehension on the part of the native people that they were merely assigning its use — not selling it outright.

The same problems existed in New Caledonia and in the Solomon Islands. In New Caledonia they were aggravated by the weight of the French presence, represented by the smart little warship flotilla in Nouméa harbour from which one would hear the bugles calling every morning as the Tricolor was raised. New Caledonia was once a penal settlement, to which many convicted Communards were transported in 1871, and some of the deportees had remained to form an exclusive little convict aristocracy in Nouméa, the capital. Other French came as colons, acquiring large areas of land, on which they reared cattle tended by black Melanesian cowboys; others were attracted by the monstrous nickel mines that were steadily paring down the mountains and polluting the rivers and the offshore waters. It was the only South Sea Island where whites seemed as numerous as natives, and were much more visible, since the Melanesians tended to stay on the land, while in Nouméa much of the manual work was done by poor whites.

The French, as they always did, tried to impose a Gallic social and political framework. The Melanesian natives were considered to be

French, and so in the schools only French was taught. A French municipal system dependent on native *maires* was established parallel to the pattern of traditional chiefly rule. It still seemed a rigid system; as well, the French settlers were racially prejudiced. The current conflict, which has reached a crescendo little more than a decade after our visit, is surprising, not because of French obstinacy but rather because of the militancy of the Melanesians, which in 1970 was confined to an activist minority, *les Foulards Rouges*.

The atmosphere in the Solomons, the straggling chain of high volcanic islands, was much more relaxed, partly because the whites had never been allowed to acquire and exploit large areas of land, but partly also because of the lack of cohesion among the inhabitants. They spoke many local languages, varied in colour from the fairly light brown of the people on easterly Malaita to the blue-black of the Shortlands Islanders in the far west, and we found great differences in the degree of acculturation.

To the west, in the Shortland Islands, on Choiseul and Vella Lavella and Gizo, most of the people seemed to have been converted to one or other of the Christian churches. And perhaps the most striking event on that part of our journey was a Christian one. We had gone into the harbour of a village on Vella Lavella where the Seventh Day Adventists had a thatched church, like a cathedral built of coconut trunks and fronds, right on the waterfront. That evening, as the boat lay moored to the jetty, we saw many people converge on the church, the men in spotless white shirts and trousers, the women in laundered cotton dresses, and the children also in fresh and frilled embroidered party garments. They came walking along the shoreline paths and paddling in little dugout canoes across the harbour.

The mate, a Polynesian from the island of Bellona, stood beside me and remarked: "They are coming tonight because one of their people will be going away with us tomorrow." The singing rose high in the church, and then a man in a blue Hawaiian shirt who had seemed to be controlling the operations of the boat, came to the rail. He appeared uneasy. "I have to go ashore when the service is over," he said. "I am arresting a man who went to his daughter, or so it is said." He went ashore, and a while later the congregation came out of the church, and followed two groups of people down to the jetty.

In one party was the police officer and his prisoner, a timid-looking man who seemed devoid of evil, and whom he merely held gently by his elbow, without handcuffs. The prisoner did not look particularly anxious, and there was no great reason for him to be so; in the South Seas generally a man who goes to jail is regarded as fortunate and perhaps even clever, since for a small amount of light work he lives well for a period of months; sentences are rarely long because of the lack of prison space, and there is no stigma attached to having gone to prison. In the other party were the prosecution witnesses, including the prisoner's wife and all his daughters, the offended one among them; jolly, dark-skinned, well-laundered girls who seemed to regard the whole trip as an outing at the expense of the government. And on the jetty was the congregation, striking up yet another joyful hymn to wish the erring brother a safe journey and a quick return.

In the eastern islands the survival of pagan life was much more evident. Even on Guadalcanal, where the colonial capital had been established at Honiara after the end of World War II, civilization was thinly spread. The road ran only part way along one coast and the interior was accessible only by foot trail or helicopter. The bush people filtered into the capital, where we would encounter them in the area known as Old Chinatown, the women with pipes in their mouths and great mops of frizzy, lime-blonded hair, and the men, bare-torsoed, with scarlet *lava-lavas*, and their mouths almost as red from chewing betel as their kilts; each wore, hung round his neck, a little closely woven bag which contained the right ingredients — the fragments of areca nut, the betel leaves, and the lime in a bamboo tube with a thin stick to dab a white speck inside the cheek while chewing. Guadalcanal is matriarchal, and one day we met a family procession whose members had just come down from their hill village; in front walked a young man in a blue kilt with a tightly and obviously artificially frizzed head of hair; behind were two girls in filthy red washed-out rags of dresses, and two completely naked small boys; in the midst of, and in control of it marched a mother figure as archetypal as the Venus of Willendorf, all fat, glossy amplitude, with bare papaw breasts and a vast belly jutting over the kilt slung low on her hips, jangling with many necklaces and stacks of bangles hand-cut from white and red shells.

Of all the islands the most complex in its traditions was Malaita. There the bush people were still mainly pagan while there were two lagoons — Lau and Langalanga — which were South Sea versions of Venice, for the people lived on artificial islands they had built of coral rocks, filling in the interstices with soil so that they could grow their coconut palms and build tight little streets of palmleaf houses. These villages were easily defensible and far enough out in salt water for the malarial mosquitos not to be able to reach them.

Malaita had a reputation for rebelliousness and violence. The last massacre of Europeans in the Solomons had taken place there in 1927. Not that the Malaitans were wholly to blame; their patience had long been tried by dishonest traders and by blackbirders — labour recruiters for

the Queensland sugar plantations who were not above kidnapping men
if they could not otherwise persuade them. I was especially warned not
to go to the north-eastern corner of the island, where a Captain Woodcock had carried out some of the worst depredations; the Melanesians
had long memories and would undoubtedly regard me as one of his clan
and therefore fair game for revenge.

The only alarming occasion on Malaita took place when we were
staying in the rest house at Maluu on the north end of the island near
the Lau lagoon. On our last evening there we and a couple of New
Zealand anthropologists got involved in a party with the native government employees, the local clerk, the teacher and the three policemen.

Somehow we accumulated fifty bottles of beer and three of whisky, all
of which were piled in the middle of a circle, and the evening began
pleasantly, exchanging tales of the megapode, the national bird of the
Solomons, which lays enormous eggs and is said — a belief all the policemen vowed to defend with their lives if need be — to lay one such egg
every day of its life once it begins to produce. The eggs are so coveted
that, on islands where the birds are attracted by the warm sand, the
laying areas are divided into squares over which people have hereditary
rights and where they build shelters to attract the birds. It is taboo to kill
the megapode or to take more than three eggs out of four.

At first there was a lyrical feeling to the occasion as we sat in a circle
on the stone flags of the terrace, with the black velvet of the night
beyond us slashed by the gold of fishing torches down the bay. The clerk
and constable began to sing the bittersweet love songs of the Langalanga
lagoon from which they both came, while the treefrogs and insects chor-
used. The songs had a lilting quality, but in the end they seemed monotonous. The tunes were almost interchangeable, and the lyrics gave the
songs their significance. To us the lyrics were incomprehensible, and so,
we realized, they were to all but the two Langalanga men who sang
them. Indeed, as the evening went on it became clear that the local
differences between Solomon Islanders were deep and enduring, and
only lightly papered over by education.

After the Langalanga men tired of singing, the teacher, who resembled
one of those Indian students in whom a Western education releases an
irrepressible didacticism, began to lecture us on the merits of rock,
which was belatedly hitting the Solomons, and to play on the gramo-
phone he had brought the strident yawpings of the West. The whole
atmosphere shifted. We discovered that the great semicircular stoop was
a magnificent dancing ground, and there we stamped in a kind of rock
war-dance, surging to and fro with arms over each other's shoulders
under the blaze of the Coleman lamp, with the policemen emitting

savage cries like those which inspired the raiding expeditions of their ancestors.

It was all excellent fun, but then, when we slumped down exhausted to drink more beer, the quarreling began. The clerk and the teacher, men from southern and northern Malaita respectively, began to insult each other; the two constables began to squabble in pidgin. I remembered against my will the lore that had been pumped into us now by half a hundred Europeans: "Watch out when the natives get our booze! They can't take it! That's when they become violent! Don't let it ever happen!" And here were we, positively encouraging it to happen! Over the next hour, wild dancing alternated with wild drinking, and maudlin fraternity with regional truculence. The atmosphere grew steadily more tense, until abruptly the police sergeant marched his unsteady troop back to the clerk's house, where we heard them shouting and breaking bottles far into the night. The next morning, when I went to pay for our room in the rest house, I found the clerk grievously hung over, yet so doggedly loyal to his job that he insisted on groaning over to his office and opening the safe to give me a receipt in accordance with government regulations. Nobody had been hurt by anything but alcohol.

The men we drank with that night were acculturated Melanesians, representatives of the class that would move into power when the islands became independent in 1978. And as I remember them I think not only of the drinking and quarreling, but even more of the presence of mind of the police sergeant who broke up the party when he thought it might get out of hand, and the conscientiousness of the clerk who insisted on doing his duty on the painful morning after.

Traditionally, on Malaita the bush people and the coast people have been enemies, divided by jealousies and vendettas, which they cherish passionately. Nevertheless, even in such a fragmented society, trade is a notable moderator of hostilities, and everywhere in the Solomons there are places where people of different clans gather for the rites of commerce. A few miles beyond Maluu to the north there was a market site on a rivermouth that had been in use as long as tradition remembered.

Since the hill people often have to walk two hours or more over switchback terrain, markets do not start early, and when we reached the rivermouth at nine o'clock trading was only just about to begin. The taboo ground was a sandy delta, and two high-prowed canoes were being beached by island women; two other similar boats were coming up the narrow estuary, propelled partly by paddle and partly by a small mastless triangular sail which one of the women held up above her head. As soon as they reached running water, the women leapt out and, wading, drew their boats up on the sand.

The bush people gathered in a grove overlooking the delta. There were about a hundred of them when we arrived, but others kept appearing in small family groups. The women carried produce, mainly the sweet potatoes that grow in the hilltop gardens, wrapped in pandanus-leaf mats; the men carried weapons — hatchets, clubs, cane knives, a few rifles, and bows and arrows in the case of the boys. None of the coast men appeared.

Looking from one group to the other, the differences were evident. The coast women were taller and fatter, with the heavy shoulders of canoe people; the bush folk were trim and muscular, with the massive calves of hill walkers. The coast women wore washed-out and shapeless cotton dresses, but the bush women mostly wore only their red cloth kilts. The bush men displayed much finery of bead armlets and porpoise-teeth jewellery, and one especially striking dandy was obviously a "big man"; he wore a black hat garnished with gold braid and with tiny gold- and silver-framed mirrors; his new red kilt was held in place by a wide leather belt studded with silver from which hung a rifle and a finely woven and geometrically patterned bag which evidently contained his smoking materials, for he puffed on a pipe and unlike most of the other men did not have a mouth red from betel chewing. While the other bush folk merely stared at us under their heavy Melanesian brows, and smiled only if we smiled first, he came silently up to us, shook my hand, elaborately raised his splendid hat to Inge, and turned back to rejoin his friends.

For a while the two groups remained apart, as the lagoon women unloaded the fresh and dried fish and octopus they had brought, and then the man in the black hat blew a whistle, and all the hill women went wading through the river to the taboo area. The trading was almost entirely in barter, the garden and forest produce of the hills for the fish of the islands. But out on the edge under the shade of the trees, half a dozen Malaitans in European dress had opened suitcases and were squatting beside their cigarettes, flashlights, knives, stick tobacco, plastic trinkets, chewing gum, and English biscuits; it was the only corner of the market where cash changed hands.

Compared to markets almost anywhere else in the world, everything proceeded quietly, the bargaining carried on almost in whispers. And yet there was a sense of latent violence, projected by the group of armed men, with their great mops of hair and their barbaric jewellery, looking on silently from the shadows of the grove; a past of nervous watchfulness seemed to find expression in their attitudes.

XXVII

A STEP INTO THE STONE AGE

IN THE MOUNTAINS OF New Guinea, we felt we were entering a different world from the archipelagos of the South Seas, which, whether coral atolls or volcanic high islands, were specks on the map compared with this vast island, bigger than France and West Germany combined, whose mountains soar to 16,000 feet. With its hundreds of tribes living in valleys segregated by the razor crests of its ranges, New Guinea is a continent in miniature, and its people were nearer to the stone age than any folk I had seen.

By the time we got there the first white men had entered the High-lands less than fifty years before, and any administration dated from the period after the area was retaken from the Japanese in World War II. Though it was near the independence that came three years later, the territory was still ruled under mandate by Australia and exploited by Australian traders and speculators.

The capital, Port Moresby, and the district headquarters of Lae on the northern coast, were shabby colonial settlements with fairly large white populations and many native Paupuans who acted as labourers and servants. The racist bias of most of the Australians was quite evident and residential sectors were effectively segregated, as were schools. I disliked these wretched little imperial enclaves intensely.

In the Highlands one encountered a dramatic difference between two ways of life: that of the new white occupiers who established the raw new settlements, and that of the natives, most of whom remained totally unacculturated pagans and belonged to a world that seemed at least ten thousand years away in time. Perhaps if we had lived there for long periods as anthropologists or government field workers, we might have established a tenuous understanding with the Highland tribesmen, but it would have been a slow and difficult process. Most of the Australians we

encountered in Goroka and Mount Hagen, the main towns of the Highlands, lived as much apart from native existence as we did in our role of
travellers.

The white people of Mount Hagen would sit in the garden of a café in
late morning when the cold night mists had burnt away and the sun had
warmed the air, and eat the ices the Italian proprietor served. Always,
along the white paling that bounded the lawn, a line of tribesmen would
stand and stare at us. And we stared back with an equal sense of remoteness at these black and almost naked men, often tall, and muscular from
walking their steep mountain paths, whose only dress would often consist of what the Australians called arse-grass, a tuft of long narrow leaves
hung fore and aft, perhaps supplemented by the skin of a small oppos-
sum hung on the chest. Yet the ornamentation that went with this sartor-
ial simplicity was often elaborate, with intricate shell and bead bracelets
clustering on the arms, and necklaces decorated with the boar's tusks which
are treasured everywhere by Melanesians.

Their mops of frizzy hair were decorated until they looked like marvellously strange hats. Some of the men would arrange elaborate montages
of feathers from the Bird-of-Paradise and other ornate species. Others
would use the wings of small and brilliant birds; others exotic flowers
arranged often with great taste and imagination in brilliant perishable
creations. Sometimes one would see a discreet but eloquent creation made
from small, delicate ferns, and one man had contrived marvellously with
the carapaces of coloured beetles. The detritus of civilization was not
despised. I saw several striking arrangements of coloured plastic ribbons,
and one intricately knotted bonnet made of discarded recorder tape.

On the verges of the mountain towns there were markets to which the
tribal people came every week. I suspect the markets were traditional
gathering places, and that the towns arose near them because this was an
easy way for traders to make contact with and government officials to
supervise the local population. The market at Goroka, on a broad open
space about a mile from the town, was a large and famous one, to which
people came from hundreds of nearby villages. A fair amount of trade
went on, partly with white people who went there to buy fruit or other
produce, but largely in barter among the tribespeople. All around the
area where the trading went on, the people gathered in little village
groups, sitting on the ground together, and one felt that many of them
had come to see and be seen. Each group was different from the next in
the arrangement of its jewellery or its garments, though few, male or
female, were far from nakedness. As well as its own style of dress, each
group had its dialect, though I heard some of them using pidgin, which
is now an official language in New Guinea.

We encountered neither smiles nor scowls, only a stare, proclaiming curiosity, perhaps a little horror at our pale eyes, but not the beginning of a relationship. The only fragmentary human contact I experienced came when a tribesman, who had departed from the usual kind of upland head-dress by wearing a biker's helmet decorated with beer labels and who carried the denuded frame of an umbrella as a sceptre, came up to me and solemnly touched a handspread of bananas I had just bought. I tore one off and gave it to him. He took it and departed without a glance or a gesture.

And yet here I experienced the most telling epiphany of our journey. We had come to a corner where only barter trading between tribesmen was going on and, to my astonishment, I saw an old man selling stone age implements that had obviously been made only a few weeks or months before. They were adzes; in each of them the long blade of beautifully polished grey-green stone, a perfect example of neolithic art, was attached with elaborate cording to the shaped and smoothed elbow from a tree branch. Another man was bargaining with the old trader and in his hands he held not the Australian silver dollars which are the only cash the tribes of the Highlands will normally accept, but shell money that had obviously been traded up from the coast; there were strings of small perforated discs and a few discs bigger than a hand. It must have been a ceremonial exchange, for shell money is not used any longer in ordinary transactions, but usually in a ritual context like a wedding; I gathered shortly afterwards that the stone adzes themselves are now used only on sacred occasions when a metal blade might offend ancestral spirits. But of such things I was not aware. It seemed that we had stumbled on a transaction from the late stone age, from the dawn of human culture. I had reached a point of origins from which there seemed nothing but to return. And immediately I found myself closing off my perceptions of the South Pacific. With that final epiphany I had seen enough. I wrote the last page of my travel journal on that day.

We soon flew from Mount Hagen to Port Moresby, and started on the long journey back to Vancouver. That day was my sixtieth birthday, and on the plane out of Port Moresby I sat with a tall Sepik snake-man mask between my knees which Inge had bought me from a dealer in Mount Hagen. When I explained to the Fijian air hostess why I was carrying it, she embraced and kissed me on the cheeks with all the warmth of which her admirable people are capable, and it seemed that I was back from the shades of the Neolithic past into the present of human intermingling. I am sure that, perhaps at the cost of a regrettable loss of fanciful millinery, the strange alien people I encountered in the Highlands of New Guinea will soon be adapting themselves to a world that offers more choices than the tribe can ever allow, and also more risks.

XXVIII

DOING JUSTICE TO THE DEAD

I N VANCOUVER AT THE END of May, 1972, I still thought of a
future as regularly interrupted as the past by expeditions like that to
the South Sea. Gordon Babineau and I used to speculate on future
journeys we might propose to the CBC like following the course of the
Norsemen from Denmark through the Faroe islands and Iceland to Labrador
and Newfoundland; tracing the triumphal and tragic expedition of
Alexander through the Middle East to the Indus and back to Babylon; or
making films on the kingdoms of the Himalayas — Nepal and Bhutan,
Sikkim and Ladakh. But all these plans went unfulfilled. It would be
almost a decade before — on our fifth trip to India — Inge and I again made
a long journey.

Certainly there was no immediate prospect of considerable travels
since I would have to write and record the scripts for the South Seas
films, and to turn the journey into a travel book.

Shortly before leaving for the South Pacific I had also been approached by Jacob Epstein of Quadrangle Press in New York with the
proposal that I should write a work of historical detection, to be called
Who Killed the Empire? This fitted not only with our extensive travels but
also my developing interest in imperialism and its effects. So I agreed to
do the book, for which Anthony Shiel, who had now bought up Christy
& Moore and succeeded John Smith as my agent, negotiated a contract
for English rights with Jonathan Cape. All this meant I had committed
myself to a long period of work.

We were as glad to be back as we were to start our wandering. There
had been only three days in the whole four and a half months in the
South Seas when we really rested. Yet I did not find it easy to settle down to
work. For one thing, we had returned to find a house that our temporary
custodian, a highly recommended Shakespearian scholar, had left filthier

than the worst New Guinea hut. In the evening of our return, my slippers came off my feet from sticking in the accumulated grease on the kitchen floor, the house was malodorous, the refrigerator was full of furry stinking remnants, and it took four days of prodigious cleaning before I could settle down to reducing the vast pile of correspondence and other urgent tasks that awaited me.

Some of the correspondence was pleasant, like the letters from Shiel and Pringle telling of the critical success of *Dawn and the Darkest Hour*, my book on Aldous Huxley, which had come out while I was away. Two at least of the tasks were melancholy ones.

Abe Rotstein had asked me whether I would invite Paul Goodman to do something for *Canadian Forum*. For thirty years I had known Paul well through correspondence, though we had never seen each other. In the 1940s, when he was poor and unknown, he would send me manuscripts on anarchism for *Freedom* or NOW, typed on cheap yellow paper and smudgily corrected with thick carpenters' pencils, and we had both written in Dwight Macdonald's magazine, *Politics*. I had seen his style develop over the years from congestion to clarity. During the 1960s Paul and I, like Colin Ward in England, had moved to the verges of the orthodox anarchist movement. Paul was especially attracted towards an approach based on the liberation of education from compulsion and rigidity. Though we agreed on such matters — Paul had a fine intuitive sense of ways in which one could work on the fringes of existing society and change it by infiltration — I never regarded him as a particularly logical thinker. He was right more often by instinct than by reason, but this did not take away from the fact that he was much the most original of post-war anarchist thinkers.

I did not get an article from Paul for the *Canadian Forum* because he died of a heart attack before he had answered my letter, and instead Abe published my article celebrating and mourning Goodman. About the same time another American writer died whom I had admired but never known, though references in his writings suggest that he knew my work, and in those days people were always finding resemblances between our approaches as critics. This was Edmund Wilson. We had independently derived our approaches from the European man-of-letters tradition of criticism, and our similarity lay mainly in our shared difference from the academic critics. When he died, I was asked to give a long talk on Wilson for the CBC. He was one of the great contemporary critics. As I remarked to Rotstein, about Wilson and Goodman: "There are some seasons when the stars fall out of one's sky."

THAT SUMMER WAS PARTICULARLY populous with visitors. One day Robert Fulford and Al Purdy arrived independently of each other.

Inge and I invited them to dinner together, and Al arrived tipsy, with a drunken second-hand bookseller in tow. It might have been a disastrous evening, but it was not, for Purdy tends to be a better conversationalist when his brain is irrigated with alcohol, and we had an evening full of original and erratic conversation, in which fine insights into literature were given word.

Much as I enjoyed such visitors, I found myself resisting the social occasions that are often considered necessary to the literary life. After my heart attack in 1966, I had already abandoned giving public lectures, but now I was beginning to find that the more I was published by Canadian houses and became thought of as a Canadian writer, the more I was expected to perform in public. I began to feel exploited. I was given an award in connection with International Book Week as B.C.'s leading non-fiction author; the joker came in the paragraph of the letter announcing the honour, in which I was asked to participate in "interviews with award winning authors on radio and television and in the press, appearances in book stores and at special programs in public libraries in the Greater Vancouver area."

I began to feel hunted by the well-meaning friends of literature. Just before I left for the South Seas Dave Godfrey had accepted for his publishing house, New Press, my volume of essays, *The Rejection of Politics*. Susan Helwig, who was running promotion for New Press, wrote in September to tell me that Dave would be coming out to Vancouver when the book was published and intended to arrange a series of receptions and parties to launch it. Perhaps I should have been appreciative, as most writers would have been — but instead I protested vehemently.

"I have already taken down my *How to Stay Alive in the Woods* and my *Whole Earth Almanac* and started my preparations to depart for Omenica or the Queen Charlottes or somewhere equally remote when the end of October comes round! But seriously, why does Dave think I obstinately live in Vancouver, and even there a reclusive life so far as whatever passes for a literary world is concerned?"

The Rejection of Politics was published in November, and it foundered with the death of New Press as an independent concern, for it appeared just before Dave Godfrey's abandonment of the publishing house he had created and the beginning of its Odyssey as the subsidiary of larger enterprises. *The Rejection of Politics* was the victim of this situation, and nothing I might have done to help it by attending receptions would have made any difference, for virtually no effort was made to sell the book, and for this reason it remains among the least known and least profitable of my works.

Herbert Read: The Stream and the Source, came out in London at almost the same time as *The Rejection of Politics* in Toronto, and it gained much more attention, for it got excellent reviews. But it did not sell so well as *The Crystal Spirit* or *Dawn and the Darkest Hour*, and unlike them it did not find an American publisher, and this was because it appeared at the time when Read's prestige had already entered its rapid decline.

Faber & Faber had become Read's main publishers because they — or T.S. Eliot, as their most forceful director — recognized the excellence of his work as a poet, an essayist and, in rare movements of the spirit, as the onetime novelist of *The Green Child* and the lyrical autobiographer of *Annals of Innocence and Experience*, and they wanted a book that would celebrate these aspects. What Fabers and I had not sufficiently recognized was that, as with so many writers, Read's reputation was something different from his achievement. It was the product of that uncertain, restless side of his nature — the rogue side — that led him to seek money and fame by writing popularizing books and going on endless lecture tours, which he justified as a kind of missionary activity. That activity had its uses, but they were ephemeral and had nothing to do with his genuine achievements as an imaginative writer or even a serious critic. My book dealt with that Read who continued to create and imagine behind his reputation — the reputation that in life made him a celebrity. When he died the celebrity dwindled quickly, but the works remained.

Meanwhile, I was finding *Who Killed the British Empire?* more complicated than I had anticipated. If I wished to find the right answers, I had to ask the right questions, since nobody else had tackled quite so ambitiously the reasons for the Empire's fall. The phenomenon was much too complex to be attributed to the will of any one person, even so great and influential a figure as Gandhi, or to some simple general hypothesis like the failure of will among the rulers.

I grew certain that the processes which brought to an end what is often known as the Second Empire (which came into being after the departure of the thirteen American colonies), did not begin in twentieth century India, but early in the nineteenth century in Canada, which was the first of the settlement colonies to struggle — from the 1830s onward — for the responsible government that would lead to local autonomy and eventual independence. But I also recognized that the death of the British Empire, like the deaths of the Roman Empire and the Persian Empire before it, had in fact been a suicide carried out with the help of willing accomplices anxious to divide up the inheritance.

To show this process and its magnitude, I constructed a panorama of the Empire in 1930, the year when it had attained its maximum extent of territory, and when no English schoolboy believed the sun would ever set on that splendid necklace of red patches that encircled the classroom globe. From this point I proceeded backward a century or more to show how in its very accumulation the empire had embodied the forces that would bring its disintegration, and then went forward from 1930 to show how the visible decline began, and, in far less time than seemed predictable, was brought to its conclusion. All this involved a great deal of work, so that it was early spring of 1973 before I finished it.

In the meantime, to vary my work and earn ready money, I had undertaken extra tasks. One was a series of four lectures for the CBC Ideas program on writers who offered teachings of philosophic pessimism. I included Nietzsche and Spengler, Julian Benda, Ortega y Gasset and Albert Camus, and I ended with a study of H.G. Wells, the enthusiastic utopian idealist whose most telling novels, such as *The Island of Dr. Moreau* and *The Sleeper Awakes*, were shadowed by a deep pessimism that made him a true ancestor — though neither would willingly have admitted it — of the George Orwell who wrote *Nineteen Eighty-Four*. I was drawn to these thinkers by a sense of the importance of reasoned pessimism in confronting the vagaries of destiny. I owed this attitude to my reading of French absurdist writers like Malraux and Camus, and to the Buddhist teaching, that from the elimination of desire and illusion comes the peace of the true philosopher. As well, I inherited an inclination to place little trust in the future which my mother had embodied in her favourite heretical beatitude, "Blessed is he who expecteth nothing, for he shall not be disappointed." Now that I had abandoned the apocalyptic expectations of my more naive anarchist phase, I found that a reasoned pessimism was an excellent standpoint from which to consider practical improvements in society. Ceasing to look forward to great victories, I found it easier to concentrate on small gains. Having once dreamt that humanity would soon experience cataclysmic liberation, I became content with improvements that would better the lives of a few, and during this same winter Inge and I (Inge especially) devoted much time to settling in the semi-rural communities outside Vancouver a handful of Tibetan refugee families whom the Canadian government had at last grudgingly allowed to emigrate. We found them jobs and homes, and we begged paintings from our artist friends to put on a show in Vancouver that earned us enough money to provide for them until they were settled in their work and houses. They were mostly simple peasants — some of them former nomad herdsman — with little or no English, but in Canada as in India they showed powers of adaptation, and most of them prospered, clinging to their Mahayanist religions and their language.

The other considerable task I undertook at this time was an offshoot from *Anarchism*. That had been translated into Italian as *L'Anarchia* and published in Milan by the unfortunate Giangiacomo Feltrinelli, who developed such an interest in the radical books he issued during the 1960s that he became a political activist and blew himself up with a bomb he was carrying for one of the violent groups that flourished in Italy at this time. Though the publisher died in this sadly absurd way, the house of Feltrinelli continued, and *L'Anarchia* has sold well. It attracted the editors of the new version of the *Encyclopedia Italiana*, and they asked me to write a long essay on anarchism. This involved a certain ingenuity, since I had only shortly beforehand written an equally long essay for *The Encyclopedia Britannica* to replace the famous but now outdated piece that Kropotkin had written for the great 9th edition of the *Britannica*, and I had to write an entirely different text using what was essentially the same basic material.

All this slowed down *Who Killed the British Empire?*, but in some ways I was glad of this for it meant that I took more thought. At the same time I had to condense a mass of material into one volume, while Gibbon had taken eight to perform a similar account of the Roman Empire. At last I saw the end of the book in sight and forced myself to complete it by booking a flight to Zurich on the 25th April.

The past year had represented a climatic point in my life as a writer. Up to now, I had originated the publication of my books mainly in Britain, and I was still regarded by people in London as an English writer who happened to reside in Canada and by Canadians as a kind of British expatriate whose local loyalties could not entirely be trusted, and this in spite of *Canadian Literature*.

When we set off for Zurich it looked as though the pattern would be continued, for the next book on my list was the account of our travels in the South Seas which Faber were publishing, and early in 1973 I had been corresponding with Alan Pringle about future plans. We agreed tentatively on a book on the literature of politics in England, and we also discussed my autobiography. But none of these plans was to work out, at least in the way Alan and I had envisaged them. The book on the literature of politics was not and probably never will be written, and the writing of my autobiography was delayed until my relationship with Faber had come to an end and I had become, in publication as well as in residence and sentiment, a Canadian writer.

XXIX

MEDALS AND MEN

INGE'S PARENTS HAD BEEN INSPIRED, on reaching eighty, to make yet another start in their lives, and having earlier on pulled up roots in Weimar rather than continue to live under Communist rule, they decided now to leave the semi-industrial ambiance of the Frankfurt region where they had been living since their flight to West Germany, and find a rural retreat in Bavaria.

When we drove from Zurich, our destination was a place called Bad Fussing, about 30 kilometres west of Passau. When we approached it we were a little shocked to find that it was not in the heart of the mountains, which Otto's old Alpine enthusiasms had led us to expect, but on the flat alluvial plain of the Inn valley. We failed to find it on the map we carried; the reason was not its smallness but its newness, for the place dated from a mere ten years back when mineral springs were discovered in the fields near Safferstetten, a village we found still as dung-smelling and rustic as it must always have been when we drove through it towards the white blocks of the hotels, apartment buildings and modernist church towers of this community whose streets were laid out in North American quadrilaterals over what a decade ago had been good grazing land and maize fields.

For the rest of the long lives of Otto and Gertrud Bad Fussing was to become one of the focal points of our life. It was an exclusively German resort; I found it a lugubrious place reminding me of Huxley's spa story, "After the Fireworks", but even more of *The Magic Mountain* if one could imagine Mann's mountain levelled to a plain. Its permanent population seemed to consist of aged arthritics, who found in the newness and rawness of the place an earnest of longevity; it would take at least fifteen years for the trees that lined the new streets to become mature, and I suspect they imagined their lives would be similarly extended, for when old people change their ways of life it is usually for magical reasons. But apart from these permanent residents there was a shifting population taking advantage of the German Medical Plans, whom we would encounter in the hotels, which were cheap and good because they did not cater to foreign tourists; they were amiable middle-class people who combined taking the waters with a bit of a holiday. There was a big circular open-air bath in the centre of the town where they would sit for hours, looking like people in a George Grosz painting, fat lobster-red men smoking cigars among the rising steam and buxom Brunnhildes in flowery bathing suits. A whole clique of sly "bath-doctors" and domineering masseurs preyed upon them. I never joined in their aqueous pursuits, but I continued to find the place interesting in its special Teutonic combination of hypochondria and vulgarity.

Still, it is possible that I would not have put up so long with the place if I had not found its surroundings so rustically appealing. North of it lay wooded country of little hill ranges and shaded flowery valleys known as the Holzland; over the Inn stretched a little-travelled corner of Upper Austria whose beechwooded hills undulated through the Sauwald to the high clifftops from which one could look down into the castled cleft of the Danube valley. It was full of old farms and villages laced together by gravel roads lined with blossoming pear trees; deer grazed in herds on the edges of the woods, and when we arrived the storks were settling to nest on the church towers. In almost every village they were preparing for May Day by erecting tall peeled poles decorated with wreaths of ribbons and fir twigs.

The tallest pole was that which the girls were entwining with elaborate serpentines of leaves in a village with the promising name of Oberfuck-ing. We went back to Oberfucking on May Day in the hope of witness-ing a saturnalia, but though the young men slapped their shoesoles with high vigour as they danced around the pole, there was nothing for strangers but red Burgenland wine and bratwurst cooked on char-coal outside the gates of the farmhouses. Farther on, in the little town of Ried, peasant bands played in the square, dancers kissed each other as they stepped in elegant minuets from the days of Maria Theresa, a child of ten won the great raffle for the 100 foot pole, and municipal politicians in knee-breeches talked of the glories of Franz Josef's reign. Later that day, crossing back into Bavaria, we stopped for dinner in a town in the foothills of the Bohemian forest, with Czech watchtowers looking down from the divide — which is also the border — and ate baked carp and barbel from the Danube. As he served us tall glasses of wheat beer, made locally and drunk with floating chunks of lemon, the inn-keeper remarked that life was better in the good old Kaiser's time. It was a nostalgic part of Europe, resentful of the present in which it prospers.

A few days later we all wandered through the Tirol, over the Arlberg Pass and down into the eastern cantons of Switzerland. Familiar Appenzell with its cheese and fine painted houses. Zug with its astrological clocks and its lakeside menus of stuffed pike and kirschtorte. Einsiedeln, with the immense pilgrimage church, where peasants with vast spade beards and flower-embroidered blouses from Mittenwald were clambering up the tall steps into the gilded intricacies, the vistas of paint and porcelain, whence vast organs thundered Bach's harmonies towards the snowy mountains. Brienz with its weather-battered wood inn where they served delicious white asparagus from Vaucluse with raw ham from the Grisons.

In Basel, I visited one of its great banking houses. There were three deep floors below ground level, and on each floor was a vault as big as a large church, its walls lined with safety deposit boxes. Each vault was guarded by tall suave gentlemen in expensive suits who had the manner and look of ambassadors, and haunted by obsessive elderly men riffling through parchments or counting the gold roubles and crowns of vanished empires, or caressing miniature ingots the size and shape of chocolate bars. One was at the heart of global finance, of the machine that controls so much of our fates, and neither the machine nor the heart seemed to beat.

Nevertheless, I felt that some of the spirit of that temple of Midas had descended on me when we got home and I found among my mail first a puzzling doggeral poem in praise of beer from Roy Daniells, and then a letter from the Canada Council telling me that I had been selected as one of the three winners of the Molson Prize, which carried with it $15,000 tax free. I was naturally delighted by the news, since the award was given me, as the citation stated, not merely for what might be regarded as my contribution to cultural nationalism, the founding of *Canadian Literature*, but also for "the abundance of ideas" in my books and for the quality of my prose. It was a recognition of the craft, and for that I was grateful.

Early in June Inge and I went to Ottawa for the presentation of the Molson awards to me and the other two recipients, the economist John Deutsch and the painter Alfred Pellan. Ottawa was at its muggiest, with the temperature at 85 degrees, and the ceremony, which had been planned with the Canada Council's usual discretion and good taste, was given an air of drama when nature contributed a violent thunderstorm through whose torrential rains the guests had to find their way to the Château Laurier.

Back at home I settled down for a long season of work. After the unfamiliarly frenetic pace which life in Europe seemed to have taken on, I was grateful for the peace it was still possible to find in cities like Vancouver. I spent the early summer on the South Sea films, which demanded a combination of words and visual images in such a way that neither became dominant and the images were not lost behind what the film men called with horror "the hedge of words". Unlike radio, phrases became more important than arguments, and everything verbal had to be directed towards enhancing rather than supplanting the visual. Here, I think, my past as a poet and the early influence of imagism on my work came in useful. I knew already that statement was not the only use for the word.

I spent many hours in the CBC studios before I even started writing scripts, first going through the unprocessed rushes of the films with the producer and the editor to outline the vital sequences, and then watching the edited films to determine the points where my narrative should intervene. Next I wrote the passages I would speak, timing them to the second. A last fine-tuning would take place when my voice was recorded. It was an exact and disciplined kind of writing, and I felt the strain of this kind of meticulous and, for the writer, somewhat self-effacing work. I was glad to get back into orally-oriented writing when the people who ran *Ideas* at CBC invited me to present a series of four talks on anarchism.

At times I had had doubts as to whether my words and the images Gordon and Mike offered would ever fit together in the seamless garment of a perfect film. But in fact the series — which we called *In the South Seas* in conscious imitation of Robert Louis Stevenson — turned out a great success. It was bought not merely by television networks in Australia and New Zealand, in whose home territory its subject lay, but also in the United States, Britain, and many European countries, including Czechoslovakia, while a version prepared for showing in Quebec found its way to France. It was popular among viewers in Canada; never in fact has any work of mine interested such a variety of people. Our neighbours, my doctor and my dentist, the tellers in our bank and people in shops, quite apart from literary and academic friends, volunteered their praise and asked for more of the same thing. The films seemed to achieve a felicitous combination of giving information and satisfying daydreams.

After all this, Gordon and I had no doubt that soon we would be going off on other such ventures together; we had not reckoned that the internal politics of the CBC are too Byzantine for such criteria as excellence, international acceptance or domestic popularity to count for very much. The balance of funding between Toronto and the outer regions was much more important to bureaucratic minds. We did not give up easily in our efforts to gain approval for our series on the Himalayan kingdoms and there were times over the years we pursued the idea (rather like K. trying to gain access to the Castle) when the CBC mandarins encouraged us. In the end, after I had approached important people in Nepal and Bhutan, Knowlton Nash, who was in charge of public affairs on CBC television, abruptly rejected the proposal without any explanation or consideration for the loss of face I incurred vis-à-vis my Asian contacts. Clearly the funds that might have made an extraordinary visual document of a rapidly changing part of the world were needed for programs planned by Toronto producers, and we in Vancouver were given to understand that we had had our turn with the South Sea films and could expect no more. The intrinsic merit of our suggestions seemed to be irrelevant.

I was still working on *South Sea Journey*, and I found the pattern of the cultures we encountered almost as intricate to navigate as the reefs of the island groups, so that it was only in the following February that I typed the last page of what turned out to be my longest travel book, so long that when they published it Fabers made the mistake of leaving out Inge's excellent photographs of the islands in order to cut costs.

Much of the summer of 1973 was occupied with a 15,000 word essay which Carl Klinck had invited me to write on new poetry for the second edition of the *Literary History of Canada*. In recent years there had been in Canada such a "verbal explosion", as Northrop Frye termed it, that the editors were devoting a whole extra volume merely to the thirteen years between 1960 and 1973. Even so, when I accepted Carl's invitation I did not quite realize what I had undertaken. For the poets had been even more prolix over this period than the prose writers, and I found that, apart from anthologies, no less than 1,100 books of verse had been published by 590 authors in Canada during the period. The revival of poetry in the 1960s had taken on a great deal of the era's general participatory populism, with dozens of small presses and little magazines suddenly appearing, edited and produced by the poets themselves, sometimes elegantly designed but often in smudgy mimeographed form, and with poets wandering over the land and presenting their work to large audiences. It was like a return to the days of the troubadours and for a little while poets like Leonard Cohen, Irving Layton and Al Purdy became almost culture heroes. The magnitude of my task bore down upon me. Even if I dealt only with those who published books, I faced suffocating problems of space. I read long into my nights, putting aside more than half the books after briefly skimming them. I still attentively read more than four hundred, and in the end wrote a sweeping survey of trends and paid closer attention to a few dozen poets who seemed to be writing the verse that might be read a generation hence. At certain periods the poets fly like ephemerae and only a few are destined to perpetuate themselves.

The fact that I carried out this monstrously concentrated task of research and reading, selection and writing was only one of the signs of my growing commitment to the Canadian literary setting and of my metamorphosis from an English-oriented writer living in Canada to a Canadian writer and — even — a western Canadian writer deeply concerned with regional issues.

More crucial was my growing interest in some of the more neglected figures of western Canadian history. One of these was Amor de Cosmos, the leader of the resistance to the monopolistic power of the Hudson's Bay Company on the west coast; during the summer of 1973 I agreed to do a brief biography of him for the Oxford University Press. But even more important was Gabriel Dumont, the Métis leader who had been Riel's general in the Northwest Rebellion of 1885.

I had long believed that Dumont was an exceptional man, and one of our few genuine Canadian heroes, and that his repute had too long been obscured by the attention devoted to Riel, the martyr, and said so in an essay published in the July, 1973 issue of *Saturday Night*. I imagined that, like most periodical articles, it might arouse a flurry of interest and then be forgotten by everyone except those with a special concern for Métis history.

In fact, the interest turned out to be a flood, and within two weeks I had been approached by three publishers who were anxious for me to do a book on Dumont. I felt like Buridan's ass, faced not with two but with three bales of hay. First I had to decide whether I wanted any hay at all; did I really want to write a book on Dumont, and was there material for much more than the article I had written? I decided that if I made it a book on Dumont and his lost world, and presented not only a portrait of the man but also a picture of Métis life and society in the nineteenth century, I would find plenty of material.

Once I had made that decision, the choice of publishers did not involve much difficulty. I eliminated Doubleday immediately because I felt it would be inappropriate for the subsidiary of an American publishing house to be bringing out this essentially Canadian book, and then I picked Hurtig rather than Macmillan because I knew he was a good publisher, generous with authors, and good at distributing books and keeping backlists alive, but even more because I felt that such a western book should be published in Edmonton rather than in Toronto.

In the autumn of 1973 an editorial I had written in *Canadian Literature* involved me in a passing and not altogether happy relationship with *Maclean's* magazine. In the editorial I had discussed some popular magazines, to most of which I had contributed, and their attitude towards literature. Particularly I was interested in the way they used the services of writers, as distinct from journalists. I pointed out that fiction writers and poets were often invited to write articles for such magazines, but that the work to which they owed their names — stories and poems — was rarely published.

Almost immediately I received a letter from Peter Newman, who had read my editorial with some anger and accused me of "attacking" *Maclean's* and of a "haughty dismissal of our continuing efforts." I pointed out that analysis was not attack, and to my astonishment received a reply in which Newman not only accepted what I had said, but invited me to become *Maclean's* regular book reviewer for a trial period, writing an article a month. I accepted, though I should have given more weight to Newman's caution that "of our four million readers only 16% have a university education", for I found myself subject to the pressures to stay popular that are inevitable when one writes for a mass magazine.

The relationship continued, with growing tension, for about ten months; then I received a book for review by Richard Rohmer, with the suggestion that I give it special attention. I did, but my attention was negative since I thought it was a pretentious and unconvincing piece of fiction. My review was published, but shortly afterwards a note came from Newman terminating the trial arrangement on the grounds, which saved face for both of us, that *Maclean's* was about to become a newsmagazine and that my kind of column would not fit into the new format. From this time onward I avoided continuing relationships with such journals, though I was always willing to write occasional articles for them so long as the purpose had been clearly defined beforehand.

So, in these varied tasks, the year span over into the spring of 1974. By June I had sent the biography of Amor de Cosmos to Oxford. My small book was in fact as much a gesture of local patriotism as a biography, for the material I could find on De Cosmos was surprisingly scanty. He was a journalist rather than a writer, and left little that was autobiographical; his papers had been so thoughtlessly dispersed that the archives yielded little in the way of new information, and I was left with a tight character study rather than a biography.

By now I had been working without a break for a year, and though the Himalayan project on which Gordon Babineau and I had been relying did not mature, it was time to go somewhere away, and the signing of my contract with Mel Hurtig gave us a reason, for to write about Dumont I had to travel in his country.

XXX

LITERARY SKIRMISHES

AFTER ALL THE DIFFICULTIES into which I had got myself in the winter of 1973-4, it seemed odd to receive a letter from Al Purdy remarking on the ordered nature of my life. "I don't know," I answered, as I would probably answer even today. "Outwardly my life may look ordered. Inwardly it seems chaos. When I read your poems I feel there's a stiller centre at the heart of all the vortex than mine." I may well have been making a great mistake about Purdy's inner life as he had about mine, and I suspect we had more in common than he and I thought. Other people have wondered at our friendship, but apart from such facts as that we are both autodidacts with an experience of poverty, I think we are driven men, pursued by inherited puritanical impulses that have been sublimated into a restless and insistent creativity, and one of the aspects of the restlessness we share had been the inability to stay for too long even in a chosen place. We travel, not exactly because we like to, since our travels are often appalling in discomfort or boredom. We travel because we must, and sometimes we accept absurd excuses just to keep moving.

In my case, the sense of claustrophobia after the long winter of work was so intense that even before the trip into Dumont's country I had accepted an invitation from the Université d'Ottawa to receive their Doctorate of Literature. I went to receive it at the end of May and two weeks later we set out, driving through the mountain ranges of British Columbia toward the country of the two Saskatchewan rivers that was the heartland of Dumont's life, a parkland of rolling hills and woods of birch and poplar.

The woods were in the fresh green of young leaves and the country was bright as a Cluny tapestry with early summer flowers, while the sloughs and ponds were full of migratory birds nesting. Hundreds of handsome yellow-headed and red-winged blackbirds populated the reed beds of Duck Lake and black terns skimmed over its water. Buffalo and other larger game animals were long gone, but herds of horses around the Métis farms and the Cree reservations reminded one of the days when the mounted hunters ruled the country. The landscape had changed very little in a century.

At places like the battle sites of Duck Lake and Fish Creek the lie of the land was in fact all that was left to bring to life the historic skirmishes that had taken place. At Batoche there was only the bullet-pierced church and the cemetery on top of the escarpment with its view of the South Saskatchewan and the boulder under which Dumont lies. The old village of the rebellion had left no vestige, and nothing remained at St. Laurent of the log houses among which Dumont had ruled his little hunters' republic in the 1870s. Where Dumont ran his ferry across the river, Gabriel's Crossing had been replaced by the glittering girders of Gabriel's Bridge.

Nobody was in doubt who Gabriel was, and indeed the fact that his legend had entered into the popular consciousness was evident. In the whole triangle between Saskatoon, Battleford and Prince Albert you had only to mention his Christian name for people to knew you were speaking of Dumont, though the Métis I talked to at Duck Lake and around Batoche had opinions rather than facts to offer. The question of Riel's sanity, which they passionately upheld, seemed to interest them most. I did find one grand-nephew of Dumont, a wiry little blue-eyed man who talked to me in his potato patch, but either he was not eager to talk to outsiders or he really remembered little from the early childhood seventy years ago when he had known Dumont as an ageing man near death. All he had to tell me was how the children would gather around Dumont outside his cabin door and he would put their hands on the scar on his head where he had been shot during the battle of Duck Lake. I gathered far more facts in the library at the University of Saskatchewan and in the archives that had been set up in the reconstructed NWMP fort at Battleford.

I returned to become involved in a controversy that rumbled all that summer through the Canadian literary world. Fraser Sutherland was editing a little magazine called *Northern Journey*. He had published some extracts from a self-analytical journal I had been keeping during the early 1970s, but otherwise I had no connection with the periodical, which early in 1974 published a kind of semi-fiction, "Slow Burn", by a young writer called Wigle, in which Margaret Atwood was unflatteringly introduced as a character drawn from real life; in an oblique way John Glassco was also introduced. It was a wretched piece of writing and certainly not worth the furore it created.

John Glassco sensibly decided to ignore the incident. Margaret Atwood, however, suspected she had been libelled, and got a lawyer to write to *Northern Journey* demanding an apology. Fraser Sutherland and his colleagues refused to offer one. Then Margaret took the case to the Writers' Union of Canada and Marian Engel, who was chairman, agreed to accept it as a grievance. Both John Glassco and I were perturbed by this decision, since it seemed obvious that the intention was for some kind of sanction would be applied against *Northern Journey*. And this would have two negative implications. One was that the Writers' Union approved of the libel laws of Canada, which Margaret Atwood's lawyer seemed inclined to invoke, when in fact those very laws were generally used to the detriment of writers. The other was that any attempt to apply sanctions in this case would be de facto censorship, and this, equally, was something in which a writers' organization should not involve itself. I wrote to Marian Engel in May objecting to this kind of action on the part of the officers of the union without consulting the members on what clearly seemed to me a matter of principle even more than a policy.

> If we are going beyond our primary function of protecting the material and legal interests of writers in the exercise of their profession and set ourselves up as a tribunal of professional ethics, I think this has to be discussed before it happens; personally I don't think we should be dabbling in such matters. But I don't like anything that sounds like censorship within the profession.

I became involved in correspondence with all the principals, including both Atwood and Sutherland, as well as Marian Engel, and also John Glassco, who stood ironically aloof, though he too disapproved of the WUC involving itself in a stand that bordered on censorship. I also wrote a long article analysing the situation that appeared in *Quill & Quire*. I offered to act as mediator, and Marian accepted my offer. Unfortunately her letter came when I was travelling to Batoche, and I did not reply until later, agreeing to mediate, but not to attempt arbitration. As I put it to Marian, I did so on the understanding that "no one can be expected to lose face completely, but that this means that everyone must be willing to lose a little bit of face. From a very long letter I have received from MA I believe she is working on the same principle. If I can get the others to the same point then something may be achieved. But I can't guarantee it."

The line I took was that the libel issue should be abandoned. I regarded Wigle's piece as so poorly written and in such bad taste that for purely literary reasons it should never have been published, and that the editors

XXXI

THE MUSE REVISITS

L OOKING AT THE *CANADIAN ENCYCLOPEDIA* which came out in 1985 with a modest group of articles over my signature, I find a certain ironic pleasure in the fact that Mel Hurtig had enough respect for the breadth of my knowledge to make me his first choice for the editorship of this massive and memorable work. When he rang me up one July evening in 1974 it was one of those ambivalent occasions when one feels an intense pleasure at an offer one cannot accept. Shortly after I had declined it, Mel offered the editorship to Morris Wolfe, who accepted, and I have no idea why he did not continue or why a gap of about five years ensued before James Marsh actually started in 1980 the great task of compiling the encyclopedia. When I handle its three massive volumes, I wonder whether even if I had found the time I would have had enough single-mindedness to carry anything like this to conclusion.

The autumn of 1974 was marked for me by something different from the prose of an encyclopedia, for I returned after many years to the writing of poetry. In *Letter to the Past* I tell how my cherished friend and anarchist associate, Marie Louise Berneri, unexpectedly died in her early thirties at the time of my return to Canada in April, 1949. My sudden inability to write lyric or elegiac poetry coincided with her death, and I was convinced that the emotional shock was the cause of this block. Since then, I had written no more than six short poems, though I had not ceased to write verse, which had been diverted into the looser and less immediate form of poetic drama written originally for radio. For decades I have been content to admit that my poetic life lay in the past, and it was with this feeling that I compiled the *Selected Poems* which Clarke Irwin published in 1967; the book seemed a memento of a lost life.

By the early 1970s I began to feel the desire to write lyric poetry stirring in me again. Two small events in 1973 encouraged me in such thoughts. That year I discovered a cache of poems written in the 1930s but never published; I thought they were worth resurrecting, and Robin Skelton agreed, publishing a group of nine of them in *Malahat Review*. This recognition of the validity of my past poetry was combined with the announcement in 1973 that Clarke Irwin had sold out of the *Selected Poems* and did not intend to reprint. I thought of combining them with the poems that had appeared in *Malahat*, and with some others omitted from the *Selected*, into a larger volume, and presenting it as a Collected Poems.

When Margaret Atwood was involved in small press publishing, she had encouraged me to think of the House of Anansi if I had a book which the more commercial presses might not be inclined to consider. Margaret had ceased to be active with Anansi by the time I thought of offering my poetry, but Shirley Gibson was responsive and so was James Polk who later became Anansi's chief editor. The new volume would be yet another selection, but it would be divided into sections determined by theme rather than arranged chronologically, and would be accompanied by an introduction, and by smaller prefaces to each section. As I remarked to Mike Doyle, I saw it as "a kind of poem-studded chronicle that will be one of the many circlings I am making around the matter of an autobiography." I did not promise any new poems, yet by the end of 1974 the new poems in fact came.

Clearly my eagerness to publish poetry again sprang from a desire to show that the poet who was my first literary persona had not died but was merely sleeping. And in fact he only needed the right emotional impulse to awaken him. The inability to deal with grief over death had silenced him, and it was appropriate that death should later reawaken and liberate him, for he re-emerged as an elegiac poet.

This began when a woman of dark and daunting beauty who had recently become my friend learnt during the summer of 1974 that her son was suffering from cancer. His case seemed hopeless, and I empathized with her anxiety and fear. Then we heard that Inge's father was gravely ill. We had thought of going to India in the summer of 1974 to see our Tibetan friends again, and now we decided to route our journey through Bavaria so that we could see him. We set off at the end of September.

Our time in London en route was already an anxious and saddening period, for Alan Pringle, I found, was suffering from a detached retina, and also from some more serious illness about whose nature he was reticent; in fact it was leukemia and he had only three more years to live.

We met him and his wife Margaret for lunch; it was clear that his sight was greatly impaired, and treatment from cortisone had changed his face into an almost unrecognizable leonine mask. Already he had told me that he was withdrawing from active publishing, and one reason for my visit was to be introduced to the editor who would be carrying on with *South Sea Journey* and presumably with any books I might later write for Faber. I was sad at Alan's condition, and also at the thought that some of the most fruitful and agreeable associations of my life seemed to be coming to an end. When I met his successor I immediately recognized the lack of intellectual sympathy between us. I also sensed that with Alan's departure there would be changes in Fabers' policies, and that my own shifting orientation from an England-directed to a Canada-directed writer might affect my relations with the firm. My premonitions were justified; *South Sea Journey* was to mark the end of a publishing relationship that had been fortunate and productive for so long.

When we got to Germany we found that Otto was indeed slowly sinking into twilight with a multitude of ills. His Bavarian doctors had concealed from him what was wrong, but all of us, including he, knew that he was suffering from irremediable cancer; we went through an extraordinary black charade, all knowing the truth but none of us articulating it. He was to experience remissions that would keep him miserably alive for the next five years, but the sense of imminent death was strong in him, and he spent much of the time in recollection of his past life, of the horrors of the Great War, of the terrifying moments of mountaineering, of the cruelties he had committed as a hunter and for which he blamed himself, of his childhood during the Kaiser's time in the ancient Thuringian town of Schmalkalden.

Since our presence seemed to sustain him in his time of despair, we decided not to continue to India. There were times when I could not endure the points of emotion, and I would go off, my head whirling with the images evoked by what he had been saying, to walk in the fir woods or to read in the hotel. One day I picked up a piece of paper and quickly wrote my first poem in many years: "Silent Hounds Loping", and the final stanza reads:

> Old mountaineer
> you stand
> at the white saddle
> on your way down
> from the blinding peak
> where you have seen
> guides and companions

fall past you into space,
you helpless.
It is all memory
but for you as real as your delirium
and for us as real as your tears falling
bright as if frozen
into the dark crevasse
where the men you survive
and the beasts you slaughtered
wait.

This was something quite different from the formalized poems which, in the 1930s manner, I had previously written, more fluent, and colloquial and also freer in form. I realized how much I had learnt, half-unconsciously, from the younger Canadian poets who were writing around me, as other poets of my generation like Earle Birney, Dorothy Livesay and P.K. Page had done, coming back in their second careers to write a poetry entirely unlike that of their pasts. I wrote several other poems during the next few days.

We came back to Canada early in November, to find that the son of my friend had died. To the public eye the mother carried her grief with magnificent stoicism, yet one had only to look to her haggard face, more beautiful than ever in sorrow, to see how deeply she had been hurt. I found poems continuing to enter my mind, dwelling on many aspects of the tragedy, and also on the simplification of my relationship with her, that resulted from it, a "tenderness/of touching solitudes", as I put it in a poem of that time.

Still the poems continued. By the time I sent in the final typescript of my selection in the early spring of 1975, it contained fifteen new poems, so that they filled a quarter of the book, *Notes on Visitations*.

The poetic impulse did not die away soon. I continued writing elegies and lyrics through the 1970s and into 1981, and published a series of further volumes with small presses — *Anima: Or Swann Grown Old*, a suite of bitter love poems, with Black Moss Press, *The Kestrel* with Coelfrith Press in England, and *The Mountain Road* which Fred Cogswell published in his Fiddlehead Books series, with a cover designed by my old friend Molly Bobak. The kind and scope of the poems tended to vary. By the time *The Mountain Road* appeared I had added nature poems to the elegiac and wryly erotic poems of the other volumes, including a number about birds, for I was returning to my boyhood interest in ornithology. While I continued to write in a freer form, I also wrote a few poems in regular forms, to prove to myself that I had not lost my old skills; they included a sonnet to Gabriel Dumont, a ballad in memory of W.H. Auden, and a sestina to serve as a kind of elegy for Roy Daniells, whose death in 1979 struck me with particular sorrow. Perhaps my greatest satisfaction was that at last I could write about the event that had stuck me almost poetically dumb in 1949; the death of Marie Louise. It was "To Marie Louise Berneri, 28 years dead", a long poem about the shared ideals and hopes among which our relationship had developed, and about the difference between dying with one's dreams intact and living to awaken from them. The poem ended:

> Utopia has arrived.
> You would not recognize
> or like it. We are still
> hoping for liberation,
> but do not expect it.
>
> I have been as free
> as any man, have succeeded
> in my personal aims,
> and yet I have failed
> what we both strove for.
>
> Perhaps it was the impossible
> and you could have achieved
> no more. But you were spared
> both failure and success,
> their varying corruptions,
> and you move in the mind's eye
> untouched by the knife of age,
> spared from the cancer of doubt.
>
> You are a shade
> and I am flesh
> yet which of us
> has died?

My spell of poetry writing came to an abrupt end. I began thinking once again of a Collected Poems, and Robin Skelton, the editor of *Malahat Review*, who recently had also become the editor for the Sono Nis Press in Victoria, encouraged me to compile one. I worked on it through late 1981, following the "warts-and-all" approach, since I realized that a Collected Poems is an autobiographical as well as a literary document, and that I had to include not merely the best of my poems, but also those that seemed to me meaningful in terms of my life.

This did not mean that I was impelled to include everything I had written. A mass of juvenilia was excluded, and remains in its archive awaiting scholarly necropsy. But from about 1938, I included most of what I had published. The production did justice to the poems, for Sono Nis is owned by Morriss Printing, where Dick Morriss carries on the fine craft traditions of his father, Charles Morriss, with whom I worked so long in producing *Canadian Literature*.

But few triumphs are complete, and my satisfaction at the appearance of the Collected Poems was muted by the alarming fact that no sooner had the collection been assembled and handed over to Robin Skelton than my inspiration suddenly dried up. It was as though whatever muse had liberated my poetic gifts from their long silence in 1974 had been offended by the fact that I had monumentalized my poetic career — "You wanted finality! You have it!" In fact, since then I have composed just one poem, and that was an elegy in the death of an old friend, Kenneth Rexroth. Yet I am sure that one day, once again before I die, the gods will revisit.

XXXII

FIGHTING FOR THE SOUL
OF BROADCASTING

M Y BOOK OF HISTORICAL DETECTION appeared in the late
autumn of 1974, and it virtually marked the end of my period
of launching my most successful books in London, for *South Sea
Journey*, which Faber delayed publishing until 1976, was poorly pro-
moted and enjoyed a muted reception in comparison with my earlier
travel books, whereas *Who Killed the British Empire?* aroused much interest in Britain and was well-received in the United States. The book
found a separate Canadian publisher in Fitzhenry and Whiteside, and so
began a cordial association that has continued to this day.

On *Gabriel Dumont* I worked fast and with mounting enthusiasm. The
scantiness of information regarding parts of Dumont's life, and especially
the early years, was almost an advantage, since I was forced to reconstruct episodes and sequences out of few facts and much conjecture, but
the empathy I had developed towards my hero carried me along. I was
astonished at the rapport I seemed to develop with a man who, after all,
had differed so much from me in action and also in character, and after I
finished the book at 3 a.m., just three hours off schedule, I picked up a
scrap of paper and in a surge of feeling wrote a sonnet which I included
in *Notes on Visitations*. What Dumont, a "fierce stranger" and I shared,
the poem intimates, is "that freedom is a word our hearts both sing: . . . "

Gabriel Dumont was one of those rare books that are critical successes
and also sell well. It is still in print. As a book commanding attention, it
has been exceeded by only three of my titles, *Anarchism*, *The Crystal
Spirit*, and *The Anarchist Reader*, a book that was commissioned by Fon-
tana Books in England; I worked on it after I had finished *Gabriel Dumont*.
The Anarchist Reader was a fat anthology of libertarian writings accompanied by a lengthy historical introduction, and over the years it has
served as a companion source book to *Anarchism*, so that it is not entirely

surprising that both books were recently reissued in revised editions by their respective publishers.

With the success of *Gabriel Dumont*, Mel Hurtig was anxious to publish more of my work. In later years I would write the texts for several illustrated books he published, including *A Picture History of British Columbia*, *Faces from History* and *British Columbia: A Celebration*. These were easily written books which sold well and earned me fairly good royalties, and I took them on to boil the pot, which did not mean that I dropped my standards either of writing or of historical accuracy. From the last of these books indeed I gained much creative satisfaction. My collaborator, the photographer Janis Kraulis, produced a sensitive and evocative collection of landscape photographs. My contribution was an anthology of writing about British Columbia from the early explorers down to contemporary poets and short story writers. I included almost sixty writers, and added an introduction celebrating my own attachment to British Columbia.

But in 1975 Mel and I were discussing something different. Ever since I first arrived on Vancouver Island and discovered the wealth of Coast Indian artifacts in the basement rooms of the Provincial Museum in Victoria, I had wanted to study and write about this complex of primitive cultures. I had read all the scanty literature which existed on the Coast Indian peoples, visited every museum and exhibition where their artifacts were exhibited, and had gone several times to the Indian villages of the Skeena where the last large groves of totem poles are still standing. I had written articles on aspects of Coast Indian life for many journals and included passages about them in books. But there was still a need for a good book on these extraordinary peoples that would reconstruct a history for them out of tradition and archaeology and would discuss the material and social basis of the rich complex of art and ceremony that made this group of small and vulnerable tribes perhaps the most civilized of so-called primitive men.

Hurtig responded to the idea of a book of this kind, which would be well illustrated and should be called *Peoples of the Coast*. He gave me a contract with a generous advance, and I managed to turn the CBC's rejection of our Himalayan project to my advantage. While the CBC was delaying its decision, the Canada Council had shown its faith by agreeing to contribute $6,000 in travel funds to what they recognized as a good and urgently needed project of recording fading cultures. When Knowlton Nash terminated that CBC project, I asked the Council if I might be allowed to use the grant in my research for *Peoples of the Coast*. They agreed, and so I had the funds to work at preparing the book. Mel and I worked out a fairly leisurely schedule for its writing and publication.

The interlude of research made me free to indulge myself in the varied and erratic pace of periodical writing, and during 1975 and 1976 I contributed articles on literature, art and politics to magazines as varied as *Sewanee Review* and *Georgia Straight*, *Ontario Review* and *Books in Canada*, *The American Scholar* and *Saturday Night*, *Artscanada* and *Weekend Magazine*. I wrote on subjects as varied as George Orwell, Ursula Le Guin and Jean Cocteau, on the painters Jack Wise and B.C. Binning, on the architecture of Arthur Erickson and the Spirit Dances of the Salish people, which we saw one winter night in the great smoky longhouse of a little Indian village on Vancouver Island. I also wrote book reviews for *The Times Literary Supplement*, the *Washington Post*, the *New Leader*, which began publishing my work under Hilton Kramer's editorship and has done so ever since, and for the *Globe and Mail*. My association with the *Globe and Mail* was at this time close, and its fate reflected how capricious the reviewer's relationship to a paper can be, how dependent on the journalist who happens to be in charge of the book page. In my experience with *Maclean's*, it was a matter of changing policies rather than personalities. But in the case of the Toronto *Star*, for which I reviewed regularly during the later 1960s, the departure of Peter Sypnowich from the book editorship abruptly ended my assignments; the next editor preferred to invite only Toronto writers, whom he could reach quickly on the telephone, rather than troubling with people in the rest of Canada. When Emile Capouya left the *Nation* his successor preferred to use only American critics. It was Ed O'Dacre who invited me to write for the *Globe and Mail* when I ceased to be book reviewer for *Maclean's*, and for several years books arrived regularly with his notes pencilled on yellow paper, but after he moved to another department of the *Globe* the invitations to review became sporadic. Every book editor seems to develop his own group of favourite reviewers, and the fact that the book desk is usually one step, and a minor one, in a newsman's career, for which a literary background is not even considered necessary, contributes to that unevenness of newspaper criticism in Canada.

I still continued to edit *Canadian Literature*, not without occasional problems. It is true that I had succeeded in preserving the journal's autonomy in the power struggles that attended the quick succession of presidents at the University of British Columbia during this period. I had also managed with the help of gradually increasing Canada Council grants to increase the size of the magazine, and during 1975 I began to publish verse for the first time, providing a fresh outlet for poets at a time when the literary magazines founded in the 1960s were beginning to wither away, and attracting not only younger poets but also established ones like Earle Birney, Dorothy Livesay, Irving Layton, Al Purdy and P.K. Page.

But then I was shocked to realize how vulnerable such ventures as *Canadian Literature* had become in a time of rapid inflation. For the last four years, out of friendship and a sense of loyalty to the journal, Charles Morriss had refrained from raising his charges for printing it. I was aware that his forbearance could not last indefinitely, yet I was still unprepared when he finally surrendered to the urgings of his accountant and told me that he would have to raise his bill by 40% in the coming year. This created an immediate and extreme deficit. Already, although the drastic economies of the 1980s had not yet been imposed, the universities were moving out of the pattern of rapid expansion and free spending that had characterized the 1950s and the 1960s, and I did not see any alternative to cutting the magazine drastically in size and abandoning the publication of poetry. Fortunately the Chairman of the University's Publications Committee, which vaguely supervised the finances of the magazines published at U.B.C., was the librarian, Basil Stuart-Stubbs, who had a remarkable skill in wringing blood from the stony hearts of university administrators. Basil not only found the money to cover *Canadian Literature*'s deficit, but also helped to put the magazine on a solid financial basis, so that even during the hard times that followed it was able to survive and even to grow.

I also began to tire of the inevitable difficulties of dealing with writers, and not only my tardy contributors. There were also constant complaints from writers who had been reviewed and did not like what had been said about their books. I find a letter written early in 1975 to one of these complainants, a minor fiction writer from the Maritimes who claimed that a negative review of his book was malicious, and suggested I balance it by publishing a favourable review that had appeared in another journal. In declining the suggestion, I wrote him that:

"You talk of your "reputation as a writer", but it is the writer himself who places his reputation on the line when he publishes a book; he lays it before the public and must expect opinions on it to vary. In my own experience the worst thing for a writer's reputation is not reviews that fail to praise him; it is the absence of reviews . . . silence, the most frightful criticism of all."

SINCE IT WAS OBVIOUS by now that none of the projects for film series which Gordon Babineau and I had put forward were likely to be accepted, I let myself be led into another deadend of television writing. In one of the frequent and always unsuccessful efforts to give credibility to CBC drama programs, John Hirsch was engaged to supervise the production of television plays and David Helwig, an excellent poet, was picked to act as a talent scout and editor. The idea was that there were many good Canadian authors who had never written television plays, but who might do so successfully if they were encouraged. David approached me and we decided to concentrate on the anarchists. I first thought of a triangular drama linking Bakunin's great conflict with Karl Marx over libertarian versus authoritarian socialism to his obsessive relationship with the nihilist conspirator and murderer, Sergei Nechaev. It soon became evident that it would be much better to leave Marx alone and to concentrate on the repulsive character of Nechaev (which so fascinated Dostoevsky that he modelled much of *The Possessed* on his career) and on his hold over the veteran anarchist Bakunin, with his great and noble vision of a liberated humanity and his generous impulses towards the people he knew.

David came out to Vancouver and urged me not to spare the melodrama, which amused me, since nothing in Bakunin's life was anything less than melodramatic. However, I did point out that, melodramatic as the action and the relationship of the characters might be, one could not escape the need to make this a play of ideas. In the last resort, the tortuous relationship between Nechaev and Bakunin, for all its melodrama and its psychological complexity, had to hinge on the issues of political morality.

David accepted this, and I worked out an elaborate scenario, reinstating the triangular pattern, but doing so by including the pathetic subplot of the infatuation for Nechaev which for a long time made Natalie, Alexander Herzen's daughter, his gradually disillusioned dupe. This provided in a muted way a necessary counterpoint to the bizarre relationship between Bakunin and Nechaev. David accepted the scenario, and I signed a generous contract by which I was paid two-thirds of the total amount when I submitted the first draft of the play, whether or not it was accepted. And this, as it turned out, was a good thing. I finished the play by September, 1975, and sent it off, though with misgivings about whether it was the CBC's cup of tea.

My apprehensions were justified. People who were more powerful in CBC television drama than Helwig quickly vetoed it, and I was left in the not entirely disastrous situation of being paid several thousand dollars for the first draft of a play that now reverted to me and which I was free to sell elsewhere. I did that almost immediately. Helwig told me of the play's rejection for television at the end of October, and by January I had sold it back to the CBC, in this case to the radio network, which paid me an additional $2,000 for the play conceived as a drama for voices.

It turned out a kind of meta-drama, with the author — myself — acting an essential role. I called it *The Lion and the Tiger Cub*, and I conceived it as less a conventional play than a "hybrid investigatory, documentary, dramatic program", whose theme would be not only that truth is stranger than fiction, but that life is sometimes larger than conventional forms of art can contain.

I began my own framing narration by taking the listener into my confidence, telling how I had followed up the clues to the story I was telling and how, if Dostoevsky had been unable to contain it all within a single novel, I could not do so within a conventional play. I remained the central narrator, conducting the investigation, controlling the flow. Two secondary historical figures, Natalie Herzen and the poet Nicholas Ogarev, acted as tellers of the events, speaking from memory. A series of scenes developed key episodes and revealed the leading characters in a tangled web of idealism and calculation, of ruthlessness and naïveté. It turned out an economical way of dramatic writing, for the complicity achieved in simple narrative would have taken many dramatic scenes to develop.

I enjoyed the production of *The Lion and the Tiger Cub* as much as the writing, since for the first time I was directly engaged as one of the characters, drawing my pay as an actor as well as a writer. I also entered into the actual process of production by coaching the actors in the characters of the nineteenth century Russians they were playing.

It was not only the most ambitious dramatic feature I wrote for the CBC, but also the last. Great changes were taking place within the corporation. The centralized control over programing which became evident before the end of the 1960s was greatly accelerated, so that now the regions had almost no money for funding programs to be conceived and produced locally. Toronto controlled the purse strings almost entirely, and this meant that the stations outside Toronto had almost no power of initiative, and the original CBC ideal of enabling the regions to understand each other through the exchange of locally originated programs was going by default.

Even worse than the attack on regional autonomy was the parallel attack on the quality of broadcasting. The CBC could never compete effectively in popular entertainment with the commercial stations, nor did it need to, for it had already loyal listeners who appreciated and needed its contributions to the dramatic, musical and literary arts and to high-level informational broadcasting. Those who wanted light entertainment were already well taken care of elsewhere, and were unlikely to be won over by the earnest attempt on which the CBC embarked to win a mass audience, an attempt which in effect resulted in the CBC abandoning what it did well and failing to create anything of value in its place. Unfortunately the key posts in the corporation had fallen into the hands of determined anti-elitists, who tried to introduce pseudo-democratic criteria in areas where they had no relevance. These people denounced as elitist anyone who sought to sustain the quality of programing and to continue ambitious productions in the arts and in anything that presented a challenge to the mind; in fact it was they who were elitist, in their patronizing arguments that the people had only brief attention spans.

Music programs began to appear in which fragments of important works floated in a swamp of inane commentary. After being accustomed to giving talks that lasted anywhere from fifteen minutes to an hour, I began to get requests for tiny mini-talks. When Vladimir Nabokov died in 1977 I was asked to celebrate his contribution to the world of letters in two minutes! When Elizabeth Smart died I was invited to do a one minute comment!

Writers and actors and musicians who had been involved in CBC programing saw the scope for doing serious work rapidly narrowing, and at the same time listeners and viewers were increasingly disappointed with the steady decline in quality.

One evening early in 1976 John Korner the painter and his wife Eileen gave a party to celebrate the publication of a new book of stories by David Watmough. Some writers were there, and also some CBC producers, including Rob Chesterman and Don Mowatt. We all agreed that something had to be done. People employed by the CBC promised to activate their own unions, and David Watmough and I agreed to get a campaign started among the local intelligentsia. A few evenings later, at a dinner given by the journalist Mary McAlpine, Inge and I recruited Arthur Erickson, and then we brought in the composer Barbara Pentland, the dramatist Michael Mercer and a former NFB producer now working freelance, Bill Davies; with the addition of Hilary Bursill-Hall, we formed a steering committee and set about drafting a manifesto which we circulated to those of recognized standing in the artistic and scholarly worlds. We hoped for a hundred signatures, but feeling ran so strongly that out of the 160 people we solicited more than 120 signed. When the *Vancouver Sun* devoted a whole page to the manifesto and the signatures we received immediate attention and applause. The local unions of radio and television producers, the Wire Service Guild, ACTRA and the B.C. branch of the Writers' Union voted unanimous support to our plea, and so, on a national scale, did the *Association des réalisateurs*, representing all the television producers outside Toronto. Newspapers, radio and television stations took up the issue, and the CBC's own news services gave us great support. Western Tory and N.D.P. M.Ps spoke in our favour.

The corporation itself was so disturbed that the President, Albert Johnson, came out to discuss our grievances, and we met him and his entourage of Vice-Presidents in a large meeting in the Planetarium. Johnson was a fussy little man, with wavy hair and a neat three-piece suit, whose long civil service career had schooled him in the arts of bafflement. However, the verbal battering he received did seem to impress him. When he got back to Ottawa he remarked that never in his career had he encountered a more arrogant group of people. Yet I feel we may have touched a little his conscience as a westerner. During the months that followed I encountered Johnson a couple of times, and he told me he was considering a measure of regional decentralization. But when we had another meeting with CBC representatives in November, there was no sign of change. I believed that Johnson genuinely wished to make at least moderate changes, but that he had become the prisoner of his own entrenched officials.

Though we persisted for a while in pushing our case at every opportunity, including a large feature with seven participants in the *Canadian Forum* (whose publication Johnson tried to block with a telephone call to the editor, Denis Smith), the wall of indifference we faced gradually tired us. Like many other groups that have tried to call the CBC back to its original mandate, we ceased our activity, and the CBC continued like some bureaucratic juggernaut down the slope towards its present state of dereliction. But the comradeship developed in such activities often brings its own rewards, and I cherish the friendships, with David Watmough and Michael Mercer especially, that developed during those seasons of campaigning.

XXXIII

RESTLESS SEASONS

OUR LONGER JOURNEYS MAY HAVE BEEN temporarily abandoned, yet we remained restless, and after the period of concentrated work that followed our return from the South Seas, our street began to seem like a pleasant prison. We began to accept reasons to go on smaller travels, and to think of establishing some kind of refuge away from Vancouver. From 1969 to early 1972 we had indeed owned a cottage on a hillside below the Benedictine Abbey at Mission, forty miles east of Vancouver, with a view over the Fraser Valley farmlands to the Cascade Range and an acre of ground planted with nut trees. We planned to retire there, and rented it out in the meantime. But we found the problems of being landlords so tedious that we sold it on the eve of our departure to the South Pacific. Now we established a loose circle of friends who might be inclined to share in a communal country refuge; they included Mary McAlpine, Tony Phillips, a psychologist at U.B.C., and his friend Margo who was then studying Tibetan at U.B.C., and the anthropologist Bob Anderson and his wife Kathy Mezei, a translator and critic, both of whom were teaching at Simon Fraser University. We first considered buying a granite and cedar folly on Lasquiti Island — one of the smaller Gulf Islands — but it had no reliable water supply and no ferry access.

In the following spring Inge and I set off on another trip to Europe. We drove from Vancouver through the Rockies and across the prairies in their fine late spring flowering to Winnipeg. The University of Winnipeg was giving me a doctorate, and they did it with a touch of the old fur trade extravagance, for we proceeded into the Convocation hall to the scream of the pipers playing *The Road to the Isles*. We flew on to Amsterdam, where we hired a car, and drove through Ghent and the Ardennes into Luxembourg and then down the Moselle Valley and across

Wurtemburg and Bavaria to Bad Fussing, and spent some time looking in vain for a congenial house in Upper Austria. We returned through the old towns of the Jura and through Alsace, north-eastern France and Belgium, revisiting Rheims for the light-filled splendour of its windows, and spending a day in Bruges for the sake of the Van Eyck paintings which we had never seen in their original form, and then flying back to Canada.

Having abandoned the idea of a refuge in the Gulf Islands and Austria, we decided to look for land in the Kootenays, into which the earth-minded hippies moved in large numbers during the 1960s, buying up all the cheap marginal holdings; driving back from Winnipeg on our return from Europe we stopped at Grand Forks to call on Eli Popoff, one of our Doukhobor friends, and he told us of a piece of land for sale that seemed to meet our hopes. We hurried home, and three days later we and Mary McAlpine, Tony and Margo went to look at the land. It was a hundred acres, wild yet in some parts tractable; it climbed high up a rocky mountainside which we would never be able to cultivate, but which would ensure our privacy and provide a home for wild animals, birds and plants. There were ten acres of flat land, which had once been cultivated, and could be regenerated as pastures and gardens; there was plenty of timber to build log cabins, and enough year-round water. The one disadvantage was a corner of two or three acres of cedar swamp which would have to be drained. The group of us put in a bid, and at first the negotiations seemed to be going so well that I began to write to my friends in England about the cabin Inge and I hoped to get built before the winter so that we would have a summer home to which we might eventually retire. However, at the last minute another buyer overbid us, and the deal fell through. Later I learnt from our Doukhobor friends that the man who got the land sank a great deal of money into those acres of marsh and never successfully drained them.

We did not give up our efforts, and during the summer we tried to find land on the hilly edges of the Fraser Valley. But what we wanted — a fairly large piece of land with a modest cabin we might later enlarge — had become difficult to get since business people seeking tax breaks began to buy up holdings as hobby farms. We never did find our ideal plot of land, and by the middle of 1976 the desire to find a refuge away from Vancouver had died down.

Since then I have wondered why we had this strange outburst of searching, since I am convinced that we had no real desire to find a new home. If we had seriously wanted to escape from city life, we would have gone seeking in places difficult of access from the city, places where land was actually still available, like the Skeena river country or the northern fringes of the Saskatchewan parkland. But, though we found both these areas attractive, and visited them during the period of our searching, we never attempted to find land there. Instead we looked in places where we knew cheap land was scarce and which were on or near to main roads by which we could reach Vancouver in a few hours, escaping from escape, as it were. As I said in one moment of self-knowledge to my former student Pat Barclay: "I know my own restlessness, and I fear that if I do plant myself in Grand Forks or Creston I'll eat my heart out for the busy days of old Vancouver."

Our search was not the result of any real desire to go back and live the country life, of which we had endured enough at Sooke almost three decades before, but rather a restlessness linked to the changes that were taking place in our life: the temporary abandonment of distant travel, my changeover from being an English to becoming a Canadian writer, my return to writing poetry, and the feeling it was time I gave up the editing that had so long preoccupied me. The search for a new setting seemed to sanctify all this change, and its failure symbolized the fact that the foundation of my life remained the steady writing in the old house under the ancient cherry tree.

AT THE END OF March 1976 we went to Bavaria again and stayed there for three weeks. It was the quick springtime of Central Europe, when the early summer flowers come already before the cowslips have withered, and I spent much time walking in that blossoming countryside and writing poems, and I benefitted from the regeneration that comes in a period of boredom.

Not long after we returned, Julian Symons and Kathleen arrived to stay ten days with us. Julian had been teaching at a New England college for the past year, and at the end he and Kathleen set out on a great wandering across North America, of which Vancouver was the farthest point. I arranged lectures for him at the local universities, and we had a fine time recording our memories of the 1930s in a conversation we did for the CBC. The presence of these old friends gave Inge and me an excuse to explore parts of our own city we hardly knew, and to revisit the Island and seek out the places where we had lived. I think it was this actual return to Sooke where the rural life had once been so difficult that really put an end to our passing craze for seeking a place in the country.

By early September we were on the move again. Having turned down all our proposals for films that would have taken us to distant and exotic places, the mandarins of CBC television finally decided to commission Gordon Babineau and me to prepare two films on the Doukhobors, past and present. Arriving while I was still deeply involved in the campaign to reform the CBC, the invitation seemed a placatory gesture, and I hesitated about accepting it. But I was attracted by the thought of putting my considerable knowledge of the Doukhobors to a new use that might broaden Canadian understanding of this greatly misunderstood people, and I knew also what a fine visual setting the Kootenays would provide for the film, while Gordon was anxious to achieve at least one more good production before he left the CBC. So I accepted the offer, knowing that the caustic commentary on CBC policies which I had written for the *Canadian Forum* would show that I had not been bought off.

We drove into Doukhobor country immediately after Labour Day, through the Cascades, across the lower end of the Okanagan Valley, and up over Anarchist Mountain to the Kettle Valley in which Grand Forks, the present capital of the Orthodox Doukhobors, is situated. Gordon and his cameraman, John Seal, were already there, and we spent the next two weeks between Grand Forks and Nelson, visiting all the small communities where the Doukhobors still remain although their great social-religious experiment of a Christian Communist society has long disintegrated.

Some relics of that past order survived. The most impressive were the solid and rather menacing large brick community houses in which, when the community flourished under Peter the Lordly Verigin after the Doukhobor migration from the prairies to British Columbia in 1908, groups of families had shared their lives. There were also, on the hillsides, the remnants of the communal orchards and the fragments of the wooden flumes that had irrigated them, and on a back road we found the communal flourmill, still being operated by a Doukhobor family. But the community as an organization had disintegrated long ago, during the Depression when the banks had foreclosed, and now, in the 1970s, though many of the Doukhobors still remained on the land that they had once communally owned, they did so independently, with the community really surviving as a religious and linguistic one, pacifism the only remnant of its former social radicalism.

This pattern persisted even in the narrow little valleys around the plateau of Krestova, where the remnant of the radical Sons of Freedom, the former nude paraders and arsonists, continued to live. Indeed, there had been no attempt to revive the Christian communism of Peter the Lordly's time since the days of Michael the Archangel's Vancouver Island commune which we visited in 1949.

The Doukhobors were no more easy to deal with in 1976 than I had found them in the past. It is true that they had become more integrated into Canadian society, and more permeated by its material values, which were manifest in the affluence of some of the homes they had built. Some of them, departing from the traditional Doukhobor distrust of the written word, had developed a scholarly interest in their past, like Peter Legebokoff, who was now organizing the Doukhobor Museum at Castlegar, and Eli Popoff and his son Jim, who was editing the English-language Doukhobor magazine *Mir* and operating a small bookstore and publishing house in connection with it. This group valued the work I had done.

But there were others among whom the traditional Doukhobor distrust of the outsiders, bred of generations of persecution and misunderstanding, in Canada as well as Russia, did not die away easily. John Verigin, the leader of the orthodox group, and his lieutenants in the Union of Spiritual Communities of Christ, feared that Gordon and I would lay too much stress on the more sensational activities of the Sons of Freedom. Stefan Sorokin, the leader of the Sons of Freedom, or Reformed Doukhobors, refused to see us and remained within a protecting circle of bodyguards and Dobermans the whole time we were in the locality. The lesser figures among the Sons of Freedom spoke to us only with caution, and Joe Podovinikoff, whom I had known since meeting him at Hilliers nearly thirty years before, had nursed a grudge for a quarter of a century over a slightly ironic piece I had written about Michael the Archangel. Still, in most cases we did succeed in quelling suspicion and soothing hurt pride, even Joe's, so that in the end John Verigin and some of the lesser leaders became co-operative, and we were able to film *sobranies* or religious meetings, funerals and festivals, scenes of daily life and the chaotic gatherings that were taking place among the various factions in the hope of healing rifts.

Whatever misgivings the Doukhobors may have had, their hospitality was never stinted. Once we had breakfasted, there was no need to consider how we should eat the rest of the day, since we had an endless succession of invitations. Doukhobor evening parties in particular were stupendous gastronomic events. Nowadays, in their day-to-day living, the Doukhobors tend to compromise with Canadian eating habits, but for festive occasions they cook entirely traditionally and provide what may be the best vegetarian food in the world. A Doukhobor dinner table would be crowded with ten to fifteen different dishes, cooked in an abundance of butter and cream. There would follow an evening of talk and song, and the song was always best at Eli Popoff's house, for this Finnish-looking little Doukhobor from Karelia had preserved the Russian folk songs — as distinct from the Doukhobor psalms — which the people had brought with them, and he and a group of his friends would sing them; some of them were songs now forgotten in Russia, and one of the most poignant of them purported to be Napoleon's lament as he stood on the walls of Moscow and watched the city burning. After three or four hours of song and intermittent talk, the hostess would say, "Now, let us have a snack!" and the table would be covered with another ten new dishes. There was never anything stronger than tea at these gatherings, but the atmosphere was so convivial that wine was unneeded.

We made two films, of the Doukhobors past and present, the first telling through reminiscent interviews and old photographs and news films the story of the persecution and discrimination in Russia and Canada that had led to a state of perpetual misunderstanding between the Doukhobors and political authorities of all kinds, and the second showing how the Doukhobors lived today, and how much like other Canadians most of them had become. The lesson we were doing our best to project was the failure of the assumptions of majoritarian democracy in situations where minorities existed who held their beliefs strongly enough to accept persecution rather than submit. The fact that our films were well received, so that they were repeated a year after their first showing and were taken into the National Film Board's permanent collection, was a sign that Canada had advanced along the path to a genuinely pluralist society.

When we had finished our work among the Doukhobors, Inge and I set out along the valley roads and the mountain to the Indian villages of the Skeena so that I would do some research for *Peoples of the Coast*. This time we went all the way down the Skeena to the sea at Prince Rupert; the river, hardly known even to most British Columbians, carved its way in the shadow of great mountains like the Rocher Déboulé and the Seven Sisters through some of the wildest country in western Canada. By the time we got home from this northern foray, we had travelled 3,500 miles over the roads.

Shortly afterwards I went on the year's oddest journey. Naim Kattan of the Canada Council had rung me up and told me, with great exhortations to secrecy, that the Governor General, Jules Léger, had decided to hold a colloquiam in late October to celebrate the 25th anniversary of the Massey Report, to frame suggestions to the government for future policies in the arts. A few representatives of the arts, some people from the cultural agencies, a handful of politicians, would gather at a meeting muted in its pretensions, since the Governor General did not want it to be assumed that he was attempting to usurp the prerogatives of the cabinet. Would I be willing to attend?

I was intrigued and amused. Did His Excellency realize that he was proposing to entertain the leading anarchist in Canada? I asked Naim. This was a non-political occasion, Naim answered, a kind of caprice on the part of the head of state, who really did not care what his guests' political views might be so long as they could offer some interesting ideas. I could hardly appear more prejudiced from my side than the Governor General from his, and my curiosity was aroused, so I agreed.

Inge went to see her parents in Germany while I was away, and I broke my journey at Edmonton to confer with Mel Hurtig. A couple of days later, I drove in a taxi up the avenue of old trees leading to the portico of Rideau Hall. As I got out, another cab arrived, and a figure I knew from photographs, and also from a long correspondence, emerged. It was the poet Dennis Lee. We were immediately surrounded by armed security guards, who looked as if they were about to frisk us when a young aide-de-camp appeared to rescue us and take us inside, where we found the four other representatives of the arts had arrived. Three of them I knew, the painter Alex Colville, the critic Malcolm Ross and the actor-playwright Gratien Gélinas. The fourth, the musician Murray Schaeffer, I had never met, though he taught at Simon Fraser University. That evening, at the first of several elaborate dinners, we met the Ottawa participants, among whom I was amused to see, was Al Johnson. Naim Kattan represented the Canada Council, the art historian Robert Hubbard and the poet Pierre Trottier were there as members of the Governor General's staff, and the three politicians attending were Jeanne Sauvé, then Minister of Communications, Hugh Faulkner, Secretary of State, and Gordon Fairweather, then a Tory M.P.

Rideau Hall was a haven of Victorian sybaritism. Each of the guests had a large room full of stuffed comfort, with boxes of cigarettes lying everywhere, and tins of biscuits and sweets and plates of apples in case he got hungry in the night. In the corridor outside the rooms a mobile bar stood permanently, so that one could pour oneself a drink at any time of the day or night.

The day would begin with an enormous English breakfast before we went into our morning session in the long gallery where we discussed the items of the agenda under the painted gaze of former governors-general and their ladies in portraits by Winterhalter and Millais. Léger presided at our first session, a good host, especially in view of the disabling stroke he was already suffering, but afterwards he left us to follow our own way. No one shone with great eloquence in these sessions, though Jeanne Sauvé tended to talk more than anyone else, and Faulkner and Fairweather showed themselves, for politicians, unusually intelligent and civilized, which was perhaps why they did not continue in politics.

There would follow an enormous and superbly cooked lunch, at which a few outsiders like Bernard and Sylvia Ostry and Timothy Porteous would appear, and then we would return for a somnolent afternoon session. Late in the afternoon, Naim and Dennis Lee and I would walk briskly in the frosty grounds to burn off the excess food, the doors being unlocked and locked for us by the security guards as we left and entered, so that we had a sense of living under siege. A cocktail reception for the Ottawa intelligentsia would be followed by a dinner even more lavish than the lunch, after which the Ottawa participants would leave and Robert Hubbard would take the representatives of the arts to talk until the small hours over whisky in the library. This was the part of the day I enjoyed most, for I had always found Colville and Ross excellent and versatile conversationalists, and Dennis Lee, though our political ideas differed greatly, turned out to be a sympathetic companion.

Nothing came of the colloquiam. We made some recommendations which I assume were duly forwarded to the government, but nothing more was heard of them. None of the press was present, and it sank into an Ottawa oubliette. But it left a seed of concern in my mind, so that years afterwards I felt impelled to write my book on the state and the arts in Canada, *Strange Bedfellows*, which I am sure would never have been thought of if the Governor General had not invited the anarchist to be his guest.

XXXIV

GRAND CLIMACTERIC

"I 'M HAVING SPLENDID AND inspiring dreams, which I attribute to the triumphant passage through the Grand Climacteric," I wrote to Margaret Atwood in the spring of 1976, " and in one of them last night you and I walked on a moonlit midnight through the Temple Gardens and down the Thames Embankment talking of Buddhism and the Sufis." Certainly it was a time of dreams, and some of which emerged as actual poems or as short stories which I called "Found Fictions" and published in the *Canadian Forum*, eventually making out of them a kind of dream novella called "The Train to the Border," which the *West Coast Review* published, and which is the only piece of my fiction that has satisfied me enough to release it in print.

I talked of the Grand Climacteric not entirely in jest, for the changes which took place after 1972, roughly coinciding with my 63rd year, which in ancient lore was termed the Grand Climacteric, represented a major shift in my pattern of living and in my mental perspectives. Still, the most important change lay ahead, for I decided to give up the editing of *Canadian Literature*. By this time it was seventeen years since I started to edit the journal and more than twenty since I first conceived it. Because it came at the right moment in the development of a Canadian literary tradition, and created its own ground swell of critical activity it had turned out a far better and more interesting magazine than I had ever hoped, and it had wielded an undeniable influence on the development of literary scholarship of all kinds in Canada, among other things preventing its ossification into a merely academic activity. When I looked at the shelf of more than seventy numbers, it seemed to me not merely a periodical, but a cumulative *oeuvre* in its own right, for a good magazine, with its balance of tones and interests, is as much a creation as any book, and reflects its editor's personality.

But I felt now that the time had come when my task was complete, and now I had opened the journal to poets there was nothing new I wanted to do with it. I tendered my resignation to become effective in mid-summer, 1977. The future of the magazine was the problem that most concerned me and made the giving up of the editorship something of a trauma. As I was making my decision to resign, Alan Crawley, who had died recently, was much on my mind. I remembered how he had allowed *Contemporary Verse* to die quietly when he felt it had fulfilled its purpose after twelve years of existence, and I remembered also Cyril Connolly, whose example as an editor had influenced me greatly, and who ran *Horizon* for precisely ten years before he brought it to an end.

However, *Canadian Literature* was a publication of the University of British Columbia, which had chosen and appointed me as editor, and though my efforts had been necessary for its foundation, that fact did not give me rights of life and death over it. Under my direction it had not only become a Canadian literary institution; it had also brought the University a degree of credit which I knew it would not wish to abandon. Whatever my wishes, *Canadian Literature* would continue, and all I could do was to make as sure as I could that the editorship fell into the right hands, that, as I told Dorothy Livesay, "whoever takes over will not just try to continue or to imitate, but will make a new magazine, so that there will really be a *Canadian Literature* II, reflecting a different editor's personality, since I feel a journal is as much a personal creation as a book."

But, university methods being what they are, I did not have the right to choose my successor. A committee of academics was appointed to select him, and in a way I was glad, for it did not prevent me from making my own nomination, but it did protect me from the resentment of those who might think they had a better title than the person actually appointed. As all academic committees do, this took an unconscionable time reaching what seemed a fairly straight-forward decision. In April I pasted up the last issue under my editorship, still with no hint of the committee's intent, and at the end of that month we went to Bavaria and Austria. When I returned there was still no decision, though when I had lunch with the chairman of the selection committee I gathered that the probable choice would be the candidate I considered an ideal successor. Indeed, with the first issue of the new dispensation due in August I had to consult him, as if he were appointed. It was not until two weeks before I actually stepped down that W.H. New, who had already made a name for himself as a fine critic, was officially appointed editor. On the 7th July I wrote to P.K. Page:

It was a lovely poem you included in your letter, but I won't be tempted to use it in *Canadian Literature*, since a week ago I handed it over to Bill New to edit. I think he'll make a good job of it, and after 18 years — though I had very mixed feelings when I made the decision to give up a year ago — I'm really rather happy to look back on it as something done, and enjoy the time for other things.

OTHER THINGS WERE NOT lacking, for at a productive stage in one's life any vacuum of time seems to attract its tasks. By the time I gave up *Canadian Literature*, I had completed *The Anarchist Reader* and *Peoples of the Coast*, and both appeared in 1977. Though otherwise it was well received, by anthropologists and general readers, *Peoples of the Coast* aroused the jealous anger of ethnologists at the Provincial Museum in Victoria, who had meant to write such a book themselves, but had neither the initiative nor, indeed, the talent to carry it out. Their verbose attack in a vast collectively written review and the counter attack with which I routed them provided many pages of gladiatorial entertainment that winter for the readers of *B.C. Studies*.

But there were new tasks also that were already beginning to occupy me in that summer of 1977. Two priests — an Anglican and a Roman Catholic — were organizing a Thomas Merton Festival in Vancouver, and they suggested to me that I write a study of this famous monk and poet to coincide with their event. I was interested, since I had not written a major critical study since *Herbert Read: The Stream and the Source*, and Merton — with whom I shared an interest in Tibetan Buddhism and a friendship with the Dalai Lama — intrigued me as a poet and a personality. So when both a Canadian publisher (Douglas & McIntyre) and an American one (Farrar, Strauss and Giroux) decided to commission the book, I began work on it. At the same time Robert Fitzhenry approached me with the idea that I do a cultural study of my fellow countrymen, to be called *The Canadians*; Fitzhenry had already brought out Canadian editions of *Who Killed the British Empire?* and *South Sea Journey*, but this would be my first title to originate with him.

Thus 1977 crowned the changes in my pattern of living that freed me once again to the life of writing, since anything resembling retirement was out of the question so as long as I continued to think in words. And the past was duly celebrated as I moved into my different future. The University of British Columbia conferred on me its Doctorate of Literature for my service to Canadian writing. The Senate voted me a Professor Emeritus, though it was many years since I had entered a classroom. And the University of British Columbia Press published a *festscrift* entitled *A Political Art* which Bill New had gathered and edited.

It was the last that pleased me most, for the contributions were voices speaking from every phase and period of my life. The friends of my early writing life in the 1930s and 1940s were there: Julian Symons, Roy Fuller and Derek Savage, Kathleen Raine and Denise Levertov. Colin Ward spoke from my anarchist days, Robert Heilman from my brief American interlude, and Mulk Raj Anand and Bhalchandra Rajan were there to commemorate my long association with India. The people in the visual arts who had become such valued friends appeared in force: Jack Shadbolt, Gordon Smith and Arthur Erickson, John Korner, Alistair Bell and Bob Steele, and P.K. Page in her painterly persona as P.K. Irwin. Mo Steinberg, Don Stephens and Bill New were reminders of my loose but lasting relationship with the English Department at U.B.C. Most numerous were the Canadian writers from several generations with whom my editing of *Canadian Literature* had drawn me into such inspiring contact: Margaret Laurence, Jack Ludwig and Ramsay Cook, Naim Kattan, George Bowering and Tom Marshall, Tom Wayman and Al Purdy, Seymour Mayne and John Robert Colombo. Finally, but far from least, Ivan Avakumovic, my friend for thirty years and my collaborator in two important books, ended the volume with a bibliography of my writings. It was a moving record of a lifetime of friendships and associations, even more than a tribute, and it was rendered all the more pleasing by the care which Dick Morriss had taken with the design and printing of the book, and by the linocut decorations by my long dead friend George Kuthan that were reproduced from the early issues of *Canadian Literature*.

I sang my own ironic elegy to the period in an acrostic poem which I contributed to the first issue of *Canadian Literature* that Bill New edited. The basic sentence was: GEORGE WOODCOCK HANDS OVER TO BILL NEW, but the poem was really a reflection on the need at times to abandon even the best of works to rediscover one's true and basic self, and the first verse, I think, renders faithfully my feeling in that momentous summer of ending and beginning.

> Going away is a kind of returning,
> Entering into a mirror of oneself,
> Or perhaps plunging into a sea cavern to
> Recover what the years had hidden away.
> Given that the task has been good, we all still
> End with the longing for liberation.

EPILOGUE

I HAVE ENDED THIS second volume of my autobiography, like the first, at an important turning point in my life. Partly this is because such an ending gives a clear shape to the book, and autobiography is as much concerned with form as any other kind of literary art. But partly also it is because autobiography is a type of writing that can only succeed where memory and imagination come together, and for that to happen time and a degree of forgetting must have taken place, a kind of marination in which the irrelevant details are dissolved and the true structure of the past emerges like the skeleton of a leaf at the end of winter.

In this sense autobiography is much nearer to fiction than it was once assumed. Literalness is no more a necessary virtue in it than it is in translation. It does not invent, as fiction does, but it does select, and perhaps it is the art that most of all deserves Wordsworth's definition of "emotion recollected in tranquillity", though to *emotion* we should in this instance perhaps add *action*. Clearly the details that will be preserved, and given a significance they perhaps did not seem to have at the time of action, will be those that best illuminate the form which the life has taken on in memory, and that form will of course be dominated by the purpose that has guided the autobiographer's life. Thus the kind of detail he will choose — or which memory in its process of endless selection will offer him — will be quite different if he is a writer than it would be if he were a scientist or a painter.

Like most forms of writing, autobiography combines the intentional and the given, and in the process of creation the writer's deliberate strategies join the unconscious selectivity of memory and the guiding force of the imagination to produce what one calls, recognizing the fictional element in selection and shaping, the "story" of one's life. And it is because this process takes time that a real autobiography, unlike the kind

[296]

of memoirs that a ghost writer compiles for a politician, cannot be written immediately after the event, and that I bring this volume to an end almost ten years ago.

Looking back over that interval I see that the impulse of my life has not really changed. Having cut away related activities like teaching and editing, and to a large extent broadcasting, I have remained a dedicated writer, working almost every day, producing not much less than I did in the past, even if I have become less of a night hawk as I have grown older, and always feeling, as I imagine most artists do while their sense of purpose is still alive, that I am only at the beginning, a perpetual learner.

I have also remained, as I became in the mid-1970s, essentially a Canadian writer, in the sense of publishing most of my books and my articles here, though I have not restricted myself to Canadian subjects, so that books like *The Canadians, The World of Canadian Writing* and *Confederation Betrayed* have been balanced by others like *Thomas Merton: Monk and Poet* and *Orwell's Message*, which deal with foreign writers, like *Letter to the Past*, the volume of autobiography telling of my childhood and young manhood in England, and like *The Marvellous Century*, the historical study of the 6th century B.C. I have tended to keep up my habit of working on more than one piece of writing at a time, so that parallel to my books I have published articles in a wide variety of journals and on as wide a variety of subjects as before.

Critics have often observed that my interests, whether literary, artistic or political, tend to be contained within an anarchistic philosophic framework which they have found more consistent than it sometimes seems to me. Yet it is true enough that my libertarian outlook has continued to influence the kind of books I write, so that my recent works have included squibs like *Confederation Betrayed*, an advocacy of a radically decentralized confederalism as the best system for Canada, and studies like *Strange Bedfellows*, which deals with the ambivalent relationship between the state and the arts in Canada, while recently I have revised and updated *Anarchism*. As much through the changes in CBC programming as owing to my own inclinations, I have done less broadcasting in recent years but it has included the most ambitious radio task of my career, the massive radio biography of George Orwell which Steve Wadhams produced and which I narrated and hosted, and which lasted for five hours when it took the air on New Year's Day. It was a celebration of my own radical past as much as of my friendship with Orwell, but it was also a vindication, as many thousands of people in Canada and the United States listened patiently to the whole programme, of my contention that there is still a great public receptive to serious broadcasting and of the trivia that most networks, including the CBC, generally offer.

And if, as this program showed, I have not abandoned my political interests, I have equally certainly not abandoned my inclination to become involved in causes. Some causes of the past have slipped away. Inge and I gave up our work for the Tibetan refugees when we realized that the majority of them were now resettled and because of their industry were at least as well off as their Indian neighbours. And we gave up the fight to reform the CBC when, some time in 1977, we realized that we were fighting a bureaucracy that seemed to grow more stubborn and unbending the more it was attacked. But the agonies of the Boat People brought us out again, to gather funds and help resettle a number of Vietnamese, Laotian and Cambodian families in Vancouver, and so did the issue of the seal hunt, which for once was a battle fought to a successful end, since our protests, including the articles I wrote in *Saturday Night* and elsewhere, helped terminate the killing of baby seals.

In 1981, moved by what some of our Indian friends were doing to alleviate the poverty of their fellow countrymen, we and a few doctors and old India hands founded the Canada India Village Aid Association, devoted to helping achieve Gandhi's aim of regenerating Indian villages as a way to end the country's ancient destitution. Working with Indian voluntary groups and greatly helped by CIDA (the Canadian International Development Agency), we have provided dispensaries in tribal regions and poor areas, built an obstetrical ward for a rural hospital, financed mobile medical units, organized programs for training paramedics and midwives, and, most recently, helped to finance the building of dams in the drought-stricken regions of Rajasthan. This work led us back again on our long travels, for in the winter of 1982-3 Inge and I set off with Toni Onley, the painter, and his wife Yukiko, on an arduous journey through India that led to my most recent book on the country, *Walls of India*, which was illustrated by Toni's paintings.

In 1985 Toni and I set out on a second journey. A synagogue had been burnt by anti-Semitic extremists in Vancouver, and Toni suggested to me that we might perform a gesture of solidarity for the victims and also provide some funds for the new synagogue if we went to Israel and together produced a parallel book to *The Walls of India*. I had been troubled before we went by some of the aspects of Israeli policy in Lebanon, but I had talked with Israelis in Canada and with Canadian Jews, and had realized that they too were by no means united in support of the actions of the military, so I had decided to go there with my mind and all my senses open. We set out, intending to fly from Munich to Tel Aviv. We spent a few days holidaying in Upper Austria and in the mountains around Saalfelden, and then returned to Munich for our flight to Israel. That day the Israeli air force bombed Tunis in an attempt to kill

Yassir Arafat, and we knew there would be retaliations. Over dinner in the Augustinerbrauhof that evening we anxiously discussed our plans, and decided that though we were willing to give our time and our talents for human understanding, we had no intention of risking our lives in the political disputes of the Levant. So we went on a long wandering through Switzerland and France, Andorra and Spain and Germany, and in the six weeks we learnt, as Toni painted and I kept a melancholy journal, how quickly the accelerating pattern of uniformity was subordinating even the most idiosyncratic regions of Europe to the homogenizing influences that ripple out from the American epicentre.

These journeys with a painter, whatever their immediate justifications, were really a product of the fascination with the relationship between the verbal and the visual arts that had long led me to seek out the friendship of painters. During the late 1950s and the 1960s I had written a great deal on Asian, Mexican and primitive art, a consideration of which had also entered into my *Peoples of the Coast*. During the 1970s I had turned to Canadian artists, writing for *Artscanada* on painters like Jack Shadbolt, Bert Binning and Jack Wise, as well as on the Canadian landscape tradition, and finally, at the end of the decade, I wrote a major study on a single painter, Ivan Eyre. My book on Eyre, which Bob Fitzhenry published in 1981, was particularly concerned with the correspondence of poetic and painterly imagery that had fascinated me ever since, long ago, I recognized the visual basis of Chinese poetry.

Not long after I completed *Ivan Eyre* I was led into another avenue of literature when Norma Gutteridge of the University of Alberta Press invited me to translate a major but largely unknown classic of Canadian history, *Le métis canadien*, which the French scholar Marcel Giraud had researched during the 1930s and had spent the years of the Occupation writing in Paris. Giraud was an ethnologist as well as a historian, but he fortunately wrote in a very clear, jargon-free style, and his book was far more detailed than any Canadian book to date on the Métis. I had dabbled in translation in the past, had put a bad French novel into better English to earn a hundred pounds in the 1940s, and had translated a few poems and some small French texts to include in *The Anarchist Reader*. But *Le métis canadien* was a massive work, far more ambitious than anything I had undertaken before. I bargained for time, and for payment. It was agreed that I could take three years to do the work, and the Canada Council provided a generous translation grant. So I agreed, and worked steadily, translating a page or two almost every day, and finished in less than my three years. The task fitted in very well with my other work, for the translation provided the variation of subject I have always liked, and the fact that I was writing directly in English at the same time helped to keep the prose of my translation in tone, so that in the end I felt I was doing what in my mind every good translator should, producing a work that read as if it had been written originally in my own language. When the book finally appeared in 1986, its two volumes consisted of just over a thousand pages of prose, apart from the notes. And far from tiring me of translation it gave me a zest for more, so that one of the projects I now have in mind for the future is the retranslation of the novelist I increasingly consider the best of them all, Marcel Proust.

As I write these last sentences, I can see no immediate dwindling in the urge that compels me to continue writing, the urge I sometimes imagine as Pater's "hard, gemlike flame" whose constant burning is "success in life." William Hazlitt began one of his essays with the statement that "No young man believes he shall ever die." There is a sense, I have found, in which old and still active artists and writers also proceed, in their work at least, in the confidence that the future is open, that in a sense they shall never die, even if as men or women they live daily with that awareness of mortality the body will not let them forget.

It is not what is done that counts in the end, but the understanding with which it is done, the acting without regard for the fruits of action of which Krishna talked in the *Bhagavad Gita*, the joy of achievement without the desire to achieve, which the true Buddhists know. As one grows older and continues to work, it is not for the financial gains, which may be large or non-existent, or for the fame, to which one becomes steadily more indifferent, or even for the eventual artifacts, but for the joy of creation itself.